COMMONWEALTH

COMMONWEALTH

Michael Hardt | Antonio Negri

**THE BELKNAP PRESS OF
HARVARD UNIVERSITY PRESS**

Cambridge, Massachusetts
London, England

First Harvard University Press paperback edition, 2011

Library of Congress Cataloging-in-Publication Data

Hardt, Michael, 1960–
    Commonwealth / Michael Hardt, Antonio Negri.
        p. cm.
    Sequel to "Empire" and "Multitude."
    Includes bibliographical references and index.
    ISBN 978-0-674-03511-9 (cloth : alk. paper)
    ISBN 978-0-674-06028-9 (pbk.)
1. International organization. 2. International cooperation. 3. Globalization.
I. Negri, Antonio, 1933– II. Title.
    JZ1318.H368 2009
    321.02—dc22   2009012652

CONTENTS

PREFACE: THE BECOMING-PRINCE
OF THE MULTITUDE

People only ever have the degree of freedom that their audacity wins from fear.

—Stendhal, *Vie de Napoléon*

Power to the peaceful.

—Michael Franti, "Bomb the World"

War, suffering, misery, and exploitation increasingly characterize our globalizing world. There are so many reasons to seek refuge in a realm "outside," some place separate from the discipline and control of today's emerging Empire or even some transcendent or transcendental principles and values that can guide our lives and ground our political action. One primary effect of globalization, however, is the creation of a common world, a world that, for better or worse, we all share, a world that has no "outside." Along with nihilists, we have to recognize that, regardless of how brilliantly and trenchantly we critique it, we are destined to live in *this* world, not only subject to its powers of domination but also contaminated by its corruptions. Abandon all dreams of political purity and "higher values" that would allow us to remain outside! Such a nihilist recognition, however, should be only a tool, a point of passage toward constructing an alternative project. In this book we articulate an ethical project, an ethics of democratic political action within and against Empire. We investigate what the movements and practices of the multitude have been and what they can become in order to discover the social relations and institutional forms of a possible global democracy. "Becoming-Prince" is the process of the multitude learning the art of self-rule and inventing lasting democratic forms of social organization.

A democracy of the multitude is imaginable and possible only because we all share and participate in the common. By "the common" we mean, first of all, the common wealth of the material world—the air, the water, the fruits of the soil, and all nature's bounty—which in classic European political texts is often claimed to be the inheritance of humanity as a whole, to be shared together. We consider the common also and more significantly those results of social production that are necessary for social interaction and further production, such as knowledges, languages, codes, information, affects, and so forth. This notion of the common does not position humanity separate from nature, as either its exploiter or its custodian, but focuses rather on the practices of interaction, care, and cohabitation in a common world, promoting the beneficial and limiting the detrimental forms of the common. In the era of globalization, issues of the maintenance, production, and distribution of the common in both these senses and in both ecological and socioeconomic frameworks become increasingly central.[1]

With the blinders of today's dominant ideologies, however, it is difficult to see the common, even though it is all around us. Neoliberal government policies throughout the world have sought in recent decades to privatize the common, making cultural products—for example, information, ideas, and even species of animals and plants—into private property. We argue, in chorus with many others, that such privatization should be resisted. The standard view, however, assumes that the only alternative to the private is the public, that is, what is managed and regulated by states and other governmental authorities, as if the common were irrelevant or extinct. It is true, of course, that through a long process of enclosures the earth's surface has been almost completely divided up between public and private property so that common land regimes, such as those of indigenous civilizations of the Americas or medieval Europe, have been destroyed. And yet so much of our world is common, open to access of all and developed through active participation. Language, for example, like affects and gestures, is for the most part common, and indeed if language were made either private or public—that is, if large portions of our words, phrases, or parts of speech were subject to private ownership or public authority—then language would lose its powers of expression, creativity, and communication. Such an example is meant not to calm readers, as if to say that the crises created by private and public controls are not as bad as they seem, but rather to help readers begin to retrain their vision, recognizing the common that exists and what it can do. That is the first step in a project to win back and expand the common and its powers.

The seemingly exclusive alternative between the private and the public corresponds to an equally pernicious political alternative between capitalism and socialism. It is often assumed that the only cure for the ills of capitalist society is public regulation and Keynesian and/or socialist economic management; and, conversely, socialist maladies are presumed to be treatable only by private property and capitalist control. Socialism and capitalism, however, even though they have at times been mingled together and at others occasioned bitter conflicts, are both regimes of property that exclude the common. The political project of instituting the common, which we develop in this book, cuts diagonally across these false alternatives—neither private nor public, neither capitalist nor socialist—and opens a new space for politics.

Contemporary forms of capitalist production and accumulation in fact, despite their continuing drive to privatize resources and wealth, paradoxically make possible and even require expansions of the common. Capital, of course, is not a pure form of command but a social relation, and it depends for its survival and development on productive subjectivities that are internal but antagonistic to it. Through processes of globalization, capital not only brings together all the earth under its command but also creates, invests, and exploits social life in its entirety, ordering life according to the hierarchies of economic value. In the newly dominant forms of production that involve information, codes, knowledge, images, and affects, for example, producers increasingly require a high degree of freedom as well as open access to the common, especially in its social forms, such as communications networks, information banks, and cultural circuits. Innovation in Internet technologies, for example, depends directly on access to common code and information resources as well as the ability to connect and interact with others in unrestricted networks. And more generally, all forms of production in decentralized networks, whether or not computer technologies are involved, demand freedom and access to the common. Furthermore the content of what is produced—including ideas, images, and affects—is easily reproduced and thus tends toward being common, strongly resisting all legal and economic efforts to privatize it or bring it under public control. The transition is already in process: contemporary capitalist production by addressing its own needs is opening up the possibility of and creating the bases for a social and economic order grounded in the common.

The ultimate core of biopolitical production, we can see stepping back to a higher level of abstraction, is not the production of objects for subjects, as commodity production is often understood, but the production of subjectivity itself. This is the terrain from which our ethical and political project must set out. But how can an ethical production be established on the shifting ground of the production of subjectivity, which constantly transforms fixed values and subjects? Gilles Deleuze, reflecting on Michel Foucault's notion of the *dispositif* (the material, social, affective, and cognitive mechanisms or apparatuses of the production of subjectivity), claims, "We belong to the *dispositifs* and act within them." If we are to act within them, however, the ethical horizon has to be reoriented from identity to becoming. At issue "is not what we are but rather what we are in the process of becoming—that is the Other, our becoming-other."[2] A key scene of political action today, seen from this vantage point, involves the struggle over the control or autonomy of the production of subjectivity. The multitude makes itself by composing in the common the singular subjectivities that result from this process.

We often find that our political vocabulary is insufficient for grasping the new conditions and possibilities of the contemporary world. Sometimes we invent new terms to face this challenge, but more often we seek to resurrect and reanimate old political concepts that have fallen out of use, both because they carry powerful histories and because they disrupt the conventional understandings of our present world and pose it in a new light. Two such concepts that play particularly significant roles in this book are poverty and love. The poor was a widespread political concept in Europe, at least from the Middle Ages to the seventeenth century, but although we will do our best to learn from some of those histories, we are more interested in what the poor has become today. Thinking in terms of poverty has the healthy effect, first of all, of questioning traditional class designations and forcing us to investigate with fresh eyes how class composition has changed and look at people's wide range of productive activities inside and outside wage relations. Seen in this way, second, the poor is defined by not lack but possibility. The poor, migrants, and "precarious" workers (that is, those without stable employment) are often conceived as excluded, but really, though subordinated, they are completely within the global rhythms of biopolitical production. Economic statistics can grasp the condition of poverty in negative terms but not the forms of life, languages, movements, or capacities for innovation they generate. Our challenge will be to find ways to translate the productivity and possibility of the poor into power.

Walter Benjamin, with his typical elegance and intelligence, grasps the changing concept of poverty already in the 1930s. He locates the shift, in a nihilistic key, in the experience of those who have witnessed destruction, specifically the destruction wrought by the First World War, which casts us in a common condition. Benjamin sees, born out of the ruins of the past, the potential for a new, positive form of barbarism. "For what does poverty of experience do for the barbarian? It forces him to start from scratch; to make a new start; to make a little go a long way; to begin with a little and build up further."[3] The "barbaric" productivity of the poor sets out to make a common world.

Love provides another path for investigating the power and

productivity of the common. Love is a means to escape the solitude of individualism but not, as contemporary ideology tells us, only to be isolated again in the private life of the couple or the family. To arrive at a political concept of love that recognizes it as centered on the production of the common and the production of social life, we have to break away from most of the contemporary meanings of the term by bringing back and working with some older notions. Socrates, for example, reports in the *Symposium* that, according to Diotima, his "instructor in love," love is born of poverty and invention. As he tries to elaborate what she taught him, he claims that love tends naturally toward the ideal realm to achieve beauty and wealth, thus fulfilling desire. French and Italian feminists argue, however, that Plato has Diotima all wrong. She guides us not toward the "sublimation" of poverty and desire in the "fullness" of beauty and wealth, but toward the power of becoming defined by differences.[4] Diotima's notion of love gives us a new definition of wealth that extends our notion of the common and points toward a process of liberation.[5]

Since poverty and love might appear too weak to overthrow the current ruling powers and develop a project of the common, we will need to emphasize the element of force that animates them. This is in part an intellectual force. Immanuel Kant, for example, conceives of Enlightenment in terms of a force that can banish the "fanatical visions" that result in the death of philosophy and, moreover, can win out over every policing of thought. Jacques Derrida, following this "enlightened" Kant, brings reason back to the force of doubt and recognizes the revolutionary passion of reason as emerging from the margins of history.[6] We too believe that such intellectual force is required to overcome dogmatism and nihilism, but we insist on the need to complement it with physical force and political action. Love needs force to conquer the ruling powers and dismantle their corrupt institutions before it can create a new world of common wealth.

The ethical project we develop in this book sets out on the path of the political construction of the multitude with Empire. The multitude is a set of singularities that poverty and love compose in the reproduction of the common, but more is required to describe the dynamics and *dispositifs* of the becoming-Prince of the multitude. We will not pull out of our hats new transcendentals or new definitions of the will to power to impose on the multitude. The becoming-Prince of the multitude is a project that relies entirely on the immanence of decision making within the multitude. We will have to discover the passage from revolt to revolutionary institution that the multitude can set in motion.

With the title of this book, *Commonwealth,* we mean to indicate a return to some of the themes of classic treatises of government, exploring the institutional structure and political constitution of society. We also want to emphasize, once we recognize the relation between the two terms that compose this concept, the need to institute and manage a world of common wealth, focusing on and expanding our capacities for collective production and self-government. The first half of the book is a philosophical and historical exploration that focuses successively on the republic, modernity, and capital as three frameworks that obstruct and corrupt the development of the common. On each of these terrains, however, we also discover alternatives that emerge in the multitude of the poor and the circuits of altermodernity. The second half of the book is a political and economic analysis of the contemporary terrain of the common. We explore the global governance structures of Empire and the apparatuses of capitalist command to gauge the current state and potential of the multitude. Our analysis ends with a reflection on the contemporary possibilities for revolution and the institutional processes it would require. At the end of each part of the book is a section that takes up from a different and more philosophical perspective a central issue raised in the body of the text. (The function of these sections is similar to that of the Scholia in Spinoza's *Ethics.*) These together with the Intermezzo can also be read consecutively as one continuous investigation.

Jean-Luc Nancy, setting out from premises analogous to ours, wonders if "one can suggest a 'Spinozian' reading, or rewriting, of

[Heidegger's] *Being and Time.*"[7] We hope that our work points in that direction, overturning the phenomenology of nihilism and opening up the multitude's processes of productivity and creativity that can revolutionize our world and institute a shared common wealth. We want not only to define an event but also to grasp the spark that will set the prairie ablaze.

PART 1

REPUBLIC (AND THE MULTITUDE
OF THE POOR)

I'm tired of the sun staying up in the sky. I can't wait until the syntax
of the world comes undone.
> —Italo Calvino, *The Castle of Crossed Destinies*

1.1

REPUBLIC OF PROPERTY

> The two grand favourites of the subjects, liberty and property (for which most men pretend to strive), are as contrary as fire to water, and cannot stand together.
>
> —Robert Filmer, "Observations upon Aristotle's Politiques"

> Thus, at its highest point the political constitution is the constitution of private property.
>
> —Karl Marx, *Critique of Hegel's Philosophy of Right*

On an Apocalyptic Tone Recently Adopted in Politics

A kind of apocalypticism reigns among the contemporary conceptions of power, with warnings of new imperialisms and new fascisms. Everything is explained by sovereign power and the state of exception, that is, the general suspension of rights and the emergence of a power that stands above the law. Indeed evidence of such a state of exception is easy to come by: the predominance of violence to resolve national and international conflicts not merely as last but as first resort; the widespread use of torture and even its legitimation; the indiscriminate killing of civilians in combat; the elision of international law; the suspension of domestic rights and protections; and the list goes on and on. This vision of the world resembles those medieval European renditions of hell: people burning in a river of fire, others being torn limb from limb, and in the center a great devil engorging their bodies whole. The problem with this picture is that its focus on transcendent authority and violence eclipses and mystifies the really dominant forms of power that continue to rule over us today—power embodied in property and capital, power embedded in and fully supported by the law.

In popular discourse the apocalyptic vision sees everywhere the rise of new fascisms. Many refer to the U.S. government as fascist, most often citing Abu Ghraib, Guantanamo, Faluja, and the Patriot Act. Others call the Israeli government fascist by referring to the continuing occupations of Gaza and the West Bank, the use of assassinations and bulldozers as diplomacy, and the bombing of Lebanon. Still others use "islamofascism" to designate the theocratic governments and movements of the Muslim world. It is true, of course, that many simply use the term "fascism" in a general way to designate a political regime or movement they deplore such that it comes to mean simply "very bad." But in all these cases when the term "fascist" is employed, the element it highlights is the authoritarian face of power, its rule by force; and what is eclipsed or mystified, instead, is the daily functioning of constitutional, legal processes and the constant pressure of profit and property. In effect, the bright flashes of a series of extreme events and cases blind many to the quotidian and enduring structures of power.[1]

The scholarly version of this apocalyptic discourse is characterized by an excessive focus on the concept of sovereignty. The sovereign is the one who rules over the exception, such authors affirm, and thus the sovereign stands both inside and outside the law. Modern power remains fundamentally theological, according to this view, not so much in the sense that divine notions of authority have been secularized, but rather in that sovereign power occupies a transcendent position, above society and outside its structures. In certain respects this intellectual trend represents a return to Thomas Hobbes and his great Leviathan that looms over the social terrain, but more fundamentally it replays the European debates of the 1930s, especially in Germany, with Carl Schmitt standing at its center. Just as in the popular discourses, here too economic and legal structures of power tend to be pushed back into the shadows, considered only secondary or, at most, instruments at the disposal of the sovereign power. Every modern form of power thus tends to be collapsed into sovereignty or fascism, while the camp, the ultimate site of control both inside and outside the social order, becomes the paradigmatic topos of modern society.[2]

These apocalyptic visions—both the scholarly analyses of sovereign power and the popular accusations of fascism—close down political engagement with power. There are no forces of liberation inherent in such a power that, though now frustrated and blocked, could be set free. There is no hope of transforming such a power along a democratic course. It needs to be opposed, destroyed, and that is all. Indeed one theological aspect implicit in this conception of sovereignty is its Manichean division between extreme options: either we submit to this transcendent sovereignty or we oppose it in its entirety. It is worth remembering that when Left terrorist groups in the 1970s claimed that the state was fascist, this implied for them that armed struggle was the only political avenue available. Leftists today who talk of a new fascism generally follow the claim with moral outrage and resignation rather than calls for armed struggle, but the core logic is the same: there can be no political engagement with a sovereign fascist power; all it knows is violence.

The primary form of power that really confronts us today, however, is not so dramatic or demonic but rather earthly and mundane. We need to stop confusing politics with theology. The predominant contemporary form of sovereignty—if we still want to call it that—is completely embedded within and supported by legal systems and institutions of governance, a republican form characterized not only by the rule of law but also equally by the rule of property. Said differently, the political is not an autonomous domain but one completely immersed in economic and legal structures. There is nothing extraordinary or exceptional about this form of power. Its claim to naturalness, in fact its silent and invisible daily functioning, makes it extremely difficult to recognize, analyze, and challenge. Our first task, then, will be to bring to light the intimate relations between sovereignty, law, and capital.

We need for contemporary political thought an operation something like the one Euhemerus conducted for ancient Greek mythology in the fourth century BC. Euhemerus explained that all of the myths of gods are really just stories of historical human actions that through retelling have been expanded, embellished, and cast up to the heavens. Similarly today the believers imagine a sovereign power that stands above us on the mountaintops, when in fact the dominant forms of power are entirely this-worldly. A new political Euhemerism might help people stop looking for sovereignty in the heavens and recognize the structures of power on earth.[3]

Once we strip away the theological pretenses and apocalyptic visions of contemporary theories of sovereignty, once we bring them down to the social terrain, we need to look more closely at how power functions in society today. In philosophical terms we can think of this shift in perspective as a move from *transcendent* analysis to *transcendental* critique. Immanuel Kant's "Copernican revolution" in philosophy puts an end to all the medieval attempts to anchor reason and understanding in transcendent essences and things in themselves. Philosophy must strive instead to reveal the transcendental structures immanent to thought and experience. "I call all cognition transcendental that is occupied not so much with objects but rather with our mode of cognition of objects insofar as this is to be possible *a priori*."[4] Kant's transcendental plane thus occupies a position not wholly in the immediate, immanent facts of experience but not wholly outside them either. This transcendental realm, he explains, is where the conditions of possibility of knowledge and experience reside.

Whereas Kant's transcendental critique is focused primarily on reason and knowledge, ours is aimed at power. Just as Kant sweeps away the preoccupations of medieval philosophy with transcendent essences and divine causes, so too must we get beyond theories of sovereignty based on rule over the exception, which is really a holdover from old notions of the royal prerogatives of the monarch. We must focus instead on the transcendental plane of power, where law and capital are the primary forces. Such transcendental powers compel obedience not through the commandment of a sovereign or even primarily through force but rather by structuring the conditions of possibility of social life.

The intuition that law functions as a transcendental structure led entire schools of juridical and constitutional thought, from Hans Kelsen to John Rawls, to develop Kantian formalism in legal theory.[5] Property, which is taken to be intrinsic to human thought and action, serves as the regulative idea of the constitutional state and the rule of law. This is not really a historical foundation but rather an ethical obligation, a constitutive form of the moral order. The concept of the individual is defined by not *being* but *having;* rather than to a "deep" metaphysical and transcendental unity, in other words, it refers to a "superficial" entity endowed with property or possessions, defined increasingly today in "patrimonial" terms as shareholder. In effect, through the concept of the individual, the transcendent figure of the legitimation of property is integrated into the transcendental formalism of legality. The exception, we might say, is included within the constitution.

Capital too functions as an impersonal form of domination that imposes laws of its own, economic laws that structure social life and make hierarchies and subordinations seem natural and necessary. The basic elements of capitalist society—the power of property concentrated in the hands of the few, the need for the majority to sell their labor-power to maintain themselves, the exclusion of large portions of the global population even from these circuits of exploitation, and so forth—all function as an a priori. It is even difficult to recognize this as violence because it is so normalized and its force is applied so impersonally. Capitalist control and exploitation rely primarily not on an external sovereign power but on invisible, internalized laws. And as financial mechanisms become ever more fully developed, capital's determination of the conditions of possibility of social life become ever more extensive and complete. It is true, of course, that finance capital, since it is so abstract, seems distant from the lives of most people; but that very abstraction is what gives it the general power of an a priori, with increasingly universal reach, even when people do not recognize their involvement in finance markets—through personal and national debt, through financial instruments that operate on all kinds of production from soybeans to computers and through the manipulation of currency and interest rates.

Following the form of Kant's argument, then, our transcendental critique must show how capital and law intertwined together—what we call the republic of property—determine and dictate the conditions of possibility of social life in all its facets and phases. But ours is obviously an unfaithful, tendentious appropriation of Kant, which cuts diagonally across his work. We appropriate his critical perspective by recognizing that the formal structure of his epistemological schema corresponds to that of the power of property and law, but then, rather than affirming the transcendental realm, we seek to challenge it. Kant has no interest in overthrowing the rule of capital or its constitutional state. In fact Alfred Sohn-Rethel goes so far as to claim that Kant, particularly in the *Critique of Pure Reason,* strives "to prove the perfect normalcy of bourgeois society," making its structures of power and property appear natural and necessary.[6]

But our quarrel here is not really with Kant. We merely want to use the tools he provides us to confront today's dominant powers. And we should highlight, finally, how the practical consequences of this transcendental critique of the republic of property overcome the powerlessness and bitter resignation that characterize the "transcendent" analyses of sovereignty and fascism. Our critique of capital, the republican constitution, and their intersection as transcendental forms of power does not imply either absolute rejection or, of course, acceptance and acquiescence. Instead our critique is an active process of resistance and transformation, setting free on a new footing the elements that point toward a democratic future, releasing, most significantly, the living labor that is closed within capital and the multitude that is corralled within its republic. Such a critique thus aims at not a return to the past or creation of a future ex nihilo but rather a process of metamorphosis, creating a new society within the shell of the old.

Republican Rights of Property

The term "republicanism" has been used in the history of modern political thought to name a variety of different, competing, often

conflicting political tendencies. Thomas Jefferson, late in his life, reflecting on the early years of the American Revolution, remarks,
"We imagined everything republican which was not monarchy."[7]
There was certainly an equal if not greater range of political positions designated by the term in the English and French revolutionary periods. But one specific definition of modern republicanism
eventually won out over the others: a republicanism based on the
rule of property and the inviolability of the rights of private property, which excludes or subordinates those without property. The
propertyless are merely, according to Abbé Sieyès, "an immense
crowd of *bi-ped instruments,* possessing only their miserably paid
hands and an absorbed soul."[8] There is no necessary or intrinsic link
between the concept of republic and the rule of property, and indeed one could try to restore alternative or create new notions of
republic that are not based on property. Our point is simply that the
republic of property emerged historically as the dominant concept.[9]

The course of the three great bourgeois revolutions—the English, the American, and the French—demonstrates the emergence
and consolidation of the republic of property. In each case the establishment of the constitutional order and the rule of law served to
defend and legitimate private property. Later in this chapter we explore how the radically democratic processes of the English Revolution were blocked by the question of property: a "people of property" faced off against "a multitude of the poor." Here, instead, we
focus briefly on the role of property in the U.S. and French revolutions.

Just a decade after the Declaration of Independence affirms the
constituent power of the American Revolution and projects a mechanism of self-government expressed through new, dynamic, and
open political forms, the *Federalist* and the debates surrounding the
drafting of the Constitution limit and contradict many of these
original elements. The dominant lines in the constitutional debates
aim to reintroduce and consolidate the sovereign structure of the
state and absorb the constituent drive of the republic within the dynamic among constitutional powers. Whereas in the Declaration

constituent power is defined as fundamental, in the Constitution it is understood as something like a national patrimony that is the property and responsibility of the government, an element of constitutional sovereignty.

Constituent power is not stripped from constituted public law but, rather, blocked (and expelled from the practices of citizenship) by the relations of force that the Constitution is built on, most important the right to property. Behind every formal constitution, legal theorists explain, lies a "material" one, where by material constitution is understood the relations of force that ground, within a particular framework, the written constitution and define the orientations and limits that legislation, legal interpretation, and executive decision must respect.[10] The right to property, including originally the rights of slaveholders, is the essential index of this material constitution, which bathes in its light all other constitutional rights and liberties of U.S. citizens. "The Constitution," writes Charles Beard in his classic analysis, "was essentially an economic document based upon the concept that the fundamental private rights of property are anterior to government and morally beyond the reach of popular majorities."[11] Many scholars have contested Beard's claim that the founders in drafting the Constitution were protecting their own individual economic interests and wealth, but what remains unchallenged and entirely convincing in his analysis is that the participants in the debate saw the Constitution as founded on economic interests and the rights of property. "The moment the idea is admitted into society that property is not as sacred as the laws of God," writes John Adams, for example, "and that there is not a force of law and public justice to protect it, anarchy and tyranny commence."[12] The sacred position of property in the Constitution is a central obstacle to the practice and development of constituent power.

One extreme but significant example of the effect of the right of property on the Constitution is the way it transforms the meaning of the right to bear arms. This right is affirmed in the seventeenth- and eighteenth-century Anglo-American tradition as the collective right to achieve and defend freedom, and it calls for the constitution of popular armies or militias rather than standing armies, which are understood to be necessarily tyrannical.[13] In the United States this tradition has been almost entirely obliterated, and the Second Amendment has been given the opposite meaning: that each is the enemy of all; that each must be wary of those who want to steal her or his property. From the transformation of the right to bear arms in the defense of private property follows a general reversal of all the central constitutional concepts. Freedom itself, which many cast as characteristic of U.S. political thought, in contrast to the principles of justice, equality, and solidarity of the revolutionary French experience, is reduced to an apology for capitalist civilization. The centrality of the defense of property also accounts for the pessimistic conception of human nature, which is present but secondary in the revolutionary period and comes to the fore in the constitutional debates. "But what is government itself," James Madison writes, for example, "but the greatest of all reflections on human nature? If men were angels, no government would be necessary."[14] Freedom becomes the negative power of human existence, which serves as a bulwark against the descent of the innate conflicts of human nature into civil war. But at the bottom of this notion of natural conflict is the struggle over property. The armed individual is the only guarantor of that freedom. *Homo politicus* becomes nothing other than *Homo proprietarius.*

In the case of the French Revolution, the centrality of property rights develops in an extraordinarily dynamic and at times violent way. A simple look at the successive revolutionary French Constitutions (and, specifically, the Declarations of the Rights of Man and Citizen that serve as their prologues) from 1789 to 1793 and 1795 gives a first indication of how the development of constitutional thought is constantly governed by the demands of property. For example, the right to property is affirmed in almost identical terms in all three versions (in Article 2 of the 1789 and Article 1 of the 1793 and 1795 Constitutions), but whereas in 1789 and 1793 the right to property is linked with the right of "resistance to oppression," in 1795 it is related only to "security." As far as equality is concerned, whereas in Article 6 of 1789 and Article 4 of 1793 it is defined as a basic right of each subject (and thus also applies to property), in Article 6 of 1795 the mandate of equality is subordinated to the rule of the majority of citizens or their representatives. Equality becomes increasingly formal, increasingly defined as a legal structure that protects wealth and strengthens the appropriative, possessive power of the individual (understood as property owner).

A more substantial and complex view of the centrality of property in the republic emerges when we focus on how the traditional conception of "real rights"—*jus reale,* the right over things—is rediscovered in the course of the French Revolution. These "real rights," property rights in particular, are clearly no longer those of the ancien régime insofar as they no longer establish a static table of values and set of institutions that determine privilege and exclusion. In the French Revolution "real rights" emerge from a new ontological horizon that is defined by the productivity of labor. In France, however, as in all the bourgeois revolutions, these real rights have a paradoxical relation to emerging capitalist ideology. On the one hand, real rights are gradually given greater importance over the universal, abstract rights that seemed to have prominence in the heroic Jacobin phase. Private property at least points toward the human capacity to transform and appropriate nature. Article 5 of the 1795 Constitution, for example, reads, "Property is the right to enjoy and use one's own goods, incomes, the fruit of one's labor and industry." As the revolution proceeds, however, there is a shift in the point of reference from the abstract terrain of the general will to the concrete one of the right and order of property.[15] On the other hand, real rights, which constitute the foundation of rents and incomes, are opposed to "dynamic rights," which stem directly from labor, and although dynamic rights appear to predominate over real rights in the early revolutionary period, gradually real rights become hegemonic over the dynamic ones and end up being central. Landed property and slave property, in other words, which appear initially to have been subordinated as archaic conditions of production, cast aside in favor of the dynamic rights associated with capitalist ideol-

ogy, come back into play. Moreover, when the right to property becomes once again central within the constellation of new rights affirmed by the bourgeois revolutions, it no longer stands simply as a
real right but becomes the paradigm for all the fundamental rights.
Article 544 of the 1804 Code Civil, for example, gives a definition
of property that characterizes notions still common today: "Ownership is the right to enjoy and dispose of things in the most absolute
manner, provided they are not used in a way contrary to law or
regulations."[16] In the dominant line of European political thought
from Locke to Hegel, the absolute rights of people to appropriate
things becomes the basis and substantive end of the legally defined
free individual.

The centrality of property in the republican constitution can
be substantiated from a negative standpoint by looking at the Haitian Revolution and the extraordinary hostility to it. By liberating
the slaves, of course, Haitian revolutionaries should be considered
from the perspective of freedom more advanced than any of their
counterparts in Europe or North America; but the vast majority of
eighteenth- and nineteenth-century republicans not only did not
embrace the Haitian Revolution but struggled as well to suppress it
and contain its effects. For the subsequent two centuries in fact, historians have excluded Haiti from the great pantheon of modern republican revolutions to such an extent that even the memory of the
revolutionary event has been silenced. The Haitian Revolution was
an unthinkable event from the perspective of contemporary Europe
and the United States, centrally, no doubt, because of deeply embedded ideologies and institutions of racial superiority, but we should
also recognize that the Haitian Revolution was unthinkable because
it violated the rule of property. A simple syllogism is at work here:
the republic must protect private property; slaves are private property; therefore republicanism must oppose the freeing of the slaves.
With the example of Haiti, in effect, the republican pretense to value
freedom and equality directly conflicts with the rule of property—
and property wins out. In this sense the exclusion of the Haitian
Revolution from the canon of republicanism is powerful evidence

of the sacred status of property to the republic. It may be appropriate, in fact, that Haiti be excluded from the list of republican revolutions, not because the Haitian Revolution is somehow unworthy of the republican spirit but, on the contrary, because republicanism does not live up to the spirit of freedom and equality contained in the Haitian rebellion against slavery![17]

The primacy of property is revealed in all modern colonial histories. Each time a European power brings new practices of government to its colonies in the name of reason, efficiency, and the rule of law, the primary "republican virtue" they establish is the rule of property. This is evident, for example, in the "Permanent Settlement" established in Bengal by British colonial authorities and administrators of the East India Company in the late eighteenth century to guarantee the security of property, especially landed property, and bolster the position of the Zamindar, the existing Bengali propertied class, thereby solidifying taxation and revenue. Ranajit Guha, in his analysis of the debates leading to the settlement, puzzles over the fact that such a quasi-feudal land settlement could have been authored by bourgeois Englishmen, some of whom were great admirers of the French Revolution. Guha assumes that European bourgeoisies compromise their republican ideals when ruling over conquered lands in order to find a social base for their powers, but in fact they are just establishing there the core principle of the bourgeois republics: the rule of property. The security and inviolability of property is so firmly fixed in the republican mentality that colonial authorities do not question the good of its dissemination.[18]

Finally, with the construction of the welfare state in the first half of the twentieth century, public property gains a more important role in the republican constitution. This transformation of the right to property, however, follows the capitalist transformation of the organization of labor, reflecting the increasing importance that public conditions begin to exert over the relations of production. Despite all the changes, the old dictum remains valid: *l'esprit des lois, c'est la propriété*. Evgeny Pashukanis, writing in the 1920s, anticipates this development with extraordinary clarity. "It is most obvious," Pashukanis claims,

> that the logic of juridical concepts corresponds with the logic of the social relationship of commodity production, and that the history of the system of private law should be sought in these relationships and not in the dispensation of the authorities. On the contrary, the logical relationships of domination and subordination are only partially included in the system of juridical concepts. Therefore, the juridical concept of the state may never become a theory but will always appear as an ideological distortion of the facts.[19]

For Pashukanis, in effect, all law is private law, and public law is merely an ideological figure imagined by bourgeois legal theorists. What is central for our purposes here is that the concept of property and the defense of property remain the foundation of every modern political constitution. This is the sense in which the republic, from the great bourgeois revolutions to today, is a republic of property.

Sapere Aude!

Kant is a prophet of the republic of property not so much directly in his political or economic views but indirectly in the form of power he discovers through his epistemological and philosophical inquiries. We propose to follow Kant's method of transcendental critique, but in doing so we are decidedly deviant, unfaithful followers, reading his work against the grain. The political project we propose is not only (with Kant) an attack on transcendent sovereignty and (against Kant) a critique aimed to destabilize the transcendental power of the republic of property, but also and ultimately (beyond Kant) an affirmation of the immanent powers of social life, because this immanent scene is the terrain—the only possible terrain—on which democracy can be constructed.

Our affirmation of immanence is not based on any faith in the immediate or spontaneous capacities of society. The social plane of immanence has to be organized politically. Our critical project is thus not simply a matter of refusing the mechanisms of power and wielding violence against them. Refusal, of course, is an important and powerful reaction to the imposition of domination, but it alone does not extend beyond the negative gesture. Violence can also be a crucial, necessary response, often as a kind of boomerang effect, redirecting the violence of domination that has been deposited in our bones to strike back at the power that originated it. But such violence too is merely reactive and creates nothing. We need to educate these spontaneous reactions, transforming refusal into resistance and violence into the use of force. The former in each case is an immediate response, whereas the latter results from a confrontation with reality and training of our political instincts and habits, our imaginations and desires. More important, too, resistance and the coordinated use of force extend beyond the negative reaction to power toward an organizational project to construct an alternative on the immanent plane of social life.

The need for invention and organization paradoxically brings us back to Kant, or, really, to a minor voice that runs throughout Kant's writings and presents an alternative to the command and authority of modern power. This alternative comes to the surface clearly, for example, in his brief and well-known text "An Answer to the Question: 'What is Enlightenment?'"[20] The key to emerging from the state of immaturity, the self-sustained state of dependency in which we rely on those in authority to speak and think for us, and establishing our ability and will to speak and think for ourselves, Kant begins, recalling Horace's injunction, is *sapere aude,* "dare to know." This notion of Enlightenment and its defining injunction, however, become terribly ambiguous in the course of Kant's essay. On the one hand, as he explains the kind of reasoning we should adopt, it becomes clear that it is not very daring at all: it compels us dutifully to fulfill our designated roles in society, to pay taxes, to be a soldier, a civil servant, and ultimately to obey the authority of the sovereign, Frederick II. This is the Kant whose life is so regularly ordered, they say, that you can set your watch by the time of his morning walk. Indeed the major line of Kant's work participates in that solid European rationalist tradition that considers Enlightenment the process of the "emendation of reason" that coincides with and supports the preservation of the current social order.

On the other hand, though, Kant opens the possibility of reading the Enlightenment injunction against the grain: "dare to know" really means at the same time also "know how to dare." This simple inversion indicates the audacity and courage required, along with the risks involved, in thinking, speaking, and acting autonomously. This is the minor Kant, the bold, daring Kant, which is often hidden, subterranean, buried in his texts, but from time to time breaks out with a ferocious, volcanic, disruptive power. Here reason is no longer the foundation of duty that supports established social authority but rather a disobedient, rebellious force that breaks through the fixity of the present and discovers the new. Why, after all, should we dare to think and speak for ourselves if these capacities are only to be silenced immediately by a muzzle of obedience? Kant's critical method is in fact double: his critiques do determine the system of transcendental conditions of knowledge and phenomena, but they also occasionally step beyond the transcendental plane to take up a humanistic notion of power and invention, the key to the free, biopolitical construction of the world. The major Kant provides the tools for stabilizing the transcendental ordering of the republic of property, whereas the minor Kant blasts apart its foundations, opening the way for mutation and free creation on the biopolitical plane of immanence.[21]

This alternative within Kant helps us differentiate between two political paths. The lines of the major Kant are extended in the field of political thought most faithfully today by theorists of social democracy, who speak about reason and Enlightenment but never really enter onto the terrain where daring to know and knowing how to dare coincide. Enlightenment for them is a perpetually unfinished project that always requires acceptance of the established social structures, consent to a compromised vision of rights and democracy, acquiescence to the lesser evil. Social democrats thus never radically question the republic of property, either blithely ignoring its power or naïvely assuming that it can be reformed to generate a society of democracy and equality.

The social democratic projects of Jürgen Habermas and John Rawls, for example, aim to maintain a social order based on transcendental, formal schema. Early in their careers Habermas and Rawls both propose more dynamic concepts oriented toward social transformation: Habermas works with a Hegelian notion of intersubjectivity that opens the possibility for radical productive subjective capacity, and Rawls insists on a "difference principle" whereby social decisions and institutions should benefit most the least advantaged members of society. These proposals, albeit in different ways, suggest a dynamic of social transformation. In the course of their careers, however, these possibilities of social transformation and subjective capacity are diluted or completely abandoned. Habermas's notions of communicative reason and action come to define a process that constantly mediates all social reality, thus accepting and even reinforcing the given terms of the existing social order. Rawls constructs a formal, transcendental schema of judgment that neutralizes subjective capacities and transformative processes, putting the emphasis instead on maintaining the equilibrium of the social system. The version of social democracy we find in Habermas and Rawls thus echoes the notion of Enlightenment of the major Kant, which, despite its rhetoric of emendation, reinforces the existing social order through schemas of transcendental formalism.[22]

Anthony Giddens and Ulrich Beck propose a version of social democracy whose basis is much more empirical and pragmatic. Whereas Habermas and Rawls require a point of departure and mediation that is in some sense "outside" the social plane, Giddens and Beck start "inside." Giddens, adopting a skeptical standpoint, attempts to fashion from the empirical and the phenomenal level an adequate representation of society in the process of reform, working, one could say, from the social to the transcendental plane. When society refuses to comply, however, when ghettos in revolt and social conflicts sprouting all around make it impossible to maintain an idea of reformist mediation emerging directly from social reality, Giddens takes recourse to a sovereign power that can bring to conclusion the process of reform. Paradoxically, Giddens introduces a transcendental project and then is subsequently forced to violate it with such an appeal to a transcendent power. Ulrich Beck, more than Giddens and indeed more than any other social democratic theorist, is willing to set his feet solidly in the real social field and deal with all the ambiguous struggles, the uncertainty, fear, and passions that constitute it. Beck is able to recognize, for example, the dynamics of workers' struggles against the factory regime and against factory closings. Although he can analyze the exhaustion of one social form, however, such as the modernity of the factory regime of production, he cannot grasp fully the emergence of new social forces. His thinking thus runs up against the fixity of the transcendental structure, which even for him ultimately guides the analysis. Modernity gives way to hypermodernity in Beck's view, which is really, in the end, only a continuation of modernity's primary structures.[23]

Analogous social democratic positions are common among contemporary theorists of globalization as diverse as David Held, Joseph Stiglitz, and Thomas Friedman. The Kantian resonances are not as strong here, but these theorists do preach reform of the global system without ever calling into question the structures of capital and property.[24] The essence of social democracy in all these various figures is the proposition of social reform, sometimes even aimed at equality, freedom, and democracy, that fails to draw into question—and even reinforces—the structures of the republic of property. In this way social democratic reformism dovetails perfectly with the reformism of capital. Social democrats like to call their modern project unfinished, as if with more time and greater efforts the desired reforms will finally come about, but really this claim is completely illusory because the process is blocked from the outset by the unquestioned transcendental structures of law and property. Social democrats continue faithfully the transcendental position of the major Kant, advocating a process of Enlightenment in which, paradoxically, all elements of the existing social order stay firmly in place.

Reforming or perfecting the republic of property will never lead to equality and freedom but only perpetuate its structures of inequality and unfreedom. Robert Filmer, a lucid seventeenth-century reactionary, recognizes clearly, in the passage that serves as an epigraph to this chapter, that liberty and property are as contrary as fire and water, and cannot stand together.

Such neo-Kantian positions may appear harmless, even if illusory, but at several points in history they have played damaging roles, particularly in the period of the rise of fascism. No one, of course, is blameless when such tragedies occur, but from the late nineteenth century to the 1920s and 1930s neo-Kantianism constituted the central ideology of bourgeois society and European politics, and indeed the only ideology open to social democratic reformism. Primarily in Marburg (with Hermann Cohen and Paul Natorp) and Heidelberg (with Heinrich Rickert and Wilhelm Windelband) but also in Oxford, Paris, Boston, and Rome, all the possible Kantian variations blossomed. Seldom has an ideological concert been as widespread and its influence as profound over an entire system of *Geisteswissenschaften*. Corporate bosses and syndicalists, liberals and socialists divided the parts, some playing in the orchestra, others with the chorus. But there was something profoundly out of tune in this concert: a dogmatic faith in the inevitable reform of society and progress of spirit, which meant for them the advance of bourgeois rationality. This faith was not based on some political will to bring about transformation or even any risk of engaging in struggle. When the fascisms emerged, then, the transcendental consciousness of modernity was immediately swept away. Do we have to mourn that fact? It does not seem that contemporary social democratic thinkers with their transcendental illusion have any more effective response than their predecessors to the risks and dangers we face, which, as we said earlier, are different from those of the 1930s. Instead the illusory faith in progress masks and obstructs the real means of political action and struggle while maintaining the transcendental mechanisms of power that continue to exercise violence over anyone who dares to know and act rather than maintaining the rules of an Enlightenment that has become mere routine.

We will try instead in the pages that follow to develop the method of the minor Kant, for whom daring to know requires simultaneously knowing how to dare. This too is an Enlightenment project, but one based on an alternative rationality in which a methodology of materialism and metamorphosis calls on powers of resistance, creativity, and invention. Whereas the major Kant provides the instruments to support and defend the republic of property even up to today, the minor Kant helps us see how to overthrow it and construct a democracy of the multitude.

1.2

PRODUCTIVE BODIES

In girum imus nocte
Et consumimur igni.
(We traveled through the night
And were consumed / redeemed by fire.)
—Guy Debord

From the Marxist Critique of Property . . .

Karl Marx develops in his early work—from "On the Jewish Question" and the "Critique of Hegel's Philosophy of Right" to his "Economic and Philosophical Manuscripts"—an analysis of private property as the basis of all capitalist legal structures. The relationship between capital and law defines a paradoxical power structure that is at once extraordinarily abstract and entirely concrete. On the one hand, legal structures are abstract representations of social reality, relatively indifferent to social contents, and on the other, capitalist property defines the concrete conditions of the exploitation of labor. Both are totalizing social frameworks, extending across the entire social space, working in coordination and holding together, so to speak, the abstract and concrete planes. Marx adds to this paradoxical synthesis of the abstract and the concrete the recognition that labor is the positive content of private property. "The relation of private property contains latent within itself," Marx writes,

> the relation of private property as *labour,* the relation of private property as *capital* and the *connection* of these two. On the one hand we have the production of human activity as *labour,* i.e. as

an activity wholly alien to itself, to man and to nature, and hence to consciousness and vital expression, the *abstract* existence of man as a mere *workman* who therefore tumbles day after day from his fulfilled nothingness into absolute nothingness, into his social and hence real non-existence; and on the other, the production of the object of human labour as *capital,* in which all the natural and social individuality of the object is *extinguished* and private property has lost its natural and social quality (i.e. has lost all political and social appearances and is not even *apparently* tainted with any human relationships).[25]

Private property in its capitalist form thus produces a relation of exploitation in its fullest sense—the production of the human as commodity—and excludes from view the materiality of human needs and poverty.

Marx's critical approach in these early texts is powerful but not sufficient to grasp the entire set of effects that property, operating through law, determines over human life. Many twentieth-century Marxist authors extend the critique of private property beyond the legal context to account for the diverse material dynamics that constitute oppression and exploitation in capitalist society. Louis Althusser, for one, clearly defines this shift in perspective, configuring it in philological and scholastic terms as a break within Marx's own thought from his youthful humanism to his mature materialism. Althusser recognizes, in effect, a passage from the analysis of property as exploitation in terms of a transcendental form to the analysis of it in terms of the material organization of bodies in the production and reproduction of capitalist society. In this passage critique is, so to speak, raised to the level of truth and at the same time superseded, as philosophy gives way to politics. In roughly the same period Max Horkheimer, Theodor Adorno, and other authors of the Frankfurt School, especially when they confront the conditions of U.S. capitalist development, operate a corresponding shift within Marxism: emphasizing the breakdown of the conceptual boundary between structure and superstructure, the consequent construction of mate-

rially effective ideological structures of rule (corresponding to Althusser's "ideological state apparatuses"), and the accomplishment of
the real subsumption of society within capital. The result of these
diverse interventions is a "phenomenologization" of critique, that is,
a shift to consider the relationship between critique and its object as
a material *dispositif*, within the collective dimension of bodies—a
shift, in short, from the transcendental to the immanent.[26]

This shift moves toward a perspective that had been difficult to
recognize within the Marxist tradition: the standpoint of bodies.
When we credit this shift to Althusser and the Frankfurt School, we
do so rather maliciously because we are convinced that the real passage, which is only intuited or suspected on the scholastic level of
such authors, is accomplished on the level of theory developed
within militancy or activism. The journals *Socialisme ou barbarie* in
France and *Quaderni rossi* in Italy are among the first in the 1960s to
pose the theoretical-practical importance of the standpoint of bodies in Marxist analysis. In many respects the investigations of worker
and peasant insurgencies in the South Asian journal *Subaltern Studies*
develop along parallel lines, and certainly there are other similar experiences that emerge in the Marxist analyses of this period throughout the world. Key is the immersion of the analysis in the struggles
of the subordinated and exploited, considered as the matrix of every
institutional relationship and every figure of social organization. "Up
to this point we have analyzed capital," Mario Tronti writes in the
early 1960s, but "from now on we have to analyze the struggles as
the principle of all historical movement."[27] Raniero Panzieri, who
like Tronti is a central figure in *Quaderni rossi,* adds that although
Marxism is born as sociology, the fundamental task is to translate
that sociological perspective into not just political science but really
the science of revolution. In *Socialisme ou barbarie,* to give another
example, Cornelius Castoriadis emphasizes that revolutionary research constantly has to follow and be redefined by the forms of the
social movements. And finally Hans-Jürgen Krahl, in the midst of
one of those extraordinary discussions at the heart of the German
socialist youth movements that precede the events of 1968, insists on

the break with every transcendental concept of the revolutionary
process such that every theoretical notion of constitution has to be
grounded in concrete experience.[28]

It is interesting in this context to look back at the 1970 Situationist manifesto titled "Contribution à la prise de conscience d'une
classe qui sera la dernière." What is fascinating about this avant-garde
text is certainly not its ridiculous Dadaist declarations or its sophisticated "Letterist" paradoxes but rather the fact of its being an investigation of the concrete conditions of labor, one that is able to grasp
in initial and partial but nonetheless correct terms the separation of
labor-power from the control of capital when immaterial production becomes hegemonic over all the other valorization processes.
This Situationist worker investigation anticipates in some extraordinary ways the social transformations of the twenty-first century. Living labor oriented toward producing immaterial goods, such as cognitive or intellectual labor, always exceeds the bounds set on it and
poses forms of desire that are not consumed and forms of life that
accumulate. When immaterial production becomes hegemonic, all
the elements of the capitalist process have to be viewed in a new
light, sometimes in terms completely inverted from the traditional
analyses of historical materialism. What was called "the transition
from capitalism to communism" takes the form of a process of liberation in practice, the constitution of a new world. Through the
activity of conducting a worker investigation, in other words, the
"phenomenologization" of critique becomes revolutionary—and
we find Marx redivivus.

This entry of the phenomenology of bodies into Marxist theory, which begins by opposing any ideology of rights and law, any
transcendental mediation or dialectical relationship, has to be organized politically—and indeed this perspective provides some of the
bases for the events of 1968. This intellectual development recalls in
some respects the scientific transformations of the Italian Renaissance three centuries earlier. Renaissance philosophers combined
their critique of the scholastic tradition with experiments to understand the nature of reality, combing the city, for example, for animals

to dissect, using their bistoury and scalpels to reveal the functioning of individual bodies. So too the theorists in the 1950s and 1960s, when, one might say, modernity arrives at its conclusion, recognize the necessity not only to develop a philosophical critique of the Marxist tradition but also to ground it in militant experience, using the scalpels that reveal, through readings of the factory and social struggles, the new anatomy of collective bodies.

Many different paths trace this passage in European Marxist theory. The fundamental genealogy no doubt follows the development of workers' struggles inside and outside the factories, moving from salary demands to social demands and thus extending the terrain of struggle and analysis to reach all corners of social life. The dynamic of struggles is not only antagonistic but also constructive or, better, constituent, interpreting a new era of political economy and proposing within it new alternatives. (We will return in detail to this economic transformation and the constituent struggles within it in Part 3.) But other important intellectual developments undoubtedly allow and force European Marxist theorists to move toward a standpoint of bodies. The work of Simone de Beauvoir and the beginnings of second wave feminist thought, for example, focus attention powerfully on the gender differences and hierarchies that are profoundly material and corporeal. Antiracist thought, particularly emerging from the anticolonial struggles in these years, put pressure on European Marxist theory to adopt the standpoint of bodies to recognize both the structures of domination and the possibilities for liberation struggles. We can recognize another, rather different path toward the theoretical centrality of the body in two films by Alain Resnais from the 1950s. *Night and Fog* and *Hiroshima mon amour* (written by Marguerite Duras) mark the imaginary of a generation of European intellectuals with the horrors of the Jewish Holocaust and the atomic devastation in Japan. The threat and reality of genocidal acts thrusts the theme of life itself onto center stage so that every reference to economic production and reproduction cannot forget the centrality of bodies. Each of these perspectives—feminist thought, antiracist and anticolonial thought, and the consciousness of genocide—forces Marxist theorists of that generation to recognize not only the commodification of laboring bodies but also the torture of gendered and racialized bodies. It is no coincidence that the series of classic studies of the discontent and poverty of the human spirit—from Freud to Marcuse—can be read as an encyclopedia of colonial-capitalist violence.

The paradox, though, is that even in the moment of capital's triumph in the 1960s, when bodies are directly invested by the mode of production and the commodification of life has rendered their relations entirely abstract, that is the point when, immediately within the processes of industrial and social production, bodies spring back onto center stage in the form of revolt. This returns us to the primordial necessity of bourgeois society we analyzed earlier, that is, the right of property as the basis of the republic itself. This is not the exception but the normal condition of the republic that reveals both the transcendental condition and the material foundation of the social order. Only the standpoint of bodies and their power can challenge the discipline and control wielded by the republic of property.

... To the Phenomenology of Bodies

Philosophy is not always the owl of Minerva, arriving at dusk to illuminate retrospectively a waning historical period. Sometimes it anticipates history—and that is not always a good thing. In Europe reactionary philosophies have often anticipated and posed the ideological bases for historical events, including the rise of fascisms and the great totalitarianisms of the twentieth century.[29] Consider, for example, two authors who dominate European thought in the first decades of the century and effectively anticipate the totalitarian events: Henri Bergson and Giovanni Gentile. Their work helps us trace another important genealogy that brings us back to the phenomenology of bodies with a new and powerful perspective.

The essential anticipatory element of this stream of early-twentieth-century European thought, which has a profound influence on reactionary political ideologies, is its invention of a philosophy of life that poses at its center an ethics of radical action. Vitalism, which unleashes a destructive fury on the critical tradition, transcendental epistemologies, and Kantian liberal ideology, has such influence in part because it corresponds to some of the dominant political and economic developments of the times. Capitalist command has been thrown into crisis by the first serious expressions of the workers' movement as a subversive force, and capital's stable values seem to be threatened by a chaotic relativism. Capitalist ideology needs to return to its beginnings, reaffirming its values, verifying its decision-making powers, and destroying every obstacle posed by mechanisms of social mediation. Such a context provides fertile soil for a blind and proud voluntarism. Vitalism, which Bergson configures as flux and Gentile as a dialectic without negativity, presents a powerful ideology for affirming a hegemonic will. Transcendental abstraction pays the price as the conception of history is forced to mold itself to the teleology of power. Bergson ends his life a Catholic and Gentile a fascist: that is how history reenters their thought. When history is believed to be threatened by an absolute relativism, religious values or voluntaristic affirmations seem the only alternative.

The great historicist thinkers of the period are also caught between these two poles: either relativism or a religious/voluntarist escape. The lines are already clear, for example, in the late-nineteenth-century exchanges between Wilhelm Dilthey and Graf Paul Yorck von Wartenburg. For Yorck relativism means cynicism and materialism, whereas for Dilthey it opens the possibility of a vital and singular affirmation within and through the historical process.[30] This debate prefigures, in epistemological terms and in the relationship between history and event, the tragedies of twentieth-century Europe in which the event and transcendence take horrifying forms in the long "European civil war" and historicism comes to mean simply political disorientation, in the various figures of fascism and populism. The destruction of the critical tradition and the dissolution of neo-Kantianism is one necessary prerequisite for the vitalist positions to become hegemonic in the confused scene of European cultural and political debates.

Phenomenology emerges in this context to operate an anti-Platonic, anti-idealist, and above all anti-transcendental revolution. Phenomenology is posed primarily as an attempt to go beyond the skeptical and relativist effects of post-Hegelian historicism, but at the same time it is driven to rediscover in every concept and every idea modes of life and material substance. Reflecting on the complex legacy of Kantianism and the violent consequences of vitalism, phenomenology pulls critique away from transcendental abstraction and reformulates it as an engagement with lived experience. This immersion in concrete and determinate being is the great strength of twentieth-century phenomenology, which corresponds to the transformation of Marxism that we traced earlier, from the critique of property to the critique of bodies.

Martin Heidegger marks out one influential path of phenomenology, but one that fails to arrive at the critique and affirmation of bodies that interests us here. His thought is permeated by a brooding reflection over the failure of modernity and destruction of its values. He brings phenomenology back to classical ontology not in order to develop a means to reconstruct being through human productive capacities but rather as a meditation on our telluric condition, our powerlessness, and death. All that can be constructed, all that resistances and struggles produce, is here instead disempowered and found "thrown" onto the surface of being. What phenomenology casts out—including Bergsonian vitalism, Gentile's voluntarism, and historicist relativism—Heidegger brings in the back door, positing it as the fabric of the present constitution of being. Heidegger's notion of *Gelassenheit,* letting go, withdrawing from engagement, for example, not only brings back the earlier vitalism and voluntarism by confusing history with destiny but also reconfigures them as an apology for fascism. "Who would have thought reading *Being and Time,*" Reiner Schürmann reflects, "that a few years later Heidegger would have entrusted the *Da-sein* to someone's will? This institution of a contingent will that rules over the *Da* determines the anthropology, the theology, and the populism of Heidegger's thought."[31] The critique and affirmation of bodies that characterizes phenomenology's revolution in philosophy thus gets completely lost in Heidegger.

This Heideggerian trajectory, however, should not obscure the much more important path of phenomenology that extends from Edmund Husserl to Maurice Merleau-Ponty. Even though closed in the speculative cage of the transcendental, imposed by the German academy, Husserl spends his life trying to break down the consistency of the subject as individual and reconstruct subjectivity as a relation with the other, projecting knowledge through intentionality. (This project leads him in the 1930s to denounce the development of the European sciences and the crisis of their ethical content, when capitalism and national sovereignty, imperialism, and war have usurped their goals and meaning.) In Merleau-Ponty being-inside the concrete reality of bodies implies an even more fundamental relation to alterity, being among others, in the perceptive modalities and the linguistic forms of being. And the experience of alterity is always traversed by a project to construct the common. Immanence thus becomes the exclusive horizon of philosophy, an immanence that is opposed not only to metaphysical transcendence but also to epistemological transcendentalism. It is no coincidence, then, that this path of phenomenology intersects at this point, in Merleau-Ponty and others, with Marxist critiques of law and the rule of property, of human rights as a natural or originary structure, and even of the concept of identity itself (as individual, nation, state, and so forth). Phenomenology, of course, is not the only philosophical tendency in this period to cast aside transcendental critique and operate such a construction from below that affirms the resistance and productivity of bodies; we have elsewhere investigated similar propositions, for example, in the materialist traditions that bring together a constitutive Spinozist ethics with a Nietzschean critique of fixed values. But phenomenology highlights perhaps more strongly than others the fundamental relation between corporeality and alterity.

Tracing the genealogy of phenomenology through the work of Merleau-Ponty in this way also provides us with a particularly illuminating perspective on the work of Michel Foucault. In his analyses of power we can already see how Foucault adopts and pushes forward the central elements, posing being not in abstract or transcendental figures but in the concrete reality of bodies and their alterity.[32] When he insists that there is no central, transcendent locus of power but only a myriad of micropowers that are exercised in capillary forms across the surfaces of bodies in their practices and disciplinary regimes, many commentators object that he is betraying the Marxist tradition (and Foucault himself contributes to this impression). In our view, though, Foucault's analyses of bodies and power in this phase of his work, following a line initiated by Merleau-Ponty, really make good on some of the intuitions that the young Marx could not completely grasp about the need to bring the critique of property, along with all the transcendental structures of capitalist society, back to the phenomenology of bodies. Foucault adopts many disguises—*larvatus prodeo*—in his relationship with Marxism, but that relationship is nonetheless extremely profound.

The phenomenology of bodies in Foucault reaches its highest point in his analysis of biopolitics, and here, if you focus on the essential, his research agenda is simple. Its first axiom is that bodies are the constitutive components of the biopolitical fabric of being. On the biopolitical terrain—this is the second axiom—where powers are continually made and unmade, bodies resist. They have to resist in order to exist. History cannot therefore be understood merely as the horizon on which biopower configures reality through domination. On the contrary, history is determined by the biopolitical antagonisms and resistances to biopower. The third axiom of his research agenda is that corporeal resistance produces subjectivity, not in an isolated or independent way but in the complex dynamic with the resistances of other bodies. This production of subjectivity through resistance and struggle will prove central, as our analysis proceeds, not only to the subversion of the existing forms of power but also to the constitution of alternative institutions of liberation.

Here we can say, to return to our earlier discussion, that Foucault carries forward the banner of the minor Kant, the Kant who not only dares to know but also knows how to dare.

The Vanishing Bodies of Fundamentalism

"Fundamentalism" has become a vague, overused term, which refers most often to belief systems that are rigid and unyielding. What unites the various fundamentalisms to a surprisingly large degree, however, is their peculiar relation to the body. At first glance one might assume that fundamentalisms provide an extreme example of the corporeal perspective that is central to biopolitics. They do indeed focus extraordinary, even obsessive attention on bodies, making all their surfaces along with their intake and output, their habits and practices the object of intense scrutiny and evaluation. When we look a bit closer, though, we see that fundamentalist vigilance about the body does not allow for the productivity of bodies that is central to biopolitics: the construction of being from below, through bodies in action. On the contrary, the preoccupation of fundamentalisms is to prevent or contain their productivity. In the final analysis, in fact, fundamentalisms make bodies vanish insofar as they are revealed to be not really the objects of obsessive attention but merely signs of transcendent forms or essences that stand above them. (And this is one reason why fundamentalisms seem so out of step with contemporary power structures: they refer ultimately to the transcendent rather than the transcendental plane.) This double relation to the body—at once focusing on it and making it disappear—is a useful definition for fundamentalism, allowing us to bring together the various disparate fundamentalisms on this common point and, through contrast, cast into sharper relief the characteristics and value of the biopolitical perspective.

The major religious fundamentalisms—Jewish, Christian, Muslim, and Hindu—certainly all demonstrate intense concern for and scrutiny of bodies, through dietary restrictions, corporeal rituals, sexual mandates and prohibitions, and even practices of corporeal mortification and abnegation. What primarily distinguishes fundamentalists from other religious practitioners, in fact, is the extreme importance they give to the body: what it does, what parts of it appear in public, what goes into and comes out of it. Even when fundamentalist norms require hiding a part of the body behind a veil, headscarf, or other articles of clothing, they are really signaling its extraordinary importance. Women's bodies are obviously the object of the most obsessive scrutiny and regulation in religious fundamentalism, but no bodies are completely exempt from examination and control—men's bodies, adolescents' bodies, infants' bodies, even the bodies of the dead. The fundamentalist body is powerful, explosive, precarious, and that is why it requires constant inspection and care.

The religious fundamentalisms are also united, however, at the same time, in their ultimate dissolution of bodies into the transcendent realm. The fundamentalist religious focus on the body really looks through it like an x ray to grasp the soul. If dietary restrictions were merely a matter of the health of the body, of course, they would simply constitute an elaborate nutritionist's guide, and dictates about consumption of pork or beef or fish would rely on issues of calories and food-borne diseases. What goes into the body, however, is really important for what it does and means for the soul—or rather for the subject's belonging to the religious community. These two issues are in fact not very distant, because the health of the soul from this perspective is just one index of gauging identitarian belonging. Similarly the clothing covering the body is an indication of inner virtue. The ultimate eclipse of the body, though, is clearest in fundamentalist notions of martyrdom. The body of the martyr is central in its heroic action, but that action really points to a transcendent world beyond. Here is the extreme point of the fundamentalist relation to the body, where its affirmation is also its annihilation.

Nationalist fundamentalisms similarly concentrate on bodies through their attention to and care for the population. The nationalist policies deploy a wide range of techniques for corporeal health and welfare, analyzing birthrates and sanitation, nutrition and housing, disease control and reproductive practices. Bodies themselves constitute the nation, and thus the nation's highest goal is their promotion and preservation. Like religious fundamentalisms, however, nationalisms, although their gaze seems to focus intently on bodies, really see them merely as an indication or symptom of the ultimate, transcendent object of national identity. With its moral face, nationalism looks past the bodies to see national character, whereas with its militarist face, it sees the sacrifice of bodies in battle as revealing the national spirit. The martyr or the patriotic soldier is thus for nationalism too the paradigmatic figure for how the body is made to disappear and leave behind only an index to a higher plane.

Given this characteristic double relation to the body, it makes sense to consider white supremacy (and racism in general) a form of fundamentalism. Modern racism in the nineteenth and twentieth centuries is characterized by a process of "epidermalization," embedding racial hierarchies in the skin—its color, smells, contours, and textures.[33] Although white supremacy and colonial power are characterized by a maniacal preoccupation with bodies, the corporeal signs of race are not entirely stable and reliable. The one who passes for white but is not poses the greatest anxiety for the white supremacist, and indeed the cultural and literary history of the United States is filled with angst created by "passing" and racial ambiguity. Such anxieties make clear, though, that white supremacy is not really about bodies, at least not in any simple way, but rather looks beyond the body at some essence that transcends it. Discourses on blood that gesture toward ancestry and lineage, which constitute the primary common link between racisms and nationalisms, are one way this essential difference beyond the body is configured. Indeed recent racial discourse has migrated in certain respects from the skin to the molecular level as biotechnologies and DNA testing are making possible new characterizations of racial difference, but these molecular corporeal traits too, when seen in terms of race, are really only indexes of a transcendent racial essence.[34] There is finally always something spiritual or metaphysical about racism. But all this should not lead us to say that white supremacy is not about bodies after all. Instead, like other fundamentalisms it is characterized by a double relation to the body. The body is all-important and, at the same time, vanishes.

This same double relation to the body indicates, finally, how economism should be considered a type of fundamentalism. At first sight economism too is all about bodies in their stark materiality insofar as it holds that the material facts of economic relations and activity are sufficient for their own reproduction without the implication of other, less corporeal factors such as ideology, law, politics, culture, and so forth. Economism focuses primarily on the bodies of commodities, recognizing as commodities both the material goods produced and the material human bodies that produce and carry them to market. The human body must itself constantly be produced and reproduced by other commodities and their productive consumption. Economism in this sense sees only a world of bodies—productive bodies, bodies produced, and bodies consumed. Although it seems to focus exclusively on bodies in this way, however, it really looks through them to see the value that transcends them. Hence "the metaphysical subtleties and theological niceties" of economism in both its capitalist and socialist forms.[35] From this perspective actual bodies, of humans and other commodities, are ultimately not the object of economism; what really matters is the quantity of economic value that stands above or behind them. That is why human bodies can become commodities, that is, indifferent from all other commodities, in the first place, because their singularity disappears when they are seen only in terms of value. And thus economism too has a typically fundamentalist relation to the body: the material body is all-important and, at the same time, eclipsed by the transcendent plane of value.

We need to follow this argument, however, through one final twist. Even though all of these fundamentalisms—religious, nationalist, racist, and economistic—ultimately negate the body and its power, they do, at least initially, highlight its importance. That is something to work with. The deviation from and subversion of the fundamentalist focus on the body, in other words, can serve as the point of departure for a perspective that affirms the needs of bodies and their full powers.

With regard to religious fundamentalism, one of the richest and most fascinating (but also most complex and contradictory) examples is the biopolitical potential that Foucault glimpses in the Islamic popular movements against the shah's government in the year leading up to the Iranian Revolution. On commission from the Italian newspaper *Corriere della Sera,* he makes two week-long visits to Iran in September and November 1978 and writes a series of brief essays in which he recounts in simple, often moving prose the development of the uprising against the regime, offering basic political analyses of the relations of force in the country, the importance of Iran's oil in the cold war, the political power of the shah, the brutality of the repression, and so forth. In the essays Foucault, of course, does not endorse political Islam, and he clearly insists that there is nothing revolutionary about the Shiite clergy or Islam as such, but he does recognize that, as it had in Europe and elsewhere in other historical instances, religion defines the form of struggle in Iran that mobilizes the popular classes. It is easy to imagine, although he does not use these terms, that Foucault is thinking about the biopolitical powers of Islamic fundamentalism in the Iranian resistance. Just two years earlier he published the first volume of his *History of Sexuality,* and soon afterwards he would deliver his lectures at the Collège de France on the birth of biopolitics. So it comes as no surprise that in these essays he is sensitive to the way that in the popular movements religious forces regulate with such care daily life, family ties, and social relations. In the context of the rebellion, he explains, "religion for them was like the promise and guarantee of finding something that would radically change their subjectivity."[36] We have no intention of blaming Foucault for the fact that after the overthrow of the shah a repressive theocratic regime took power, a regime against which he protested. What we find most significant in his articles instead is how he recognizes in the religious fundamentalism of the rebellion and its focus on bodies the elements of a biopolitical power that, if deployed differently, diverted from its closure in the theocratic regime, could bring about a radical transformation of subjectivity and participate in a project of liberation.

For nationalism we do not need any such complex example to recognize the potentially progressive elements contained within it.

Particularly during the course of national liberation struggles, nationalisms have served as the workbench for the experimentation of numerous political practices.[37] Think, for example, of the intensely corporeal nature of oppression and liberation that Frantz Fanon analyzes while working as a psychiatrist in the midst of the Algerian Revolution. The violence of colonialism that runs throughout its institutions and daily regimens is deposited in the bones of the colonized. Dr. Fanon explains that, as in a thermodynamic system, the violence that goes in has to come out somewhere: it is most commonly manifested in the mental disorders of the colonized—a violence directed inward, self-inflicted—or in forms of violence among the colonized, including bloody feuds among tribes, clans, and individuals. The national liberation struggle, then, is for Fanon a kind of training of the body to redirect that violence outward, back whence it came, against the colonizer.[38] Under the flag of revolutionary nationalism, then, tortured, suffering bodies are able to discover their real power. Fanon is well aware, of course, that once independence has been achieved, the nation and nationalism become again an obstacle, closing down the dynamics that the revolution had opened. Nationalism can never fully escape fundamentalism, but that should not blind us to the fact that, particularly in the context of national liberation struggles, nationalism's intense focus on bodies suggests biopolitical practices that, if oriented differently, can be extraordinarily powerful.

We have to approach the fundamentalism of white supremacy a bit ironically to see how it provides an opening toward a biopolitical practice through its focus on the body. The Black Power movement in the United States in the 1960s and 1970s, to give one example, transforms and revalues the epidermalization of human differences that grounds racist thought. Black Power focuses on the surfaces of the body—skin color, hair quality, facial features, and so forth—but not to whiten skin or straighten hair. Becoming black is the aim, because not only is black beautiful but also the meaning of blackness is the struggle for freedom.[39] This is not so much an antiracist discourse as a counterracist one, one that uses the focus on bodies as a means to affirm blackness. We should note, though, that this boomerang of counterracism does not couple the focus on bodies with some transcendent, metaphysical moment in which bodies vanish and the dominant element is really some essential, spiritual blackness—or rather, in the cases when it does, it becomes yet another fundamentalism. Counterracism that remains tied to the material, to the beauty and power of bodies, opens the possibility for a biopolitical practice.

Finally, Marx reveals the possibility of subverting economism in his early readings of classical political economy. He grasps the intense focus on bodies and their productivity in the work of Adam Smith and others, but he also recognizes how that productivity of laboring bodies is narrowed and finally eclipsed when bodies become merely producers of value for capital. This inspires some of the most lyrical passages in Marx's work, in which he tries to restore the full productivity of bodies across all the domains of life. Labor, freed from private property, simultaneously engages all our senses and capacities, in short, all our "*human* relations to the world—seeing hearing, smelling, tasting, feeling, thinking, contemplating, sensing, wanting, acting, loving."[40] When labor and production are conceived in this expanded form, crossing all the domains of life, bodies can never be eclipsed and subordinated to any transcendent measure or power.

In each of these frameworks, then, the intense concentration on the body that characterizes fundamentalism offers an opening for a biopolitical perspective. Biopolitics thus is the ultimate antidote to fundamentalism because it refuses the imposition of a transcendent, spiritual value or structure, refuses to let the bodies be eclipsed, and insists instead on their power.

1.3

THE MULTITUDE OF THE POOR

> A Common-wealth is ... the Government of the whole multitude of the base and poorer sort, without respect to the other Orders.
> —Sir Walter Raleigh, *Maxims of State*

> The humor and the wit of the mariners, renegades, and castaways are beyond the cultivated inter-changes of those who sit around mahogany tables. They have to be. Hangman's nooses hang loose around the necks of countless millions today, and for them their unfailing humor is an assertion of life and sanity against the ever-present threat of destruction and a world in chaos.
> —C. L. R. James, *Mariners, Renegades, and Castaways*

Multitude: The Name of the Poor

Since the dominant form of the republic is defined by property, the multitude, insofar as it is characterized by poverty, stands opposed to it. This conflict, however, should be understood in terms of not only wealth and poverty but also and more significantly the forms of subjectivity produced. Private property creates subjectivities that are at once individual (in their competition with one another) and unified as a class to preserve their property (against the poor). The constitutions of the great modern bourgeois republics mediate this balance between the individualism and class interests of property. The poverty of the multitude, then, seen from this perspective, does not refer to its misery or deprivation or even its lack, but instead names a production of social subjectivity that results in a radically plural and open body politic, opposed to both the individualism and the exclusive, unified social body of property. The poor, in other words, refers not to those who have nothing but to the wide multiplicity of all those who are inserted in the mechanisms of social production regardless of social order or property. And this conceptual conflict is also a political conflict. Its productivity is what makes the multitude of the poor a real and effective menace for the republic of property.

The essential foundations for understanding the constitutive relation between multitude and poverty in this way are established in the political struggles of seventeenth-century England. The term "multitude" acquired then an almost technical meaning in popular political discourse and pamphlets to name all those gathered together to form a political body regardless of rank and property.[41] It is understandable that multitude, defined in this way, comes to connote the lowest rank of society and the propertyless, since they are the most visibly excluded from the dominant political bodies, but really it is an open, inclusive social body, characterized by its boundlessness and its originary state of mixture among social ranks and groups. Nahum Tate in *Richard the Second* (1681), for example, his rewriting of Shakespeare, gives an idea of this mixed social body when he describes the multitude with a list of occupations: "Shoomaker, Farrier, Weaver, Tanner, Mercer, Brewer, Butcher, Barber, and infinite others with a Confused Noise."[42] But even Tate's multiplicity of trades, which could serve as a reference to a nascent working class, does not adequately capture the multitude's unbounded nature—its being without regard to rank or property—or its power as a social and political body.

We begin to see more clearly the defining relation to poverty of the multitude in the 1647 Putney Debates between the Levellers and factions of the New Model Army on the nature of a new constitution for England and particularly on the right of suffrage. The Levellers argue strongly against the restriction of the vote to those who own property. Colonel Thomas Rainsborough, speaking for them, does not use the term "multitude," but in his arguments he does present the poor as an unbounded and mixed political body. "I think that the poorest he that is in England," Rainsborough affirms, "has a life to live as the greatest he; and therefore truly, sir, I think it's clear, that every man that is to live under a government ought first by his own consent to put himself under that government; and I do think that the poorest man in England is not at all bound in a strict sense to that government that he has not had a voice to put himself under."[43] Rainsborough is gesturing toward a political body when he refers to this extreme point, "the poorest he," but this is not a subject that is limited to or even defined by this lack. Rather this multitude of the poor is a political body without distinction of property, a mixed body that is unbounded, which would include Tate's list of tradesmen but not be limited to them. For Rainsborough, furthermore, this conception of the poor as an open and inclusive political body directly supports and even necessitates universal (or at least extended) suffrage and equal representation. And indeed Commissary Ireton of the army, Rainsborough's primary interlocutor in the Putney Debates, immediately recognizes the threat to the rule of property posed by this conception of the political subject. If the vote belongs to everyone, Ireton reasons, why should not all property belong to everyone? That is indeed exactly where the logic leads.

Tracing the history of the term "multitude" presents a philological conundrum because there is little textual record of the political speech and writing of the proponents of the multitude. The vast majority of references in the archive of seventeenth-century English texts are negative, written by those who want to destroy, denigrate, and deny the multitude. The term is almost always preceded by a derogatory adjective to double the weight against it: the lawless multitude, the headless multitude, the ignorant multitude, and so forth. Robert Filmer and Thomas Hobbes, to cite two prominent figures, seek to deny not only the rights of the multitude but also its very existence. Filmer, arguing on scriptural grounds, cast as if they were historical, contests the claims, made by authors such as Cardinal Bellarmine, that the multitude because of common natural right has the power to determine the civil order. Power was given not equally by natural right to the entire multitude, he contends, but to Adam, the father, whose authority passes rightly to all patriarchs. "There never was any such thing as an independent multitude, who at first had a natural right to a community," Filmer proclaims. "This is but a fiction or fancy of too many in these days."[44] Hobbes challenges the existence of the multitude on more directly political grounds. The multitude is not a political body, he maintains, and for it to become political it must become a people, which is defined by its unity of will and action. The many, in other words, must be reduced to one, thereby negating the essence of the multitude itself: "When the multitude is united into a body politic, and thereby are a people . . . and their wills virtually in the sovereign, there the rights and demands of the particulars do cease; and he or they that have the sovereign power, doth for them all demand and vindicate under the name of *his,* that which before they called in the plural, *theirs.*"[45] Filmer and Hobbes are representative of the dominant stream of seventeenth-century English political thought, which gives us only a negative reflection of or reaction to the multitude. But certainly the intensity of that reaction—the fear and hatred inspired in Filmer and Hobbes—is testimony to the power of the cause.

Another strategy for investigating the politics of the multitude in seventeenth-century English thought is to turn to the field of physics, since the same set of basic laws were thought to apply equally to physical and political bodies. Robert Boyle, for example, challenges the dominant view that all existing bodies are compounds of homogeneous, simple elements by arguing instead that multiplicity and mixture are primary in nature. "Innumerable swarms of little bodies," he writes, "are mov'd to and fro," and "Multitudes" of corpuscles are "driven to associate themselves, now with one Body, and presently with another."[46] All bodies are always already mixed multitudes and constantly open to further combination through the logic of corpuscular association. Since physical and political bodies obey the same laws, Boyle's physics of unbounded multitudes immediately implies an affirmation of the political multitude and its mixed body. And indeed it should be no surprise that Hobbes, understanding this threat, argues vociferously against Boyle.[47]

To complete this connection between the physical and political notions of the multitude, we have to travel across the English Channel to Holland. Baruch Spinoza's physics, like Boyle's, opposes any atomism of pure bodies and focuses instead on processes of mixture and composition. There is no need here to enter into the details of their different epistemologies—between a rationalist-mechanist theory and a corpuscular-experimental conception—since both authors conceive of nature as composed through encounters among elementary particles.[48] Encounters result either in decomposition into smaller bodies or composition into a new, larger body. In Spinoza's politics the multitude is a similarly mixed, complex body that is composed by the same logic of clinamen and encounter. The multitude is thus an inclusive body in the sense that it is open to encounters with all other bodies, and its political life depends on the qualities of these encounters, whether they are joyful and compose more powerful bodies or whether they are sad and decompose into less powerful ones. This radical inclusiveness is one element that clearly marks Spinoza's multitude as a multitude of the poor—the poor conceived, once again, as not limited to the lowest in society but open to all regardless of rank and property. Spinoza, finally, makes the essential and decisive step of defining this multitude as the only possible subject of democracy.[49]

To understand better this connection between the multitude and poverty we should step back a few centuries to see how the same spectacle of the multitude of the poor confronts the tribunals of civil and church authorities in Renaissance Italy. The mendicant order of Francis of Assisi preaches the virtue of the poor in order to oppose both the corruption of church power and the institution of private property, which were intimately connected. The Franciscans give prescriptive value to the mottos of Gratian's *Decretum*—"iure naturali sunt omnia omnibus" (by natural law all belongs to everyone) and "iure divino omni sunt communia" (by divine law all things are common)—which themselves refer to basic principles of the church fathers and the Apostles, "habebant omnia communia" (keep all things in common) (Acts 2:44). A bitter debate, foreshadowing the events of Putney three centuries later, emerges between the papacy and the Franciscans (and within the Franciscan order) pitting those who affirm the rule of property, and thus negate the communion dictated by natural law, against the Franciscan groups which believe that only on the basis of common wealth can a good and just society be created on earth. Only a few years later, in fact, in 1324, Marsilius of Padua would pose poverty as the sole basis for not only Christian perfection but also, what primarily interests us, democratic society.[50]

Throughout the centuries of modernity the term "multitude" is not used in other parts of the world with the technical political sense it acquires in seventeenth-century England, but the specter of a multitude of the poor circulates around the globe and threatens the rule of property everywhere it takes root. It appears, for example, in the great sixteenth-century peasant wars waged by Thomas Münzer and the Anabaptists against the German princes.[51] In the rebellions against European colonial regimes, from the 1781 Tupac Katari attack on Spanish rule in La Paz to the 1857 Indian rebellion against the rule of the British East India Company, the multitude of the poor challenges the republic of property. And at sea, of course, the multitude populates the maritime circuits of production and trade, as well as the pirate networks that prey on them. The negative image is in this case, too, the one most strongly conveyed to us: the multitude is a many-headed hydra that threatens property and order.[52] Part of the threat of this multitude is its multiplicity, composed at times of combinations of sailors, maroons, servants, soldiers, tradesmen, laborers, renegades, castaways, pirates, and numerous others circulating through the great oceans. The threat is also, though, that this multitude will undermine property and its structures of rule. When men of power and property warn about the dangerous hydra loose in the seas, they are not telling fairy tales but trying to grasp and neutralize a real and powerful political threat.

Jacques Rancière, finally, understands the nature of politics itself in terms very close to those we find in the seventeenth-century debates about the multitude. For Rancière "the whole basis of politics is the struggle between the poor and the rich" or, more precisely, he goes on to say, the struggle between those who have no part in the management of the common and those who control it.[53] Politics exists when those who have no right to be counted, as Rancière says, make themselves of some account. The part of those who have no part, the party of the poor, is an excellent initial definition of the multitude, as long as we add immediately that the party of the poor is by no means homologous to the party of the rich. The party of the rich makes false claim to universality, pretending in the guise of the republic of property to represent the entire society, when in fact it is based only on an exclusive identity, the unity and homogeneity of which is guaranteed by the ownership of property. The party of the poor, in contrast, is not an identity of one exclusive portion of society but rather a formation of all those inserted in the mecha-nisms of social production without respect to rank or property, in all their diversity, animated by an open and plural production of sub-jectivity. By its very existence the multitude of the poor presents an objective menace to the republic of property.

Who Hates the Poor?

It often seems as if everyone hates the poor. Certainly the rich do, usually casting their loathing in moral terms—as if poverty were the sign of some inner failure—or sometimes masking it in terms of pity and compassion. Even the not-quite-so-poor hate the poor, in part because they see in them an image of what they might soon become. What stands behind the hatred of the poor in its different forms is fear, since the poor constitute a direct threat to property— not only because they lack wealth and might even be justified in stealing it, like the noble Jean Valjean, but also because they have the power to undermine and overthrow the republic of property. "The vile multitude not the people is what we want to exclude," pro-claims Adolphe Thiers in a session of the French National Assembly in 1850. The multitude is dangerous and must be banished by law, Thiers continues, because it is so mobile and impossible to grasp as a unified object of rule.[54] Every such instance of hatred and fear should be read in an inverted way, as an affirmation, or at least an acknowledgment, of the power of the poor.

Alongside the history of practical maneuvers—dividing the poor, depriving them of the means of action and expression, and so forth—is the equally long record of ideological efforts to tame, undermine, and nullify the power of the poor. It is interesting that so many of these ideological operations have been conducted within the context of Christian theology and doctrine, perhaps precisely because the threat posed by the poor to the rule of property has been experienced so intensely within Christianity. Pope Benedict XVI, in his 2006 encyclical *Deus caritas est,* seeks directly to challenge the scriptural bases of and mystify ideologically the power of the poor. He claims that the apostolic mandate to share all things in common is impractical in the modern world and moreover that the Christian community should not engage such questions of social justice but leave them for governments to resolve. What he advocates instead is charitable activity on behalf of the poor and suffering, casting the poor as objects of pity rather than powerful subjects. There is nothing very original in Benedict XVI's operation. He is just the newest epigone in a long line of Christian ideological crusaders against the poor.[55]

One pinnacle (or nadir) of the ideological effort to cancel the power of the poor through mystification is the brief June 1945 lecture by Martin Heidegger titled simply "Poverty" ("Die Armut"). The scene of the lecture is dramatic and significant. Since March of that year, when French troops crossed the Rhine, Heidegger and some of his colleagues from the philosophy department of the University of Freiburg have taken refuge in the Wildenstein castle in the hills of the Black Forest east of the city, where they continue to give lectures. By late June the arrival of French troops at the castle is imminent, and Heidegger is undoubtedly well aware that the Soviet army is on the banks of the Elba, Vienna has fallen, and Berlin cannot be far behind. He chooses for his final lecture to comment on a sentence from Hölderlin, written in the final years of the eighteenth century, during the French Revolution: "With us, everything is con-

centrated on the spiritual, we have become poor to become rich."
And in the margins of the manuscript at the point where he first
cites this sentence, he adds, "Why, in the present moment of world
history, I choose to comment on this sentence for us will be made
clear by the commentary itself." Heidegger, looking into the face of
a disaster of historic proportions—the end of the Nazi project, the
end of Germany and the German people as he conceives them,
and the advance of communism—responds with an ontological discourse on poverty.[56]

Let us begin by exploring the philosophical content of the lecture, even though Heidegger has already indicated that its full meaning will only be revealed in relation to its moment of world history.
Heidegger proceeds, following his usual method, by questioning
each key term in Hölderlin's sentence. What does Hölderlin mean
by "us"? The answer is easy: we Germans. What does he mean by
"spiritual"? Readers of Heidegger will not be surprised by this either: by spiritual he means the essential ontological relation, that is,
the fact that human essence is defined by its relation to Being. This
concentration on the spiritual, then, this accent on Being, prepares
Heidegger for an ontological reading of poverty and wealth in the
second half of the sentence. Poverty, he begins, does not really have
to do with possessions, as normal usage would suggest, whereby
poverty would be a state of not having material necessities. Poverty
refers not to having but to being. "The essence of poverty resides in
a being. Being truly poor means: being in such a way that we lack
nothing, except the non-necessary."[57] At this point Heidegger risks
coming to a banal conclusion that poverty is defined by necessity
and thus constraint, whereas wealth, which offers the privilege of
engaging the non-necessary, is capable of freedom. Such a conception, though, in addition to being banal, cannot explain the causality
of Hölderlin's phrase that leads from becoming poor to becoming
rich.

Heidegger solves the riddle, as he often does, with recourse to
German etymology. The old German word *frî*, from which *freie* or
"free" derives, means to preserve or protect, allowing something to

reside in its proper essence. Freeing something, he continues, means guarding its essence against any constraints of necessity. The freeing of freedom, then, reverses or transforms necessity: "Thus necessity is in no way, as all of Metaphysics understands it, the opposite of freedom, but rather only freedom is in itself necessity converted." This allows Heidegger to turn the trick. It is true, of course, that the poor lack the non-necessary, which is at the center of freedom. "What we lack we do not have, but it is what we lack that has us." We recognize this to the extent that "everything is concentrated on the spiritual," that is, on the relation to Being at the essence of humanity. Even in our lacking we belong, in some sense, through our relation to Being, to the freedom of the non-necessary: "Once the essence of humanity holds properly to the relation between freeing Being and humanity, that is, once human essence lacks the non-necessary, then humanity becomes poor in the true sense."[58] Becoming poor leads to becoming rich because poverty itself marks a relation to Being, and in that relation, necessity is converted into freedom, that is, the preservation and protection of its proper essence. Being-poor is thus in itself, Heidegger concludes, being-rich.

Those not initiated into the intricacies of Heideggerian philosophy might well ask at this point, Why go through such gymnastics just to confuse the distinction between poverty and wealth? The answer, as Heidegger himself tells us in his marginal note at the beginning, has to be found in the "world-historical" situation he is facing, specifically the impending Nazi defeat and the approaching Soviet troops. Remember that Heidegger elsewhere in his work expresses his anticommunism in ontological terms. A decade earlier, for example, in his *Introduction to Metaphysics,* he claims that from the metaphysical standpoint, the United States and the Soviet Union are really united in projects of unleashed technique. These are clearly peoples, in his view, for whom everything is not concentrated on the spiritual. But why in June 1945 should Heidegger decide to investigate the ontological position of poverty? The answer seems to be that he considers a certain notion of poverty to be the essence of communism and its primary appeal, so he wants to combat the enemy on its home turf. Indeed Heidegger's battle against communism becomes explicit in the final pages of the lecture. The poor are not opposed to the rich, as he imagines communism to claim, but rather the real meaning of poverty can be discovered only from the "spiritual" perspective that recognizes the relation of human essence to Being.[59]

This is certainly a bizarre and ineffective challenge to communist ideology, but what concerns us more here is the way Heidegger mystifies the power of the poor and how in the guise of saving the concept of poverty he really condemns it. Even though the poor are dignified in Heidegger's eyes by their relation to Being, they remain completely passive in this relation, like powerless creatures in the face of an all-powerful god. In this respect Heidegger's approach to the poor is really only a more sophisticated version of Pope Benedict XVI's charity. The poor can be an object of pity and generosity when, and only when, their power has been completely neutralized and their passivity is assured. And the fear of the poor that is thinly veiled behind this benevolent façade is immediately linked to a fear of communism (embodied for the pope in liberation theology).

Heidegger makes the explicit link between poverty and communism, but one should also remember how often hatred of the poor serves as a mask for racism. In Heidegger's case one can imagine a speculative argument, following Adorno, about the link in Nazi Germany between the authoritarian personality and anti-Semitism.[60] And if we switch to the context of the Americas, it is almost always the case that hatred of the poor expresses a thinly veiled or displaced racism. Poverty and race are so intimately linked throughout the Americas that this hatred is inevitably intermingled with disgust for black bodies and a revulsion toward darker-skinned people. "Race differences and class differentials have been ground together in this country in a crucible of misery and squalor," Henry Louis Gates Jr. and Cornell West write about the United States, "in such a way that few of us know where one stops and the other begins."[61] Everywhere there is hatred of the poor there is likely to be racial fear and hatred lurking somewhere nearby.

Another connection, which is not so obvious, links Heidegger's ontological subordination of the poor to Carl Schmitt's political theology and his affirmation of transcendent sovereign power. Such a connection might seem counterintuitive since Heidegger is so insistent about the end of metaphysics and refuses to locate Being as a transcendent essence, which would, in the realm of ontology, occupy an analogous position to Schmitt's political sovereign. The link appears clearly, however, at the other end of the spectrum, in their denigration and fear of the power of immanence. Schmitt's notion of sovereign power and his theory of the Führer seek to contain politically, just as Heidegger's analysis denigrates ontologically, the multitude of the poor and its power. This is one moment when it is not insignificant or anecdotal fact that both Schmitt and Heidegger support the Nazi regime. There should by no means be a prohibition on learning from reactionary thinkers, and indeed many leftist scholars have relied heavily on the work of Schmitt and Heidegger in recent years, but one should never forget that they are reactionaries, a fact that unfailingly comes out in their work.[62]

What Heidegger and Schmitt do not challenge but simply mystify and try to contain is an ontological relation of the poor that points in the opposite direction, based on the innovation, the subjectivity, and the power of the poor to intervene in the established reality and create being. This may be spiritual in the sense that it poses a relation between humanity and being, but it is also equally material in its corporeal, material constructive practices. This is the ontological power of the poor that we want to investigate—one that is at the center of a notion of communism that Heidegger and Schmitt would have no idea how to confront.

Poverty and Power

In the course of the great bourgeois revolutions of the seventeenth and eighteenth centuries, the concept of the multitude is wiped out from the political and legal vocabulary, and by means of this erasure the conception of republic (*res publica* rather than *res communis*) comes to be narrowly defined as an instrument to affirm and safeguard property. Property is the key that defines not only the republic but also the people, both of which are posed as universal concepts but in reality exclude the multitude of the poor.

This exclusion is the essential content of Hobbes's conceptual division between the multitude and the people. The king is the people, Hobbes declares, because the people, in contrast to the multitude, is a unified subject and can thus be represented by a single person. On the surface his distinction is simply geometrical: the people is one (and thus capable of sovereignty), whereas the multitude is plural (and thus incoherent, unable to rule itself). This is just a translation of the debate about the physics of bodies, which we saw in relation to Boyle and Spinoza, with a small extension to indicate the political consequences. We need to ask at this point, however, what stands behind the unity of the people for Hobbes? In seventeenth-century English political discourse it is not unusual to conceive of "the people" as "freeholders," that is, those with sufficient independent property to qualify to vote for members of parliament. The glue that holds this people together, in other words, and whose lack dictates the plurality of the multitude, is property. Hobbes makes even clearer in *Behemoth* the function of property to expel the poor from the people. The only glory of merchants, he writes, "whose profession is their private gain," is "to grow excessively rich by the wisdom of buying and selling" and "by making poor people sell their labour to them at their own prices; so that poor people, for the most part, might get a better living by working in Bridewell [prison], than by spinning, weaving, and other such labour as they can do."[63] The lack of property, which excludes the poor from the people, is not a contingent fact for Hobbes but a necessary and constantly reproduced condition that allows those with property to maintain and increase it. The multitude of the poor is the essential pillar that supports the people and its republic of property.

Machiavelli shows us this relationship from the other side and illuminates the resistance that animates the poor. "Strip all of us naked, you will see that we are alike," he writes in a speech invented for an anonymous rebel in the revolt of the *ciompi,* the fourteenth-century wool carders, against the *popolo grasso,* the wealthy Florentines. "Dress us in their clothes and them in ours," Machiavelli's agitator continues, referring to the rich owners of the wool factory, "and without a doubt we shall appear noble and they ignoble, for only poverty and riches make us unequal." There is no need for the poor to feel remorse for the violence of their rebellions because "where there is, as with us, fear of hunger and prison, there cannot and should not be fear of hell." Faithful servants, the orator explains, are still just servants, and good people are always poor. Now is the time, then, "not only to free ourselves from them but to become so much their superiors that they will have more to lament and fear from you than you from them."[64] Central to this passage is the fact that poverty is not a characteristic of human nature itself. In other texts Machiavelli falls into a naturalistic version of human poverty and frailty, lamenting the fate of humanity in a cruel, unfeeling universe, as Lucretius did before him and Leopardi after. "Every animal among us is born fully clad," he proclaims, for example, in *The Golden Ass.* "Only man is born naked [*ignudo*] of all protection; he has neither hide nor spine nor feather nor fleece nor bristles nor scales to make him a shield."[65] But this traditional realist line, which derives from the static character of older materialist analyses, does not satisfy Machiavelli. His materialist method needs, on the contrary, to become joyful—not only realist but also dynamic and rebellious, as in the case of the *ciompi,* against property and its institutions.

Machiavelli reveals here a fundamental alternative path within modern political thought, which poses the poor as not only the remainder left by the violent appropriation conducted by nascent powers of capital, not only prisoners of the new conditions of the production and reproduction, but also a force of resistance that recognizes itself as exploited within a regime that still bears the marks of the common: a common social life, common social wealth. The poor occupies a paradoxical position, at once excluded and included, which highlights a series of social contradictions—between poverty and wealth, in the first place, but also between subordination and production, and hierarchy and the common. What is most important about the alternative Machiavelli reveals, however, is that these social contradictions are dynamic, animated by antagonism and resistance. Key to his histories and political analyses is the progression that leads from indignation to the creation of social disorders or riots *(tumulti),* and in turn poses the conditions for the rebellion of the multitude, which is excluded from wealth but included in its production. Humanity is never naked, never characterized by bare life, but rather always dressed, endowed with not only histories of suffering but also capacities to produce and the power to rebel.

Spinoza carries forward this Machiavellian alternative and, among many other conceptual advances, highlights the corporeal aspects of this power. He not only recognizes that the body is a site where poverty and needs are expressed, but also emphasizes that in the body resides a power the limits of which are still unknown: "No one has yet determined what a Body can do."[66] He connects these two conditions, poverty and power, in a dynamic that strives toward the production of community. When Spinoza remarks on the ignorance of children, for instance, or the weakness of our bodies or the brutality of the human social condition, he always poses such states of poverty as the point of departure for a logic of transformation that moves out of solitude and weakness by means of the construction of sociality and love. The power Spinoza identifies in these various forms can be summarized as a quest for the common: just as in epistemology he focuses on "common notions" that constitute rationality and give us greater power to think, and in ethics he orients action toward common goods, so too in politics Spinoza seeks mechanisms whereby singular bodies can together compose a common power. This common power by which the multitude battles poverty and creates common wealth is for Spinoza the primary force that supports the possibility of democracy.

Marx adds one more step to this alternative trajectory, confirming Machiavelli's intuition that the power of the poor stands at the center of social rebellion and Spinoza's hypothesis that the power of the multitude is essential to the possibility of democracy. Like the others, Marx begins his reasoning with poverty, identifying the origin of the properly capitalist form of poverty in the long and varied processes of so-called primitive accumulation. When they are separated from the soil and from all other means of production, workers are doubly free: free in the sense that they are not bound in servitude and also free in that they have no encumbrances, that is, no property or even any right to access the land. The proletariat is created as a multitude of the poor. "Labor capacity," Marx writes, "denuded of the means of labour and the means of life is . . . absolute poverty as such and the worker [is] the mere personification of the labour capacity. . . . As such, conceptually speaking, he is a *pauper*." The pauper Marx is talking about here refers not just to those who live in misery on the limits of starvation but to all workers insofar as their living labor is separated from the objectified labor accumulated in capital. But nakedness and poverty is only one side of the matter. Like Machiavelli and Spinoza, Marx links the proletariat's poverty directly to its power in the sense that living labor is "the general possibility of material wealth" in capitalist society. Living labor is thus at once "absolute poverty" as object and "general possibility" as subject. Marx conceives this explosive combination of poverty and power as the ultimate threat to private property, one which resides at its very heart.[67]

Some readers are likely to object at this point that our reliance on concepts such as poverty and the multitude hopelessly confuses Marxist categories, obscuring the difference, for example, between the "precapitalist" misery that results from violent expropriation and the properly capitalist misery of wage labor and exploitation. In this way we betray Marx's materialist method and muddle the class character of his analysis. Not even the utopian socialists, our critics can exclaim, so thoroughly mystify the analysis of exploitation in Marx and scientific socialism! We maintain, though, that our approach is just as materialist as traditional Marxist analyses, but in part because of the changing nature of labor and exploitation, which we engage in detail in later chapters, we break down some of the boundaries conventionally drawn around the working class. One important change is that exploitation today tends to be no longer a productive function but rather a mere instrument of domination. This corresponds to the fact that, in different ways in various contexts around the world, as modes of life and work characterized by mobility, flexibility, and precarity are ever more severely imposed by capitalist regimes of production and exploitation, wage laborers and the poor are no longer subjected to qualitatively different conditions but are both absorbed equally into the multitude of producers. The poor, whether they receive wages or not, are located no longer only at the historic origin or the geographical borders of capitalist production but increasingly at its heart—and thus the multitude of the poor emerges also at the center of the project for revolutionary transformation.[68]

DE CORPORE 1: BIOPOLITICS AS EVENT

> I am painting, I am Nature, I am truth.
> —Gustave Courbet

To grasp how Michel Foucault understands biopower, we have to situate it in the context of the broader theory of power he develops in the period when he begins working with the concept, the second half of the 1970s, in *Discipline and Punish* (1975) and the first volume of *The History of Sexuality* (1976). In these books Foucault's notion of power is always double. He devotes most of his attention to disciplinary regimes, architectures of power, and the applications of power through distributed and capillary networks, a power that does not so much repress as produce subjects. Throughout these books, however, sometimes in what seem like asides or marginal notes, Foucault also constantly theorizes an other to power (or even an other power), for which he seems unable to find an adequate name. Resistance is the term he most often uses, but it does not really capture what he has in mind, since resistance, as it is generally understood, is too dependent on and subordinate to the power it opposes. One might suggest to Foucault the Marxist notion of "counterpower," but that term implies a second power that is homologous to the one it opposes. In our view, the other to power that runs through these books is best defined as an alternative production of subjectivity, which not only resists power but also seeks autonomy from it.

This understanding of the doubleness of power helps us approach Foucault's attempts to develop the concept of biopower.

Here too Foucault's attention is focused primarily on the power over life—or, really, the power to administer and produce life—that functions through the government of populations, managing their health, reproductive capacities, and so forth. But there is always a minor current that insists on life as resistance, an other power of life that strives toward an alternative existence. The perspective of resistance makes clear the difference between these two powers: the biopower against which we struggle is not comparable in its nature or form to the power of life by which we defend and seek our freedom. To mark this difference between the two "powers of life," we adopt a terminological distinction, suggested by Foucault's writings but not used consistently by him, between biopower and biopolitics, whereby the former could be defined (rather crudely) as the power over life and the latter as the power of life to resist and determine an alternative production of subjectivity.

The major streams of Foucault interpretation, however, do not adequately grasp the dual nature of biopolitics. One stream, which is presented first by François Ewald and later by Roberto Esposito, analyzes the terrain of biopolitics primarily from the standpoint of the normative management of populations. This amounts to an *actuarial* administration of life that generally requires viewing individuals from a statistical perspective, classifying them into large normative sets, which become more coherent the more the microsystems that compose them are de-subjectivized and made homogeneous. Although this interpretation has the merit of philological fidelity (albeit with a rather narrow perspective on Foucault's opus), it leaves us with merely a "liberal" image of Foucault and biopolitics insofar as it poses against this threatening, all-encompassing power over life no alternative power or effective resistance but only a vague sense of critique and moral indignation.[69]

A second major stream, which centers on the interpretation of Giorgio Agamben (and emerges to some extent from the work of Jacques Derrida and Jean-Luc Nancy), accepts that biopolitics is an ambiguous and conflictive terrain but sees resistance acting only at its most extreme limit, on the margins of a totalitarian form of power, on the brink of impossibility. Here such authors could easily be interpreting the famous lines from Hölderlin's poem "Patmos": "Wo aber Gefahr ist, wächst / Das Rettende auch" (Where there is danger, / The rescue grows as well). This stream of interpretation thus does to a certain extent distinguish biopolitics from biopower but leaves biopolitics powerless and without subjectivity. These authors seek in Foucault a definition of biopolitics that strips it of every possibility of autonomous, creative action, but really they fall back on Heidegger in these points of the analysis to negate any constructive capacity of biopolitical resistance. Agamben transposes biopolitics in a theological-political key, claiming that the only possibility of rupture with biopower resides in "inoperative" activity *(inoperosità)*, a blank refusal that recalls Heidegger's notion of *Gelassenheit,* completely incapable of constructing an alternative.[70]

Finally, we can construct something like a third stream of interpretation of biopolitics, even if it is generally not posed in reference to Foucault and his terminology, that includes authors who understand life with reference to naturalistic and/or transcendental invariables of existence. From this perspective there is a certain autonomy conceded to biopolitical subjectivity, for example, in the invariable logical-linguistic structures proposed by Noam Chomsky or the ontological duration of preindividual and interindividual linguistic and productive relations in authors such as Gilbert Simondon, Bernard Stiegler, and Peter Sloterdijk. But this subjectivity, though posed as resistance to the existing power structures, lacks a dynamic character because it is closed within its invariable, naturalistic framework. The biopolitical resistance of these invariables can never create alternative forms of life.[71]

None of these interpretations captures what for us is most important in Foucault's notion of biopolitics. Our reading not only identifies biopolitics with the localized productive powers of life— that is, the production of affects and languages through social cooperation and the interaction of bodies and desires, the invention of new forms of the relation to the self and others, and so forth—but also affirms biopolitics as the creation of new subjectivities that are presented at once as resistance and de-subjectification. If we remain too closely tied to a philological analysis of Foucault's texts, we might miss this central point: his analyses of biopower are aimed not merely at an empirical description of how power works for and through subjects but also at the potential for the production of alternative subjectivities, thus designating a distinction between qualitatively different forms of power. This point is implicit in Foucault's claim that freedom and resistance are necessary preconditions for the exercise of power. "When one defines the exercise of power as a mode of action upon the actions of others, when one characterizes these actions by the government of men by other men—in the broadest sense of the term—one includes an important element: freedom. Power is exercised only over free subjects, and only insofar as they are free. . . . At the very heart of the power relationship, and constantly provoking it, are the recalcitrance of the will and the intransigence of freedom."[72] Biopolitics appears in this light as an event or, really, as a tightly woven fabric of events of freedom.

Biopolitics, in contrast to biopower, has the character of an *event* first of all in the sense that the "intransigence of freedom" disrupts the normative system. The biopolitical event comes from the outside insofar as it ruptures the continuity of history and the existing order, but it should be understood not only negatively, as rupture, but also as innovation, which emerges, so to speak, from the inside. Foucault grasps the creative character of the event in his earlier work on linguistics: *la parole* intervenes in and disrupts *la langue* as an event that also extends beyond it as a moment of linguistic invention.[73] For the biopolitical context, though, we need to understand the event on not only the linguistic and epistemological but also the anthropological and ontological terrain, as an act of freedom. In this context the event marked by the innovative disruption of *la parole* beyond *la langue* translates to an intervention in the field of subjectivity, with its accumulation of norms and modes of life, by a force of subjectification, a new production of subjectivity. This irruption of the biopolitical event is the source of innovation and also the criterion of truth. A materialist teleology, that is, a conception of history that emerges from below guided by the desires of those who make it and their search for freedom, connects here, paradoxically, with a Nietzschean idea of eternal return. The singularity of the event, driven by the will to power, demonstrates the truth of the eternal; the event, and the subjectivity that animates it, constructs and gives meaning to history, displacing any notion of history as a linear progression defined by determinate causes. Grasping this relation between the event and truth allows us to cast aside the accusation of relativism that is too often lodged against Foucault's biopolitics. And recognizing biopolitics as an event allows us both to understand life as a fabric woven by constitutive actions and to comprehend time in terms of strategy.

Foucault's notion of the event is at this point easily distinguishable from the one proposed by Alain Badiou. Badiou has done a great service by posing the event as the central question of contemporary philosophy, proposing it as the locus of truth. The event, with its irreducible multiplicity, that is, its "equivocal" nature, subtracts, according to Badiou, the examination of truths from the mere form of judgment. The difference between Badiou and Foucault in this respect is most clearly revealed by looking at where, temporally, each author focuses attention with respect to the event. In Badiou an event—such as Christ's crucifixion and resurrection, the French Revolution, or the Chinese Cultural Revolution, to cite his most frequent examples—acquires value and meaning primarily *after* it takes place. He thus concentrates on the intervention that retrospectively gives meaning to the event and the fidelity and generic procedures that continually refer to it. Foucault, in contrast, emphasizes the production and productivity of the event, which requires a forward- rather than backward-looking gaze. The event is, so to speak, inside existence and the strategies that traverse it. What Badiou's approach to the event fails to grasp, in other words, is the link between freedom and power that Foucault emphasizes from within the event. A retrospective approach to the event in fact does not give us access to the rationality of insurrectional activity, which must strive within the historical processes to create revolutionary events and break from the dominant political subjectivities. Without the internal logic of making events, one can only affirm them from the outside as a matter of faith, repeating the paradox commonly attributed to Tertullian, *credo quia absurdum,* "I believe because it is absurd."[74]

The biopolitical event that poses the production of life as an act of resistance, innovation, and freedom leads us back to the figure of the multitude as political strategy. Consider, to take an example from a very different domain, how Luciano Bolis, an Italian antifascist partisan, poses in his memoir the relation between grains of sand and the resistance of the multitude (in terms reminiscent of Walt Whitman's democratic leaves of grass). Bolis is fully aware that his sacrifice is only a grain of sand in the desert among the sufferings of the multitude engaged in struggle. "I believe, though," he explains, "that it is the duty of the survivors to write the story of those 'grains of sand' because even those who, because of particular circumstances or different sensibilities, were not part of that 'multitude' understand that our Liberation and the set of values on which it stands was paid for in the form of blood, terror, and expectations, and all that stands behind the word 'partisan,' which is still today misunderstood, scorned, and rejected with vacuous complacency."[75] Biopolitics is a partisan relationship between subjectivity and history that is crafted by a multitudinous strategy, formed by events and resistances, and articulated by a discourse that links political decision making to the construction of bodies in struggle. Gilles Deleuze casts the biopolitical production of life, in a similarly partisan way, as "believing in the world" when he laments that we have lost the world or it has been taken from us. "If you believe in the world you precipitate events, however inconspicuous, that elude control, you engender new space-times, however small their surface or volume.... Our ability to resist control, or our submission to it, has to be assessed at the level of our every move."[76] Events of resistance have the power not only to escape control but also to create a new world.

As one final example of the biopolitical power of bodies, from still another domain, consider a passage from Meister Eckhart's sermon "Jesus Entered":

> Now pay attention and look! If a human were to remain a virgin forever, he would never bear fruit. If he is to become fruitful, he must necessarily be a wife. "Wife," here, is the noblest name that can be given to the mind, and it is indeed more noble than "virgin." That man should receive God in himself is good, and by this reception he is a virgin. But that God should become fruitful in him is better; for the fruitfulness of a gift is the only gratitude for the gift. The spirit is wife when in gratitude it gives birth in return and bears Jesus back into God's fatherly heart.[77]

Eckhart is trying to focus our attention on the productivity of the biopolitical event, but what baggage comes with it! To read a passage like this, one has to pass it through decades of feminist theory, like so many baths of photographic solvents: starting with Simone de Beauvoir's analysis of how Woman is a patriarchal construct that subordinates women, in large part by tethering them to biological reproductive capacities; then feminist religious scholars who reveal the particularly Christian modes of patriarchy and the persistence of the virgin/whore dichotomy; and finally feminist political theorists who demonstrate how figures of women function in the canon of European political philosophy as markers of chaos and dangerous fecundity that must be excluded from the public realm. As these masculinist and heterosexist layers are stripped away, the image from Eckhart's passage that rises to the surface is a decidedly queer one! Productivity bursts forth as man becomes female, and here Eckhart's mystical visions recall the deliriums of President Schreber, who, as Freud reports, believes he is becoming woman in order to be impregnated by God and bear a new race of humanity. Interestingly, productivity in Eckhart coincides with the moment of gender crossing. (Could Eckhart recognize the same productivity in female masculinity that he finds in male femininity?) The biopolitical event, in fact, is always a queer event, a subversive process of subjectivization that, shattering ruling identities and norms, reveals the link between power and freedom, and thereby inaugurates an alternative production of subjectivity.

The biopolitical event thus breaks with all forms of metaphysical substantialism or conceptualism. Being is made in the event. It is interesting to note the strong resonance of this notion of the biopolitical event with American Pragmatism. "If nature seems highly uniform to us," writes Charles Peirce, "it is only because our powers are adapted to our desires."[78] Pragmatists propose, in effect, a performative analysis of the biopolitical event and demonstrate that the movement of biopolitical powers functions equally in the opposite direction: our desires, in other words, are also adapted to nature. We will return to this point in *De Homine* 1 at the end of Part 2 (and readers should keep in mind that these concluding discussions can also be read separately as one continuous argument).

PART 2

MODERNITY (AND THE LANDSCAPES OF ALTERMODERNITY)

We take off into the cosmos, ready for anything. . . . And yet, if we examine it more closely, our enthusiasm turns out to be all sham. We don't want to conquer the cosmos, we simply want to extend the boundaries of Earth to the frontiers of the cosmos. . . . We have no need of other worlds. We need mirrors. We don't know what to do with other worlds.

—Stanislaw Lem, *Solaris*

2.1

ANTIMODERNITY AS RESISTANCE

> As the Indian experience shows, the formal termination of colonial rule, taken by itself, does little to end the government of colonialist knowledge.
>
> —Ranajit Guha, *A Rule of Property for Bengal*

Power and Resistance within Modernity

Modernity is always two. Before we cast it in terms of reason, Enlightenment, the break with tradition, secularism, and so forth, modernity must be understood as a power relation: domination and resistance, sovereignty and struggles for liberation.[1] This view runs counter to the standard narrative that modernity emerged from Europe to confront in the colonies the premodern, whether that be conceived as barbaric, religious, or primitive. "There is no modernity without coloniality," claims Walter Mignolo, "because coloniality is constitutive of modernity."[2] It is constitutive insofar as it marks the hierarchy at modernity's heart. Modernity, then, resides not solely in Europe or in the colonies but in the power relation that straddles the two.[3] And therefore forces of antimodernity, such as resistances to colonial domination, are not outside modernity but rather entirely internal to it, that is, within the power relation.

The fact that antimodernity is within modernity is at least part of what historians have in mind when they insist that European expansion in the Americas, Asia, and Africa be conceived not as so many *conquests* but rather as colonial *encounters*. The notion of conquest does have the advantage of emphasizing the violence and brutality of European expansion, but it tends to cast the colonized as passive. Moreover, it implies that either the previously existing civilization was wiped out and replaced by that of the colonizer, or that it was preserved intact as an outside to the colonial world. This traditional view portrays colonial Indian society, for example, as Ranajit Guha writes, "either as a replication of the liberal-bourgeois culture of nineteenth-century Britain or as the mere survival of an antecedent pre-capitalist culture."[4] Modernity lies between these two, in a manner of speaking—that is, in the hierarchy that links the dominant and the subordinated—and both sides are changed in the relation. The notion of encounter highlights the two-ness of the power relation and the processes of mixture and transformation that result from the struggle of domination and resistance.

Working from the standpoint of colonial encounters, historians document two important facts: precolonial civilizations are in many cases very advanced, rich, complex, and sophisticated; and the contributions of the colonized to so-called modern civilization are substantial and largely unacknowledged. This perspective effectively breaks down the common dichotomies between the traditional and the modern, the savage and the civilized. More important for our argument, the encounters of modernity reveal constant processes of mutual transformation.

Long before the Spanish arrive in central Mexico, for example, the Nahua (that is, the inhabitants of the Aztec realm who speak Nahuatl) constructed highly developed cities, called *altepetl,* roughly the size of Mediterranean city-states. An *altepetl* is organized according to a cellular or modular logic in which the various parts of the metropolis correspond to an orderly cyclical rotation of labor duties and payments to the sovereign. After Cuauhtémoc surrenders to Cortés in 1521, the *altepetl* is not simply replaced by European urban forms through the long process of Hispanization, but neither does it survive intact. All the early Spanish settlements and administrative forms—the *encomienda,* the rural parishes, Indian municipalities, and the administrative jurisdictions—are built on existing *altepetl* and adapted to their form.[5] Nahua civilization does not survive unchanged, then, but neither does the Spanish. Instead, along with urban structures and administrative practices, music, language, and other cultural forms are progressively mixed, flowing through innumerable paths across the Atlantic in both directions, transforming both sides.[6]

Well before the formation of the United States, to give another, more directly political example, the Iroquois developed a federalist system to manage the relations among six nations—Mohawks, Oneidas, Onondagas, Cayugas, Tuscaroras, and Senecas—with checks and balances, separation between military and civil authorities, and other features later included in the U.S. Constitution. Iroquois federalism was widely discussed and admired in the eighteenth-century United States among figures such as Benjamin Franklin and Thomas Jefferson. The material aid of Native Americans to European settlers—how to plant crops, survive harsh winters, and so forth—has been incorporated into national mythology, but U.S. political forms are usually presented as being of purely European origin.[7] The point of such examples is simply to demonstrate the mixture and mutual transformation that characterize the encounters of modernity.

The problem with these examples, however, is that they do not emphasize the violence and unequal power relation of modernity. The dominant forces of modernity encounter not mere *differences* but *resistances*. What colonial historiography primarily accomplished and what needs to be countered, as Ranajit Guha explains, "is a conjuring trick to make resistance disappear from the political history of India under British rule."[8] There is something psychotic about the idea that modernity is a purely European invention, since it constantly has to deny the role in the construction and functioning of modernity of the rest of the world, especially those parts of it subordinated to European domination. Rather than a kind of psychic repression, we might better think of this denial as an instance of *foreclosure* in the psychoanalytic sense. Whereas the repressed element or idea, psychoanalysts explain, is buried deep inside, the foreclosed is expelled outside, so that the ego can act as if the idea never occurred to it at all. Therefore, whereas when the repressed returns to the neurotic subject it rises up from the inside, the foreclosed is experienced by the psychotic as a threat from the outside. The foreclosed element in this case is not only the history of contributions to modern culture and society by non-European peoples and civilizations, making it seem that Europe is the source of all modern innovation, but also and more important the innumerable *resistances* within and against modernity, which constitute the primary element of danger for its dominant self-conception. Despite all the furious energy expended to cast out the "antimodern" other, resistance remains within.[9]

To insist that forces of antimodernity are within modernity, on the common terrain of encounter, is not to say, of course, that the modern world is homogeneous. Geographers rightly complain that, despite constant talk about space, contemporary theoretical discussions of postcoloniality and globalization generally present spaces that are anemic, devoid of real differences.[10] The center-periphery model is one framework that does capture well in spatial terms the two-ness of modernity's power relation, since the dominant center and subordinated peripheries exist only in relation to each other, and the periphery is systematically "underdeveloped" to fit the needs of the center's development.[11] Such geographies of modernity go awry, however, when they conceive resistance as external to domination. All too often Europe or "the West" is cast as homogeneous and unified, as the pole of domination in this relationship, rendering invisible the long history of European liberation struggles and class struggles.[12] And correspondingly many analyses neglect the forms of domination and control located outside Europe, conceiving them merely as echoes of European domination. This error cannot be corrected simply by multiplying the centers and peripheries—finding centers and peripheries within Europe, for instance, as well as within each subordinated country. To understand modernity, we have to stop assuming that domination and resistance are external to each other, casting antimodernity to the outside, and recognize that resistances mark differences that are within. The resulting geographies are more complex than simply the city versus the country or Europe versus its outside or the global North versus the global South.

One final consequence of defining modernity as a power relation is to undermine any notion of modernity as an unfinished project. If modernity were thought to be a force purely against barbarism and irrationality, then striving to complete modernity could be seen as a necessarily progressive process, a notion shared by Jürgen Habermas and the other social democratic theorists we discussed earlier.[13] When we understand modernity as a power relation, however, completing modernity is merely continuing the same, reproducing domination. More modernity or a more complete modernity is not an answer to our problems. On the contrary! For the first indications of an alternative, we should instead investigate the forces of antimodernity, that is, resistances internal to modern domination.

Slave Property in the Modern Republic

The history of modernity and the history of republicanism are woven together to the point where at times they become indistinguishable. Several different conceptions of republic, as we saw earlier, compete in the seventeenth and eighteenth centuries, and some of these indeed refer to something very similar to the rule of the multitude, but only one conception—the republic of property—emerges as dominant. This republic matches so well with modernity because property relations are one form—a privileged form—of the power relation that constitutes it. A particularly revealing terrain on which to investigate this intimate relation among republic, property, and modernity is, perhaps paradoxically, the history of modern slavery. Slavery is a scandal for the republic, even though, throughout the eighteenth century and well into the nineteenth, black slavery and the slave trade are prominent, even central features of republican governments throughout Europe and the Americas. In the United States slave relations and slave production are explicit cornerstones of the republic and its economy. In France and England, although there is no comparable number of slaves within national boundaries, slavery and the slave trade are integral elements of the national economies, political debates, and colonial administrations. One does not have to look far below the surface to see how firmly slavery is rooted in the republic. The question to ask, then, is why, when slavery is so inimical to standard notions of republicanism and modernity, does slavery function for so long within modern republics, not as a peripheral remnant of the past but as a central sustaining pedestal?

Slavery is a scandal for the republic, first of all, because it violates the republic's core ideological principles: equality and freedom. Other sectors of the population, such as women and those without property, are deprived of political rights and equality by republican constitutions, but the inequality and unfreedom of slaves pose the most extreme ideological contradiction. Although many eighteenth- and nineteenth-century republican texts pose slavery as the primary foil against which republican freedom and equality are defined, they generally invoke ancient slavery and ignore the slavery of their own times, the black slavery of the Americas, which supports their own societies.[14] This ideological blindness is part of an operation that attempts to make slaves disappear or, when their existence cannot be denied, cast them outside as remnants of the premodern world and thus foreign to the republic and modernity.

The second way in which slavery is a scandal for the republic is that it violates the capitalist ideology of free labor. Capitalist ideology too uses slavery as the primary negative backdrop: freedom is defined by the fact that the wage laborer owns his or her labor-power and is thus free to exchange it for a wage. As owners of their labor-power, workers, unlike slaves, can be absorbed ideologically within the republic of property. Moreover, since chattel slavery confounds the essential division between labor and property, slaves constitute the point of maximum ideological contradiction within the republic of property, the point at which either freedom or property can be preserved, but not both. Here again, republican and capitalist ideological operations seek to make slaves disappear, or cast them as mere remnants of premodern economic relations, which capital will eventually banish from history.[15]

Making slaves disappear is not so simple, though, when the question is not only ideological but also material and economic. The relation between slavery and wage labor is difficult to disentangle in the course of this history. If we limit our focus to the countries of western Europe, as do many of the histories, the development of capitalist production can be made to appear relatively separate from slave production, or, at the limit, the slave trade and slave production are seen as providing a major external source of the wealth that makes possible the emergence of industrial capital in Europe. Furthermore, as many historians have noted, the slave plantation system experiments with and perfects the production scheme, division of labor, and disciplinary regimes that the industrial factory will eventually implement. From this perspective, though, slavery and capitalism seem to form a temporal sequence, as if capital and modernity were inimical to slavery and slowly but surely put an end to it.

Once we extend our view, however, and recognize that the context essential for the birth and growth of capital resides in the wide circuits of the passage of humans, wealth, and commodities extending well beyond Europe, then we can see that slavery is completely integrated into capitalist production during at least the eighteenth century and much of the nineteenth. "The slavery of the Blacks in Surinam, in Brazil, in the southern regions of North America . . . is as much the pivot upon which our present-day industrialism turns as are machinery, credit, etc.," Marx writes. "Without slavery there would be no cotton, without cotton there would be no modern industry. It is slavery which has given value to the colonies, it is the colonies which have created world trade, and world trade is the necessary condition of large-scale machine industry."[16] Slaves and proletarians play complementary roles in the worldwide capitalist division of labor, but the slaves of Jamaica, Recife, and Alabama are really no less internal to the capitalist economies of England and France than the workers in Birmingham, Boston, and Paris. Rather than assuming that capitalist relations necessarily corrode and destroy slavery, then, we have to recognize that throughout the eighteenth and nineteenth centuries the two support each other through a massive segregation schema, with one generally located on the east side of the Atlantic and the other on the west.[17]

None of this, however, grasps the racial hierarchy that is the essence of modern slavery. Just as slavery is viewed as an aberration in the republic of property, so too is racism conceived, from a similarly ideological perspective, as an external element and a distortion of modernity, which, once again, leads to the incompleteness hypothesis, as if modernity, perfecting itself, will eventually banish racism. Recognizing the internal relation of black slavery in the republic of property, though, helps us see racism in modernity as not only an ideology but also a system of material, institutional practices: a structure of power that extends well beyond the institution of slavery. The persistence of racial hierarchies in modernity, then, not only in slavery but also in the myriad other forms they take, is not a sign that modernity is "unfinished" but instead indicates the intimate relationship between race and modernity.[18] Earlier we said that without coloniality there is no modernity, and here we can see that race plays a similarly constitutive role. The three together function as a complex—modernity, coloniality, racism—with each serving as a necessary support for the others.

Slavery might thus serve as the emblem of the psychosis of the republic of property, which preserves its ideological coherence through disavowal or foreclosure, either refusing to recognize the existence of the traumatic reality of slavery or casting it outside. This is undoubtedly part of the reason why the Haitian Revolution has been so neglected in modern history. The Haitian Revolution, after all, as we said earlier, is much more faithful to republican ideology than the English, U.S., or French revolutions, in at least one central respect: if all men are equal and free, then certainly none can be slaves. And yet Haiti seldom appears in historical accounts of the Age of Revolution. The course of the Haitian Revolution is filled with contradictory forces, tragic turns, and disastrous outcomes, but it remains, despite all this, the first modern revolution against slavery, and thus one might call it the first properly modern revolution. Saying that, however, would take the republic and modernity according to only their ideological self-definitions, not their material and institutional substance, and whereas the Haitian Revolution extends the former, it betrays the latter. Freeing slaves violates the rule of property, and legislating against racial division (as does the 1805 Haitian Constitution, Article 14 of which declares all Haitians black regardless of skin color) undermines institutionalized racial hierarchy. Perhaps it should not be surprising that the Haitian Revolution constitutes for the vast majority of European and North American republicans of its time (and our own) an unthinkable event. It has to be silenced or cast outside because it reveals the profound contradiction between the ideology and substance of republicanism and modernity.[19]

One advantage of recognizing the intimate relation between slavery and the modern republic—and more generally the doubleness of modernity—is that it highlights the power of slaves and their resistance. When the slave is conceived as an abstract category, it is often posed as a figure of absolute subjugation, a subject that has been entirely stripped of freedom. Slaves thus present a useful limit case for Foucault's claim, cited earlier, that power is exercised only over free subjects. If slaves were indeed under absolute domination, there would be no power exercised over them, according to Foucault. It sounds contradictory, of course, to claim that slaves are free. Foucault's point is that all subjects have access to a margin of freedom, no matter how narrow that may be, which grounds their capacity to *resist*. To say that power is exercised only over "free subjects," then, really means that power is exercised only over subjects that resist, subjects that even prior to the application of power exercise their freedom. Slaves are most free, from this perspective, not from sundown to sunup, when out of reach of the master's whip, but when they resist the exercise of power over them.[20] Baruch Spinoza makes a similar claim and anchors it to an ontological foundation: "Nobody can so completely transfer to another all his right, and consequently his power, as to cease to be a human being, nor will there ever be a sovereign power that can do all it pleases."[21] Slave resistance pushes to the limit the relation between poverty and power exercised as freedom.

In historical terms this reflection illuminates the decisive role played by slave revolts, rebellions, and exoduses. Slavery is overturned not by the good conscience of republican values, as if it were just a premodern remainder; nor by the progressive forces of capital, as if it were a precapitalist form that took time for capital to eliminate entirely. Instead slavery is destroyed by the resistances of slaves themselves, who make it untenable as a form of government and unprofitable as a form of production.[22] W. E. B. Du Bois provides an extreme example of this hypothesis by arguing that slaves are protagonists of their own emancipation in the United States and determine the outcome of the Civil War. In order to sabotage the economy of the plantation system and stop the flow of food and other provisions to the Confederate Army, he explains, slaves set in motion an exodus, "a general strike that involved directly in the end perhaps a half million people," which contributes to undermining the Confederate fighters.[23] Du Bois proposes this general strike as an emblem to condense the long history of slave resistance and, more important, to demonstrate how black slaves are free subjects who play a determining role not just in their own emancipation but in the course of humanity as a whole. "It was the Negro himself," Du Bois claims, "who forced the consideration of this incongruity [between democracy and slavery], who made emancipation inevitable and made the modern world at least consider if not wholly accept the idea of a democracy including men of all races and colors."[24] The resistances and revolts of slaves thus elucidate the contradiction at the heart of the republic of property and modernity as a whole.

Similar phenomena can be found in the second wave of servitude and slavery in eastern Europe that stretches from the seventeenth-century restoration of feudal relations, following the wars of religion, to the birth of the nation-state. Both Marx and Max Weber focus on this history, not only because it breaks with the deterministic theory of stages of development of the mode of production—workers in eastern Europe, after a phase of relative liberalization of their movements, are reduced again to servitude *within* the processes of the formation of the capitalist mode of production—but also because it shows how, already in the preindustrial period, the mobility and freedom of labor-power constitutes a power of resistance and antagonism that capital cannot tolerate. In fact these forms of servitude are eventually destroyed, in part, by the flight of peasants toward the metropolises of western Europe. Through exodus, the antagonism of the servant with respect to the lord is transformed into the "abstract," objective antagonism of the working class in the face of the capitalist class.[25] The point once again is that even in circumstances of servitude, "free subjects" have the power to resist, and that resistance, a force of antimodernity, is key to understanding the movements of modern history.

One thing this reflection on slave resistance makes clear is that, although slaves may undergo what Orlando Patterson calls a "social death," they remain alive in their resistance. Humans cannot be reduced to "bare life," if by that term we understand those stripped of any margin of freedom and power to resist.[26] Humans are "naked" only in the Machiavellian sense we discussed earlier: full of rage and power and hope. And this brings us back to the definition of modernity itself by highlighting the fact that its double nature is marked by not only hierarchy but also antagonism. Slave resistance is a force of antimodernity not because it goes against the ideological values of freedom and equality—on the contrary, as Du Bois makes clear, slave rebellions are among the highest instances of those values in modernity—but because it challenges the hierarchical relationship at the core of modernity's power relation. Antimodernity, conceived in this way, is internal to and inseparable from modernity itself.

The Coloniality of Biopower

Antimodernity is held under control in the power relation of modernity not only through external forms of subjugation—from the slave master's lash and the conquistador's sword to capitalist society's police and prison—but also and more important through internal mechanisms of subjectification. The techniques and instruments of the triumvirate modernity-coloniality-racism permeate and invest subordinated populations. This is not to imply, of course, that modernity consists of total and absolute control, but rather to refocus our attention once again on the resistances that are born within modernity. The pervasiveness of modern power, in other words, corresponds to the internal provenance of antimodernity.

Some of the most influential work in postcolonial studies emphasizes the effectiveness of modes of representation and ideological constructions to demonstrate the pervasive or even all-encompassing nature of colonial power. Edward Said's study of Orientalism, for example, demonstrates how representations of colonized and dominated populations—in novels, histories, administrative documents, and myriad other texts—not only legitimate the colonial hierarchy in the minds of the colonizers but also shape the consciousness of the colonized.[27] Gayatri Spivak's famous and provocative claim that the subaltern cannot speak similarly focuses on the ideological power of representations. In the conflict over the practice of *sati,* or widow burning, between British colonial ideology and traditional patriarchal ideology, widows in colonial India, Spivak argues, occupy an abject position, doubly silenced: confronted on the one side by the discourse of "white men saving brown women from brown men" and on the other by the traditional affirmation that "the women want to die." Such ideological constructs completely saturate the colonial scene, completely eclipsing, in Spivak's example, any position from which the female subaltern can speak.[28] Such analyses of ideological and representational constructions are so powerful in part because they demonstrate how coloniality is achieved and maintained not just through violence and force, which, however generalized, always remain isolable and limited, but through at least tacit consent to the colonial modes of consciousness and forms of knowledge that spread without boundaries throughout society.

Religious institutions wield some of the most powerful instruments of modern colonial ideological control. All of the major religions have a hand in this—Islam, Hinduism, and Confucianism in different ways, and today Christian evangelical and Pentecostal churches, which are expanding enormously in Africa and Latin America, play a predominant role—but the Catholic Church has to be accorded a special place, given its long history of and intimate

relation to European conquest and colonization. It is a commonplace by now that throughout the Spanish conquest and colonization of the Americas, the friars and priests of the Catholic Church
function as ideological and moral complements to the soldiers and
generals of the Spanish crown. The church not only pursues the task
of converting the heathens to Christianity but also devises elaborate
ideological structures about the nature and capacities of the native
populations, questioning their capacity for reason, their ability to
become Christian, and even their humanity. What is perhaps most
remarkable about these racist and colonialist ideological constructs
in the Catholic Church is their durability: even Pope Benedict XVI
on a visit to Brazil in 2007 could repeat them. "Christ is the Savior
for whom they were silently longing," he claims, referring to the
populations of the Americas. "They received the Holy Spirit who
came to make their cultures fruitful, purifying them and developing
the numerous seeds that the incarnate Word had planted in them,
thereby guiding them along the paths of the Gospel. In effect, the
proclamation of Jesus and of his Gospel did not at any point involve
an alienation of the pre-Columbian cultures, nor was it the imposition of a foreign culture."[29] The ideological construct, as the pope's
claims make clear, is and must be internal to the subjugated, such
that it is experienced as something that was already present, waiting
to be actualized, rather than arriving as an imposition from the outside.

It is certainly very important to critique these kinds of representations and ideological constructs, as do many colonial and postcolonial scholars, but there is a limitation to such projects. Ideology
critique always assumes that in the final analysis, even though it
is pervasive, ideology is somehow external to, or at least separable
from, the subjugated subjects (or their interests). Notions of ideology and representation, in other words, do not go far enough to
grasp the depth of the modernity-coloniality-racism complex. Generally when racism or "race thinking" is considered an ideology, for
example, it is posed as an aberration or failure of modernity and
thus, even though widespread, relatively separate from modern soci-

ety as a whole. Racism, like coloniality, however, is not only internal to but also constitutive of modernity. It is "institutional," as Stokely Carmichael and Charles Hamilton argue, in the sense that racism is not just an individual question of bias or prejudice but goes well beyond the level of ideology, that racism is embodied and expressed throughout the administrative, economic, and social arrangements of power.[30] "Such a conception," writes Barnor Hesse, "moves the emphasis away from the apparently autonomous ideological universe of codified ideas of discrete physiognomies and metaphors of autochthonous blood to 'regimes of practices.'"[31] Hesse suggests, in other words, that racism is better understood as not ideology but governmentality. This is an important shift: the power relation that defines the modernity-coloniality-racism complex is primarily a matter not of knowing but of doing; and thus our critique should focus on not the ideological and epistemological but the political and ontological. Recognizing modernity's racism and coloniality as biopower helps accomplish the shift of perspective by emphasizing that power regulates not just forms of consciousness but forms of life, which entirely invest the subordinated subjects, and by focusing attention on the fact that this power is productive—not only a force of prohibition and repression external to subjectivities but also and more important one that internally generates them.

To return to the Catholic Church, then, we might consider as a prototype of its exercise of biopower the notorious Spanish Inquisition, which by the seventeenth century is firmly established in Peru and elsewhere in the Americas as a primary pillar of the colonial regime. The Inquisition is of course an ideological structure, which develops and enforces extremely refined definitions of what it means to be a Spaniard and a Christian, discovering and exposing infidels, heretics, and enemies of the church and the crown, but it is also a highly developed bureaucracy which invents the systems of protocols, procedures, regulations, and record keeping that will later constitute modern state bureaucracies. The Lima Inquisition, rather than being a remnant of premodern irrationality, is as good a place as any to identify the birthplace of modernity insofar as it brings together race thinking, coloniality, and administrative structures, producing in a paradigmatic way the hierarchies and power relations that define modernity. The Inquisition may be an extreme example, but it poses in very clear terms how subjects are produced through the confession of truths, the observance of correct behavior, and myriad other practices and procedures. The powers of modernity-coloniality-racism have never been merely superstructural phenomena but are rather material apparatuses that run throughout the collective existence of dominated populations and invest their bodies, producing internally the forms of life.[32]

If coloniality is a form of biopower, which functions internally, producing forms of life, does this mean that resistances have no place to stand and will necessarily be defeated? Nathan Wachtel, posing this question in much more specific historical terms, asks whether the anticolonial revolts in sixteenth-century Peru were all really vanquished. "Well, yes," he responds, "if one thinks of the fortunes of war and the colonial situation. But we know that native revolts, according to the context in which they developed, could take different forms." The Araucanians in Chile adopted certain European instruments of war, whereas the Peruvian Indians relied more on traditional methods, and there were widespread small-scale passive forms of resistance. Wachtel concludes, however, that we should remain open to a reversal of the results we expect to find. Sometimes what looks like a defeat turns out to be a victory and vice versa—and indeed measuring victory and defeat in this way may not be the most useful yardstick.[33] This returns us to our more general theoretical question: Does the fact of biopower's all-encompassing reach and capillary exercise, thoroughly investing subjects, mean that there is no place for resistance? This question echoes the many objections raised against Foucault's studies of power which presume all that is internal to power is functional to it. To understand this point, though, we need the kind of reversal of perspective that Watchel indicates. We should not think of power as primary and resistance a reaction to it; instead, paradoxical as it may sound, resistance is prior to power. Here we can appreciate the full importance of Foucault's claim that power is exercised only over free subjects. Their freedom is prior to the exercise of power, and their resistance is simply the effort to further, expand, and strengthen that freedom. And in this context the dream of an outside, an external standpoint or support for resistance, is both futile and disempowering.

Our conceptual project might thus be configured as a chiasmus. One movement shifts the study of the modernity-coloniality-racism complex from the external position of ideology to the internal position of biopower. And the second travels in the opposite direction, opening up from the inside of antimodern resistances to the biopolitical struggles that are capable of rupture and the construction of an alternative.

2.2

_____

AMBIVALENCES OF MODERNITY

_____

Alegría imagined a map of the world suspended in darkness until
suddenly a tiny flame blazed up, followed by others, to form a burning necklace of revolution across the two Americas.
                                    —Leslie Marmon Silko, *Almanac of the Dead*

Marxism and Modernity

With regard to modernity the Marxist tradition is ambivalent, at
times even contradictory. It contains a strong current that celebrates
modernity as progress and denigrates all forces of antimodernity as
superstition and backwardness, but it also includes an antimodernity
line, which is revealed most clearly in the theoretical and political
positions closely tied to class struggle. Resistances to capital by
workers, peasants, and all others who come under capitalist control
constitute a central instance of antimodernity within modernity.

Karl Marx's work provides a solid basis for the view that identifies modernity with progress. In the sections of the *Grundrisse* dedicated to the analysis of "forms which precede capitalist production,"
for example, he insists on the deterministic connections that link the
Asiatic and ancient (slave) modes of production to the formation of
the capitalist mode. This teleological reading of economic history
poses divisions among economic forms and practices, which were at
times present in the same historical period, and leads everything unerringly, in Marx's time, to the centrality of the capitalist mode of
production, using the same crude evolutionary logic as when he
maintains, in a somewhat different context, that "human anatomy

contains the key to the anatomy of the ape." Marx, along with Engels, tends in many of his works to view those outside Europe as
"people without history," separate from the development of capital
and locked in an immutable present without the capacity for historical innovation.[34] This accounts for Marx's underestimation in
this period, the 1850s, of anticolonial resistances, peasant struggles,
and in general the movements of all those workers not directly engaged in capitalist production. This perspective also leads Marx to
view colonization (British rule in India, for instance) as necessary
for progress since it introduces to the colony capitalist relations of
production.[35] We should add, in this regard, that the major nine-
teenth- and early-twentieth-century European critiques of this element of Marx's work raised by historians and social scientists does
not challenge the teleological, evolutionary aspect of the analysis.
Max Weber, for example, enlarges the gamut of criteria for evaluating development to include religious, political, cultural, and other
phenomena but does not weaken the deterministic logic of progress.[36]

The modernizing and progressivist line of Marx's thought is
reproduced in a wide variety of Marxist discourses. The social democratic notion of "incomplete" modernity, which we mentioned
earlier, is based on similar assumptions, although the relation of those
thinkers to Marx is tenuous at best. The long tradition of scientific
socialism, along with the socialist policies of industrial development,
also derives from this aspect of Marx's thought. And the denigration
of figures of labor and rebellion outside the industrial working class
as precapitalist or primitive has a significant presence in the Marxist
tradition.[37]

World-systems theories present an ambiguous but nonetheless
important case of the inheritance of this line of Marx's thought. Already in Ferdinand Braudel's work, from which world-systems theories take inspiration, and even earlier in the morphological theories
of capitalist development, the world market is seen to be constituted
through a relatively linear process of expansion of the capitalist capacity to export goods. Gradually, the theory goes, capital absorbs

within itself the entire world. And this certainly has come to pass, but not in such a simple or linear fashion. It is true that the world-systems perspective does not present an absolutely linear progression in its analysis of global expansion: the spatial progression (which is linear in the sense that the capitalist integration processes are presented as irreversible) is accompanied by a temporal ascesis that describes the cyclical contradictions of capitalist expansion. Within these cycles and their rhythms (from primitive accumulation to industrial centralization up to financial accumulation and then back again, after the crisis that financial accumulation creates) the hegemonic centers of development shift geographically—previously from the coasts of the Mediterranean to those of the Atlantic and today to the Pacific region—and consequently define the spatial hierarchies and/or zones of exclusion. Even when these theories take into account cyclical variations, however, the systematic nature of capitalist development and expansion is maintained. What the schema cannot account for adequately, even when it refers to "antisystemic" movements, are the forces of antimodernity: it cannot recognize class struggle as fundamental in the determination of historical, social, and economic development; it cannot understand capital as a relation that pulls together (and cuts apart) the powers of labor and the rule of capital; and finally, it cannot adequately take into account the resistances of subjects other than those directly involved in capitalist production. The less sophisticated versions of world-systems theory rely on a conception of development through successive stages, in which each stage determines a higher degree of progress of social and economic relations. But even in the hands of its most sophisticated practitioners, world-systems theory, without access to the dark forces of antimodernity, reproduces the link between Marxism and modernity.[38]

It would be a mistake, however, to identify Marxism as a whole with a progressivist notion of modernity. When we look at the theories in the Marxist tradition closest to class struggle and revolutionary action, in fact, those dedicated to overthrowing the power of capitalist modernity and breaking with its ideology, we get an entirely different picture. The anti-imperialist theories and political projects that emerge in the early twentieth century provide one important example of antimodernity in Marxism and revolutionary communism. In Rosa Luxemburg's work the terrain of the realization and valorization of the capitalist corporation depends on the expanding limits of the capitalist market and, primarily, on the colonial boundaries. On these limits—and on capital's capacity to expand through a continual process of primitive accumulation—is accomplished, with the consolidation of collective profit, the progressive subsumption of the globe within capitalist command. But this development creates, in Luxemburg's perspective, enormous contradictions, and her notions of contradiction and crises highlight the subjective forces that arise against capitalist modernity:

> The more ruthlessly capital sets about the destruction of non-capitalist strata at home and in the outside world, the more it lowers the standard of living for the workers as a whole, the greater also is the change in the day-to-day history of capital. It becomes a string of political and social disasters and convulsions, and under these conditions, punctuated by periodical economic catastrophes or crises, accumulation can go on no longer. But even before this natural economic impasse of capital's own creating is properly reached it becomes necessary for the international working class to revolt against the rule of capital.[39]

On these boundaries of development capitalist crises are constantly generated by the forces of antimodernity, that is, proletarian revolts.

In Lenin the subjective face of capitalist crisis is even more dramatic. While the great capitalist powers are battling one another over conflicting imperialist projects in the First World War, the struggles against the war and against the capitalist logic that drives it provide a common ground for anticapitalist and anticolonial struggles. Lenin's "popular outline," *Imperialism,* in addition to offering analyses of finance capital, banks, and the like, also proposes that the interimperialist war has generated not only misery and death for the workers of the world but also the opportunity to break through the ideological barriers that have divided them. Lenin rails against the "labor aristocracy" in European countries that, with its chauvinism and reformism, effectively supports imperialism and posits the potential of a common anti-imperialist struggle that brings the "thousand million people (in the colonies and semi-colonies)" together with the "wage slaves of capitalism in the lands of 'civilization.'"[40] The power of this common struggle against capitalist modernity that animates the communist movement breaks completely with the determinism and teleology of progressivist discourses.

Mao Zedong continues this line of revolutionary communist theory and emphasizes in it the power of antimodernity. Mao recognizes that the economic and social development of China cannot be accomplished only by following the models of modernity. Reforming the structures of government and transforming the living conditions of workers to liberate them from capitalist rule requires an alternative path. Mao's elevation of the political role of the peasantry, of course, is one extremely important departure from orthodox positions, as is more generally his powerful critique of Stalinist economic thought.[41] Even in Mao's most extreme modernization projects, Wang Hui suggests, there is a strong element of antimodernity. This "antimodern theory of modernization," he explains, brings together characteristics of Chinese thought from the late Qing onwards with the antimodernity of the revolutionary communist tradition.[42]

Once we have recognized this antimodern stream in revolutionary communist thought—which, we must admit, even in the authors we cite, is always ambivalent, mixed with notions of modernity and progress—we should take another look at Marx's work, because it does not undividedly support the modernity line as we suggested earlier. In the last years of his life, the second half of the 1870s, after having worked for decades on *Capital* and throwing himself headlong into the project to create a communist International, Marx becomes interested in pre- or noncapitalist forms of property and starts reading some of the founders of modern anthropology and sociology, such as Lewis Morgan, Maksim Kovalevsky, John Phear, Henry Maine, John Lubbock, and Georg Ludwig Maurer. He develops a hypothesis that bourgeois private property is only one form of property among many others that exist in parallel, and that the rules of capitalist property are acquired only through a brutal and complex disciplinary training. He thus completely overturns the rigid theory of "precapitalist forms" that he developed in the 1850s: he draws into question the claim that economic laws act independently of historical and social circumstances and extends his perspective somewhat beyond the Eurocentric limits of his earlier views, subordinating the history of Europe to the standpoint of the entire globe, which contains within it radical differences.

Marx's break with his earlier assumptions of modern "progress" seems to be consolidated when he receives a request in the late 1870s to adjudicate between two groups of Russian revolutionaries: one side, citing Marx's own work, insists that capitalism has to be developed in Russia before the struggle for communism can begin; and the other side sees in the *mir*, the Russian peasant commune, an already existing basis for communism. Marx finds himself in an awkward position here because, whereas his major writings support the former position, his current thinking agrees with the latter. Marx tries to reconcile his views, claiming, for instance, in the draft of a letter to Vera Zasulich, that in order to consider the question, "we must descend from pure theory to Russian reality." The historical necessity of the destruction of communal property in western Europe that Marx describes in *Capital* is not, he explains in another letter of this period, a universal history that immediately applies to Russia or anywhere else. It is a mistake to "metamorphose my historical sketch of the genesis of capitalism in Western Europe into a historical-philosophical theory of general development, imposed by fate on all peoples, whatever the historical circumstances in which they are placed."[43] In Russia, in fact, the task of the revolution is to halt the "progressive" developments of capital that threaten the Russian commune. "If revolution comes at the opportune moment," Marx writes, "if it concentrates all its forces so as to allow the rural commune full scope, the latter will soon develop as an element of regeneration in Russian society and an element of superiority over the countries enslaved by the capitalist system."[44] Does this affirmation of the forces of antimodernity and what Étienne Balibar calls his "anti-evolutionist" hypothesis reveal a contradiction in Marx? If so, it seems to us a healthy contradiction, one that enriches his thought.[45]

One important element that Marx seems to intuit in this exchange but cannot articulate is that the revolutionary forms of antimodernity are planted firmly on the common. José Carlos Mariátegui is in a privileged position to recognize this aspect of antimodern resistance both within and outside Europe. After traveling to Europe in the 1920s and studying socialist and communist movements there, he returns to his native Peru and discovers that Andean indigenous communities, the *ayllus*, rest on a parallel basis. The indigenous communities defend and preserve common access to the land, common forms of labor, and communal social organization—something like, in Mariátegui's mind, the prerevolutionary Russian peasant communities that interested Marx, the *mir*. "The Indian," he writes, "in spite of one hundred years of republican legislation, has not become an individualist" but instead resists in communities, on the basis of the common.[46] Mariátegui certainly recognizes the theocratic and despotic elements of traditional Inca society, but he also finds in it a solid rooting in the common that serves as a basis for resistance. Through his contact with European communism he comes to understand the importance and potential of the indigenous populations and social forms of "Inca communism"—not, of course, as a remainder preserved intact from pre-Columbian times or as a derivative of European political movements, but as a dynamic expression of resistance within modern society. Antimodernity, within Europe and outside, should be understood first in the social expression of the common.

Socialist Development

Whereas the tradition of Marxist theory has an ambivalent relation to modernity, the practice of socialist states is tied to it more unequivocally. The three great socialist revolutions—in Russia, China, and Cuba—although the revolutionary struggles that lead to them are traversed by powerful forces of antimodernity, all come to pursue resolutely modernizing projects. The dominant capitalist countries, as numerous authors have argued, promote and impose throughout the twentieth century ideologies and economic policies of development that, although cast as a benefit to all, reproduce the global hierarchies of modernity-coloniality. The programs of the socialist states, however, are equally dedicated to this same notion of development, perversely repeating the figure and structures of power in the capitalist countries they oppose. The critique of imperialism, which remains a central ideological pillar for the postrevolutionary socialist states, is forced to go hand in hand with the promotion of developmentalist political economy.

Well before the Bolshevik victory, as we said earlier, strong theoretical veins of revolutionary thought envision the goal of socialism as not so much liberation but higher development, which is thought to repeat or even improve on the modernization of the dominant countries. The construction of a national people and a socialist state are both functional to developmentalist ideology, which eclipses any autonomous development of alternative needs and indigenous traditions. At times national economic development is posed as a purgatory that has to be traversed in order to catch up with the capitalist countries, but more often it is seen as paradise itself. To critique development, of course, does not imply rejecting prosperity (on the contrary!), just as the critique of modernity does not mean opposing rationality or enlightenment. It requires rather, as we said earlier, that we take a different standpoint and recognize how the continuation of modernity and development programs only reproduces the hierarchies that define them.[47]

The ambivalence of the modernity and developmentalism of the economic programs of the socialist states can already be recognized in Lenin's 1898 study *The Development of Capitalism in Russia*. The modern model of economic development he affirms directly conflicts in this book with his appreciation of the "premodern"—or, really, antimodern—antagonism of the subaltern classes. He tries to resolve the contradiction by deferring it: economic progress is necessary now to allow the subaltern classes to mature to the point where they can effectively challenge capitalist rule. But note that whenever Lenin tries to solve a contradiction by deferring it into the future—most notably in his theory of the withering of the state—he is merely covering over a real problem. The maturation process or transition never comes to an end, and the contradiction remains intact. Lenin in this instance lacks not the spirit of the revolutionary struggle but a sufficient analysis of the mystifying function of capitalist ideology and its notion of progress.[48] In similar fashion, the developmentalist ideologies and economic policies of the socialist states do not betray the revolutionary forces and theories that led to them but rather flatten their ambivalence by highlighting the face of modern progress and eliminating the elements of antimodernity.

It is no coincidence that in the last decades of the twentieth century, when the "great hope" of really existing socialism falls into disenchantment, the three great socialist experiments are all enveloped in a common crisis. In the case of the Soviet Union, what was its model of development if not a mirage of liberation translated into the language of capitalist development? It envisioned an exit from economic dependency through stages of development, through the awkward absorption and transfiguration of capitalist modernity into the rhetoric of socialism. Marxism was simplified into an evolutionary theory of progress from which all elements of antimodernity are excluded as backward, underdeveloped. The Soviet crisis involved all aspects of social development, along with the democratic status of the political structures, the ruling mechanisms of the bureaucratic elite, and the geopolitical situation of Soviet quasi-colonial expansion.

In China the crisis led not to collapse but to an evolution of the system that refined the strongly centralized political management of development along the lines of the capitalist organization of labor. This can be directed through socialist, bureaucratic, and centralized means or in a more socially decentralized way, giving space and support to market forces in the framework of a unified global market that offers profits and competitive advantage from wage in-equalities and poor labor conditions. The Chinese road to neoliber-alism is different from that of the capitalist countries—with limited privatization, continuing state control, the creation of new class di-visions with new hierarchies between urban and rural areas, and so forth—but no less effective. In retrospect, the current neoliberal re-gime in China helps us identify more clearly how powerful the de-velopmentalist ideology was all along within the socialist regime.

Cuba, finally, has managed so far to hold at bay the ultimate consequences of the crisis but only by freezing itself in time, becom-ing a kind of preserve of socialist ideology that has lost its original components. The enormous pressure of the crisis, though, continues to have profound effects. And Cuba constantly has to ward off the two threatening alternatives that seem to prefigure its future: the catastrophic end of the Soviet experience or the neoliberal evolu-tion of the Chinese.

This same socialist ideology also traveled for several decades through the so-called underdeveloped or developing countries, from India and East Asia to Africa and Latin America. Here too there was a strong continuity between the capitalist theories of development and the socialist theories of dependency.[49] The project of modernity and modernization became key to the control and repression of the forces of antimodernity that emerged in the revolutionary struggles. The notions of "national development" and the "state of the entire people," which constantly held out an illusory promise for the fu-ture but merely served to legitimate the existing global hierarchies, was one of the most damaging regurgitations of socialist ideology. In the name of the "unity of the entire people," in fact, were organized political operations that pretended to overcome class conflict (while merely suppressing it) and thus confused the political meanings of Right and Left, along with fascist and communist. This reactionary project of modernity (behind the mask of socialism) emerges most strongly in moments of economic crisis: it was part of the horrible experience of the Soviet 1930s, and in certain respects it is repeated again today, not in the name of the "unity of the entire people" but rather in the mad rush of Left and Right elected political forces toward parliamentary and populist "centrism," to create what Étienne Balibar calls "extremism of the center."[50]

The "mistaken standpoint" of the three great socialist experiences, to take up ironically an old term of Soviet bureaucrats, is due not so much to the fact that the progressivist norms of capitalist development were internalized in the consciousness of the ruling classes of "really existing socialism," but rather to the fact that, paradoxically, these norms were too weakly internalized. Although these experiments in socialism failed, capitalist development in Russia and China did not. After relatively brief crises those countries returned to capitalism much richer and more powerful than they were when they supposedly broke with capitalist development. "Really existing socialism" proved to be a powerful machine of primitive accumulation and economic development. Among other innovations, in conditions of underdevelopment it invented instruments (like those of Keynesianism, for instance) that capitalist states adopted only in phases of cyclical crisis; and it anticipated and normalized the tools of governance to rule over the exception that (as we will see in Part 4) continue to be used in the current global order. Considering the exhaustion of global capitalist development today, the crises of "really existing socialism" take on an acute contemporary relevance. *De te fabula narratur:* the story is really about you.

It would be wrong to forget or minimize, however, how much the victorious socialist revolutions in Russia, China, and Cuba aided and inspired anticapitalist and anti-imperialist liberation movements around the world. We should be careful that our critique of them does not simply reinforce the vulgar attempts of the dominant ideology to cancel them from memory. Each of these revolutions initiated cycles of struggles that spread throughout the world in a kind of viral contamination, communicating their hopes and dreams to other movements. It would be useful, in fact, at this point in history, to be able to measure realistically the extent to which the definitive crisis of the socialist states hindered or actually aided the course of liberation movements. If we say, in other words, that the "brief twen-

tieth century," which began in 1917, came to an end between Beijing and Berlin in 1989, that does not mean in any way that the
hope and movement for communism ended then but only that another century has begun. We will explore some of the ways that the
forces of antimodernity today act within and against the processes of
capitalist globalization and discover an escape route from the cage of
developmentalist ideology in which the socialist states were trapped.

In any case, one fact that emerges clearly from this history is
that liberation struggles can no longer be cast in terms of modernization and stages of development. The power of antimodernity,
which was unrealized in the socialist revolutions and the struggles
for national independence, comes to the fore again, intact, in our
times. Che Guevara seems to intuit this fact during the final years of
his life when he tries to break away from the structural determinism
and the historical linearity of socialist doctrine, which, he recognizes, merely reproduces the basic features of capitalist modernity.
"Pursuing the chimera of realizing socialism with the help of the
blunt weapons left to us by capitalism," he writes, leads to a dead
end. "To construct communism it is necessary to make, simultane-
ous with the new material foundation, a new humanity [el hombre
nuevo]."[51] Che certainly knows firsthand the constraints of socialist
developmentalism. He serves as president of the national bank and
minister of industries in the years after the revolution. But in 1965
he mysteriously disappears from public view and leaves to join revolutionary struggles first in the Congo and then in Bolivia, where he
is killed. Some see this decision to leave Cuba and his government
posts as a sign of a romantic's restlessness for adventure or an unwill-
ingness to roll up his sleeves and face the hard work of building a
national economy. We interpret it instead as a refusal of the bureaucratic and economic straitjacket of the socialist state, a refusal to obey
the dictates of development ideology. The new humanity he seeks to
build communism will never be found there. His flight to the jungle
is really a desperate attempt to rediscover the forces of antimodernity he knew in the liberation struggle. Today it is even more clear
than in Che's time that only movements from below, only subjec-

tivities at the base of the productive and political processes have the capacity to construct a consciousness of renewal and transformation. This consciousness no longer descends from the intellectual sectors that are organic to what was once called socialist science but rather emerges from the working classes and multitudes that autonomously and creatively propose antimodern and anticapitalist hopes and dreams.

Caliban Breaks Free of the Dialectic

Throughout modernity, often alongside the most radical projects of rationalism and enlightenment, monsters continually spring up. In Europe, from Rabelais to Diderot and from Shakespeare to Mary Shelley, monsters present figures of sublime disproportion and terrifying excess, as if the confines of modern rationality were too narrow to contain their extraordinary creative powers. Outside Europe, too, forces of antimodernity are cast as monsters in order to rein in their power and legitimate domination over them. Stories of human sacrifice among Amerindians serve as evidence for sixteenth-century Spaniards of their cruelty, violence, and madness, just as the notion of the cannibal functions for African colonizers in a later period. The witch-hunts, witch burning, and witch trials that spread widely throughout Europe and the Americas in the sixteenth and seventeenth centuries are further examples of the forces of antimodernity cast out as irrationality and superstition, betraying reason and religion. Witch-hunts often spring up, in fact, in regions that have recently been the site of intense peasant rebellion, often led by women, resisting coloniality, capitalist rule, and patriarchal domination.[52] But modernity has difficulty dealing with its monsters and tries to dismiss them as illusions, figments of an overheated imagination. "Perseus wore a magic cap so that the monsters he hunted down might not see him," Marx writes. "We draw the magic cap down over our eyes and ears so as to deny that there are any monsters."[53] The monsters are real, though, and we should open our eyes and ears to understand what they have to tell us about modernity.

Max Horkheimer and Theodor Adorno try to grasp the monsters of antimodernity—irrationalism, myth, domination, and barbarism—by bringing them into dialectical relation with enlightenment. "We have no doubt," they write, "that freedom in society is inseparable from enlightenment thinking. We believe we have perceived with equal clarity, however, that the very concept of that thinking, no less than the concrete historical forms, the institutions of society with which it is intertwined, already contains the germ of the regression [its reversal] which is taking place everywhere today."[54] They see modernity caught inextricably in an intimate relationship with its opposite, leading inevitably to its self-destruction. Horkheimer and Adorno, writing from exile in the United States in the early 1940s, are struggling to understand the Nazi rise in Germany and the mixture of rationality and barbarism in the regime. The Nazis are not anomalous in their view, however, but a symptom of the nature of modernity itself. Proletarians too, they maintain, are subject to this same dialectic, such that their projects of freedom and rational social organization are inevitably functional to the creation of a total, administered society. Horkheimer and Adorno see no moment of subsumption or resolution of this dialectic but only a constant frustration of modernity's ideals and even a progressive degradation into their opposite, so that instead of finally realizing a truly human condition, we are sinking into a new kind of barbarism.

Horkheimer and Adorno's argument is extraordinarily important for its decisive departure from the teleological modernizing line of Marxist thought, but in our view, by constructing the relation between modernity and antimodernity as a dialectic, they make two mistakes. First, the formulation tends to homogenize the forces of antimodernity. Some antimodernities, like the Nazis, do indeed constitute horrible fiends that enslave the population, but others challenge the structures of hierarchy and sovereignty with figures of uncontainable freedom. Second, by closing this relationship in a dialectic, Horkheimer and Adorno limit antimodernities to standing in opposition and even contradiction to modernity. Rather than being a principle of movement, then, the dialectic brings the relationship to a standstill. This accounts for the fact that Horkheimer and

Adorno can see no way out, leaving humanity doomed to the eternal play of opposites. Part of the problem, then, is the failure to recognize differences among figures of antimodernity, because the most powerful of them, and the ones that will interest us most, do not stand in a specular, negative relation to modernity but rather adopt a diagonal stance, not simply opposing all that is modern and rational but inventing new rationalities and new forms of liberation. We need to get out of the vicious cycle that Horkheimer and Adorno's dialectic sets up by recognizing how the positive, productive monsters of antimodernity, the monsters of liberation, always exceed the domination of modernity and point toward an alternative.

One way to break free from this dialectic is to look at the relationship from the standpoint of modernity's monsters. The savage, deformed Caliban in Shakespeare's *Tempest,* for example, is a powerful symbol of the colonized native as a terrible, threatening monster. (The name Caliban itself could be an approximate anagram for cannibal at the same time that it suggests the Caribs, the native population of Caribbean islands exterminated during the colonial period.) Prospero the magician recounts that he tried to befriend and educate the monster, but once it threatened his daughter, Miranda, he had no choice but to restrain the brute by imprisoning him within a tree. The monstrousness and savagery of the native, following the classic script, legitimates the rule of the European in the name of modernity. Caliban, however, cannot simply be killed or cast out. "We cannot miss him," Prospero explains to Miranda. "He does make our fire / fetch in our wood, and serves in office / That profit us."[55] The monster's labor is needed, and thus he must be kept inside the island society.

The figure of Caliban has also been redeployed as a symbol of resistance in twentieth-century anticolonial struggles in the Caribbean. The monstrous image created by the colonizers is revalued from the other side to tell the story of the suffering of the colonized and their liberation struggles against the colonizers. "Prospero invaded the islands," writes Roberto Fernández Retamar, "killed our ancestors, enslaved Caliban, and taught him his language to make himself understood. What else can Caliban do but use that same language—today he has no other—to curse him, to wish that the 'red plague' would fall on him. I know no other metaphor more expressive of our cultural situation, of our reality. . . . [W]hat is our history, what is our culture, if not the history and culture of Caliban?"[56] The culture of Caliban is the culture of resistance that turns the weapons of colonial domination back against it. The victory of the Cuban Revolution, then, for Retamar, is the victory of Caliban over Prospero. Aimé Césaire similarly rewrites Shakespeare's play so that now Caliban, who has for so long been lorded over by Prospero, finally wins his freedom, not only breaking the chains of his physical imprisonment but also freeing himself ideologically from the monstrous image—underdeveloped, incompetent, and inferior—that he had internalized from the colonizers. "Caliban's reason" thus becomes a figure for Afro-Caribbean thought in its distinct and autonomous development from the European canon.[57]

This anticolonial Caliban offers a way out of the dialectic in which Horkheimer and Adorno leave us trapped. From the perspective of the European colonizers the monster is contained in the dialectical struggle between reason and madness, progress and barbarism, modernity and antimodernity. From the perspective of the colonized, though, in their struggle for liberation, Caliban, who is endowed with as much or more reason and civilization than the colonizers, is monstrous only to the extent that his desire for freedom exceeds the bounds of the colonial relationship of biopower, blowing apart the chains of the dialectic.

To recognize this savage power of monsters, let us go back to another moment in European philosophy that, in addition to expressing the typical racism and fear of otherness, highlights the monster's power of transformation. Spinoza receives a letter from his friend Pieter Balling which relates that after the recent death of his son he continues disturbingly at times to hear his son's voice. Spinoza responds with a puzzling example of his own hallucinations: "One morning as the sky was already growing light, I woke from a very deep dream to find that the images which had come to me in my dream remained before my eyes as vividly as if the things had been true—especially [the image] of a certain black, scabby Brazilian whom I had never seen before."[58] The first thing to remark about this letter is its racist construction of the black, scabby Brazilian as a sort of Caliban, which most likely derives from Spinoza's second-hand knowledge of the experiences of Dutch merchants and entre-preneurs, especially Dutch Jews, who established businesses in Brazil in the seventeenth century. Spinoza, of course, is by no means alone among European philosophers in employing such racist images. Many of the most prominent authors in the canon—Hegel and Kant first among them—not only invoke non-Europeans in general and the darker races specifically as figures of unreason but also mount arguments to substantiate their lower mental capacities.[59] If we stop our reading of the letter at that point, however, we miss what is most interesting in Spinoza's monster, because he goes on to explain how it configures for him the power of the imagination. The imagination for Spinoza does not create illusion but is a real material force. It is an open field of possibility on which we recog-nize what is common between one body and another, one idea and another, and the resulting common notions are the building blocks of reason and tools for the constant project of increasing our powers to think and to act. But the imagination for Spinoza is always exces-sive, going beyond the bounds of existing knowledge and thought, presenting the possibility for transformation and liberation. His Bra-zilian monster, then, in addition to being a sign of his colonial men-tality, is a figure that expresses the excessive, savage powers of the imagination. When we reduce all figures of antimodernity to a tame dialectical play of opposite identities, we miss the liberatory possi-bilities of their monstrous imaginings.[60]

It is true, of course, that there have long existed and continue to exist today forces of antimodernity that are not liberatory at all. Horkheimer and Adorno are right to see a reactionary antimoder-nity in the Nazi project, and we can recognize it too in the various modern projects of ethnic cleansing, the white supremacist fantasies of the Ku Klux Klan, and the deliriums of world domination of U.S.

neoconservatives. The antimodern element of all these projects is their effort to break the relationship at the heart of modernity and free the dominator from dealing with the subordinated. The theories of sovereignty from Juan Donoso Cortés to Carl Schmitt are antimodern insofar as they too seek to break the relationship of modernity and put an end to the struggle at its core by liberating the sovereign. The so-called autonomy of the political proposed by these theories is really the autonomy of rulers from the ruled, freedom from the challenges and resistance of the subjugated. This dream is an illusion, of course, because rulers can never survive without the subordinated, just as Prospero cannot do without his Caliban and, ultimately, as the capitalist can never be free of those pesky workers. The fact that it is an illusion, though, does nothing to stop it continuing today to create untold tragedies. These monsters are the real stuff of nightmares.

This gives us two positive tasks for an analysis of the forces of antimodernity. The first is to pose a clear distinction between reactionary antimodern notions of power that seek to break the relationship by freeing the sovereign and liberatory antimodernities that challenge and subvert hierarchies by affirming the resistance and expanding the freedom of the subordinated. The second task, then, is to recognize how this resistance and freedom always exceed the relationship of domination and thus cannot be recuperated in any dialectic with modern power. These monsters possess the key to release new creative powers that move beyond the opposition between modernity and antimodernity.

2.3
_____

ALTERMODERNITY

_____

> *Mesrin:* Where are you from?
> *Azor:* The world.
> *Mesrin:* Do you mean my world?
> *Azor:* Oh, I don't know about that, there are so many worlds!
> —Marivaux, *La dispute*

> A world in which many worlds are possible.
> —Zapatista slogan

How Not to Get Stuck in Antimodernity

Up to this point we have explored antimodernity as a form of resistance internal to modernity in at least three senses. First, it is not an effort to preserve the premodern or unmodern from the expanding forces of modernity but rather a struggle for freedom within the power relation of modernity. Second, antimodernity is not geographically external to but rather coextensive with modernity. European territory cannot be identified with modernity and the colonial world with antimodernity. And just as the subordinated parts of the world are equally modern, so too antimodernity runs throughout the history of the dominant world, in slave rebellions, peasant revolts, proletarian resistances, and all liberation movements. Finally, antimodernity is not temporally external to modernity in the sense that it does not simply come after the exertion of modern power, as a reaction. In fact antimodernity is prior in the sense that the power relation of modernity can be exercised only over free subjects who express that freedom through resistance to hierarchy and domination. Modernity has to react to contain those forces of liberation.

At this point, however, especially after having recognized the savage, excessive, monstrous character of liberation struggles, we run into the limits of the concept and practices of antimodernity. In effect, just as modernity can never extricate itself from the relationship with antimodernity, so too antimodernity is finally bound up with modernity. This is also a general limitation of the concept and practices of resistance: they risk getting stuck in an oppositional stance. We need to be able to move from resistance to alternative and recognize how liberation movements can achieve autonomy and break free of the power relation of modernity.

A terminological cue from the globalization protest movements shows us a way out of this dilemma. When large demonstrations began to appear regularly at the meetings of leaders of the global system across North America and Europe in the late 1990s and the first years of the new millennium, the media were quick to label them "antiglobalization." Participants in these movements were uncomfortable with the term because, although they challenge the current form of globalization, the vast majority of them do not oppose globalization as such. In fact their proposals focus on alternative but equally global relationships of trade, cultural exchange, and political process—and the movements themselves constructed global networks. The name they proposed for themselves, then, rather than "antiglobalization," was "alterglobalization" (or *altermondialiste,* as is common in France). The terminological shift suggests a diagonal line that escapes the confining play of opposites—globalization and antiglobalization—and shifts the emphasis from resistance to alternative.

A similar terminological move allows us to displace the terrain of discussions about modernity and antimodernity. *Altermodernity* has a diagonal relationship with modernity. It marks conflict with modernity's hierarchies as much as does antimodernity but orients the forces of resistance more clearly toward an autonomous terrain. We should note right away, though, that the term altermodernity can create misunderstandings. For some the term might imply a reformist process of adapting modernity to the new global condition while preserving its primary characteristics. For others it might suggest alternative forms of modernity, especially as they are defined geographically and culturally, that is, a Chinese modernity, a European modernity, an Iranian modernity, and so forth. We intend for the term "altermodernity" instead to indicate a decisive break with modernity and the power relation that defines it since altermodernity in our conception emerges from the traditions of antimodernity—but it also departs from antimodernity since it extends beyond opposition and resistance.

Frantz Fanon's proposition of the stages of evolution of "the colonized intellectual" provides an initial guide for how to move from modernity and antimodernity to altermodernity. In Fanon's first stage the colonized intellectual assimilates as much as possible to European culture and thought, believing that everything modern and good and right originates in Europe, thus devaluing the colonial past and its present culture. Such an assimilated intellectual becomes more modern and more European than the Europeans, save for the dark skin color. A few courageous colonized intellectuals, however, achieve a second stage and rebel against the Eurocentrism of thought and the coloniality of power. "In order to secure his salvation," Fanon explains, "in order to escape the supremacy of white culture the colonized intellectual feels the need to return to his unknown roots and lose himself, come what may, among his barbaric people."[61] It is easy to recognize too a whole series of parallel forms that antimodern intellectuals take in the dominant countries, seeking to escape and challenge the institutionalized hierarchies of modernity along lines of race, gender, class, or sexuality and affirm the tradition and identity of the subordinated as foundation and compass. Fanon recognizes the nobility of this antimodern intellectual position but also warns of its pitfalls, in much the same way that he cautions against the dangers of national consciousness, negritude, and pan-Africanism. The risk is that affirming identity and tradition, whether dedicated to past suffering or past glories, creates a static position, even in its opposition to modernity's domination. The intellectual has to avoid getting stuck in antimodernity and pass through it to a third stage.

"Seeking to stick to tradition or reviving neglected traditions is not only going against history, but against one's people," Fanon continues. "When a people support an armed or even political struggle against a merciless colonialism, tradition changes meaning."[62] And neither does identity remain fixed, but rather it must be transformed into a revolutionary becoming. The ultimate result of the revolutionary process for Fanon must be the creation of a new humanity, which moves beyond the static opposition between modernity and antimodernity and emerges as a dynamic, creative process. The passage from antimodernity to altermodernity is defined not by opposition but by rupture and transformation.

One particularly complex field for investigating the border between antimodernity and altermodernity is the movements and discourses of indigeneity that have developed in recent decades, primarily in the Americas and the Pacific. This is, of course, a classic terrain of antimodernity: ever since the European invasions the affirmation of indigenous traditions and identities has served as a powerful weapon of defense. Paradoxically, too, claims to indigenous rights in some societies, particularly those in which rights are based on historic treaties such as in Australia, New Zealand, and Canada, are linked to the preservation of memory and tradition, and thus effectively punish deviation from identity. According to the ideology of liberal multiculturalism common to settler societies, indigenous subjects are called on or even obliged to perform an authentic identity.[63] And yet many contemporary indigenous movements and discourses manage to escape antimodernity and open toward altermodernity.

The ambiguities between anti- and altermodern positions are evident, for example, in an anthology of the writings by Latin American indigenous theorists brought together by Guillermo Bonfil Batalla in the early 1980s. The project of *indianidad* (Indian-ness) that is common to all the authors, he explains in his introduction, is really aimed at the annihilation of "the Indian." By annihilation he does not mean, of course, the physical destruction of Indians, which has indeed been a byproduct when not a direct object of modernity

over the last five hundred years. Neither does he mean by it a process in line with the "modernizing" policies of liberal oligarchies
throughout Latin America to Hispanicize and assimilate the indigenous populations, making "the Indian" disappear through intermarriage, migration, and education, such that indigenous civilizations
would be relegated to museums. The project to abolish the Indian is
instead the destruction of an identity created by the colonizers and
is thus solidly based in antimodernity. The crucial point for us,
though, comes at the next moment of the argument. One option,
once the colonial identity is abolished, is to restore the "authentic"
identities—the Quiché, the Maya, the Quechua, the Aymara, and so
forth—as they existed before the encounter with European civilization, with their traditional modes of social organization and authority. Such a notion remains squarely within the tradition of antimodernity and the second stage of Fanon's sequence. Bonfil Batalla's
discourse in this and his other works generally remains closed in the
identity formations of antimodernity, but he does nonetheless suggest an opening toward another option. "Ethnic identity is not an
abstract, ahistorical entelechy," he writes; "it is not a dimension that
is foreign to social becoming nor an eternal and immutable principle."[64] This notion of social becoming suggests the possibility of
moving out of the antimodernity of indigenism in the direction of
an indigenous altermodernity.

The novelist Leslie Marmon Silko is one of the most interesting theorists of altermodernity. Her novels demonstrate how the
theft of land, the rule of private property, the militarism, and other
aspects of modern domination continue to ruin the lives of so many
Native Americans. Most distinctive about Silko's novels, however,
are the processes of mixture, movement, and transformation that
disrupt any antimodern formations of identity and tradition. They
are filled with mestizas/mestizos, Black Indians, "half-breeds," Indians excluded from their tribes, and other hybrid figures, constantly
moving across borders through the desert. Her protagonists never
forget the past, the wisdom of the elders, and the sacred books of
their ancestors, but in order to keep tradition alive and heed the an-

cient prophecies, they constantly have to make the world anew and in the process transform themselves. Native American practices, knowledges, and ceremonies constantly need to be transformed to maintain their power. Revolution is thus, in Silko's world, the only way not simply to rebel against the destroyers and guarantee our survival but paradoxically to preserve our most precious inheritance from the past.[65]

The Zapatista campaigns for indigenous rights in Mexico provide a clear political example of this altermodernity. The Zapatistas do not pursue either of the conventional strategies that link rights to identity: they neither demand the legal recognition of indigenous identities equal to other identities (in line with a positive law tradition) nor do they claim the sovereignty of traditional indigenous power structures and authorities with respect to the state (according to natural law). For most Zapatistas, in fact, the process of becoming politicized already involves both a conflict with the Mexican state and a refusal of the traditional authority structures of indigenous communities. Autonomy and self-determination are thus the principles that guided the Zapatista strategy in negotiating the constitutional reforms in the 1996 San Andrés Accords on Indigenous Rights and Culture with the government of Ernesto Zedillo. When the government failed to honor the agreement, however, the Zapatistas began a series of projects to put its principles into action by instituting autonomous regional administrative seats (caracoles) and "good government councils" (juntas de buen gobierno). Even though the members of Zapatista communities are predominantly indigenous, then, and even though they struggle consistently and powerfully against racism, their politics does not rest on a fixed identity. They demand the right not "to be who we are" but rather "to become what we want." Such principles of movement and self-transformation allow the Zapatistas to avoid getting stuck in antimodernity and move on to the terrain of altermodernity.[66]

Altermodernity thus involves not only insertion in the long history of antimodern struggles but also rupture with any fixed dialectic between modern sovereignty and antimodern resistance. In the passage from antimodernity to altermodernity, just as tradition and identity are transformed, so too resistance takes on a new meaning, dedicated now to the constitution of alternatives. The freedom that forms the base of resistance, as we explained earlier, comes to the fore and constitutes an event to announce a new political project. This conception of altermodernity gives us a preliminary way to pose the distinction between socialism and communism: whereas socialism ambivalently straddles modernity and antimodernity, communism must break with both of these by presenting a direct relation to the common to develop the paths of altermodernity.

The Multitude in Cochabamba

Altermodernity is a matter of not only culture and civilization but also equally labor and production. Throughout the modern period, however, these fields of struggle have often been thought to be separate from and even antagonistic to each other. The stereotype in many parts of the world, which is not entirely false, is that labor struggles are led by industrial working classes engaged in modernizing projects, whereas civilizational struggles are populated by people of color and indigenous groups with antimodern agendas. From the perspective of civilizational struggles, then, the goals and policies of labor movements can be as detrimental as those of the ruling classes, repeating their racist practices and promoting their Eurocentric cultural visions; and from the perspective of labor movements, civilizational struggles are frequently seen as backward, premodern, even primitive. Many other subjectivities have also been drawn into this conflict. Peasant movements at times have been closer to the one or the other side of this divide, and gender struggles have sometimes found alliance with one or both of these sides but often have been subordinated by both. Such ideological and practical conflicts have strained and even broken apart alliances within communist, national liberation, and anti-imperialist movements. The passage from antimodernity to altermodernity, however, brings with it a significant shift whereby these fields of struggle are, at least potentially, newly aligned, not in the sense that they are unified or that one holds hegemony over others, but in that they autonomously march forward on parallel paths.

The social movements in Bolivia that paved the way for the election of Evo Morales to the presidency in 2005 are a powerful example of this parallelism of altermodernity, which highlights political forms that express the autonomy and the connection of diverse sets of demands and social subjectivities. Two peaks of this cycle of struggles were the 2000 fight over the control of water resources in Cochabamba and the surrounding valley; and the 2003 battle over the right to control natural gas resources in El Alto and the highlands. In their general outlines these are classic examples of the resistance to neoliberalism that has arisen throughout the world in recent years. In the case of Cochabamba, a mid-sized city in the interior of Bolivia, the World Bank advised the national government to eliminate subsidies required for public water service by selling the water system to foreign investors who would establish a "proper system of charging." After the government followed the advice and sold the water supply system, the foreign consortium immediately raised local water rates 35 percent, at which time the protests began. The war over gas in 2003 follows the same script. These are not isolated incidents, moreover, but merely the most visible points of a continuous high level of mobilization throughout the country from at least 2000 to 2005. What is most remarkable about these struggles is how they manage to coordinate a wide variety of economic and social demands in horizontal networks, demonstrating perhaps more clearly than any other experience the shift from antimodernity to altermodernity.

To appreciate the complexity of this situation we have to recognize how Bolivian society and the movements present multiplicities at every turn. First of all, what is at stake in these struggles is not merely an economic problem (of land, labor, and natural resources), and neither is it only a racial, cultural, or civilizational problem. It is all of these at once. Second, in each of these domains there is a multiplicity of subjectivities engaged in struggle. The sociologist René Zavaleta captures this multiplicity when he characterizes Bolivia in the 1970s as a *socieded abigarrada,* which in English could be rendered awkwardly as a many-colored, variegated, or even motley society.[67] Zavaleta views this social diversity in a negative light, as a marker of Bolivia's "premodern" character, as if modernity were defined by homogeneous classes, identities, and social institutions. By our conception, however, Bolivia is not only just as modern as France or India or Canada but also just as open to altermodernity. The diversity Zavaleta recognizes is, in the context of altermodernity, a potential key to social transformation. The question here is how the social multiplicities in question interact and, specifically, how they cooperate in common struggle. To understand this dynamic we have to look more closely at the nature of this *sociedad abigarrada* and recognize the relations among the various social singularities that compose the social movements.

The wide diversity of racial groups engaged in the struggles is obvious: in addition to those of European descent there are officially thirty-six different indigenous ethnicities or peoples in Bolivia, the most numerous of which are Aymara and Quechua, along with various populations of mixed-race heritage. This is one axis along which the movements are plural or many-colored. The forms and sectors of labor are equally diverse, but this axis cannot be understood without some knowledge of Bolivian economic history. After the revolution of 1952 worker and peasant movements organized in powerful unions, and the Bolivian miners along with a relatively small industrial labor force played a central role in national politics. The hegemony of the old working class came to an end by the late 1980s, however, owing to political and military repression and, more important, economic restructuring that transformed the Bolivian labor force. Some of the largest mines were closed, and many of the peasants who had been recruited as mine workers a generation earlier had to migrate again in search of work. As workers were increasingly forced to move from one place and one occupation to another, and as an ever larger portion of the labor force had to work without fixed contracts, the working class became more complex in composition and, like other working classes throughout the world, had to become more flexible and mobile. The resulting multiplicity of workers and working conditions makes it no longer possible to organize the class vertically in centralized structures. Miners can no longer represent hegemonically the interests of the entire Bolivian working class, just as in other countries autoworkers or steelworkers can no longer play such a role. All relations of hegemony and representation within the working class are thus thrown into question. It is not even possible for the traditional unions to represent adequately the complex multiplicity of class subjects and experiences. This shift, however, signals no farewell to the working class or even a decline of worker struggle but rather an increasing multiplicity of the proletariat and a new physiognomy of struggles. The Bolivian social movements are "many-colored," then, along at least two intersecting axes: the racial, ethnic, and cultural axis; and the axis of the various sectors of labor engaged in common struggle.[68]

A group of contemporary Bolivian scholars following Zavaleta use the term "multitude-form," in contrast to the old class-form, to name the internally differentiated struggles of altermodernity. The multitude-form is what characterizes struggles in a *sociedad abigarrada*. Whereas Zavaleta saw the multitude as passive or merely spontaneous because of its multiplicity, in contrast to the active unity of the class, these contemporary scholars understand it as the protagonist of a coherent political project. Multitude is a form of political organization that, on the one hand, emphasizes the multiplicity of the social singularities in struggle and, on the other, seeks to coordinate their common actions and maintain their equality in horizontal organizational structures. The "Coordination for the Defense of Water," for instance, which organizes the struggles in Cochabamba in 2000, is one such horizontal structure. What the recent Bolivian experiences make clear, in fact, is how the multitude-form manages to construct political organization not only among the diverse components of the working class, and not only among the multiplicity in the racial and ethnic domain, but also between these axes. "This fragmentation of the movements," Alvaro García Linera explains, "expresses the structurally segmented ethnic, cultural, political, class, and regional reality of society itself, which obliges us to reinvent the means of articulation of the social, not as a hierarchical fusion but rather as provisional horizontal networks."[69] The multitude-form is not a magic key that opens all doors, but it does pose adequately a real political problem and posit as the model for addressing it an open set of social singularities that are autonomous and equal, capable together, by articulating their actions on parallel paths in a horizontal network, of transforming society.[70]

Multitude is thus a concept of applied parallelism, able to grasp the specificity of altermodern struggles, which are characterized by relations of autonomy, equality, and interdependence among vast multiplicities of singularities. In the Bolivian struggles, as in so many others like them throughout the world, there is no single figure of labor, such as the miners, that can guide or claim to represent all the workers. Instead miners, industrial workers, peasants, unemployed people, students, domestic workers, and numerous other sectors of labor participate equally in the struggle. Similarly the Bolivian struggles are not led by non-indigenous groups or really by indigenous groups either. A multiplicity of social singularities defined more or less by their culture or ethnicity or labor position coordinate their struggles together in the multitude. The guiding principle here is the same one we saw earlier in the context of the Zapatistas: aimed at not the recognition, preservation, or affirmation of identities but the power of self-determination of the multitude. In altermodernity the obstacles and the divisions of antimodernity—particularly those between civilizational and labor struggles—have been displaced by a new physiognomy of struggles that poses multiplicity as a primary element of the political project.

The struggles of the Bolivian multitude also demonstrate another essential feature of altermodernity: its basis in the common. In the first place, the central demands of these struggles are explicitly aimed at ensuring that resources, such as water and gas, will not be privatized. The multitude of altermodernity, in this sense, runs counter to the republic of property. Second, and more important, the struggles of the multitude are based in common organizational structures, where the common is seen as not a natural resource but a social product, and this common is an inexhaustible source of innovation and creativity. In the city of El Alto, for instance, the Committees for the Defense of National Gas, which animated the struggles in 2003, functioned on the basis of already existing local practices and structures of self-rule. El Alto is a sprawling suburb of La Paz, which is inhabited primarily by Aymara populations that migrated to the capital from the rural highlands over the last twenty years. On the one hand, then, the struggles grew out of and were conditioned by the organizational patterns and the practices of self-government of rural Aymara communities, which are based on the common: common access to resources and property, common responsibilities for community affairs, and so forth. On the other hand, the neighborhood councils in El Alto, organized in a citywide federation, form another basis of self-government. The neighborhood councils supply a wide range of services not provided by the government, from education to health care and other social services, making decisions about shared resources and citizen responsibilities. When the mass mobilization broke out in 2003, then, it was not, as some assumed, a spontaneous rebellion but a mature organizational structure that grew directly out of already existing networks and well-established practices of self-government.[71]

This vision of a multitude composed of a set of singularities and based on practices of self-determination and the common is still missing one essential element of altermodernity: its constant metamorphosis, its mixture and movement. Every singularity is a social becoming. What the multitude presents, then, is not only a *sociedad abigarrada* engaged in common struggle but also a society constantly in the process of metamorphosis. Resistance and the collaboration with others, after all, is always a transformative experience. Rather than a static mosaic of many-colored parts, this society is more like a kaleidoscope in which the colors are constantly shifting to form new and more beautiful patterns, even melding together to make new colors.

Rupture and Constitution

In this chapter we have traveled some of the landscapes of altermodernity, emphasizing how they both grow out of antimodern struggles and move beyond them. The task of altermodernity, which is illustrated by some social movements experimenting with the multitude form, is not only to resist and challenge the hierarchical relationships established by modernity and the identities of antimodernity but also to create alternative social relations based on the common. Altermodernity thus shares some attributes with but is fundamentally different from the discourses of hypermodernity and postmodernity.

We could say, in a playful kind of nationalist shorthand, that Germans are primarily responsible for the concept of hypermodernity, U.S. intellectuals for postmodernity, and the French for altermodernity—although our preference for the position of altermodernity is not due to any sort of Francophilia. All of these concepts pose some kind of historical rupture in or with modernity, but the nature of that break and the possibilities it opens are different in important ways. By "hypermodernity" we mean to group together all those concepts, such as second modernity and reflexive modernity articulated by authors such as Ulrich Beck and Jürgen Habermas, that propose in the contemporary world no break with the principles of modernity but rather a transformation of some of modernity's major institutions. These perspectives do recognize well many of the structural changes of the nation-state, the deployments and regulations of labor and capitalist production, the biopolitical organization of society, the nuclear family, and so forth, but none of this implies for them a break with modernity, and indeed they do not see that as a desirable outcome. Rather they envision modernizing modernity and perfecting it by applying its principles in a reflexive way to its own institutions. This hypermodernity, however, in our view, simply continues the hierarchies that are central to modernity, putting its faith in reform, not resistance, and thus does not challenge capitalist rule, even when recognizing the new forms of the "real subsumption" of society within capital.[72]

Postmodernity marks a much more substantial rupture than hypermodernity, posing the end of the core elements of modernity, which is cause for celebration for some authors and for others lament. In our previous work we too have employed the concept of postmodernity to emphasize the importance of the historical break that presents new conditions and new possibilities in a wide variety of social fields: on the economic terrain, for example, with the reorganization of relations of production in the emergence of the hegemony of immaterial production; and on the political terrain with the decline of structures of national sovereignty and the emergence of global mechanisms of control. The term "postmodernity," however, is conceptually ambiguous since it is primarily a negative designation, focusing on what has ended. In fact many authors who affirm the concept of postmodernity can be linked to the traditions of "negative thought" and/or philosophies of *Krisis*.[73] They focus on the destructive destiny of Enlightenment and the powerlessness of reason in the face of the new figures of power; but despite their strong protest and denunciation of the incapacity of reason to react to the crisis, they have no recognition of the capacities of existing subjectivities to resist this power and strive for liberation. The philosophers of *Krisis* thus correctly grasp, perhaps in some cases without knowing it, the definitive decline of the dominant line of Enlightenment thought and its Eurocentrism, but they can only offer weak thought and aestheticism while presiding over the tomb of Enlightenment critique—and, naturally, around the tomb they start talking of theology.[74] The various theories of postmodernity, which are extraordinarily diverse, generally allude to the contemporary volatility of social norms and conventions, but the term itself does not capture a strong notion of resistance or articulate what constitutes "beyond" modernity.

Altermodernity, in contrast, marks a more profound rupture with modernity than either hyper- or postmodernity. In fact it is two removes from modernity since it is first grounded in the struggles of antimodernity and their resistance to the hierarchies at the core of modernity; and second it breaks with antimodernity, refusing the dialectical opposition and moving from resistance to the proposition of alternatives. There is no faith here that the core principles of modernity can be reformed and perfected as there is for the proponents of hypermodernity. The struggles of antimodernity have long ago washed away any residue of those illusions. And in contrast to most propositions of postmodernity, altermodernity provides a strong notion of new values, new knowledges, and new practices; in short, altermodernity constitutes a *dispositif* for the production of subjectivity.

To construct a definition of altermodernity on its own terms now and not simply in contrast to other concepts, we propose three general lines of investigation, each of which designates histories of struggle that come together in altermodernity. The first is a line of European Enlightenment or, better, an alternative line within European Enlightenment. We gave an example of this earlier by tracing the connections among Machiavelli, Spinoza, and Marx. Ever since the beginnings of bourgeois society and modern European philosophy, this line has designated the search for absolute democracy against sovereign absolutism however it is organized, even in republican guise.[75] Many of the central figures in the canon of European philosophy, such as Immanuel Kant and Friedrich Nietzsche, occupy ambiguous positions with respect to this line; but the need to critique them and European thought as a whole should never make us forget that the tradition and its major philosophers also contain extraordinarily powerful conceptions of liberation. The desire to free humanity from the weight of poverty and exploitation, superstition, and domination may at times be submerged and made unrecognizable by the dominant transcendental formation that legitimates and consolidates the power relations of modernity, but it continues nonetheless in European thought as an alternative, subterranean line.

Workers' movements throughout the world constitute a second line that, in often dramatic and sometimes tragic fashion, has run along the borders among modernity, antimodernity, and altermodernity. Here too, in both Marxist theory and socialist practice, the alternative line has often been submerged and made unrecognizable. In the dominant theories of the workers' movements the ideology of the linearity of progress and capitalist development has often been coupled with the conviction that European thought and society are the source of innovation and thus prefigure the future course of the rest of the world. The socialist states and "really existing socialism" always hid in their closets the certainty that the productive relations of capitalist modernity have to be maintained and that progress has to proceed through "stages of development." An unrelenting critique of this, however, should not blind us to the alternative line that exists throughout the tradition. We have to keep in mind the moments of powerful ambivalence that, as we saw earlier, characterize the central thinkers in the tradition: in the early and late Marx, in his attempts to recognize communism in the critique of private property and in his critiques of the Eurocentric, progressivist nature of his own theories; in the reappearing tendency in Lenin's thought to reopen the terrain of anti-imperialist struggle and pull communist action away from the structural block of capitalist development; and in the contradiction in Mao between the drive to further a radical anticapitalist revolution with the construction of a new civilization based on the common and the bureaucratic construction of a market economy and authoritarian state, a tension that runs from the guerrilla war against the Japanese and the Long March to the Great Leap Forward and the Cultural Revolution. (Perhaps, in fact, the best approach to understanding the 1989 Tiananmen revolt is to read the demands of the Beijing students and workers as an attempt to renew the radical hope of this democratic line against the sirens and violence of the new structures of capitalist discipline and management that the party hierarchy was in the process of imposing.) Despite the defeats and catastrophes of this tradition, though, in the reality of revolutionary experience in the liberation struggles against exploitation and hierarchy, and in all the moments of antimodern resistance there has also been present an alternative path that poses the possibility of breaking definitively with the relation of command that modernity invented. Years from now we may be able to look back and see that the result of really existing socialism and its collapse was to demonstrate how the social relationship between exploitation and domination that seemed only to define the organization of labor actually permeates the entire society. Within the experiences of really existing socialism, in other words, the passage to the rule of biopower took its complete form, and thus the forces of biopolitics emerge here too, configuring the lines of altermodernity.

A third line links together the forces of antimodernity that resist coloniality, imperialism, and the innumerable permutations of racialized rule. We described earlier the danger that such movements get stuck in a reactive, oppositional position and never get out of the dialectic with modernity. But an even graver danger is that successful revolts end up reproducing the hierarchical power relations of modernity. How many victorious national liberation struggles have led to the construction of postcolonial states that merely perpetuate capitalist relations of property and command on the basis of a small group of elites, conforming to the position of the nation at the bottom of the global hierarchy and accepting the fact that large portions of their population are condemned to misery! And yet within the traditions of antimodernity there always lives the possible emergence of altermodern forces and forms, especially, as we have seen, whenever the common appears as the basis and goal of struggles— not only the common as a given element such as land or natural resources but also and more important the common as a result such as networks of social relations or forms of life.

None of these three lines, however, is alone sufficient to construct an adequate definition of altermodernity. Our hypothesis is that the forces of antimodernity in each of these three domains, continually defeated and contained in the past, can be reproposed today as altermodernity when they link with the lines of resistance in the other domains. The capitalist totality is not, as it seemed to many, the point of arrival or end of history where all antagonisms can be absorbed, but rather the limit on which resistances proliferate throughout the sphere of production and all the realms of social life. The three lines have to be woven together in such a way as to recognize the metamorphosis, the anthropological transformation that altermodernity requires. As Frantz Fanon and Che Guevara affirmed, in different contexts, in order to defeat modernity and go beyond antimodernity, a new humanity must be created.

This passage from anti- to altermodernity illuminates some aspects of the contemporary role of the intellectual. First, although critique—of normative structures, social hierarchies, exploitation, and so forth—remains necessary, it is not a sufficient basis for intellectual activity. The intellectual must be able also to create new theoretical and social arrangements, translating the practices and desires of the struggles into norms and institutions, proposing new modes of social organization. The critical vocation, in other words, must be pushed forward to move continually from rupture with the past toward charting a new future. Second, there is no place for vanguards here or even intellectuals organic to the forces of progress in the Gramscian sense. The intellectual is and can only be a militant, engaged as a singularity among others, embarked on the project of co-research aimed at making the multitude. The intellectual is thus not "out in front" to determine the movements of history or "on the sidelines" to critique them but rather completely "inside." The function of the intellectual today, though in many ways radically different, shares some aspects with the one developed in the context of the patristics in the first centuries of Christianity. That was in many respects a revolutionary movement within an Empire that organized the poor against power and required not only a radical break with traditional knowledge and customs but also an invention of new systems of thought and practice, just as today we must find a way out of capitalist modernity to invent a new culture and new modes of life. Let's call this, then, only half facetiously, a *new* patristic, in which the intellectual is charged with the task not only to denounce error and unmask illusions, and not only to incarnate the mechanisms of new practices of knowledge, but also, together with others in a process of co-research, to produce a new truth.

DE HOMINE 1: BIOPOLITICAL REASON

Imagine people who could only think aloud. (As there are people who can only read aloud.)

—Ludwig Wittgenstein, *Philosophical Investigations*, no. 331

In his *History of Madness,* Foucault not only details how madness is invented through a series of enclosures and exclusions of mentalities and populations, and not only, by revealing this history, seeks to undermine the sovereign rule of reason, but also points toward another truth that lies beyond madness. "Is it possible," Foucault speculates, "that the production of the truth of madness is manifest in forms that are not those of relations of knowledge?"[76] The perspective of altermodernity lies in that other rationality, which extends beyond the reason/madness couple. But what is the truth *beyond* madness? Or more simply, how is this *other* possible and where can it be found?

One logical response to these questions is to look for a truth and a rationality *outside*. As soon as one cites Foucault's study of madness, in fact, one should extend it beyond the European limits of his thought to analyze the effects of colonial reason on and the attribution of madness to the colonized.[77] Some of the most powerful critiques of epistemology in the latter half of the twentieth century do establish standpoints outside or elsewhere, grounded in identity and the position of the subordinated. "Caliban's reason" and decolonial epistemologies are examples that confront Eurocentrism; and feminist epistemologies have challenged the force of gender domination in the production of thought and knowledge.[78]

One of the great contributions of these frameworks has been to unmask the false universality and objectivity of traditional epistemologies, demonstrating that those systems of knowledge are embedded within the hierarchies and power relations that characterize modernity.

The external standpoint and the foundation in identity that give such epistemological critiques their power can also, as many of the practitioners are keenly aware, prove to be a limitation. Donna Haraway, for example, warns that any search for a standpoint outside, based in identity, is tinged with the dream of returning to a Garden of Eden, a site of absolute purity.[79] Another way of posing this danger, to use the slogan we derived from Fanon earlier, is that such projects risk getting stuck in antimodernity. In epistemology as in politics, we need to focus on the forces of critique and resistance that are inside modernity and from this internal position discover the means to create an alternative. The passage from anti- to altermodernity, in the epistemological context, must lead to a biopolitical conception of rationality.

Two intuitions serve us as initial guides for exploring the terrain of biopolitical reason. First, *the experience of the common* provides a framework for breaking the epistemological impasse created by the opposition of the universal and the particular. Once we have critiqued the false universals that characterize dominant modern rationality, any new attempt to promote universal truths is rightly viewed with suspicion, because the critique has unmasked not only those specific claims to universality but also the transcendent or transcendental basis on which universal truths are proclaimed. It is not sufficient, though, in reaction to this, simply to limit ourselves to particular knowledges with no claim to truth. The common cuts diagonally across the opposition between the universal and the particular. Normal usage of the terms "common sense" and "common knowledge" captures some of what we have in mind insofar as they extend beyond the limitations of the particular and grasp a certain social generality, but these terms generally view the common as something passive, already given in society. We concentrate instead, following Spinoza's conception of "common notions," on the *production and productivity* of the common through collective social practices. Like the universal, the common lays claim to truth, but rather than descending from above, this truth is constructed from below.[80]

This leads directly to our second guiding intuition: that epistemology has to be grounded on the terrain of struggle—struggle that not only drives the critique of the present reality of domination but also animates the constitution of another reality. Saying that truth is constructed from below means that it is forged through resistance and practices of the common. Our conception of the biopolitical and its development, then, is not just analogous to the political passage from antimodernity to altermodernity, as we suggested earlier. It is in some sense the same process of struggle seen now through a different attribute—a biopolitical struggle that produces at once a new reality and a new truth.

Discovering a basis for knowledge in the common involves, first of all, a critique of the pretense of objectivity of the scientific tradition, but one that, of course, does not search for an outside to that tradition. This critique instead arises from the inside, through what Foucault calls "the insurrection of knowledges . . . against the centralizing power-effects that are bound up with the institutionalization and workings of any scientific discourse organized in a society such as ours."[81] The critique of the objectivity of science, which is allied with the politics of truth that has supported and developed colonial, capitalist, masculinist, and imperial practices of domination, has now become conventional and widely accepted, at least within progressive scholarly circles. What interests us specifically, though, and is revealed especially from the internal, insurrectionary perspective, is that a common subject is formed here that has nothing to do with the transcendental.

The emergence of the common, in fact, is what has attracted so many authors to the epistemological and political possibilities opened by Ludwig Wittgenstein's notions of language games and forms of life. "So you are saying that human agreement decides what is true and what is false?" Wittgenstein asks himself rhetorically. And he responds: "It is what human beings *say* that is true and false; and they agree in the *language* they use. That is not agreement in opinions but in form of life [*Lebensform*]."[82] We should highlight two aspects of Wittgenstein's operation. First, by grounding truth in language and language games, he removes truth from any fixity in the transcendental and locates it on the fluid, changeable terrain of practice, shifting the terms of discussion from knowing to doing. Second, after destabilizing truth he restores to it a consistency. Linguistic practice is constituent of a truth that is organized in forms of life: "to imagine a language means to imagine a form of life."[83] Wittgenstein's concepts manage to evade on one side individual, haphazard experience and, on the other, transcendental identities and truths, revealing instead, between or beyond them, the common. Language and language games, after all, are organizations and expressions of the common, as is the notion of a form of life. Wittgensteinian biopolitics moves from knowledge through collective practice to life, all on the terrain of the common.[84]

Numerous other instances in the philosophical tradition of the critique of epistemology are similarly linked to the common. Earlier, for example, we explored briefly that path in phenomenology that leads from Merleau-Ponty to Levinas and Derrida, in which the critique of knowledge is combined with an analytics of *Mitsein* (being-with), which is, of course, another powerful conception of the common. The question, however, is not simply reference to the common but where the common is posed—whether the common is, on the one hand, naturalized or in some other way hypostatized or, on the other, grounded in collective practice. Consider, for example, the kind of hypostasis that is familiar to functionalist anthropology and sociology. Philippe Descola characterizes such functionalism as a perspective in which all of the constitutive elements of a natural set agree—based on a definite place—serving to perpetuate a stable totality.[85] Just as Claude Lévi-Strauss asserts that "every use of the concept of identity must begin with the critique of this notion," that is, the critique of every "substantial identity" or natural totality, so too every use of the notion of the common must begin with its critique.[86] The common is thus in the paradoxical position as being a ground or presupposition that is also the result of the process. Our analysis, then, from this point on in our research, should be aimed at not "being common" but "making the common."

Some contemporary anthropologists, pursuing a path parallel to ours, arrive at a similar conclusion about the role of the common in an alternative, biopolitical rationality, which goes beyond the division between nature and culture, between *Naturwissenschaften* and *Geisteswissenschaften*. Eduardo Viveiros de Castro, for example, uses the unmodern ontology of Amerindians of the Brazilian Amazon as a standpoint to critique the tradition of modern epistemology. He provocatively poses the Amerindian perspective as an inversion of a series of conventional modern philosophical positions to explain the consequences of the fact that Amerindians conceive animals and other nonhumans as "persons," as kinds of humans, such that human interactions with what would normally be called "nature" take a form something like "social relations." As a result, whereas modern philosophy (from Kant to Heisenberg) posits that the point of view creates the object, here the point of view creates the subject; and whereas modern philosophy conceives of one nature and many cultures, here there is one culture (all are in some sense human) but many natures (occupying different worlds). Viveiros de Castro thus discovers, in contrast to the "multiculturalism" of modern philosophy, an Amerindian "multinaturalism": "One culture, multiple natures—one epistemology, multiple ontologies. Perspectivism implies multinaturalism, for a perspective is not a representation. A perspective is not a representation because representations are a property of the mind or spirit, whereas the point of view is located in the body," and "what I call 'body' is not a synonym for distinctive substance or fixed shape; body is in this sense an assemblage of affects or ways of being that constitute a *habitus*."[87] Multiple ontologies do not imply fixed divisions between beings. Rather Viveiros de Castro describes, in his study of Araweté cosmology, a universe where Becoming is prior to Being and where the relation to alterity is not just a means of establishing identity but a constant process: becoming-jaguar, becoming other.[88] Our aim here—and Viveiros de Castro's too—is not to advocate an un-modern Amerindian ontology but rather to use that perspective to critique modern epistemology and push it toward an altermodern rationality. As we saw in the route we took through Wittgenstein, here too what is required is a shift of emphasis from knowing to doing, generating a multiplicity of beings constantly open to alter-ity that are revealed through the perspective of the body, which is an assemblage of affects or ways of being, which is to say, forms of life—all of which rests on a process of making the common.

Bruno Latour arrives by different means at a similar affirma-tion that the common must be constructed, but he is satisfied at that point simply to conclude: we must organize the *tâtonnement,* that is, the groping trial and error of experience. We agree with La-tour that, between nature and culture, we always experience the world in fragments, but we insist on a much stronger power, not to recompose some lost totalities but to translate them into the fabric of a common experience and *through practice* to constitute from them a new form of life.[89]

When we place so much weight on the common, as we do here, some are likely to object that this amounts to an assumption of sameness or identity that denies or negates difference. We should emphasize, on the contrary, that when the common appears in the thought of Wittgenstein or Viveiros de Castro, it brings with it an affirmation of singularities. Wittgenstein's conceptions of language games and forms of life present the common only insofar as they engage alterity: the common is composed of interactions among singularities, such as singularities of linguistic expression. The same is true for the Amerindian multiple ontologies and the processes of becoming that Viveiros de Castro describes. Differences in perspec-tive mark differences over not only opinions or principles but also what world we inhabit—or really they indicate that we inhabit dif-ferent worlds. And yet every world is defined by becomings, con-stantly engaged with alterity. Whereas identity and difference stand in opposition, the common and singularity are not just compatible but mutually constitutive.

We are now in the position to offer provisionally three characteristics that a biopolitical reason would have to fulfill: it would have to put rationality at the service of life; technique at the service of ecological needs, where by ecological we mean not simply the preservation of nature but the development and reproduction of "social" relations, as Viveiros de Castro says, between humans and nonhumans; and the accumulation of wealth at the service of the common. That makes it clear (to move now through the same three items in inverse order) that economic valorization is no longer possible except on the basis of the social appropriation of common goods; that the reproduction of the lifeworld and its physical environment is no longer possible except when technologies are directly controlled by the project of the common; and that rationality can no longer function except as an instrument of the common freedom of the multitude, as a mechanism for the institution of the common.

All of this remains lifeless and inert, however, unless biopolitical reason is grounded on the terrain of collective practice, where the state of being-in-common is transformed into a process of making the common. The collective practice of biopolitical reason has to take the form of *strategic investigation,* a form of militancy. This is necessary, first of all, because, as we argued in *De Corpore* 1, in the biopolitical context truth is born and dies as an event of being, produced by a common experience. Spinoza jokes at one point that in order to speak the truth of the sestertius or the imperial (two different coins) that I have in my hand and grasp their value, I have to refer to the common voice that gives them monetary value. Truth can only be proclaimed out loud. In *De Homine* 1, however, we see that truth must be not only proclaimed but also acted, which Spinoza identifies with the formula *experientia sive praxis,* the principle of a truth formed by the activism of subjects who want to live a common life. No transcendent or transcendental force can stand between subjects and truth, citizens and their power. "With regard to political theory," Spinoza writes, "the difference between

Hobbes and myself . . . consists in this, that I always preserve the
natural right in its entirety, and I hold that the sovereign power in a
State has right over a subject only in proportion to the excess of its
power over that of a subject. This is always the case in a state of nature."[90] Said out loud, the truth is produced in action made in common, without intermediaries.

The kind of strategic investigation we have in mind resembles,
on the one hand, the traditional Marxist "factory investigation" that
inquired into the conditions and relations of workers with a combination of sociological detachment and political goals, but remained fundamentally external to the situation, in the hands of the
party intellectual elite.[91] It also resembles, on the other, the kind of
interactive production of knowledge common to the "teach-ins" of
the 1960s, which was indeed conceived as a kind of ethical practice
entirely invested in the common fabric of the social situation, but
one which was not effectively mobilized as political action.[92] Closer
to the strategic investigation we have in mind is a third conception,
which incorporates elements of these two but goes beyond them:
Foucault's use of the notion of *dispositifs,* that is, the material, social,
affective, and cognitive mechanisms active in the production of subjectivity. Foucault defines the *dispositif* as a network of heterogeneous elements oriented by a strategic purpose:

> By *dispositif* I understand a sort of formation, let's say, whose
> primary function, at a given historical moment, is to respond
> to a demand [*urgence*]. The *dispositif* thus has an eminently stra-
> tegic function [which means that] it involves a certain manip-
> ulation of relations of force, a rational and concerted interven-
> tion in those relations of force, either to develop them in
> some direction or to block them or to stabilize and utilize
> them. The *dispositif* is thus always inscribed in a power relation
> [*un jeu de pouvoir*], but always also tied to one or several limits
> of knowledge, which derive from it and, at the same time,
> condition it.[93]

Foucault's notion of strategic knowledge allows us to conceive the
collective production of the common as an intervention in the cur-

rent relations of force aimed at subverting the dominant powers and reorienting forces in a determinate direction. The strategic production of knowledge in this sense implies immediately an alternative production of subjectivity. The dynamic of the *dispositif* not only extends from a knowledge process to the prescription of subjectivity but also is always open to the constitution of the common, internal, one might say, to history and life, and engages in the process of revolutionizing them. Biopolitical reason is thus defined by a kind of ontological resonance between the *dispositifs* and the common.

All we have just said via Foucault, however, has also been reached via a series of different routes through the discussions internal to the movements of the multitude in the last few decades. One of these routes took off from the crisis of the industrial workers' movements and their scientific knowledges in the 1960s. Intellectuals within and outside the factories struggled to appropriate the process of knowledge production from the party hierarchy, developing a method of "co-research" to construct together with workers alternative knowledges from below that are completely internal to the situation and intervene in the current power relations.[94] Another route has been forged by professors and students who take their work outside the universities both to put their expertise at the service of social movements and to enrich their research by learning from the movements and participating in the production of knowledge developed there. Such militant research is conceived not as community service—as a sacrifice of scholarly value to meet a moral obligation—but as superior in scholarly terms because it opens a greater power of knowledge production.[95] A third route, which has developed primarily among the globalization movements in recent years, adopts the methods of "co-research" developed experimentally in the factories and applies them to the entire terrain of biopolitical production. In social centers and nomad universities, on Web sites and in movement journals, extraordinarily advanced forms of militant knowledge production have developed that are completely embedded in the circuits of social practice.[96] By all these routes, strategic investigation is always the production of knowledge through *dispositifs*. It is active engagement with the production of subjectivity in order to transform reality, which ultimately involves the production of new truths. "Revolutionary dreams erupt out of political engagement," writes Robin Kelley; "collective social movements are incubators of new knowledge."[97] Strategic investigation is really something you cannot talk about without doing it.

We keep looking for confirmations and verifications of our practice in reality, hoping they will be revolutionary, Enzo Melandri says, but really there is no shortage of confirmations. What are lacking are revolutions. We have to stop focusing on the haystack and find the needle. This will succeed or fail with the fluctuating fortunes of revolution.[98]

PART 3

CAPITAL (AND THE STRUGGLES OVER COMMON WEALTH)

> Therefore we require, and we resolve to take both Common land,
> and Common woods to be a livelihood for us, and look upon you as
> equal with us, not above us, knowing very well that *England,* the land
> of our Nativity, is to be a common Treasury of livelihood to all, with-
> out respect to persons.
>
> —Gerrard Winstanley et al.,
> "A Declaration from the Poor Oppressed People of England"

3.1

METAMORPHOSES OF THE
COMPOSITION OF CAPITAL

The effect of writing in a foreign language on our mind is like the
effect of repeated perspectives in a camera obscura, in which the
camera obscura is able to render with precision distinct images that
correspond to real objects and perspectives in such a way *that the effect
depends on the camera obscura rather than on the real object*.

—Giacomo Leopardi, *Zibaldone*

The Technical Composition of Biopolitical Labor

Economic production is going through a period of transition in
which increasingly the results of capitalist production are social relations and forms of life. Capitalist production, in other words, is becoming biopolitical. Before we start inventing new tools for this
new situation, we should return to Marx's method for grasping the
current state of economic life: to investigate the composition of capital, which involves distinguishing the proportion and role of labor-
power and constant capital in the contemporary production processes. And, specifically, we need to investigate first the "technical
composition" of capital or, really, the technical composition of labor
to ascertain who produces, what they produce, and how they produce in today's global economy. Determining the general outlines of
the technical composition of labor will give us a basis for not only
recognizing the contemporary forms of capitalist exploitation and
control but also gauging the means at our disposal for a project of
liberation from capital.

Three major trends emphasized by scholars of political economy give us a good first approximation of the current transformations that labor is undergoing in many parts of the world. First is the trend toward the hegemony or prevalence of immaterial production in the processes of capitalist valorization.[1] "The immaterial dimension of the products," André Gorz asserts, their symbolic, aesthetic, and social value, "predominates over their material reality."[2] Images, information, knowledge, affects, codes, and social relationships, for example, are coming to outweigh material commodities or the material aspects of commodities in the capitalist valorization process. This means, of course, not that the production of material goods, such as automobiles and steel, is disappearing or even declining in quantity but rather that their value is increasingly dependent on and subordinated to immaterial factors and goods. The forms of labor that produce these immaterial goods (or the immaterial aspects of material goods) can be called colloquially the labor of the head and heart, including forms of service work, affective labor, and cognitive labor, although we should not be misled by these conventional synecdoches: cognitive and affective labor is not isolated to specific organs but engages the entire body and mind together. Even when the products are immaterial, in other words, the act of producing remains both corporeal and intellectual. What is common to these different forms of labor, once we abstract from their concrete differences, is best expressed by their biopolitical character. "If we had to hazard a guess on the emerging model in the next decades," posits Robert Boyer, "we would probably have to refer to the *production of man by man* and explore right away the institutional context that would permit its emergence."[3] And as Christian Marazzi notes, the current passage in capitalist production is moving toward an "anthropogenetic model," or in other words, a biopolitical turn of the economy. Living beings as fixed capital are at the center of this tranformation, and the production of forms of life is becoming the basis of added value. This is a process in which putting to work human faculties, competences, and knowledges—those acquired on the job but, more important, those accumulated outside work interacting with automated and computerized productive systems—is directly productive of value.[4] One distinctive feature of the work of head and heart, then, is that paradoxically the *object* of production is really a *subject,* defined, for example, by a social relationship or a form of life.

The second major trend of the technical composition of labor is the so-called feminization of work, which generally refers to three relatively separate changes. First, quantitatively, it indicates the rapid increase in the proportion of women in the wage labor market over the last two or three decades in both the dominant and subordinated parts of the world. Second, the feminization of work marks a qualitative shift in the working day and thus the temporal "flexibility" of labor for both women and men. There has been a rapid decline of the regularly divided working day that had been achieved by many workers, especially in Europe and some of the other dominant countries, which allowed for eight hours of work, eight hours of leisure, and eight hours of sleep. Part-time and informal employment, irregular hours, and multiple jobs—aspects that have long been typical of labor in the subordinated parts of the world—are now becoming generalized even in the dominant countries. Third, the feminization of work indicates how qualities that have traditionally been associated with "women's work," such as affective, emotional, and relationship tasks, are becoming increasingly central in all sectors of labor, albeit in different forms in different parts of the world. (And this dovetails with the predominance of biopolitical production that constitutes the first trend.) The traditional economic division between productive and reproductive labor breaks down in this context, as capitalist production is aimed ever more clearly at the production of not only (and perhaps not even primarily) commodities but also social relationships and forms of life. As the temporal division between work time and the time of life is becoming confused, the productive power of labor is being transformed into a power to generate social life. We can accept the term "feminization" to indicate these changes as long as it is said with a bitter irony, since it has not resulted in gender equality or destroyed the gender division of labor. On the contrary! Affective labor is required of women disproportionately on and off the job. In fact any woman who is not willing to do affective labor on call—smile appropriately, tend to hurt feelings, knit social relationships, and generally perform care and nurturing—is viewed as a kind of monster. Despite their massive entry into the wage labor force, furthermore, women are still primarily responsible in countries throughout the world for unpaid domestic and reproductive labor, such as housework and child care, as well as bearing a greater burden of informal-sector jobs in both rural and urban areas. Women's double workday is a powerful obstacle to greater education and access to better and better-paid work. The transformations of labor along the lines of some qualities traditionally associated with women's work and the increasing entry of women into the wage labor force have in most cases resulted in worsening conditions for women (as well as men). The misleading aspects of the term "feminization" are one reason we find it more useful, as long as we keep in mind the gendered nature of these processes, to understand these shifts as labor *becoming biopolitical,* which emphasizes the increasingly blurred boundaries between labor and life, and between production and reproduction.[5]

The third major trend of the technical composition of labor is the result of new patterns of migration and processes of social and racial mixture. All levels of capitalist enterprises in the dominant countries, from huge corporations to small businesses, from agribusiness to manufacturing, from domestic labor to construction, need constant flows of both legal and illegal migrants to supplement the local labor force—and this continually generates ideological conflicts within the capitalist classes, as we will see later, constrained as they are by their pocketbooks to favor migrant flows but opposed to them in their moral, nationalist, and often racist consciousnesses. There are also enormous south-to-south international flows of labor and massive migrations within single countries, often in very specific sectors of production. These migrations transform labor markets in quantitative terms, making them properly global, even though, of course, movements of labor are not free but highly constrained to specific routes, often entailing extreme dangers. At the same time, labor markets are also qualitatively transformed. On the one hand, the gender of labor migration is shifting such that women are constituting an increasing portion of the flows, both to take jobs traditionally designated for women—such as domestic work, sex work, elder care, and nursing—and also to occupy low-skill, labor-intensive positions in manufacturing sectors, such as electronics, textiles, footwear, and toys, where young female workers are now predominant. This shift goes hand in hand with the "feminization" of work, often combined with the racial stereotype of the "nimble fingers" of women in the global South. "Ideas of *flexibility, temporality, invisibility,* and *domesticity* in the naturalization of categories of work," writes Chandra Mohanty, "are crucial in the construction of Third-World women as an appropriate cheap labor force."[6] On the other hand, labor migration is (and has always been) characterized by racial division and conflict. Migrations sometimes highlight the global racial divisions of labor by crossing their boundaries, and at other times, especially in the dominant countries, racial hierarchies become flashpoints for conflict. Migration, however, even when it creates conditions of extraordinary hardship and suffering, always holds the potential to subvert and transform racial division, in both economic and social terms, through exodus and confrontation.

These three major trends pose significant challenges to traditional concepts and methods of political economy in large part because biopolitical production shifts the economic center of gravity from the production of material commodities to that of social relations, confusing, as we said, the division between production and reproduction. Intangible values and intangible assets, as economists call them, pose a problem because the methods of economic analysis generally rely on quantitative measures and calculate the value of objects that can be counted, such as cars, computers, and tons of wheat. The critique of political economy, too, including the Marxist tradition, has generally focused on measurement and quantitative methods to understand surplus value and exploitation. Biopolitical products, however, tend to *exceed* all quantitative measurement and take *common* forms, which are easily shared and difficult to corral as private property. If we return to Marx in this new light, we find that the progression of definitions of capital in his work actually gives us an important clue for analyzing this biopolitical context. Although wealth in capitalist society first appears as an immense collective of commodities, Marx reveals that capital is really a process of the creation of surplus value via the production of commodities. But Marx develops this insight one step further to discover that in its essence capital is a *social relation* or, really, the constant reproduction of a social relation via the creation of surplus value via the production of commodities. Recognizing capital as a social relation gives us a first key to analyzing biopolitical production.

Michel Foucault appreciates all the strangeness and richness of the line of Marx's thinking which leads to the conclusion that "l'homme produit l'homme." He cautions that we should not understand Marx's phrase as an expression of humanism. "For me, what must be produced is not man as nature designed it, or as its essence prescribes; we must produce something that does not yet exist and we cannot know what it will be." He also warns not to understand this merely as a continuation of economic production as conventionally conceived: "I do not agree with those who would understand this production of man by man as being accomplished like the production of value, the production of wealth, or of an object of economic use; it is, on the contrary, destruction of what we are and the creation of something completely other, a total innovation."[7] We cannot understand this production, in other words, in terms of the producing subject and the produced object. Instead producer and product are both subjects: humans produce and humans are produced. Foucault clearly senses (without seeming to understand fully) the explosiveness of this situation: the biopolitical process is not limited to the reproduction of capital as a social relation but also presents the potential for an autonomous process that could destroy capital and create something entirely new. Biopolitical production and the three major trends we have outlined obviously imply new mechanisms of exploitation and capitalist control, and we will explore these in more detail next, but we should keep an eye out from the beginning, following Foucault's intuition, for how biopolitical production, particularly in the ways it exceeds the bounds of capitalist relations and constantly refers to the common, grants labor increasing autonomy and provides the tools or weapons that could be wielded in a project of liberation.

Biopolitical Exploitation

By revealing the general outlines of the technical composition of labor—who produces, what they produce, and how—we have addressed the first half of Marx's method for investigating the composition of capital with respect to the emerging form of biopolitical production. Now we turn to the "organic composition" of capital, which consists of the relation between variable capital and constant capital or, to put it in terms that suggest the "organic" metaphor for Marx, between living labor and dead labor (in the form of machines, money, raw materials, and commodities). Investigating contemporary capital's organic composition will have to address the new conditions of the production of surplus value in the biopolitical context as well as the new forms of exploitation. The organic composition, in other words, refers not only to the "objective" conditions of capitalist production but also and more significantly to the "subjective" conditions contained in the antagonistic relationship between capitalists and workers, which are expressed in exploitation and revolt.

Capitalist accumulation today is increasingly external to the production process, such that exploitation takes the form of *expropriation of the common*. This shift can be recognized in two primary guises. Scholars who critique neoliberalism often emphasize that increasingly today capitalist accumulation is a predatory operation that functions through dispossession, by transforming into private property both public wealth and wealth held socially in common.[8] Naomi Klein uses the notion of "disaster capitalism," for example, to analyze the model of neoliberal economic policy applied in many countries throughout the world that takes advantage of a moment of shock, whether consciously generated militarily and politically or arrived at due to environmental disaster, to facilitate the massive privatization of public industries, public welfare structures, public transportation networks, and so forth.[9] Scholars studying subordinated regions and especially those countries where state structures are particularly weak, including many parts of Africa, highlight cases in which neoliberal accumulation involves expropriation of the common primarily in the form of natural resources. Extraction processes—of oil, diamonds, gold, and other materials—thrive in war-torn regions without sovereign states and strong legal structures. Foreign capitalist firms, often employing few local workers, extract wealth and transport it out of the country in ways reminiscent of the looting conducted under colonial regimes in the past.[10] It is not surprising, then, that Marxist scholars have focused new attention in recent years on the concept of primitive accumulation, since that concept allowed Marx to understand the accumulation of wealth outside the capitalist production process, through the direct expropriation of human, social, and natural wealth—selling African slaves to plantation holders, for example, or looting gold from the Americas. Contemporary Marxist scholars generally deviate from Marx, however, as we saw in Part 2, by showing that there is no linear historical relation between such mechanisms of primitive accumulation and capitalist production processes, no progressive history of development in which the former gives way to the latter, but rather a constant back-and-forth movement in which primitive accumulation continually reappears and coexists with capitalist production. And insofar as today's neoliberal economy increasingly favors accumulation through expropriation of the common, the concept of primitive accumulation becomes an even more central analytical tool.[11]

This first guise of the expropriation of the common, which focuses on neoliberal policies in terms of dispossession and expropriation, however, does not provide us sufficient means to analyze the organic composition of capital. Although it articulates fully the state policies and fortunes of dead labor, it says little about the other element necessary for an investigation of the organic composition of capital: the productivity of living labor. To put it differently, political

economists (and the critics of political economy) should not be satisfied with accounts of neoliberalism that pose capitalist accumulation as merely or primarily the expropriation of existing wealth.
Capital is and has to be in its essence a *productive* system that generates wealth through the labor-power it employs and exploits.

A second guise of the expropriation of the common, which
centers on the exploitation of biopolitical labor, allows us to pursue
much better a Marxian investigation of the organic composition of
capital. The three major trends of the transformation of the technical composition of labor that we outlined earlier all are engaged in
the production of common forms of wealth, such as knowledges,
information, images, affects, and social relationships, which are subsequently expropriated by capital to generate surplus value. Note
right away that this second guise refers primarily to a different notion of the common than does the first. The first is a relatively inert,
traditional notion that generally involves natural resources. Early
modern European social theorists conceive of the common as the
bounty of nature available to humanity, including the fertile land to
work and the fruits of the earth, often posing it in religious terms
with scriptural evidence. John Locke, for example, proclaims that
"God, as King David says, Psal. cxv. 16. has given the earth to the
children of men; given it to mankind in common."[12] The second
notion of the common is dynamic, involving both the product of
labor and the means of future production. This common is not only
the earth we share but also the languages we create, the social practices we establish, the modes of sociality that define our relationships, and so forth. This form of the common does not lend itself to
a logic of scarcity as does the first. "He who receives an idea from
me," Thomas Jefferson famously remarks, "receives instruction himself without lessening mine; as he who lights his taper at mine,
receives light without darkening me."[13] The expropriation of this
second form of the common—the artificial common or, really, the
common that blurs the division between nature and culture—is the
key to understanding the new forms of exploitation of biopolitical
labor.

When analyzing biopolitical production we find ourselves being pulled back from exploitation to alienation, reversing the trajectory of Marx's thought—without, however, returning us to the humanism of his youth. Biopolitical production does present in newly prominent ways the characteristics of alienation. With regard to cognitive and affective labor, for example, capital alienates from the worker not just the product of labor but the laboring process itself, such that workers do not feel their own their capacities for thinking, loving, and caring when they are on the job.[14] But this pull to the category of alienation is also due to the fact that some characteristics closely tied to exploitation, particularly those designating capital's productive role, have faded. Capital—although it may constrict biopolitical labor, expropriate its products, even in some cases provide necessary instruments of production—does not organize *productive cooperation*. With reference to large-scale industry, Marx recognizes that the essential role of the capitalist in the production process, which is clearly linked to the mechanisms of exploitation, is to provide cooperation, that is, bring workers together in the factory, give them the tools to work together, furnish a plan to cooperate, and enforce their cooperation. The capitalist ensures cooperation, Marx imagines, like the general on the battlefield or the conductor of the orchestra.[15] In biopolitical production, however, capital does not determine the cooperative arrangement, or at least not to the same extent. Cognitive labor and affective labor generally produce cooperation autonomously from capitalist command, even in some of the most constrained and exploited circumstances, such as call centers or food services. Intellectual, communicative, and affective means of cooperation are generally created in the productive encounters themselves and cannot be directed from the outside. In fact, rather than providing cooperation, we could even say that capital *expropriates cooperation* as a central element of exploiting biopolitical labor-power. This expropriation takes place not so much from the individual worker (because cooperation already implies a collectivity) but more clearly from the field of social labor, operating on the level of information flows, communication networks, social codes, linguistic innovations, and practices of affects and passions. Biopolitical exploitation involves the expropriation of the common, in this way, at the level of social production and social practice.

Capital thus captures and expropriates value through biopolitical exploitation that is produced, in some sense, *externally* to it. It is no coincidence that as biopolitical production is becoming hegemonic, economists more frequently use the notion of "externalities" to understand the increase and decrease of value. A well-educated population, they say, for example, is a positive externality for a corporation operating in a specific country, just as a poorly educated one is a negative externality: the productivity of the corporation is raised or lowered due to factors completely external to it.[16] We will return in greater detail later to the question of externalities, but we can hypothesize here that economists are recognizing the increasing importance of factors external to capital because in fact, to reverse the conventional economic formulation, capital is increasingly external to the productive process and the generation of wealth. In other words, biopolitical labor is increasingly autonomous. Capital is predatory, as the analysts of neoliberalism say, insofar as it seeks to capture and expropriate autonomously produced common wealth.

To pose this same point in different economic terminology and from a slightly different perspective, the exploitation of labor-power and the accumulation of surplus value should be understood in terms of not profit but *capitalist rent*.[17] Whereas profit is generated primarily through internal engagement in the production process, rent is generally conceived as an external mode of extraction. In the 1930s John Maynard Keynes predicted and welcomed the prospect of the "euthanasia of the rentier" and thus the disappearance of the "functionless investor" as a primary figure of capital. He understood "the rentier aspect of capitalism as a transitional phase which will disappear when it has done its work." The future of capital belonged to the capitalist investor actively engaged in organizing and overseeing production.[18] Instead, in the contemporary networks of biopolitical production, the extraction of value from the common is increasingly accomplished without the capitalist intervening in its production. This renewed primacy of rent provides us an essential insight into why finance capital, along with the vast stratum that Keynes denigrates as functionless investors, occupies today a central position in the management of capitalist accumulation, capturing and expropriating the value created at a level far abstracted from the labor process.

One final remark on Marx's concepts: we have found useful at several points in our work Marx's notion of the real subsumption of labor within capital, by which he means a moment when capital no longer simply absorbs within its disciplinary apparatus and production processes preexisting labor activities created outside capital (this is merely a formal subsumption), but actually creates new, properly capitalist forms of labor, integrating labor fully, so to speak, into the capitalist body. In the biopolitical context capital might be said to subsume not just labor but society as a whole or, really, social life itself, since life is both what is put to work in biopolitical production and what is produced. This relationship between capital and productive social life, however, is no longer *organic* in the sense that Marx understood that term because capital is increasingly external and has an ever less functional role in the productive process. Rather than an organ functioning within the capitalist body, biopolitical labor-power is becoming more and more autonomous, with capital simply hovering over it parasitically with its disciplinary regimes, apparatuses of capture, mechanisms of expropriation, financial networks, and the like. The rupture of the organic relationship and the growing autonomy of labor are at the heart of the new forms of crisis of capitalist production and control, to which we now turn our attention.

Crises of Biopolitical Production and Control

Capital is in crisis. So what? We read about crises in the newspaper every day: stock market crises, credit crises, mortgage crises—all kinds of crises. Some people will lose money and others will get rich. There once was a time when people believed that the objective disequilibria of the capitalist economy, its cycles, and its endemic crises of production, circulation, and realization would eventually lead to collapse. Instead, as the most astute analysts of capital have long told us, capital works by breaking down or, rather, through creative destruction achieved by crises. In contemporary neoliberal economic regimes, in fact, crisis and disaster have become ever more important as levers to privatize public goods and put in place new mechanisms for capitalist accumulation.[19] But not all capitalist crises are the same.[20] Whereas *objective* economic crises can be functional to capitalist accumulation, crises that are *subjective* and political (or, really, equally economic and political) pose a real threat to capital. Such a crisis is emerging today in the context of biopolitical production, in which the powers of the new technical composition of labor-power cannot be contained by the capitalist modes of control; in fact the exercise of capitalist control is increasingly becoming a fetter to the productivity of biopolitical labor.

Before sketching the outlines of the current crisis, we should recall the basic terms of a similar crisis of capitalist control that emerged in the 1970s after the labor struggles and social struggles of the 1960s had undermined the bases of the welfare state model in the dominant countries. The crisis of the state and capitalist production at that time was caused not only by workers' struggles that constantly demanded higher wages, a greater redistribution of wealth, and improvements of the quality of life of the working classes, but also by a generalized insubordination of workers together with a series of other social movements, more or less coordinated, making ever-increasing social and political demands. Samuel Huntington had at least some inkling of the danger when he lamented that "blacks, Indians, Chicanos, white ethnic groups, students, and women" making demands on the state were creating not only a fiscal and economic crisis but also and more important a crisis of control.[21] It is important to situate such crises, however, in relation to other crises and to the resulting transformations of capital and the state. The welfare state itself served for several decades as an effective response to crises generated primarily by workers' struggles in the early twentieth century, but in the 1970s its mechanisms could no longer control the new social and economic forces that had emerged.

In response to the crisis of the 1970s there was a shift from the welfare state to the neoliberal state and biopolitical forms of production and control.

We read these historical developments in terms of a constant, mutually determining relation between capitalist structures of rule and the struggles for liberation. (We hesitate to call this relation dialectical because there is no synthetic resolution but only a back-and-forth movement.) On the one hand, workers' and social struggles determine the restructuring of capital, and on the other, that restructuring conditions the terms of future struggles. In each era of capitalist development, in other words, with each transformation of the technical composition of labor, workers use the means at their disposal to invent new forms of revolt and autonomy from capital; and in response to this, capital is forced to restructure the bases of production, exploitation, and control, transforming once again the technical composition; at which point once again workers discover new weapons for new revolts; and so forth. Our hypothesis, then, is that today we are arriving at another such moment of crisis.

For a first approximation of the current biopolitical crisis we can return to the three general trends in the transformation of labor we spoke of earlier. Each trend indicates strategies of the capitalist control of labor-power, but in each case we find that the mechanisms of control contradict the productivity of biopolitical labor and obstruct the creation of value, thereby exacerbating the crisis. With regard to the first trend, the development of cognitive, affective, and biopolitical forms of labor, strategies of capitalist command develop intensively and extensively. Intensive strategies primarily divide and segment the common field of productive cooperation, establishing something like command outposts by which private and/or state agencies monitor and regulate social production processes through various techniques of discipline, surveillance, and monitoring. Other intensive strategies drain the common that serves as the basis for biopolitical production, for example, by dismantling institutions of public education through the privatization of primary education and the defunding of secondary education. Extensive strategies are

typified by the workings of finance, since it does not directly intervene in the productive networks but spreads over, expropriating
and privatizing the common wealth embedded in the accumulated
knowledges, codes, images, affective practices, and biopolitical relationships that they produce. Capital's appropriative processes thus
stand opposed to the common that biopolitical labor creates socially.
In this respect the financial world, in its relative separation, mimics
(or really mirrors and inverts) the movements of social labor-power.
When we recognize the common as not object but subject of development, however, it is clear that the multitude striving to maintain
and reproduce its "forms of life" cannot be treated with the traditional regimes of discipline and control. As the U.S. subprime mortgage crisis and the subsequent global economic crises demonstrate,
when the state is forced to bail out banks in order to correct the
excesses of private initiative and guarantee social welfare, the conflict between capital and living labor begins to take place on the terrain of finance.

Here we run into the first contradiction, because the intensive
and extensive strategies of control both destroy the common, the
former segmenting or draining the common bases of production
and the latter privatizing the common results. The productivity of
biopolitical labor is reduced every time the common is destroyed.
Consider, for example, the production of scientific knowledge, a
very specialized field but one that shares the basic characteristics of
biopolitical production as a whole. For scientific knowledge to be
produced, the relevant information, methods, and ideas, which result
from past scientific activity, must be open and accessible to a broad
scientific community, and there must be highly developed mechanisms of cooperation and circulation among different laboratories
and researchers through journals, conferences, and the like. When
new knowledge is produced, it too must be made common so that
future scientific production can use it as a basis. Biopolitical production must in this way establish a virtuous cycle that leads from the
existing common to a new common, which in turn serves in the
next moment of expanding production. The segmentation and ex-

propriation of the common, however, inevitably destroy this virtuous cycle such that capital becomes increasingly a fetter on biopolitical production.

A second strategy of capitalist control, which corresponds to the "feminization" of work, is the imposition of precarity, organizing all forms of labor according to the infinite modalities of market flexibility. In Europe and Japan, where in the latter half of the twentieth century large portions of the labor force experienced relatively stable, guaranteed employment with a strictly regulated working day, the process of labor becoming precarious over the past few decades has been particularly visible. Workers are increasingly forced to move among multiple jobs, both over the course of a working career and in the course of a working day. A central aspect of precarity, then, is that it imposes a new regime of time, with respect to both the working day and the working career—or, to put it another way, precarity is a mechanism of control that determines the temporality of workers, destroying the division between work time and nonwork time, requiring workers not to work all the time but to be constantly available for work.[22] The precarity of labor, of course, is not new for women and racial minorities in the dominant countries or the vast majority of workers, male and female, in the subordinate countries, where nonguaranteed, informal labor arrangements have long been the norm. Now precarity is becoming generalized at all levels of the labor force throughout the world, and indeed taking some new, extreme forms. An anecdotal anthropological example illustrates this extreme precarity. In a neighborhood on the outskirts of Monrovia, Liberia, Danny Hoffman reports, a man named Mohammed organizes and deploys thousands of young men at a time, many of them former combatants in Liberia or Sierra Leone, for a variety of informal occupations. One day he sends men to work temporarily at an illegal diamond mine in southeastern Liberia; another day he deploys men to work on a rubber plantation in another part of the country; he can even send two thousand men to a specific site to pose as ex-combatants for a disarmament program to receive funds from a UN agency; and his men are constantly available for military

operations. These men constitute an extreme case of precarious labor: a *population flottante* that is infinitely flexible and mobile, perpetually available for any work.[23] It is no longer helpful to think of
this as an industrial reserve army or a reserve army of any sort since
there is no "standing army" to which it refers, that is, no guaranteed,
stable labor force. Or rather, under control regimes of precarity, the
entire labor force becomes a reserve army, with workers constantly
on call, at the disposal of the boss. Precarity might thus be conceived
as a special kind of poverty, a temporal poverty, in which workers are
deprived of control over their time.

Labor precarity poses the second contradiction since it inverts
the control of time required for biopolitical production. The production of ideas, images, or affects is not easily limited to specific
times of the day, and thus biopolitical production tends to erode the
conventional divisions of the working day between work time and
nonwork time. The productivity of biopolitical labor, and specifically the creativity involved in biopolitical production, requires the
freedom of the producers to organize their own time; but the control imposed by precarity takes time away, such that when you are
working in a precarious situation none of your time is your own.
You can, of course, think and produce affects on demand, but only
in a rote, mechanical way, limiting creativity and potential productivity. The contradiction, then, lies between the productivity of biopolitical labor when allowed to organize time autonomously and
the fetters imposed on it by precarity, which strips it of control.

A third strategy of capitalist control, which corresponds to
the increasing migrations and mixtures of labor-power, involves the
construction of barriers, physical and social, to channel and halt
flows of labor. The reenforcing of existing borders and the creation
of new ones is often accompanied by a kind of moral, even civilizational panic. Fears of the United States being overrun by Mexicans
or Europe by Muslims are mixed with and support strategies to
block labor mobility. The old tools of racism and racial segregation
are sharpened as weapons of control in both dominant and subordinated countries throughout the world. Erecting barriers takes place

not only at national borders but also and perhaps more important within each country, across metropolitan spaces and rural landscapes, segmenting the population and preventing cultural and social mixture. In addition to the walls erected against migrations at the border, we should also focus on the effects of illegal status on populations within the country. Being clandestine not only deprives people of social services and the rights of citizenship but also discourages them from circulating in and mixing freely with other segments of the society. Just as precarity creates a poverty of time, so too geographical and social barriers intensify a poverty of space.

The contradiction for production posed by blocking migrations and creating divisions is obvious, at least in one of its aspects. When governments in the dominant countries "succeed" in keeping illegal migrants out, businesses immediately decry the shortage of labor: who will pick the tomatoes and apples, who will care for the elderly and do the domestic work, who will work in the sweatshops when there are no illegal workers? "It would be easier, where property is well secured," Bernard Mandeville remarked over two hundred years ago, "to live without money than without poor; for who would do the work?"[24] The contradiction regarding movement and mixing is repeated even more intensely at a deeper level. To raise productivity, biopolitical production needs not only control over its movements but also constant interactions with others, with those who are culturally and socially different, in a situation of equality. Contemporary economists talk a lot about creativity, in sectors such as design, branding, specialized industries, fashion, and the culture industries, but generally neglect the fact that the creativity of biopolitical labor requires an open and dynamic egalitarian culture with constant cultural flows and mixtures.[25] Control through the closure of space and the imposition of social hierarchies is a fetter to productivity. The contradiction from this perspective is really a conflict between inclusion and exclusion and is manifest at the governmental level by the crisis of both dominant models of integration: the republican-assimilationist strategy most often associated with France and the multicultural strategy typical of Britain. (The United States has experimented with and pioneered both strategies, combining them in different measures.) These models are in crisis because, despite claims to the contrary, their shared goal is to create and maintain social hierarchies and close social space, which impedes biopolitical production.

All three of these contradictions point to the fact that capital's strategies and techniques of exploitation and control tend to be fetters on the productivity of biopolitical labor. Capital fails to generate a virtuous cycle of accumulation, which would lead from the existing common through biopolitical production to a new expanded common that serves in turn as the basis of a new productive process. Instead, each time capital intervenes to control biopolitical labor and expropriate the common, it hampers the process, forcing it to limp along, handicapped. This is not, of course, an entirely new phenomenon. Since Marx's time the critique of political economy has focused on the contradiction between the social nature of capitalist production and the private nature of capitalist accumulation; but in the context of biopolitical production the contradiction is dramatically intensified, as if raised to a higher power.

3.2

_____

CLASS STRUGGLE FROM CRISIS

TO EXODUS

_____

> I've had enough of a sober tone,
> It's time to play the real devil again.
> —Johann Wolfgang von Goethe, *Faust*

The Open Social Relation between Labor and Capital

In the context of biopolitical production we have found that capital should be understood not simply as a social relation but as an *open* social relation. Capital previously has held together within itself labor-power and the command over labor, or in Marxian language, it has been able to construct an organic composition of variable capital (the wage labor force) and constant capital. But today there is a growing rupture within the organic composition of capital, a progressive decomposition of capital in which variable capital (and particularly biopolitical labor-power) is separating from constant capital along with its political forces of command and control. Biopolitical labor tends to generate its own forms of social cooperation and produce value autonomously. In fact the more autonomous the social organization of biopolitical production, the more productive it is. Capital thus has ever more difficulty creating a coherent cycle of production and synthesizing or subsuming labor-power in a process of value creation. Perhaps we should no longer even use the term "variable capital" to refer to this labor-power since its productive relation to constant capital is ever more tenuous.

Should we thus declare capital doomed, finished? Has the revolution already begun? Or in more technical terms, has variable capital definitively liberated itself from the clutches of constant capital? No; crisis, as we said earlier, does not mean collapse, and the contradictions of capital, however severe, never in themselves imply its demise or, moreover, create an alternative to capitalist rule. Instead the rupture within capital and the emerging autonomy of biopolitical labor present a political opening. We can *bet* on the rupture of the relation of capital and build politically on the emerging autonomy of biopolitical labor. The open social relation presented by capital provides an opportunity, but political organization is required to push it across the threshold. When Abbé Sieyès on the eve of the French Revolution asks what is the value of the Third Estate—everything! but politically it is worth nothing!—he launches a political and philosophical polemic based on a similar threshold presented by the economic situation. The Third Estate, which was emerging as the center of social production, was no longer willing to accept its subordination and pay taxes to the ruling powers of the ancien régime. What we have to develop after having sketched the broad outlines of biopolitical production, exploitation, and control are the terms of class struggle today: on what resources is it based, what are the primary social lines of conflict, and what are the political forms available for its organization?

Let us start with some basics. The emerging autonomy of biopolitical labor with respect to capital, which pries open the social relation of capital, rests primarily on two facts. First is the newly central or intensified role of the *common* in economic production, as both basis and product, which we have already explored in part. Second is the fact that the productivity of labor-power increasingly *exceeds* the bounds set in its employment by capital. Labor-power has always exceeded its relation to capital in terms of its potential, in the sense that people have the capacity to do much more and produce much more than what they do at work. In the past, however, the productive process, especially the industrial process, has severely restricted the actualization of the potential that exceeds capital's bounds. The auto worker, for example, has extraordinary mechanical and technological skills and knowledges, but they are primarily site specific: they can be actualized only in the factory and thus in the relation with capital, aside from some tinkering with the car in the garage at home. The affective and intellectual talents, the capacities to generate cooperation and organizational networks, the communication skills, and the other competences that characterize biopolitical labor, in contrast, are generally not site specific. You can think and form relationships not only on the job but also in the street, at home, with your neighbors and friends. The capacities of biopolitical labor-power exceed work and spill over into life. We hesitate to use the word "excess" for this capacity because from the perspective of labor-power or from the standpoint of society as a whole it is never too much. It is excess only from the perspective of capital because it does not produce economic value that can be captured by the individual capitalist—even though, as we will see shortly, such production does produce economic value that can be captured by capital at a broader social level, generally as externalities.

At this point we can hazard a first hypothesis: class struggle in the biopolitical context takes the form of exodus. By exodus here we mean, at least initially, a process of *subtraction* from the relationship with capital by means of actualizing the potential autonomy of labor-power. Exodus is thus not a refusal of the productivity of biopolitical labor-power but rather a refusal of the increasingly restrictive fetters placed on its productive capacities by capital. It is an expression of the productive capacities that exceed the relationship with capital achieved by stepping through the opening in the social relation of capital and across the threshold. As a first approximation, then, think of this form of class struggle as a kind of maroonage. Like the slaves who collectively escape the chains of slavery to construct self-governing communities and quilombos, biopolitical labor-power subtracting from its relation to capital must discover and construct new social relationships, new forms of life that allow it to actualize its productive powers. But unlike that of the maroons, this exodus does not necessarily mean going elsewhere. We can pursue a line of flight while staying right here, by transforming the relations of production and mode of social organization under which we live.

Class struggle does still, of course, involve resisting capitalist command and attacking the bases of capitalist power, which we will address in more detail later, but it also requires an exodus from the relationship with capital and from capitalist relations of production. And although the requirements for *resistance* are immediately given to workers in the labor relation itself—workers always have the power to say no, to stop providing their labor to capital, and their ability to subvert the production process is constantly present in their very capacity to produce—the requirements for *exodus* are not so evident. Exodus is possible only on the basis of the common— both access to the common and the ability to make use of it—and capitalist society seems driven to eliminate or mask the common by privatizing the means of production and indeed all aspects of social life. Before turning to questions of political organization, then, we need to investigate more fully the existing forms of the common available in society today.

Specters of the Common

Specters of the common appear throughout capitalist society, even if in veiled and mystified forms. Despite its ideological aversion, capital cannot do without the common, and today in increasingly explicit ways. To track down these specters of the common, we will need to follow the path of productive social cooperation and the various modes of abstraction that represent it in capitalist society. Revealing some of these really existing forms of the common is a first step toward establishing the bases for an exodus of the multitude from its relation with capital.

One vast reservoir of common wealth is the metropolis itself. The formation of modern cities, as urban and architectural historians explain, was closely linked to the development of industrial capital. The geographical concentration of workers, the proximity of resources and other industries, communication and transportation systems, and the other characteristics of urban life are necessary elements for industrial production. Throughout the nineteenth and twentieth centuries the growth of cities and the qualities of urban space were determined by the industrial factory, its needs, rhythms, and forms of social organization. Today we are witnessing a shift, however, from the *industrial* to the *biopolitical metropolis*. And in the biopolitical economy there is an increasingly intense and direct relation between the production process and the common that constitutes the city. The city, of course, is not just a built environment consisting of buildings and streets and subways and parks and waste systems and communications cables but also a living dynamic of cultural practices, intellectual circuits, affective networks, and social institutions. These elements of the common contained in the city are not only the prerequisite for biopolitical production but also its result; the city is the source of the common and the receptacle into which it flows. (We will explore more fully the dynamics of the biopolitical metropolis in *De Corpore* 2, following Part 4.)

One lens for recognizing the common wealth of the metropolis and the efforts to privatize it is provided by urban real estate economics, a field in desperate need of demystification. It is useful to remember that ground rent and the value of land presented great difficulties for classical political economists. If labor is the source of all wealth, according to Adam Smith's axiom, then what accounts for the value of land or real estate more generally? Labor is incorporated into the land, of course, by working the soil and constructing on it, but that clearly does not account adequately for the value of real estate, especially in an urban environment. To say that land rent is a monopoly price does not address the central problem either. Real estate value cannot be explained internally but can be understood only with reference to external factors.[26]

Contemporary real estate economists are fully aware, of course, that the value of an apartment or a building or land in a city is not represented exclusively by the intrinsic characteristics of the property, such as the quality and size of its construction, but is also and even primarily determined by externalities—both negative externalities, such as air pollution, traffic congestion, noisy neighbors, high levels of criminality, and the discotheque downstairs that makes it impossible to sleep on Saturday nights; and positive externalities, such as proximity to playgrounds, dynamic local cultural relations, intellectual circuits of exchange, and peaceful, stimulating social interactions. In these externalities we encounter a specter of the common. The main preoccupation of these economists is that externalities fall outside the realm of property relations and are thus resistant to market logic and exchange. In efficient free markets, they claim, people make rational decisions, but when there are "market distortions," when externalities come into play and social costs do not equal private costs, market rationality is lost and "market failure" results. The crazy thing is that especially in urban environments the value of real estate is determined primarily by externalities. Market failure is the norm. The most orthodox neoliberal economists thus spend their time inventing schemes to "rationalize" the situation and privatize the common so it can be traded and will obey market rules, seeking ways to monetize pollution or traffic, for instance, in order to make the social costs equal to the private costs and thus restore logic to market exchanges.[27]

Parenthetically we should note that the important and growing role of externalities allows us to rethink some of the standard assumptions of political economy. Just as there is today an inversion of the progression traditionally assumed by political economists from rent to profit, as we said earlier, so too is there an inversion of the presumed tendency from "absolute rent" (based on mere appropriation) to "relative rent" (based on the value of labor added to the property). To the extent that work done to the property has increasingly less significant effect in relation to the "common work" external to it—in the general social circuits of biopolitical production and reproduction of the city—the tendency is today moving back from relative toward absolute rent.[28]

Real estate agents, the everyday practitioners of trading urban value, with their feet solidly on the ground and their hands greedily clutching their pocketbooks, do not need any complicated theories to understand the dominant role of the common. Their mantra—

"location, location, location"—is their way of expressing the strategy to minimize the negative externalities and maximize the positive. Location is merely a name for proximity and access to common wealth—not only with respect to the park but also the quality of neighborhood relations, the pathways of communication, the intellectual and cultural dynamics, and so forth. Real estate agents do not need to privatize externalities and "rationalize" the markets. With an eye to the common, they are very capable of making money from the metropolis and its "irrationality."

Our aim, though, is not to give advice on how to get rich with real estate, but to track down the specters of the common. The theories of real estate economics, along with the practices of real estate agents, demonstrate how the metropolis itself is an enormous reservoir of the common, of not only material but also and moreover immaterial factors, both good and bad. What the economists do not understand, though, is where common wealth comes from. The common may be external from the perspective of the market and the mechanisms of capitalist organization, but it is completely *internal* to the processes of biopolitical production. The wealth produced in common is abstracted, captured, and privatized, in part, by real estate speculators and financiers, which, as we saw earlier, is a fetter to further production of the common. This dilemma is illustrated by the classic dialectic of urban artist neighborhoods and gentrification: poor artists move into a neighborhood with low property values because they cannot afford anything else, and in addition to producing their art they also produce a new cityscape. Property values rise as their activity makes the neighborhood more intellectually stimulating, culturally dynamic, and fashionable, with the result that, eventually, artists can no longer afford to live there and have to move out. Rich people move in, and slowly the neighborhood loses its intellectual and cultural character, becoming boring and sterile. Despite the fact that the common wealth of the city is constantly being expropriated and privatized in real estate markets and speculation, the common still lives on there as a specter.[29]

Finance is another vast realm in which we can track down

specters of the common. Georg Simmel remarks that the qualities of the metropolis are the very same qualities that money demands: a detailed division of labor, impersonal encounters, time synchronicity, and so forth.[30] What really underlies these various characteristics to a large extent is the power of abstraction. Finance capital is an enormous engine of abstraction that simultaneously represents and mystifies the common as if reflecting it in a distorted mirror.[31]

Finance capital has long been criticized for amplifying economic risks and for not producing anything—and after the global crisis of 2008 vilification of finance has become extremely widespread. Finance is casino capitalism, its critics charge, little more than a legal form of gambling with no social utility. The dignity of industrial capital, they claim, is that it directly engages productive forces and produces value in material products, whereas the products of finance are fictional, making money from money, remaining abstract from and thus parasitical on the production of real value. Such criticisms are partly true—even though financial instruments are used for risk management as well as speculation and the biopolitical economy is increasingly oriented toward immaterial products. But they do not grasp the essential nature of finance. If financial speculation is to be conceived as gambling, it is an intelligent, informed type of gambling in which the investor, like someone who bets on horse races who gauges the animal's physical condition and that of the racetrack, has to judge the future performance of a sector of production through a variety of indicators, some of them very abstract. Finance capital is in essence an elaborate machine for *representing* the common, that is, the common relationships and networks that are necessary for the production of a specific commodity, a field of commodities, or some other type of asset or phenomenon. This representation involves an extraordinary process of abstraction from the common itself, and indeed financial products take on ever more abstract, esoteric forms such that they may refer not to production directly but to representations of future production or representations of representations. Finance's powers of abstraction are dizzying, and that is why mathematical models become so central. Abstraction itself, though, is possible only because of the social nature of the wealth being represented. With each level of abstraction financial instruments grasp a wider social level of networks that directly or indirectly cooperate in the production process. This power of abstraction, in other words, rests on and simultaneously mystifies the common.[32]

The role of finance with respect to other forms of capital has expanded exponentially in recent decades. Giovanni Arrighi interprets this as a cyclical phenomenon parallel to the rise of finance centered in Britain in the late nineteenth century and earlier moments.[33] It is more important in our view, however, to link finance's rise with the concurrent emerging centrality of biopolitical production. Insofar as biopolitical labor is autonomous, finance is the adequate capitalist instrument to expropriate the common wealth produced, external to it and abstract from the production process. And finance cannot expropriate without in some way representing the product and productivity of common social life. In this respect finance is nothing but the power of money itself. "Money represents pure interaction in its purest form," Georg Simmel writes. "It makes comprehensible the most abstract concept; it is an individual thing whose essential significance is to reach beyond individualities. Thus, money is the adequate expression of the relationship of man to the world, which can only be grasped in single and concrete instances, yet only really conceived when the singular becomes the embodiment of the living mental process which interweaves all singularities and, in this fashion, creates reality."[34] Finance grasps the common in its broadest social form and, through abstraction, expresses it as value that can be exchanged, mystifying and privatizing the common in order to generate profits. We have no intention of celebrating or condemning finance capital. We propose instead to treat it as a field of investigation for tracking down the specters of the common lurking there.

Both our examples, the real estate market and finance, reveal a tense and ambivalent relation between abstraction and the common. Before bringing this discussion to a close, though, we might illuminate this ambivalence by looking briefly at Marx's approach to capital's powers of abstraction. Abstraction is essential to both the functioning of capital and the critique of it. Marx's point of departure in *Capital,* in fact, is his analysis of abstract labor as the determining foundation of the exchange-value of commodities. Labor in capitalist society, Marx explains, must be abstracted from the concrete labors of the tailor, the plumber, the machinist to be considered as labor in general, without respect to its specific application. This abstract labor once congealed in commodities is the common substance they all share, which allows for their values to be universally commensurable, and which ultimately allows money to function as a general equivalent. Too many readers of Marx, eager to discern political coordinates from the opening pages of the text, correlate these distinctions to political positions: for concrete labor and against abstract labor, for use-value and against exchange-value. Marx views abstraction, however, with ambivalence. Yes, abstract labor and the system of exchange are mechanisms for extracting surplus value and maintaining capitalist control, but the concept of abstract labor—representing what is common to labor in different occupations—is what makes it possible to think the working class. Without abstract labor there is no working class! This is yet another example of the ways in which capital, by pursuing its own interests and guaranteeing its essential functions, creates the tools to resist and eventually overcome the capitalist mode of production. Capitalist abstraction always rests on the common and cannot survive without it, but can only instead constantly try to mystify it. Hence the ambivalence of abstraction.

Corruption and Exodus

Every social institution rests on the common and is defined, in fact, by the common it draws on, marshals, and creates. Social institutions are thus essential resources for the project of exodus. But we should remember that not all forms of the common are beneficial. Just as, in the language of economists, some externalities are positive and others negative, some forms of the common increase our powers to think and act together, as Spinoza might say, and others decrease them. Beneficial forms are motors of generation, whereas detrimental forms spread corruption, blocking the networks of social interactions and reducing the powers of social production. Exodus thus requires a process of selection, maximizing the beneficial forms of the common and minimizing the detrimental, struggling, in other words, against corruption. Certainly capital constitutes one form of the corruption of the common, as we have seen, through its mechanisms of control and expropriation, segmenting and privatizing the common, but relatively independent forms of the corruption of the common are found too in the ruling social institutions.

The three most significant social institutions of capitalist society in which the common appears in corrupt form are the family, the corporation, and the nation. All three mobilize and provide access to the common, but at the same time restrict, distort, and deform it. These are social terrains on which the multitude has to employ a process of selection, separating the beneficial, generative forms of common from the detrimental and corrupt.

The family is perhaps the primary institution in contemporary society for mobilizing the common. For many people, in fact, the family is the principal if not exclusive site of collective social experience, cooperative labor arrangements, caring, and intimacy. It stands on the foundation of the common but at the same time corrupts it by imposing a series of hierarchies, restrictions, exclusions, and distortions. First, the family is a machine of gender normativity that constantly grinds down and crushes the common. The patriarchal structure of family authority varies in different cultures but maintains its general form; the gender division of labor within the family, though often critiqued, is extraordinarily persistent; and the heteronormative model dictated by the family varies remarkably little throughout the world. The family corrupts the common by imposing gender hierarchies and enforcing gender norms, such that any attempt at alternative gender practices or expressions of alternative sexual desires are unfailingly closed down and punished.

Second, the family functions in the social imaginary as the sole paradigm for relationships of intimacy and solidarity, eclipsing and usurping all other possible forms. Intergenerational relationships are inevitably cast in the parent–child model (such that teachers who care, for example, should be like parents to their students), and same-generation friendships are posed as sibling relationships (with a band of brothers and sorority sisters). All alternative kinship structures, whether based on sexual relationships or not, are either prohibited or corralled back under the rule of the family. The exclusive nature of the family model, which carries with it inevitably all of its internal hierarchies, gender norms, and heteronormativity, is evidence of not only a pathetic lack of social imagination to grasp other forms of intimacy and solidarity but also a lack of freedom to create and experiment with alternative social relationships and nonfamily kinship structures.[35]

Third, although the family pretends to extend desires and interests beyond the individual toward the community, it unleashes some of the most extreme forms of narcissism and individualism. It is remarkable, in fact, how strongly people believe that acting in the interests of their family is a kind of altruism when it is really the blindest egotism. When school decisions pose the good of their child against that of others or the community as a whole, for example, many parents launch the most ferociously antisocial arguments under a halo of virtue, doing all that is necessary in the name of their child, often with the strange narcissism of seeing the child as an extension or reproduction of themselves. Political discourse that justifies interest in the future through a logic of family continuity—how many times have you heard that some public policy is necessary for the good of your children?—reduces the common to a kind of projected individualism via one's progeny and betrays an extraordinary incapacity to conceive the future in broader social terms.[36]

Finally, the family corrupts the common by serving as a core institution for the accumulation and transfer of private property. The accumulation of private property would be interrupted each generation if not for the legal form of inheritance based on the family. Down with the family!—not, of course, in order for us to become isolated individuals but instead to realize the equal and free participation in the common that the family promises and constantly denies and corrupts.

The corporation is another form in which the common is both generated and corrupted. Capitalist production in general is an enormous apparatus for developing the common networks of social cooperation and capturing their results as private accumulation. For many workers, of course, the workplace is the only site outside the family where they experience cooperation with others and collective projects, the only place where they escape the individualism and isolation of contemporary society. Producing together in a planned way stimulates the "animal spirits," as Marx says, and thus generates in the workplace the rewards and pleasures of sociality and productive exchange. Predictably, corporations encourage workers to attribute the stimulation and satisfaction they experience at work to the corporation itself, with consequent feelings of dedication and loyalty. What is good for the corporation, the ideological refrains goes, is good for all of us. It is true, and one should not deny the fact, that work in capitalist society does engage the common and provide a site for social and productive cooperation—in varying degrees, of course, and often much less at the lower levels of the workforce. As we have already explained at length, however, the common engaged and generated in production is not only expropriated but also fettered and corrupted through capital's imposition of hierarchy and control. What we should add here instead is that the corporation is remarkably similar to the family in some of the ways it generates and corrupts the common. The two institutions can easily appear as oases of the common in the desert of contemporary society. At work as in the family, though, cooperative relationships are subject to strict internal hierarchies and external limitations. As a result, many who try to flee the horrors of the family run into the welcoming embrace of the corporation, and vice versa, others flee the corporation, seeking refuge in the family. The much-discussed "balance" between work and family is really an alternative between lesser evils, between two corrupt forms of the common, but for too many in our societies these are the only social spaces that provide access, however distorted, to the common.[37]

Finally, the nation too is a social institution in which the common is both deployed and corrupted. Many certainly do experience belonging to the nation as a terrain of the common, which engages the collective cultural, social, and political expressions of the population. The nation's claim as the central terrain of social life is heightened in times of crisis and war, when the population is called to set aside differences in the interest of national unity. More than a shared history or a set of linguistic and cultural traditions, the nation is, according to Benedict Anderson's influential formulation, an imagined community, which is another way of saying a deployment of the common. What a sad indication of the wretched state of our political alternatives, though, that the nation becomes the *only* community imaginable, the only form for expressing social solidarity and escaping from individualism! How pathetic it is when politics can be conducted *only* in the name of the nation! In the nation too, of course, just as in the family and the corporation, the common is submitted to severely restrictive operations: the nation is defined internally and externally by hierarchies and exclusion. The nation inevitably functions through the construction and enforcement of "a people," a national identity, which excludes or subordinates all those who are different. It is true that the nation and its people, along with their centripetal mechanisms that unify the social field, have in some cases, particularly in anticolonial and anti-imperialist struggles, functioned as part of liberation projects; but even then the nation and national consciousness present "pitfalls," as Frantz Fanon says, that may be recognized fully only after the furors of battle die down. Calls to sacrifice for the glory and unity of the nation and the people always have a fascist ring in our ears, since we have so often heard them, in dominant and subordinate countries alike, as the repeated refrain of authoritarian, totalitarian, and militaristic adventures. These are just some of the corruptions the common suffers at the hands of the nation.[38]

In spite of the revulsion they inspire in us, we should remember that the family, the corporation, and the nation do engage and mobilize the common, even if in corrupted form, and thereby provide important resources for the exodus of the multitude. All these institutions present networks of productive cooperation, resources of wealth that are openly accessible, and circuits of communication that simultaneously whet the desire for the common and frustrate it. The multitude must flee the family, the corporation, and the nation but at the same time build on the promises of the common they mobilize. Keep in mind that opening and expanding access to the common in the context of biopolitical production means seizing control of the means of production and reproduction; that it is the basis for a process of subtraction from capital and the construction of autonomy of the multitude; and that this project of exodus is the primary form class struggle takes today.

Our readers with a taste for combat may be reluctant to accept a notion of class struggle as exodus because it does not have enough fight in it. Not to worry. Moses learned long ago that those in power do not just let you go without a fight. And, more important, exodus does not mean getting out as naked life, barefoot and penniless. No; we need to take what is ours, which means reappropriating the common—the results of our past labors and means of autonomous production and reproduction for our future. That is the field of battle.

KAIROS OF THE MULTITUDE

_____

> The gradual crumbling that left unaltered the face of the whole is cut
> short by a sunburst which, in one flash, illuminates the features of the
> new world.
>
> —G. W. F. Hegel, *Phenomenology of Spirit*

What a Multitude Can Do

All the objective conditions are in place: biopolitical labor constantly
exceeds the limits of capitalist command; there is a breach in the
social relation of capital opening the possibility for biopolitical labor
to claim its autonomy; the foundations of its exodus are given in the
existence and constant creation of the common; and capital's mechanisms of exploitation and control increasingly contradict and fetter
biopolitical productivity. But there are also countervailing objective
conditions: new capitalist mechanisms find novel ways to expropriate and privatize the common, and the old social institutions cease-
lessly corrupt it. Where does all this leave us? Analysis of objective
conditions take us this far but no further. Capitalist crisis does not
proceed automatically to collapse. The multiplicity of singularities
that produce and are produced in the biopolitical field of the common do not spontaneously accomplish exodus and construct their
autonomy. Political organization is needed to cross the threshold and
generate political events. The *kairos*—the opportune moment that
ruptures the monotony and repetitiveness of chronological time—
has to be grasped by a political subject.

    We propose the multitude as an adequate concept for organizing politically the project of exodus and liberation because we are convinced that, in the current biopolitical context even more than before, traditional organizational forms based on unity, central leadership, and hierarchy are neither desirable nor effective.[39] The multitude proposition has now been debated in intellectual and political circles for several years, and we can take advantage of these discussions to evaluate and refine the concept. The critiques and challenges we have found most productive center generally on two fundamental questions: one regarding the multitude's capability to take coherent political action and a second about the progressive or liberatory character of its actions.

The best critics of the concept of multitude regarding the first line of questions accept our assessment that, especially in the biopolitical context, society is composed of a radical plurality, or rather a multiplicity of irreducible singularities. The question is whether and how these singularities can act together politically. At play fundamentally is the concept of the political itself. Pierre Macherey, for instance, explains quite rightly that politics requires the ability to make decisions on not an individual but a social level. "How can the flesh of the multitude become a body?" he asks. "The intervention of a political entity is necessary, an entity in this case that, while maintaining the rhizomatic structure of the multitude, must itself be collective and refuse any vertical form of ordering, and in that way remain faithful to its immanent destiny that requires it to unfold on a plane of horizontality. How then can the multitude organize itself, without sacrificing the autonomy of the singularities that compose it?"[40] Macherey sees the multiplicity of the multitude as posing a political obstacle or challenge because he assumes that acting as a political body and making decisions requires unity. He thus sees any political project for the multitude caught in a contradiction: either sacrifice its horizontal multiplicity and adopt a unified vertical organization, thereby ceasing to be a multitude; or maintain its structure and be incapable of political decision and action.

Ernesto Laclau similarly considers the immanence and plurality of the multitude a barrier to its capacity for politics. He agrees

that today there exists the initial condition of the multitude: the social field is radically heterogeneous. He explains, then, still along the
lines of the multitude, that political action requires that the singularities on the plane of immanence engage in a process of articulation to define and structure political relations among them. Laclau
diverges, though, when he insists that in order for articulation to
take place, a guiding hegemonic force must emerge above the plane
of immanence that is able to direct the process and serve as a point
of identification for all the singularities. Hegemony represents the
plurality of singularities as a unity and thus transforms the multitude
into a people, which because of its unity is deemed capable of political action and decision making: "The political operation *par excel-
lence* is always going to be the construction of a 'people.'"[41] Like Macherey, Laclau sees the multitude as a figure on the road to politics
but not yet a political figure.

A second line of questioning concerns primarily not whether
the multitude can act politically but the direction of its political actions—not the form, so to speak, but the content of the multitude's
politics. Specifically, these authors see no reason to assume that the
political decisions and action of the multitude will be oriented toward liberation. Paolo Virno, for example, one of those who has
most fruitfully advanced the concept of the multitude, considers its
politics profoundly ambivalent since the multitude is endowed in his
view with roughly equal measures of social solidarity and aggressiveness. Just as a long tradition of political philosophy warns it is
naïve or irresponsible to assume that humans in the state of nature
are unfailingly good, Virno emphasizes the ambivalence of the "state
of nature" characterized by biopolitical production. The powerful
new tools in the possession of the multitude—linguistic tools, along
with tools of communication, affect, knowledge, and so forth—have
no necessary predisposition to the good but can just as easily be used
for ill. Virno thus advocates a "realist" position, insisting that any discussion of the positive political capacities of the multitude be accompanied by a sober look at the negative.[42]

Étienne Balibar similarly insists that the concept of the multitude lacks internal political criteria that would guarantee its actions a progressive orientation or antisystemic character. It may just as likely contribute to the systems of global exploitation as resist and contest them. Like Virno, Balibar emphasizes the ambivalent standpoint of the multitude, which he explains, for example, in terms of the double meaning of fear of the multitude. Both the fear the multitude feels and the fear it inspires can lead, in his view, in varying political directions. The multitude may be a sound sailing vessel, to lend Balibar a metaphor, but without a rudder there is no way to predict where it will end up.[43]

Slavoj Žižek and Alain Badiou take this questioning of the multitude's political orientation one step further, posing it as not ambivalent but aligned with the forces of domination. Žižek charges that the multitude, even in the guise of anticapitalist struggles, really mimics and supports capitalist power, and he traces the flaw of multitude thinking back to Marx. Marx's error, he suggests, is to believe that capital creates its own gravediggers, that the developments of capitalist society and production create within capital itself an antagonistic political subject, the proletariat, capable of revolution. Žižek maintains, however, that the apparent antagonisms and alternatives that capital produces internally really end up supporting the system. He focuses, for example, on how capital creates proliferating multiplicities in the realm of the market and consumption, through the infinite variety of its commodities and the desires they elicit. From this perspective, then, the multiplicities of the multitude and its horizontal network structures mirror capital's own decentered and deterritorializing deployment, and thus, even when thought to be resisting it, the multitude's actions inevitably repeat and reproduce capitalist rule. Radical transformation and, specifically, revolutionary opposition to capitalist rule, Žižek insists, will never emerge, as the multitude does, from within capital itself.[44]

Whereas Žižek credits the mistakes of multitude thinking to an error in Marx, Badiou traces them to the work of Foucault and his conception of resistance. Since resistance is constantly engaged with power, Badiou reasons, it never escapes power, and moreover never recognizes the necessity for the event to break with power. Any conception of a creative, antisystemic multitude, he claims, is only a dreamy hallucination *(un rêverie hallucinée)*. "That which goes by the name 'resistance,' in this instance, is only a component of the progress of power itself." The existing movements of the multitude thus amount to little in Badiou's estimation. "All we've seen are very ordinary performances from the well-worn repertoire of petit-bourgeois mass movements, noisily laying claim to the right to enjoy without doing anything, while taking special care to avoid any form of discipline. Whereas we know that discipline, in all fields, is the key to truths."[45] Badiou's critique of the multitude is in effect an extension and generalization of Žižek's: whereas Žižek, indicating Marx's error, charges that the multitude in the guise of contesting capital merely mimics and supports its rule, Badiou, referring to Foucault, maintains that the multitude and other projects of resistance are really only components of the progress of power itself.

The Common Nature of the Multitude

These questions and critiques regarding the political capacities and orientation of the multitude are useful because they help us focus on and clarify the extent to which the concept is adequate to organizational projects of liberation in our biopolitical reality. In order to respond to these questions we have to show how the multitude is not a spontaneous political subject but a project of political organization, thus shifting the discussion from *being* the multitude to *making* the multitude. Before addressing them directly, though, we need to explore some of the philosophical and political bases of the concept of multitude, investigating in particular the way the multitude interacts with and transforms nature.

Like "the people," the multitude is the result of a process of political constitution, although, whereas the people is formed as a unity by a hegemonic power standing above the plural social field, the multitude is formed through articulations on the plane of immanence without hegemony. We can see this difference from another perspective by recognizing that these two processes pose different relations between politics and the state of nature. A long tradition of political theory tells us that the construction of hegemony or sovereignty requires a passage from the anarchy of the state of nature to the political life of the civil state. The constitution of the multitude, however, confounds this division between the state of nature and the civil or political state: it is thoroughly political while never leaving behind the state of nature. This is not as paradoxical as it seems once we see the metamorphosis of nature at work in the constitution of the multitude.

Feminist scholars, appreciating the political obstacle posed by a notion of nature as fixed and immutable, separate from and prior to cultural and social interaction, have demonstrated how nature is constantly constructed and transformed. Judith Butler, for example, challenges the traditional sex-gender distinction by questioning the fixity of nature. The major stream of feminist theory throughout its second wave investigates how gender is malleable and socially constructed, Butler explains, but assumes that sex differences are natural, biological, and hence immutable. She argues instead that, in addition to gender, sex too is socially constructed, that sex and sexual differences are, following Foucault, discursive formations. This is not to deny that sex is directly linked to biology and bodies, but rather to suggest that what we know and think about sex, our mode of apprehension of it, is inextricably embedded in determinate social discourses.[46] Other feminist scholars pursue this argument in scientific and biological terms to demonstrate that nature modulates according to social constructs and practices. Anne Fausto-Sterling, for instance, explores how nature and bodies are constantly transformed through social interactions and, specifically, how what we understand as sex and sexual difference are entirely embedded in social and cultural practices and consciousness. Even human bone structure, she argues, which we think of as one of the elements of the body most fixed in nature, requires specific triggers for development and modifies differently depending on complex relations to bodily practices during growth, many of which are defined by specific gender practices. Culture shapes bones.[47] This does not mean that there is no such thing as nature, but rather nature is constantly transformed by social and cultural interactions. The claim that nature is subject to mutation is closely related to the philosophical proposition of a constituent ontology—the notion, that is, that being is subject to a process of becoming dictated by social action and practices. God or being or nature, in Spinoza's vocabulary, is not separate from and prior to the interaction of modes in the world but rather entirely constituted by them.[48]

These investigations of the plasticity and mutability of nature really refer to the common—and indeed nature is just another word for the common. But it is important to keep in mind the distinction between the two notions of the common we cited earlier. Whereas the traditional notion poses the common as a natural world outside of society, the biopolitical conception of the common permeates equally all spheres of life, referring not only to the earth, the air, the elements, or even plant and animal life but also to the constitutive elements of human society, such as common languages, habits, gestures, affects, codes, and so forth. And whereas according to the traditional notion, for thinkers like Locke and Rousseau, the formation of society and the progress of history inevitably destroy the common, fencing it off as private property, the biopolitical conception emphasizes not only preserving the common but also struggling over the conditions of producing it, as well as selecting among its qualities, promoting its beneficial forms, and fleeing its detrimental, corrupt forms. We might call this an ecology of the common—an ecology focused equally on nature and society, on humans and the nonhuman world in a dynamic of interdependence, care, and mutual transformation. Now we are better positioned to understand how the becoming political of the multitude does not require leaving behind the state of nature, as the tradition of sovereignty insists, but rather calls for a metamorphosis of the common that operates simultaneously on nature, culture, and society.

The metamorphosis of the common leads us directly to the problem of the production of subjectivity. It is useful to remember how heated the so-called postmodernism debates became in the

1980s and 1990s around this question. On one side were postmodernists who focused generally on the production of consciousness. In some respects their position repeated the classic Frankfurt School thesis that alienated consciousness is produced in capitalist society, its culture industries, its mandate to consumption, and its commodity culture, but replaced the gloom of the Frankfurt School with a more cheerful disposition. The claim that subjectivity is produced in the circuits of commodified capitalist culture seemed to some to herald a weak notion of freedom based on play and contingency. On the other side were modernist defenders of the subject in the name of not only reason, reality, and truth but also the possibilities of a politics of liberation. A stable subject residing outside the functioning of power was thought to be necessary as a ground for politics in class politics, race politics, feminism, and other identity domains. These two sides, which we have painted in admittedly reductive terms, monopolized the most visible debates, but a third approach, much closer to our own, was developed in the same period by Foucault, Deleuze, and Guattari. These authors focus on the social mechanisms of the production of subjectivity in institutional architectures, psychoanalytic discourse, state apparatuses, and so forth, but they do not greet the recognition that subjectivity is produced through apparatuses of power with either celebration or despair. They regard the production of subjectivity rather as the primary terrain on which political struggle takes place. We need to intervene in the circuits of the production of subjectivity, flee from the apparatuses of control, and construct the bases for an autonomous production.[49]

The politics of the production of subjectivity helps us understand better the economic process of the metamorphoses of the common, which we analyzed earlier. The biopolitical production of ideas, codes, images, affects, and social relationships directly treats the constituent elements of human subjectivity: this terrain is precisely where subjectivity is born and resides. One might still conceive of economic production as an engagement of the subject with nature, a transformation of the object through labor, but increasingly the "nature" that biopolitical labor transforms is subjectivity itself. This relation between economic production and subjectivity thus cuts out the ground from under traditional notions of the labor process and creates a potentially vertiginous loop. We can cut through some of these seeming paradoxes, though, by approaching the production process in terms of metamorphoses of the common. And it should be obvious that this kind of economic process, central to biopolitical production, is also an ontological process through which nature and subjectivity are transformed and constituted.

Multitude should be understood, then, as not a being but a making—or rather a being that is not fixed or static but constantly transformed, enriched, constituted by a process of making. This is a peculiar kind of making, though, insofar as there is no maker that stands behind the process. Through the production of subjectivity, the multitude is itself author of its perpetual becoming other, an uninterrupted process of collective self-transformation.

From Being to Making the Multitude

Once we shift our perspective from being the multitude to making the multitude, and once we recognize the multitude as a constant process of metamorphosis grounded in the common, we are in a better position to respond to the questions and critiques of the concept we outlined earlier. The first set of questions deems the multitude incapable of politics because it is not unified by hegemony. At issue here is whether only hegemonic, unified subjects or also horizontally organized multiplicities are capable of political action. We can answer these questions by referring to our earlier economic investigations. Biopolitical production takes place and can only take place on the terrain of the common. Ideas, images, and codes are produced not by a lone genius or even by a master with supporting apprentices but by a wide network of cooperating producers. Labor tends to be increasingly autonomous from capitalist command, and thus capital's mechanisms of expropriation and control become fetters that obstruct productivity. Biopolitical production is an orchestra keeping the beat without a conductor, and it would fall silent if anyone were to step onto the podium.

The model of biopolitical economic production serves us here as an analogy for political action: just as a wide social multiplicity produces immaterial products and economic value, so too is such a multitude able to produce political decisions. It is much more than an analogy, though, because the same capacities that are set in play, which are necessary for the one, are also sufficient for the other. The ability of producers autonomously to organize cooperation and produce collectively in a planned way, in other words, has immediate implications for the political realm, providing the tools and habits for collective decision making. In this respect the division between economic production and political action posed by authors such as Hannah Arendt completely breaks down. Arendt's conception of politics focuses on plurality and freedom, characterizing political action as a realm of singularities that communicate and cooperate in a common world. She distinguishes this from the economic realm of *Homo faber,* which is separated off in the workplace and driven instrumentally toward making a product. The economic producer, she reasons, is inclined to denounce the action and speech that define politics as idleness and useless chatter. Work is driven narrowly toward a telos, such that "the strength of the production process is entirely absorbed in and exhausted by the end product," whereas the strength of the political process is never exhausted in a product but rather grows "while its consequences multiply; what endures in the realm of human affairs are these processes, and their endurance is as unlimited, as independent of the perishability of material and the mortality of men as the endurance of humanity itself."[50] Arendt is clearly referring to an economic paradigm of material production, with the factory as her primary model, but once we shift our gaze to biopolitical production, we clearly see that all of the qualities she attributes to the political apply equally to the economic: the cooperation of a wide plurality of singularities in a common world, the focus on speech and communication, and the interminable continuity of the process both based in the common and resulting in the common. This is one reason for using the term "bio*political*" to name this form of production, because the economic capacities and acts are themselves immediately political. We should note here that Arendt also distinguishes a third fundamental human activity, which she calls labor. The labor she has in mind corresponds to the biological functioning of the body and thus the production of vital necessities. Both the condition and goal of this labor, she explains, is thus life itself. Arendt primarily uses this concept of labor, of course, as a foil to distinguish the political realm, separating it from the world of needs, but here again we can see that her distinctions are progressively breaking down. Politics has probably never really been separable from the realm of needs and life, but increasingly today biopolitical production is aimed constantly at producing forms of life. Hence the utility of the term "*bio*political." Focusing on the making of the multitude, then, allows us to recognize how its productive activity is also a political act of self-making.

We are now finally in a position to respond easily to the first set of questions about the political capacities of the multitude. It is true that the organization of singularities required for political action and decision making is not immediate or spontaneous, but that does not mean that hegemony and unification, the formation of a sovereign and unified power—whether it be a state, a party, or a people—is the necessary condition for politics. Spontaneity and hegemony are not the only alternatives. The multitude can develop the power to organize itself through the conflictual and cooperative interactions of singularities in the common. Even if one recognizes this tendency, it is reasonable to question whether the multitude is ready for such responsibilities, whether it has become sufficiently endowed with the capacities to organize, act, and decide politically. Remember Lenin's warning on the eve of October 1917: never make revolution on the basis of some ideal or imagined population. The Russian people are not ready to rule themselves, he claims, but need a hegemonic force to guide them through the transition period. They have been trained at work to need subordination, supervision, and managers: they have a boss on the job, and thus they need a boss in politics.[51] The logic of Lenin's warning puts all the more pressure on our demonstration earlier of both the tendential hegemony of biopolitical production in the contemporary economy and the qualities and capacities that come with it. If one can realistically establish the capacities for self-organization and cooperation in people's daily lives, in their work, or more generally in social production, then the political capacity of the multitude ceases to be a question.

The second set of questions, which regard the political orientation of the multitude, progressive or regressive, resisting the current system of power or supporting it, is not so easily addressed. In earlier chapters we proposed a conception of resistance that is prior to power since power is exercised only over free subjects, and thus, although situated "within and against," resistance is not condemned to reinforce or repeat the structures of power. We also presented a biopolitical notion of the event, different from the conception that events come only "from the outside," and thus our sole political duty is to be faithful to them and their truth, to maintain discipline after the event arrives. Those who follow this notion of the event can only wait with a kind of messianic fervor for another event to come. Biopolitical events instead reside in the creative acts of the production of the common. There is indeed something mysterious about the act of creation, but it is a miracle that wells up from within the multitude every day.

Resistance and the creation of events, however, do not yet establish the political orientation of the multitude. The characteristics of the common and the multitude's relation to it give us some indications of how to proceed. Pierre Macherey identifies the rebellious character of the common, which always exceeds the limits of power. "By common life," he writes, "one must thus understand all the figures of collective creation that put to work cooperation and collaboration, the network that, once set in motion, can extend infinitely. That is why common life exceeds every system and every fixed order, to which it is necessarily rebellious."[52] The fact that the multitude, based in the common, always exceeds the limits of power indicates its incompatibility with the ruling system—and its antisystemic nature in that sense—but does not yet establish its liberatory political orientation.

One facet of the political direction of the multitude lies in its exodus from all corrupt derivations of the common accumulated in social institutions, including the family, the corporation, and the nation. The multitude must select the beneficial and flee the detrimental forms of the common. What is corrupt about the common in these institutions, we can see now, is that through hierarchies, divisions, and limits, they block the production of subjectivity and, moreover, the production of the common. Through its selection and exodus the multitude must set the common in motion, opening up again its processes of production.

The political orientation also should be defined in the *making* of the multitude, conceived not only as its political constitution but also as its economic production. In the context of biopolitical production, by working on the common and producing the common, the multitude constantly transforms itself. This brings to mind Marx's admiration for Charles Fourier's utopian insight that the proletariat is a subject in transformation, transformed through labor but also and moreover through social, cooperative, inventive activity in the time left free from the constraints of work. "The process," Marx explains, extending Fourier's insight, "is then both discipline, as regards the human being in the process of becoming; and, at the same time, practice, experimental science, materially creative and objectifying science, as regards the human being who has become, in whose head exists the accumulated knowledge of society."[53] The self-transformation of the multitude in production, grounded in the expansion of the common, gives an initial indication of the direction of the self-rule of the multitude in the political realm.

All of these elements, however, animated by biopolitical events, fleeing corrupt forms of the common, and dedicated to furthering the production of the common in its beneficial forms, do not yet specify adequately the political orientation of the multitude. We need at this point to engage directly with the question of organization because that is the terrain on which the progressive, liberatory, antisystemic character of the multitude will have to be verified and consolidated in its own durable institutions. This will be one of the primary tasks for us to address, first in *De Singularitate* 1 and the Intermezzo that follow this section and then throughout the second half of the book: a theory of political organization adequate to the multitude. The terrain of organization is where we must establish that the multitude can be a revolutionary figure and indeed that it is the only figure today capable of revolution.

DE SINGULARITATE 1:

OF LOVE POSSESSED

Let your loves be like the wasp and the orchid.
—Gilles Deleuze and Félix Guattari

All the theoretical elements we have accumulated thus far—from the multitude of the poor to the project of altermodernity and from the social productivity of biopolitical labor to the exodus from capitalist command—despite all their power, risk lying inert beside one another without one more element that pulls them together and animates them in a coherent project. What is missing is love. Yes, we know that term makes many readers uncomfortable. Some squirm in their seats with embarrassment and others smirk with superiority.[54] Love has been so charged with sentimentality that it seems hardly fit for philosophical and much less political discourse. Leave it to the poets to speak of love, many will say, and wrap themselves in its warm embrace. We think instead that love is an essential concept for philosophy and politics, and the failure to interrogate and develop it is one central cause of the weakness of contemporary thought. It is unwise to leave love to the priests, poets, and psychoanalysts. It is necessary for us, then, to do some conceptual housecleaning, clearing away some of the misconceptions that disqualify love for philosophical and political discourse and redefining the concept in such a way as to demonstrate its utility. We will find in the process that philosophers, political scientists, and even economists, despite the imagined cold precision of their thinking, are really often speaking about love. And if they were not so shy they would tell us as much. This will help us demonstrate how love is really the living heart of the project we have been developing, without which the rest would remain a lifeless heap.

To understand love as a philosophical and political concept, it is useful to begin from the perspective of the poor and the innumerable forms of social solidarity and social production that one recognizes everywhere among those who live in poverty. Solidarity, care for others, creating community, and cooperating in common projects is for them an essential survival mechanism. That brings us back to the elements of poverty we emphasized earlier. Although the poor are defined by material lack, people are never reduced to bare life but are always endowed with powers of invention and production. The real essence of the poor, in fact, is not their lack but their power. When we band together, when we form a social body that is more powerful than any of our individual bodies alone, we are constructing a new and common subjectivity. Our point of departure, then, which the perspective of the poor helps reveal, is that love is a process of the production of the common and the production of subjectivity. This process is not merely a *means* to producing material goods and other necessities but also in itself an *end*.

If such a statement sounds too sentimental, one can arrive at the same point through the analysis of political economy. In the context of biopolitical production, as we have demonstrated in the course of Part 3, the production of the common is not separate from or external to economic production, sequestered neither in the private realm nor in the sphere of reproduction, but is instead integral to and inseparable from the production of capital. Love—in the production of affective networks, schemes of cooperation, and social subjectivities—is an economic power. Conceived in this way love is not, as it is often characterized, spontaneous or passive. It does not simply happen to us, as if it were an event that mystically arrives from elsewhere. Instead it is an action, a biopolitical event, planned and realized in common.

Love is productive in a philosophical sense too—productive of being. When we engage in the production of subjectivity that is love, we are not merely creating new objects or even new subjects in the world. Instead we are producing a new world, a new social life. Being, in other words, is not some immutable background against which life takes place but is rather a living relation in which we constantly have the power to intervene. Love is an ontological event in that it marks a rupture with what exists and the creation of the new. Being is constituted by love. This ontologically constitutive capacity has been a battlefield for numerous conflicts among philosophers. Heidegger, for instance, strenuously counters this notion of ontological constitution in his lecture on poverty that we read earlier. Humanity becomes poor to become rich, he argues, when it lacks the nonnecessary, revealing what is necessary, that is, its relation to Being. The poor as Heidegger imagines them in this relation, however, have no constitutive capacity, and humanity as a whole, in fact, is powerless in the face of Being. On this point Spinoza stands at the opposite end from Heidegger. Like Heidegger, he might say that humanity becomes rich when it recognizes its relation to being, but that relation for Spinoza is entirely different. Especially in the mysterious fifth book of Spinoza's *Ethics,* we constitute being actively through love. Love, Spinoza explains with his usual geometrical precision, is joy, that is, the increase of our power to act and think, together with the recognition of an external cause. Through love we form a relation to that cause and seek to repeat and expand our joy, forming new, more powerful bodies and minds. For Spinoza, in other words, love is a production of the common that constantly aims upward, seeking to create more with ever more power, up to the point of engaging in the love of God, that is, the love of nature as a whole, the common in its most expansive figure. Every act of love, one might say, is an ontological event in that it marks a rupture with existing being and creates new being, from poverty through love to being. Being, after all, is just another way of saying what is ineluctably common, what refuses to be privatized or enclosed and remains constantly open to all. (There is no such thing as a private ontology.) To say love is ontologically constitutive, then, simply means that it produces the common.

As soon as we identify love with the production of the common, we need to recognize that, just like the common itself, love is deeply ambivalent and susceptible to corruption. In fact what passes for love today in ordinary discourse and popular culture is predominantly its corrupt forms. The primary locus of this corruption is the shift in love from the common to the same, that is, from the production of the common to a repetition of the same or a process of unification. What distinguishes the beneficial forms of love instead is the constant interplay between the common and singularities.

One corrupt form of love is identitarian love, that is, love of the same, which can be based, for example, on a narrow interpretation of the mandate to love thy neighbor, understanding it as a call to love those most proximate, those most like you. Family love—the pressure to love first and most those within the family to the exclusion or subordination of those outside—is one form of identitarian love. Race love and nation love, or patriotism, are similar examples of the pressure to love most those most like you and hence less those who are different. Family, race, and nation, then, which are corrupt forms of the common, are unsurprisingly the bases of corrupt forms of love. From this perspective we might say that populisms, nationalisms, fascisms, and various religious fundamentalisms are based not so much on hatred as on love—but a horribly corrupted form of identitarian love.

An initial strategy to combat this corruption is to employ a more expansive, more generous interpretation of the mandate to love thy neighbor, reading the neighbor not as the one nearest and most like you but, to the contrary, as the other. "The neighbor is therefore . . . only a place-keeper," says Franz Rosenzweig. "Love is really oriented toward the embodiment of all those—men and things—that could at any moment take this place of its neighbor, in the last resort it applies to everything, it applies to the world."[55] The mandate to love thy neighbor, then, the embodiment of each and every commandment for the monotheistic religions, requires us to love the other or, really, to love alterity. And if you are not comfortable with scriptural exegesis as explanation, think of Walt Whitman's poetry, in which the love of the stranger continually reappears as an encounter characterized by wonder, growth, and discovery. Nietzsche's Zarathustra echoes Whitman when he preaches that higher than love of neighbor is "love of the farthest."[56] Love of the stranger, love of the farthest, and love of alterity can function as an antidote against the poison of identitarian love, which hinders and distorts love's productivity by forcing it constantly to repeat the same. Here then is another meaning of love as a biopolitical event: not only does it mark rupture with the existent and creation of the new, but also it is the production of singularities and the composition of singularities in a common relationship.

A second form of corrupt love poses love as a process of unification, of becoming the same. The contemporary dominant notion of romantic love in our cultures, which Hollywood sells every day, its stock in trade, requires that the couple merge in unity. The mandatory sequence of this corrupted romantic love—couple-marriage-family—imagines people finding their match, like lost puzzle pieces, that now together make (or restore) a whole. Marriage and family close the couple in a unit that subsequently, as we said earlier, corrupts the common. This same process of love as unification is also expressed in many different religious traditions, especially in their mystical registers: love of God means merging in the divine unity. And it is not so surprising that such notions of mystical union often use the conventional language of romantic love, invoking the betrothed, divine marriage, and so forth, because they are aimed at the same goal: making the many into one, making the different into the same. Similarly, various forms of patriotism share this notion of setting (or pushing) aside differences and alterity in order to form a united national people, a national identity. This second corruption of love as unification is intimately related, in fact, to the first identitarian corruption of love: love of the same, love making the same.

One philosophical key to our argument here, which should be clear already, is that the dynamic of multiple singularities in the common has nothing to do with the old dialectic between the many and the one. Whereas the one stands opposed to the many, the common is compatible with and even internally composed of multiplicities. This compatibility between the common and multiplicity can be understood in simple terms (perhaps too simple) when posed in the field of political action: if we did not share a common world, then we would not be able to communicate with one another or engage one another's needs and desires; and if we were not multiple singularities, then we would have no need to communicate and interact. We agree in this regard with Hannah Arendt's conception of politics as the interaction and composition of singularities in a common world.[57]

Promoting the encounters of singularities in the common, then, is the primary strategy to combat love corrupted through identity and unification, which brings the production of subjectivity to a halt and abrogates the common. Sameness and unity involve no creation but mere repetition without difference. Love should be defined, instead, by the encounters and experimentation of singularities in the common, which in turn produce a new common and new singularities. Whereas in the ontological context we characterized the process of love as *constitution,* here in a political context we should emphasize its power of *composition.* Love composes singularities, like themes in a musical score, not in unity but as a network of social relations. Bringing together these two faces of love—the constitution of the common and the composition of singularities—is a central challenge for understanding love as a material, political act.

We began this discussion by claiming that economic production is really a matter of love, but we are perfectly aware that economists do not see it that way. Economists, in fact, have long celebrated Bernard Mandeville's early-eighteenth-century satire *The Fable of the Bees* as an anti-love anthem, proof that there is no possible connection between economics and love. Mandeville tells of a beehive that is wealthy and powerful but ridden with all order of private vices, including deceit, greed, laziness, and cowardice. The hive moralists constantly rail against vice to no avail. Finally the god

of the hive, weary of the constant harping, makes all the bees virtuous and eliminates vice, but as soon as he does so, the work of the
hive comes to a halt and the society of the hive falls apart. The fable
is aimed, obviously, at social moralists and rationalist utopians.
Mandeville, like Machiavelli and Spinoza before him, insists that,
instead of preaching how people *should be,* social theorists must
study how people *are* and analyze the passions that actually animate
them.

Mandeville's fable scandalized eighteenth-century English society, as it was meant to, but some, including Adam Smith, read it as
a confirmation of capitalist ideology. Smith takes Mandeville's polemic that vice, not virtue, is the source of public benefit—people
work out of greed, obey the law out of cowardice, and so forth—to
support the notion that self-interest is the basis of market exchanges
and the capitalist economy. If each acts out of self-interest, then the
public good will result from market activity as if guided by an invisible hand. Smith, of course, a stalwart advocate of sympathy and
other moral sentiments, is not advocating vice but simply wants to
keep misplaced moral imperatives and well-intentioned public control out of the economy. What Smith bans most adamantly from the
marketplace is the common: only from private interests will the
public good result. "It is not from the benevolence of the butcher,
the brewer, or the baker, that we expect our dinner," Smith famously writes, "but from their regard to their own interest. We address ourselves, not to their humanity but to their self-love, and
never talk to them of our own necessities but of their advantages."[58]
Our love for one another has no place in the realm of economic
exchanges.

We get a rather different, updated fable of economic life when
we focus on not the society within the hive but bee pollination activity outside it. For honeybees, flowers located within flying distance of the hive constitute a positive externality. Bees fly from one
apple blossom to another, one cherry blossom to another, gathering
nectar to transport back to the hive. As a bee collects nectar, its legs
rub pollen off the anther of the flower, and when it proceeds to an-

other, some of the pollen from its legs rubs off on the stigma of the
next flower. For the flowers, then, bee activity is a positive externality, completing the cross-pollination necessary to produce fruit. The
economic fable of these bees and flowers suggests a society of mutual aid based on positive externalities and virtuous exchanges in
which the bee provides for the needs of the flower and, in turn, the
flower fulfills the bee's needs.[59]

We can imagine Mandeville and Smith frowning at this fable
because of its suggestion of virtue and purposeful mutual aid as the
basis of social production. We are hesitant about the bee pollination
fable too, but for a different reason: the kind of love it promotes.
Bees and flowers do indeed suggest a kind of love, but a static, corrupt form. (We know, we're anthropomorphizing the bees and
flowers, projecting human traits and desires onto them, but isn't that
what all fables do?) The marriage between bee and flower is a
match made in heaven; they are the two halves that "complete"
each other and form a whole, closing the common down in sameness and unity. But isn't this union a model of the productivity of
the common, you might ask? Doesn't it produce honey and fruit?
Yes, you might call this a kind of production, but it is really just the
repetition of the same. What we are looking for—and what counts
in love—is the production of subjectivity and the encounter of singularities, which compose new assemblages and constitute new
forms of the common.

Let's switch species, then, to write a new fable. Certain orchids
give off the odor of the sex pheromone of female wasps, and their
flowers are shaped like the female wasp sex organs. Pollination is
thus achieved by "pseudocopulation" as male wasps move from one
orchid to the next, sinking their genital members into each flower
and rubbing off pollen on their bodies in the process. "So wasps
fuck flowers!" Félix Guattari exclaims with rather juvenile glee in a
letter to Gilles Deleuze. "Wasps do this work just like that, for nothing, just for fun!"[60] Guattari's delight at this example is due in part
to the fact that it undercuts the industriousness and "productivism"
usually attributed to nature. These wasps aren't your dutiful worker

bees; they aren't driven to produce anything. They just want to have fun. A second point of interest for Guattari is undoubtedly the way this pollination story reinforces his lifelong diatribe against the corruptions of love in the couple and the family. Wasps and orchids do not suggest any morality tale of marriage and stable union, as bees and flowers do, but rather evoke scenarios of cruising and serial sex common to some gay male communities, especially before the onslaught of the AIDS pandemic, like passages from the writings of Jean Genet, David Wojnarowicz, and Samuel Delany. This is not to say that cruising and anonymous sex serve as a model of love to emulate for Guattari (or Genet, Wojnarowicz, or Delany), but rather that they provide an antidote to the corruptions of love in the couple and the family, opening love up to the encounter of singularities.

When the wasp and orchid story appears in print in Deleuze and Guattari's *A Thousand Plateaus,* several years after Guattari's initial letter, the fable has been refined and cast in the context of evolutionary discourse. Deleuze and Guattari insist, first of all, that the orchid is not imitating the wasp or trying to deceive it, as botanists often say. The orchid is a becoming-wasp (becoming the wasp's sexual organ) and the wasp is a becoming-orchid (becoming part of the orchid's system of reproduction). What is central is the encounter and interaction between these two becomings, which together form a new assemblage, a wasp-orchid machine. The fable is devoid of intentions and interests: the wasps and orchids are not paragons of virtue in their mutual aid, nor are they models of egotistic self-love. Deleuze and Guattari's machinic language allows them to avoid asking "What does it mean?" and focus instead on "How does it work?" The fable thus tells the story of wasp-orchid love, a love based on the encounter of alterity but also on a process of becoming different.[61]

Mandeville's bees (at least according to Smith's reading) are the model for a capitalist dream of individual free agents trading labor and goods in the marketplace, intent on their own self-interest and deaf to the common good. The dutiful worker bees, in contrast, joined with their flowers in a virtuous union of mutual aid, are the stuff of socialist utopia. All of these bees, however, belong to the bygone era of the hegemony of industrial production. Wasps who love orchids, instead, point toward the conditions of the biopolitical economy. How could these wasps be a model for economic production, you might ask, when they don't produce anything? The bees and flowers produce honey and fruit, but the wasps and orchids are just hedonists and aesthetes, merely creating pleasure and beauty! It is true that the interaction of wasps and orchids does not result primarily in material goods, but one should not discount their immaterial production. In the encounter of singularities of their love, a new assemblage is created, marked by the continual metamorphosis of each singularity in the common. Wasp-orchid love, in other words, is a model of the production of subjectivity that animates the biopolitical economy. Let's have done with worker bees, then, and focus on the singularities and becomings of wasp-orchid love!

A FORCE TO COMBAT EVIL

There are more things in heaven and earth, Horatio,
Than are dreamt of in your philosophy.
—William Shakespeare, *Hamlet*

As a motor of association, love is the power of the common in a double sense: both the power that the common exerts and the power to constitute the common. It is thus also the movement toward freedom in which the composition of singularities leads toward not unity or identity but the increasing autonomy of each participating equally in the web of communication and cooperation. Love is the power of the poor to exit a life of misery and solitude, and engage the project to make the multitude. As we continue our study, we will have to identify how this march of freedom and equality can be made lasting, strengthened, and consolidated in the formation of social and political institutions.

All of this sounds good, you might say, for a political theory designed for angels, not humans, but people do not always act on the basis of love, and they often destroy the common. Is it not more realistic, then, rather than assuming that humans are fundamentally good, to conceive of them as fundamentally evil? Indeed such a "realist" or, really, pessimistic position is the dominant view in Euro-Atlantic political philosophy, from Thomas Hobbes's notion of a "war of all against all" to Helmuth Plessner's proposition of a political anthropology in which humans are characterized by "potentially unlimited intraspecies aggressiveness."[1] From this perspective, a political anthropology based on love, which does not take into account the evil that lurks in human hearts, is naïve at best. Believing that people are what we want them to be and that human nature is fundamentally good is dangerous, in fact, because it undermines the political and conceptual tools necessary to confront and restrain evil. By focusing instead on how dangerous humans are, such authors maintain, and specifically on how human nature is characterized by discord, violence, and conflict, such a theory can treat this evil, contain it, and thereby construct a society that holds evil in check.

We agree that a realist perspective, with its mandate for political thought to understand humanity as it is, not as we want it to be, is extremely important. Humans are not naturally good. In the terms we developed in the last chapter, this corresponds to the ambivalence of the common and love, that is, the fact that they can take negative as well as positive forms. And furthermore the spontaneous actions of a multitude of people, as we said, are not necessarily anti-systemic or oriented toward liberation. In fact people often struggle for their servitude, as Spinoza says, as if it were their salvation.[2]

The problem with the pessimistic conceptions of political anthropology, however, is that after justly dismissing any fundamental goodness, they pose evil as an equally fundamental, invariable element of human nature. Evil is posed by some in religious terms as transcendent (sin, for example) and by others as a transcendental element (a radical evil that marks a limit of human society). Saint Paul manages to grasp these two formulations in a single verse: "I would not have known sin except through law" (Romans 7:7). If evil is radical, then one must try to neutralize and contain it; even if evil and sin are recognized as "necessary illusions" that result from the "sleep of reason," as Kant says, they must be regulated. The form of law (and thus the practices and theoretical mechanisms that grant law the function of controlling the entire set of social behaviors according to a priori norms) has always in this metaphysical frame constituted the transcendental complement of an ontology of radical evil.[3] In most political discussions, though, metaphysical foundations are not required. The evil in human nature is simply confirmed empirically: look at all the evil that humans have done and continue to do every day—the wars, the cruelty, the suffering! This amounts to something like a secular theodicy: How can humans be good when there is so much evil in the world and when they so often act in evil ways? Whether on religious, philosophical, and/or empirical bases, then, pessimistic political anthropologies treat evil as an invariant feature of human nature, which must be constantly restrained and contained in society.

What we are confronting here, though, is a poorly posed question. It is a mistake to ask whether human nature is good or evil, first of all, because good and evil are contingent evaluations, not invariants. They are judgments that arise after the exercise of the will. Spinoza, for example, like Nietzsche after him, explains that humans do not strive for something because they deem it good but instead deem it good because they strive for it. Foucault poses Spinoza's point in more clearly political terms when he claims, in a debate with Noam Chomsky, that the question of justice—just war in this case—arises only after political action: the proletariat does not make war on the ruling class because it considers that war just but rather considers class war just because it wants to overthrow the ruling class.[4] To say that good and evil, like just and unjust, are relative terms that depend on relations of force is not to say that they do not exist, but rather simply that they are not fixed, invariable foundations.

Whether human nature is good or evil is a poorly posed question also because basing the analysis of political anthropology on invariants of any sort leads to a dead end. The question is not what invariant defines human nature, in other words, but *what human nature can become.* The most important fact about human nature (if we still want to call it that) is that it can be and is constantly being transformed. A realist political anthropology must focus on this process of metamorphosis. This brings us back to the issue of making the multitude, through organization and self-transformation. Questions of good and evil can only be posed after the making of the multitude is initiated, in the context of its project.

By arguing against the fixity of evil in human nature, we do not intend to make it impossible to use the term. Evil does exist. We see it all around us. But the problem of evil has to be posed in such as way that its genealogy can be understood, thereby giving us a key to combating it. The pessimistic view of political anthropology registers the existence of evil but by treating it as an invariant blocks any attempt to understand its genesis: evil just is.

Our proposition for political anthropology is to conceive of evil as a derivative and distortion of love and the common. Evil is the corruption of love that creates an obstacle to love, or to say the same thing with a different focus, evil is the corruption of the common that blocks its production and productivity. Evil thus has no originary or primary existence but stands only in a secondary position to love. We spoke earlier of corruptions of love in racisms, nationalisms, populisms, and fascisms; and we similarly analyzed not only the destruction of the common through capitalist expropriation and privatization but also institutionalized corruptions of the common in the family, the corporation, and the nation. This double position of evil as corruption and obstacle presents us with some initial criteria for our investigation.

Having posed the problem of evil in this way allows us to return to Spinoza's conception, which served us as the model for a politics of love. We should start with this typically Spinozian geometrical sequence: at the level of sensations he identifies a striving *(conatus)* of and for life; this striving is built upon and directed in desire *(cupiditas),* which functions through the affects: and desire in turn is strengthened and affirmed in love *(amor),* which operates in reason. The movement of this sequence involves not negation—striving is not negated by desire, or desire by love—but rather a progressive accumulation, such that desire and love are increasingly powerful strivings for life. And this process is immediately political since the object of all the terms of this sequence is the formation of collective social life and, more generally, the constitution of the common. "Since fear of solitude exists in all men," Spinoza writes, "because no one in solitude is strong enough to defend himself, and procure the necessaries of life, it follows that men naturally aspire to the civil state; nor can it happen that men should ever utterly dissolve it."[5] This passage resembles those of other seventeenth- and eighteenth-century authors who theorize the negation of the state of nature in the formation of society, but the key difference is that Spinoza poses this as a positive, cumulative progression: the striving toward freedom and the common resides at the most basic level of life; then desire sets in motion the construction of the common; and finally love consolidates the common institutions that form society. Human nature is not negated but transformed in this sequence.

Spinoza, however, is the ultimate realist. He recognizes that the social construction of the common through love does not function unimpeded and that humans are the authors of the obstacles. On the surface his explanation is that humans create these impediments and evil in general out of ignorance, fear, and superstition. Since to combat evil, then, one must overcome ignorance and fear and destroy superstition, education in the truth of the intellect and the correct exercise of the will are the antidotes to evil. But any Stoic could tell us that! Spinoza's difference resides at a deeper level where the education or training of the mind and body are grounded in the movement of love. He does not conceive evil, as does Augustine, for instance, as a privation of being; nor does he pose it as a lack of love. Evil instead is love gone bad, love corrupted in such a way that it obstructs the functioning of love. Consider ignorance, fear, and superstition, then, not just as the lack of intelligence but as the power of intelligence turned against itself, and equally the power of the body distorted and blocked. And since love is ultimately the power of the creation of the common, evil is the dissolution of the common or, really, its corruption.

This gives us a Spinozian explanation for why at times people fight for their servitude as if it were their salvation, why the poor sometimes support dictators, the working classes vote for right-wing parties, and abused spouses and children protect their abusers. Such situations are obviously the result of ignorance, fear, and superstition, but calling it false consciousness provides meager tools for transformation. Providing the oppressed with the truth and instructing them in their interests does little to change things. People fighting for their servitude is understood better as the result of love and community gone bad, failed, and distorted. The first question to ask when confronting evil, then, is, *What specific love went bad here? What instance of the common has been corrupted?* People are powerfully addicted to love gone bad and corrupt forms of the common. Often, sadly, these are the only instances of love and the common they know! In this context it makes sense that Spinoza thinks of ethics in a medical framework—curing the ills of the body and mind, but more important, identifying how our intellectual and corporeal powers have been corrupted, turned against themselves, become self-destructive. Maybe this ethical and political therapeutic model explains why Freud was so fascinated by Spinoza.

But this is not only a therapeutic model. Ethics and politics come together in an "ontology of force," which eliminates the separation between love and force that so many metaphysical, transcendental, and religious perspectives try to enforce. From a materialist perspective instead, love is the propositional and constituent key to the relationship between being and force, just as force substantiates love's powers. Marx, for example, speaks of the "winning smiles" of matter and its "sensuous, poetic glamour," writing, "In Bacon [and in the Renaissance in general] materialism still holds back within itself in a naïve way the germs of a many-sided development." These forms of matter are "forces of being," endowed with "an impulse, a vital spirit, a tension," even a "torment of matter."[6] There is something monstrous in the relationship between love and force! But that *monstruum,* the overflowing force that embodies the relationship between self and others, is the basis of every social institution. We have already seen how Spinoza poses the development of institutions in the movement from the materiality of *conatus* or striving all the way to rational, divine love, composing isolated singularities in the multitude. We find something similar, albeit from a completely different perspective, in Wittgenstein's meditations on pain, which is incommunicable except though constructing a common linguistic experience and, ultimately, instituting common forms of life. Spinozian solitude and Wittgensteinian pain, which are both signs of a lack of being, push us toward the common. Force and love construct together weapons against the corruption of being and the misery it brings.[7]

Love is thus not only an ontological motor, which produces the common and consolidates it in society, but also an open field of battle. When we think of the power of love, we need constantly to keep in mind that there are no guarantees; there is nothing automatic about its functioning and results. Love can go bad, blocking and destroying the process. The struggle to combat evil thus involves a training or education in love.

To clarify, then, we should individuate and bring together three operations or fields of activity for the power of love. First, and primarily, the power of love is the constitution of the common and ultimately the formation of society. This does not mean negating the differences of social singularities to form a uniform society, as if love were to mean merging in unity, but instead composing them in social relation and in that way constituting the common. But since the process of love can be diverted toward the production of corrupt forms of the common, since love gone bad creates obstacles that block and destroy the common—in some cases reducing the multiplicity of the common to identity and unity, in others imposing hierarchies within common relations—the power of love must also be, second, a force to combat evil. Love now takes the form of indignation, disobedience, and antagonism. Exodus is one means we identified earlier of combating the corrupt institutions of the common, subtracting from claims of identity, fleeing from subordination and servitude. These two first guises of the power of love—its powers of association and rebellion, its constitution of the common and its combat against corruption—function together in the third: making the multitude. This project must bring the process of exodus together with an organizational project aimed at creating institutions of common. And all three of these guises are animated by the training or *Bildung* of the multitude. There is nothing innate or spontaneous about love going well and realizing the common in lasting social forms. The deployment of love has to be learned and new habits have to be formed through the collective organization of our desires, a process of sentimental and political education. Habits and practices consolidated in new social institutions will constitute our now transformed human nature.

It should be clear at this point that love always involves the use of force or, more precisely, that the actions of love are themselves deployments of force. Love may be an angel, but if so it is an angel armed. We saw earlier that the constitutive power of love and its creation of the common imply what we might call an ontological force involved in the production of being, the production of reality. The combative figure of love's force becomes clearer, though, when we focus on the revolt against and exodus from hierarchical institutions and the corruptions of the common. And furthermore making the multitude and forming its institutions of the common entail what might be called a constituent political force. But really these three forces of love are not separate. They are merely different guises of love's power.

The link between love and force, we should be clear, does not come with any guarantees either. We know that the racial, patriarchal, identitarian, and other corruptions of love are not lacking in force. In fact they often wield a surplus of force as if to cover over their deviation from love's dedication to the common. Is the force of love, then, indistinguishable from the force of its corruptions? No; worrying about the use of force in this way is a false scrupulousness. We can easily enumerate several criteria available for distinguishing love's force. First, the content of the link between love and force is the common, which composes the interaction of singularities in processes of social solidarity and political equality. Second, the direction of love's force is oriented toward the freedom of those singularities. Third, the organizational forms of this exercise of force are always open, constitutive, and horizontal, such that every time it is solidified in fixed vertical relations of power, love exceeds it and overflows its limits, reopening organization again to the participation of all. Fourth, the relation between love and force is legitimated in the consensus of singularities and the autonomy of each, in a relationship of reciprocity and collective self-rule. Fifth, this force is always directed toward consolidating this process in institutions that can allow it to continue ever more powerfully. And the list could go on.

The real difficulties are not at the conceptual level of distinguishing criteria but in the political field where we must conduct the battle. Even when we understand clearly the powers of love and its corruptions, even when we face with open eyes the evil in our societies, the love gone bad and the corrupt forms of the common to which we and others are addicted, there is no guarantee of success. Giacomo Leopardi, in his famous poem *Lenta ginestra,* captures the fragility of love and the singularities struggling in common against the seemingly ineluctable destiny of death and destruction. The looming volcano Vesuvius towers above threateningly, but the delicate flowers of the Scotch broom continue indefatigably to push up its slopes. It would be easy to enter the struggle if we were guaranteed victory beforehand. Leopardi celebrates the fact that love constantly battles, regardless of the enormity of the forces stacked against us. Victory is possible and fear of the volcano defeated only when hope is organized to construct human community.[8]

Finally, let us return to the pessimistic political anthropologies we set out from in order to emphasize the political difference marked by our conception of evil and the means to combat it. Even among authors whose work is very close to ours, we recognize a recent tendency to link a notion of evil as an invariant of human nature to a politics aimed at restraining evil. One fascinating occasion for developing this line of reasoning is a passage in Paul's epistles that proposes the figure of the *katechon* (the one that restrains). The *katechon,* Paul explains, restrains "the lawless one," a satanic figure, and thus holds off the apocalypse until its proper time (2 Thessalonians 2:1–12). This mysterious "restrainer" has generally been interpreted in Christian theology as a sovereign power: in the early Christian era Tertullian identifies the *katechon* as the Roman Empire, and in the twentieth century Carl Schmitt proposes that it is a Christian Empire. Regardless of the specific referent, these authors concur that the *katechon* is a lesser evil that protects us against a greater one. This notion corresponds perfectly to the implications of a pessimistic political anthropology. If we accept that evil or intraspecies aggressiveness or some such element is an invariant of human nature, then restraining evil will be one if not *the* central task of politics, limiting us to a politics of the "lesser evil."[9]

Our conception of evil as a corruption of and obstacle to love in the creation of the common leads instead to a politics of not restraining but combating evil. Since evil is secondary to love, we are not limited to external containment but have access to its inner mechanisms. Love is the battlefield for the struggle against evil. Moreover, the primacy of love indicates the power we have in this fight. If evil were primary, we would be helpless against it. We would need to trust in an Empire to restrain it and hold death at bay. But since evil derives from love, the power of evil is necessarily less. Love is stronger than death. And thus acting through love we have the power to combat evil. Such a politics of love has no need to accept the rule of a lesser evil. This is not to say we should imagine we can defeat evil once and for all—no, the corruptions of love and the common will continue. What it means, though, is that the battle is ours to fight and win.

In the second half of this book, from this point on, we seek to discover within the movements of the multitude the mechanisms of the common that produce new subjectivity and form institutions. But before leaving this discussion we should consider one terrible historical experience of the relation between love and force in the socialist and Bolshevik conceptions of the party. The premise is rational and understandable: nothing is possible when we are isolated and only unity makes effective and multiplies the value of indignation and individual revolt. Militants thus go forward hand in hand to create a compact group, armed with knowledge and passion. That would be the spark to transform society. The conclusion, though, is false: surreptitiously but implacably the party's determinations of norms and measures, its decisions (even the right to life and death) become separated from the experience of the movements and absorbed by the logic of capitalist alienation, turning bureaucratic and tyrannical. What should give force to multiplicity is transformed into the violence of identity. Unity is projected as a transcendent value, and the slogan of revolution serves to corrupt the common. No, the party will not defeat evil. Today the memory of that corruption only pushes us further to discover a force to combat evil.

PART 4

EMPIRE RETURNS

And perhaps the great day will come when a people, distinguished by wars and victories and by the highest development of a military order and intelligence, and accustomed to make the heaviest sacrifices for these things, will exclaim of its own free will, "We break the sword," and will smash its entire military establishment down to its lowest foundations.

—Friedrich Nietzsche, *Human, All Too Human*

4.1

———————

BRIEF HISTORY OF A FAILED COUP D'ÉTAT

————————————

> We shall run the world's business whether the world likes it or not.
> The world can't help it—and neither can we, I guess.
> —Joseph Conrad, *Nostromo*

Let the Dead Bury the Dead

The most significant event of the first decade of the new millennium for geopolitics may be the definitive failure of unilateralism. At the end of the last millennium a genuinely new global situation had emerged, which set in motion new processes of governance and began to establish new structures of global order. A new Empire was being formed that was qualitatively different from the previously existing imperialisms, which had been based primarily on the power of nation-states. Instead of engaging directly the formation of Empire, however, the dominant forces on the global scene, the U.S. government in particular, denied and repressed the novelty, conjuring up specters from the past, forcing dead figures of political rule to stumble across the stage and replay outdated dreams of grandeur. Ambitions of imperialist conquest, nationalist glory, unilateral decision making, and global leadership were all revived, with horrifyingly real violence. Within the United States, where these fantasies were most powerful, what had seemed in the past to be alternatives—isolationism, imperialism, and internationalism—were resuscitated and woven together, turning out merely to be different faces of the same project, all stitched together with the thread of U.S. exceptionalism. It took only a few years, though, for these ghostly figures to collapse in a lifeless heap. The financial and economic crisis of the early twenty-first century delivered the final blow to U.S. imperialist glory. By the end of the decade there was general recognition of the military, political, and economic failures of unilateralism.[1] There is no choice now but to confront head-on the formation of Empire.

The decade put an end to dreams of a unipolar world. The conventional narrative of international relations scholars is that the twentieth century witnessed a major transformation from a multipolar world ruled by a set of dominant nation-states—which traces its roots back to the Peace of Westphalia but emerged in truly global form through the European, U.S., and Japanese imperialist projects—to the bipolar world defined by the two cold war superpowers. The collapse of the Soviet Union and the end of the cold war opened an alternative, in the minds of many scholars and policymakers, between a return to some form of multipolarity or the creation of a unipolar system centered on the United States, the sole superpower, a single imperialist with no competitors or peers. The attempt and failure to establish U.S. hegemony and unilateral rule in the course of the decade, however, proved the vision of a unipolar world to be an illusion. At this point even the strategists of U.S. power are beginning to recognize that what the collapse of unipolarity signals is not a return to any previous bipolar or multipolar arrangement but the emergence of a new order. "At first glance," explains Richard Haass, former director of policy planning at the U.S. State Department,

> the world today may appear to be multipolar. The major powers—China, the European Union (EU), India, Japan, Russia, and the United States—contain just over half the world's people and account for 75 percent of global GDP and 80 percent of global defense spending. Appearances, however, can be deceiving. Today's world differs in a fundamental way from one of classic multipolarity: there are many more power centers, and quite a few of these poles are not nation-states. Indeed,

one of the cardinal features of the contemporary international system is that nation-states have lost their monopoly on power and in some domains their preeminence as well. States are being challenged from above, by regional and global organizations; from below, by militias; and from the side, by a variety of nongovernmental organizations (NGOs) and corporations. Power is now found in many hands and in many places.

According to Haass, therefore, none of the conventional geometries—unipolar, bipolar, or multipolar—adequately describes the emerging global order. "The principal characteristic of twenty-first-century international relations," he continues, "is turning out to be nonpolarity: a world dominated not by one or two or even several states but rather by dozens of actors possessing and exercising various kinds of power. This represents a tectonic shift from the past."[2] It has now become uncontroversial, even commonplace, to pose the contemporary global order, which has in fact been forming since the end of the cold war, as characterized by a distribution of powers, or more precisely a form of network power, which requires the wide collaboration of dominant nation-states, major corporations, supranational economic and political institutions, various NGOs, media conglomerates, and a series of other powers. It is quickly becoming common sense, in other words, that the problem of the twenty-first century is the problem of Empire.[3]

Was it a lost decade, then? After this detour through resurrected imperialist adventures and unilateral pretenses, which "perfected" the imperialist machine only to demonstrate its definitive obsolescence, are we right back where we were before? We need to look a bit more closely at the failures of unilateralism and the impossibility of multilateralism to see how the formation of Empire has proceeded through this process—both how its shape has clarified and how it has moved in new directions.

The attempt to create a unipolar order centered on the United States was really a coup d'état within the global system, that is, a dramatic subordination of all the "aristocratic" powers of the emerging imperial order, such as the other dominant nation-states and the supranational institutions, in order to elevate the "monarchical" power of the United States. The coup d'état was an effort to transform the emerging form of Empire back into an old imperialism, but this time with only one imperialist power. The primary events and ultimate failure of the coup have by now been thoroughly chronicled by journalists and scholars. Plans for a "New American Century" were in place well before the attacks on the World Trade Center and the Pentagon on September 11, 2001, but every coup needs a trigger, a catastrophic event that legitimates taking the reins of power. The rhetoric of a "war on terror" justified a state of emergency in the imperial system, and the coup was set in motion in the attempt to concentrate the powers of the global order in the hands of the United States, establishing unilateral control, raising or lowering the status of nation-states according to their alignment with the will of Washington, undermining the capacities and autonomy of the international and supranational institutions, and so forth. On the emerging imperial system was imposed a central authority through which all global decisions were to pass. The invasions and occupations of Afghanistan and Iraq were the centerpiece, but the coup also involved a series of economic and political operations at various levels in the global system. The military failures were thus the most visible but by no means the only measure of the collapse of the coup. From this perspective, then, it is not true, as so many tirelessly repeat, that everything changed on September 11. The rhetoric of a historic break facilitated the forces of the coup, but we can see clearly now, after the coup has failed and the dust cleared, that the attacks and the subsequent unilateralist adventures, however horrifying and tragic, were not in fact moments of radical change but steps in the formation of Empire.[4]

It is no coincidence that in the heady early days of the coup some of the planners and supporters began to sing the praises of past imperialist formations, especially those of the United States and Britain. Whereas for several decades the term "imperialist" had functioned as an insult across the political spectrum almost comparable to the accusation of "fascist," suddenly a small but significant group of pundits and politicians publicly embraced imperialism! Others, even when shying away from using the term, resurrected all the conventional apologies for imperialism: its ability to remake the global environment, its civilizing influence, its moral superiority, and so forth. More prudent scholars and policymakers accepted as given the coup d'état and its success but warned against its excesses and sought to make its reign more humane and long-lasting. Typical of this effort were the various discussions of hegemony that cautioned against the dangers of relying too heavily on "hard power" and recommended strong doses of "soft power."[5] Running throughout these various positions, however, despite their differences, was an imperialist conception of political order.

The visionaries most dedicated to the coup and most convinced of its success were the so-called neoconservatives, a much-publicized group of journalists, pseudo-academics, and government officials who have a strong presence in the mainstream and conservative sectors of the U.S. media. These ideologues are "idealists" in the sense that they share a vision of a global political order in which the United States holds overwhelming power, unilaterally decides political issues for other nations, and thereby guarantees global peace. And they are equally apocalyptic, warning about the dire consequences of not following their dictates. "There is no middle way for Americans" in the war on terror, write David Frum and Richard Perle ominously. "It is victory or holocaust."[6] These ideologues are fundamentally against Empire—against, that is, collaboration with the wide network of powers in the emerging imperial formation—and for imperialism. Their war cry, in effect, is "Imperialism or death!"

Though long on vision, neoconservatives are remarkably short on substance. In their hubris they pay little attention to the necessary bases for exercising imperialist power and maintaining unilateral hegemony. Their plans rely heavily on military power, but they fail to invent or develop new military capacities, putting their faith simply in a strategic transformation, as we will see in the next section. They show astonishingly little concern, furthermore, for economic planning. At times they ally themselves with proponents of neoliberal economics, but that remains peripheral to their vision. The essence of their agenda is political: establishing and exercising the unilateral capacity of the United States to "shape the global environment," to organize and dictate global political affairs. Even in the political realm, though, neoconservatives disregard the need to gain moral and political authority. They seem to take for granted that nation-states and other significant powers will unquestioningly consent to the wishes of Washington. The neoconservatives, in short, strike the pose of the great British imperialists of a bygone era, but without the substance to support their dreams—without the force to maintain domination or the consent to sustain hegemony—they strike only a farcical figure.[7] They embarked on a very strange project: to assert hegemony without concern for, and even scorning the necessary prerequisites for, that hegemony itself.

After the failure of the coup d'état became apparent, the neoconservatives scattered into separate camps. The most intelligent and most opportunistic try to save their careers by shifting their positions—for example, reasserting the power of nation-states for global order—and claiming they never really agreed with the coup in the first place. The hardliners instead remain convinced of the vision and simply blame the Bush administration or others for carrying it out poorly, focusing most often on military errors made in Iraq.[8] The coup did not, of course, fail only because of incompetence. U.S. unilateralism and its imperialist projects were already dead before the coup forced them to their feet to thrash about for a few bloody years. Perhaps the neoconservative ideologues are the adequate gravediggers for an ideology that was already defunct.

One other oddly symmetrical historical anomaly of this period is the explosion of scholarly and popular books on the Left that analyzed the coup as a return to imperialism. For a couple of years, roughly from 2003 to 2005, such books dominated the shelves of bookstores. There is no new world order, they explain, no new form of Empire, and thus (what a relief!) no need for new concepts and theories. Global order and domination continue to be defined, as they were throughout the twentieth century, by U.S. imperialism. These arguments are correct on the surface, of course, since the coup was indeed an attempt to resurrect imperialism, but profoundly mistaken in substance. The tradition of dead generations still weighs like a nightmare on the brain of the living. In effect these scholars were duped by the boasting of the instigators of the coup, accepting at face value their resurrected figures and pretenses to imperialist power. Such theories of a new (or not so new) U.S. imperialism are really an inverted repetition of U.S. exceptionalism, such that the United States is an exception here not, as the U.S. celebrants and apologists would have it, because of its virtue and vocation for freedom and democracy but rather because of its will to dominate, and moreover, since many nation-states share that will, its power to do so. The time has come, though, to let the dead bury the dead.[9]

The Exhaustion of U.S. Hegemony

Now that the coup d'état has failed and the attempt to establish the unilateral control of the United States over global affairs has been all but aborted, we need to detail the breakdown in military, economic, political, and moral affairs in order to analyze the current state in which this leaves the imperial system. The military failure is most visible and dramatic. The invasion of Afghanistan and the quick collapse of the Taliban government were really only a prelude. Iraq would be the proving ground where the United States demonstrates it can "go it alone," in defiance of the United Nations and some of its primary traditional allies. Baghdad is conquered quickly with little resistance, forces of the United States and its allies spread throughout the national territory, and a U.S. occupying administration is established. By the summer of 2003 the mission has been accomplished: unilateral military power has proved its effectiveness, and the coup d'état seems to stand on firm ground. The victor starts looking around for new arenas (Syria? Iran?) in which to exert its power.

Over the course of the next few years, however, the presumed military victory is swept away: at first with drips and drops of resistance to the occupation forces, then periodic showers, and finally massive downpours. Afghanistan, which was once reported to be successfully under the control of the occupying forces and the appointed government, is soon revealed to be rocked by serious conflicts. In Iraq the occupying military forces and their counterparts in the newly created Iraqi government are forced into the position of the boy with his finger in the dike. As death tolls rise, so do the possibilities of a flood and unrestricted civil war. The eventual "surge" of U.S. forces and decline of violence in Iraq cannot change the fact that has been revealed. On the proving ground of Iraq, unilateral military power has not demonstrated its ability to create and guarantee global order but has, on the contrary, shown its complete inability to do so. Even if the United States eventually declares victory, unilateralism was defeated in Iraq.

In retrospect the failure in Iraq highlights two well-established truths of military thought. The first demonstrates the necessary size and composition of a conquering and occupying army. A primary element of the unilateral project in Iraq was the military strategy often referred to as the "revolutionary in military affairs" (RMA) or "defense transformation." This strategy, which was most publicly supported at the time by U.S. Secretary of Defense Donald Rumsfeld, often against the objections of generals and the military establishment, is based on two primary strategic innovations: reducing troop levels through the coordinated use of information and weapons technologies in combat; and reorganizing military formations to make them lighter, more mobile, and more flexible. The 2003 "victory of Baghdad" and the seeming success of this strategy briefly inspired dreams of cyborg and robot armies that could vanquish enemies with no soldiers lost (no U.S. soldiers, that is). As Iraqi resistance grew, however, the effectiveness of the strategy was quickly undermined. It became obvious that the relatively small army organized in technologically equipped mobile units is a powerful offensive weapon but unable to defend established positions, or rather, in journalistic jargon, it can win the war but not the peace. The traditional view that occupations require large numbers returned as common sense. By early 2007, with Rumsfeld ousted as secretary of defense, the U.S. government effectively abandons the core strategies of the "revolutionary in military affairs" and begins instead a dramatic escalation of troops in Iraq.[10]

A second traditional military view reconfirmed by the defeat in Iraq highlights the vast difference in subjectivity on the two sides of conflict. Armed resistance, particularly armed resistance against an occupying army, is a terrific engine of the production of subjectivity. The occupation creates an extraordinary willingness among Iraqis to risk harm and death, sometimes taking horrible, barbaric forms. It teaches us, once again, that the presence of the occupier is sufficient to produce resistance. For the occupying army, however, there is no such production of subjectivity, regardless of all the ideological campaigns to link the war to the September 11 attacks and, more generally, to create "terrorism" or radical Islam as a unified global enemy. At certain points in the past, patriotism enabled a production of subjectivity that could support a foreign war effort, but today the effectiveness of that mechanism is limited. Occupying armies now tend, in one way or another, to be populated by mercenaries. Machiavelli recognized long ago the superiority of a "people in arms" to any mercenary army because of the production of subjectivity that drives it. And no technological advantage will ever address that subjective imbalance.

These two obstacles for U.S. unilateralist military strategy—the limitations of technological transformations and the imbalance in subjectivity—coincide powerfully in urban warfare. Military strategists are well aware that insurgencies and resistances will increasingly be located in metropolises and that the technological apparatus mobilized by the RMA is ill equipped for this environment.[11] In the labyrinthine passageways of the urban landscape it is difficult to fight and kill at a distance. The metropolis is also a factory for the production of subjectivity, as we argue in *De Corpore* 2 at the end of this section of the book. The well-established spaces of the common, the circuits of communication, and the social habits that form the metropolis serve as powerful multipliers of the production of subjectivity in resistance. A metropolis can ignite overnight, and the blazes stubbornly refuse to be extinguished.

Defeat in one campaign, of course, does not disprove a military strategy. Some are bound to say that the fiasco was due merely to tactical errors, such as dismissing former Baath Party officials, disbanding the Iraqi military, or failing to counter the resistance quickly enough. We can rest assured, too, that the strategists in the U.S. military and its allied think tanks are busy working—with the aid of abstract theories and video game simulations—to reformulate the RMA for urban environments and achieve goals like "persistent area dominance" through technological and strategic innovations.[12] Israeli military theorists also are hard at work developing effective strategies to control urban environments without exposing troops to risk.[13] It is already clear, though, that regardless of future innovations and refinements, this strategy cannot support a unilateral military project of the United States.

The primary architects of the U.S. war in Iraq may be naïve or inexpert military strategists, but they are undoubtedly lucid political thinkers. They are conscious that large numbers of U.S. casualties are certain to undermine domestic support. They are also thinking ahead, beyond Afghanistan and Iraq, to the future requirements of a unilateral global order. There is no way that the U.S. military can match up to other major powers, such as Russia and China, in the logic of the old military strategy. It simply does not have the numbers. The promise of the new strategy is that it can overcome the numerical imbalance and turn asymmetry to its advantage. Such a technological-strategic advantage, its authors believe, is the only hope for creating long-lasting unilateral military control. Although they answer the needs of the political logic, however, these strategies have proved unable to hold up militarily, even against relatively small, poorly equipped militias like those in Afghanistan and Iraq.

The international political hegemony of the United States has also rapidly declined during the period of the coup and its failure. Some of the architects of the 2003 Iraq invasion probably did expect U.S. tanks to be greeted in Baghdad with flowers and kisses and, moreover, other nation-states to be grateful to the United States for taking leadership in the war. It will soon be hard to remember that during significant periods of the twentieth century, especially during the most intense years of the cold war, the United States enjoyed a hegemonic position in many parts of the world. The ideological explanation of U.S. hegemony has been predicated on the notion that the United States acts consistently, both domestically and abroad, to promote and defend freedom and democracy. We know well, however, the long history of the U.S. government undermining democratically elected governments and supporting dictatorships, through overt and covert operations, from Guatemala and Chile to the Philippines and Indonesia.[14] The real cause for consent to U.S. hegemony rested on the fact that other nation-states believed the actions of the United States consistently advanced their own national interests, or rather the interests of those in power. This is a delicate balance, though, because material interests are necessarily coupled with the "idealistic" ideological rationale and cannot survive without it.[15] As Cicero said of Rome, U.S. global leadership often sounded to its allies more like *patrocinium* than *imperium*.

The photos of Abu Ghraib prison can serve as a symbol for the erosion of the moral and political authority of the United States and the inversion of its image from defender of freedom and democracy to violator of basic rights and international law. For decades, of course, critical voices have protested the way the U.S. military has trained death squads and encouraged the use of torture. The photos of U.S. soldiers torturing and mocking prisoners in Iraq, however, completely shattered what remained of its virtuous image, shifting focus to the widespread use of terror and torture as a political and military tool by the United States, in Guantanamo and other irregular prisons, and underlining the fact that the U.S. government approves and promotes the use of torture in violation of international law. "We are in danger of losing something much more important than just the war in Iraq," Thomas Friedman warns after the publication of the Abu Ghraib photos. "We are in danger of losing America as an instrument of moral authority and inspiration in the world."[16] The United States is certainly not the greatest violator of rights or proponent of torture, but its image can no longer function as a paradigm for the promotion of rights and law, freedom and democracy.

The ideological cover of U.S. hegemony probably wore thin, we suspect, because its substance had already emptied out. Other powers had determined, in other words, that the international action of the United States—its wars, its unilateral adventures, its economic models, and so forth—no longer consistently advanced their own interests. We will have to analyze this shift more closely in the next section in terms of economic interests, but for the moment it is sufficient to recognize how the failure of the coup d'état coincides with the decline of the hard and soft power of the United States, that is, the defeat of its military strategy and the collapse of its moral and political authority.

What Is a Dollar Worth?

The breakdown of U.S. unilateralism and the failure of the United States' attempted coup d'état within the imperial system is not merely a function of military might or strategy. Together with political and moral authority, economic strength is part of the "soft power" necessary for hegemony. The economic, military, and political/moral aspects of the unilateralist project operate according to independent logics but mutually reinforce one another, bolstering one another during the ascent of power and dragging one another down in decline. In the broadest terms, the success of hegemonic power in the economic sphere, at least in contemporary capitalist conditions, rests on its ability to guarantee profits on a general level among capitalists, not only for its own national interests but also for those of its allied powers. Gauging economic hegemony is certainly an inexact science, but we can read symptoms from a variety of arenas in a growing chorus of "no confidence" votes for unilateral U.S. economic control.

Although the military defeat of the United States in Iraq is most visible, its economic failure is perhaps more significant and provides a powerful illustration of the impossibility of the unilateralist project. Control of Iraqi oil reserves is undoubtedly important, but the primary economic objective of the occupation was to conduct a radical experiment in neoliberal transformation.[17] The occupation administration in Iraq led by Paul Bremer was given the charge to destroy the existing social structures of the Iraqi economy, including labor rights, state-owned industries, and welfare systems—raze the economic terrain, so to speak, create a clean slate, and from there, from point zero, invent a pure neoliberal economy. Bremer's regime, however, was thwarted by a variety of stiff economic resistances (in addition to its own incompetence). It quickly learned the difficulty of privatizing the economic goods of the country and selling them to foreign corporations. Foreign corporations are reluctant to buy, on the one hand, because the continuing violence in the country makes business all but impossible and, on the other, because they fear that international law will not recognize as legitimate their ownership of national industries and resources sold by an occupying regime. Creation of a pure neoliberal economy also proved impossible because Iraqi workers resist privatization. Naomi Klein reports, in fact, that some workers fired from state industries immediately enlisted in the military resistance. In addition to failing militarily in Iraq, then, the U.S. unilateral project failed economically—failed, that is, to create a new economic regime that could generate and guarantee profits. Iraq is an example of the general strategy of radical neoliberal transformation coupled with U.S. military control and political hegemony in the unilateralist project.[18]

The essential question, although it is impossible to answer directly in a satisfactory way, is whether U.S. unilateralism—with its "war on terror," its political hegemony, and its economic policies—is good for business and favors the profits of global capital. That is not to ask, obviously, whether it favors a handful of specific corporations, such as Halliburton or Bechtel, but whether it benefits collective capital as a whole. One useful way to approach this question is to focus on the abilities of the United States to impose its wishes on the other nation-states in international economic agreements. The

United States, in fact, is experiencing increasing difficulty gaining consent to its economic hegemony. There has been mounting resistance, for example, to U.S. proposals at the so-called Doha round of World Trade Organization meetings, beginning in Doha in 2001 and Cancún in 2003, and continuing for several years. Each annual meeting is pronounced a failure when a deadlock develops, most often over farm subsidies in the dominant nations and access to industrial and agricultural markets. The most noteworthy symbolic defeat for the United States in this regard was perhaps its failure to gain Latin American support of the Free Trade Area of the Americas (FTAA) agreement. For so much of the last century Washington could rely on "its backyard" and count on the support of the Latin American nations for its economic projects. At Mar del Plata in 2005, however, Latin American governments were able, at least in part, to declare their independence from U.S. economic hegemony. This is not just a political affirmation of national sovereignty but also and more significantly an indication that the ruling elites of these countries no longer view U.S. hegemony as beneficial to their economic interests. All of these discrete failures, then, these resistances to the will of Washington, from Baghdad and Doha to Mar del Plata, can be read as a series of votes of "no confidence" in the soft power of the United States—symptoms of the failure of its unilateral economic project.

The most fundamental indicator of international economic hegemony may be the position and function of the national currency. The dominance of the dollar has been demonstrated, for several decades, by its role as the primary currency of exchange and reserve in the global economy, which represented international confidence in the U.S. economy and consent to U.S. economic leadership. This does not mean that the dollar has constantly maintained a high value with respect to other currencies. In fact the manipulation of exchange rates often serves the dominant power as a mechanism to resolve internal economic problems on the international scene. The dollar today does still function as the global currency, but this may be merely an aftereffect of its past glory. "U.S. hegemony, as opposed to sheer domination," writes Giovanni Arrighi, "in all likelihood has already ended; but, just as the pound sterling continued to be used as an international currency three to four decades after the end of British hegemony, so may the dollar."[19] Maybe someday in the future the euro or the yuan or some combination of currencies will ascend to the dominant position, but by that time the dollar's hegemony will already be long past.

The U.S. mortgage crisis beginning in 2007 and the subsequent global financial and economic crises demonstrate some important facets of the current global position of the U.S. economy. On the one hand, it reveals the extent to which the achievements of the New Deal and the welfare structures in the U.S. economy have been dismantled largely by drawing on global finance markets. Globalization has served to stabilize and underwrite U.S. economic policies of privatization. When U.S. homeowners find it impossible to pay their mortgages, on the other hand, it becomes clear how much capitalists throughout the world are affected by the U.S. crisis. The hegemony of the U.S. market, while still attracting global investment, has been dramatically weakened. The value of the dollar depends increasingly on not the productivity of the country of which it is the monetary symbol but the ability to blackmail global finance markets.[20]

The various strands of the failure of the United States' unilateral project came together as a perfect storm in the aftermath of Hurricane Katrina in 2005. The corruption and incompetence of the government agencies charged with responding to the emergency were really just the surface effects of a social structure deprived systematically for years. The effects of failed neoliberal economic projects, which had been felt around the world, now appeared dramatically on domestic soil. The furor caused when some journalists and politicians called the displaced populations "refugees" is indicative of the anxiety aroused by the confusion between inside and outside when U.S. viewers are confronted by images they are accustomed to associating with the subordinate regions of the world. The aftermath of Hurricane Katrina also exposed the continuing racial

divisions of the United States and the strong correspondence between race and poverty. The catastrophe served as a reminder of not
only the high percentage of African Americans living without adequate resources in areas such as Louisiana and Mississippi, but also
how government agencies and the media react differently to different racial populations. In the weeks after the hurricane the racism of
the United States at every level of society, from governmental structures to common prejudices, was vividly on display. Finally, the Katrina disaster marked a turning point in the U.S. population's support for the Iraq war. Some commentators pointed out the direct
connections—money spent on war had deprived the national infrastructure, the Mississippi and Louisiana National Guard deployed in
war zones was unavailable for disaster relief, and so forth—but we
suspect that the connection in public opinion functioned more
powerfully at a more abstract and profound level. By the summer of
2005, just two years after the celebrations of imperialist glory in the
"victory of Baghdad," cracks in the unilateral projects were showing
everywhere, and the disaster following Katrina was confirmation.
Events would drag on for years, but it was already obvious that the
coup d'état had failed.

AFTER U.S. HEGEMONY

> The provinces generally go, in the changes they make, from order to disorder and then pass again from disorder to order, for worldly things are not allowed by nature to stand still.
>
> —Machiavelli, *Florentine Histories*

Interregnum

The failure of the U.S. unilateral project leads many analysts to search about for successor candidates to global hegemony. Will a new caliphate emerge that can order large parts of the globe on the basis of Muslim unity under theocratic control? Will Europe now united reclaim its dominant position and dictate global affairs? Or is the rest of the world just waiting for the moment when China is ready to exert its unilateral hegemony? We find all these notions of "new pretenders to the throne" implausible, however, because they are based on the assumption that the form of global order remains imperialist and that, although the United States is incapable of achieving unilateral hegemony, some other nation-state or sovereign power is. The breakdown of U.S. unilateralism demonstrates, in our view, the failure not only of a U.S. project but also and more important of unilateralism itself. The form of global order has irreversibly shifted. We are living today in a period of transition, an interregnum in which the old imperialism is dead and the new Empire is still emerging.

Giovanni Arrighi offers one of the most trenchant and astute analyses of the waning of U.S. hegemony. The rising period of a hegemonic power in the global economic system, according to Arrighi's reading of cycles of accumulation, is characterized by steady investment in new productive processes, whereas the shift from production to finance is a symptom of decline. The financialization of the U.S. economy since the 1970s thus signals an "autumnal" phase, parallel in his view to the period of diminishing British economic hegemony almost a century earlier. The military failures of the United States, coordinated with its retreating economic hegemony, are further evidence of decline for Arrighi, such that the Vietnam War, not long after the decoupling of the dollar from the gold standard and the first oil crisis, marked its *signal* crisis and the occupation of Iraq its *terminal* crisis. Arrighi thus hypothesizes that the U.S.-led cycle of global accumulation will be succeeded by a new cycle centered in East Asia (with Japan seen at the helm in his earlier work and China in his more recent). It is a mistake, however, to read Arrighi's argument, even though some elements in his work do point in this direction, as projecting that China or any other nation-state will repeat the form of U.S. hegemony, which itself repeated the British, and further back the Dutch, the Genoese, and the Venetian. Instead the new cycle of accumulation requires a new global political order and a reorganization of the geography and mode of operation of world capital. China will not be the new imperialist power, in other words, and neither will there emerge a global mega-state that repeats the features of nation-state hegemony on a larger scale. The most innovative aspect of Arrighi's analysis, in fact, is his proposal of an emerging "world-market society based on greater equality among the world's civilizations," which he articulates through a creative and attentive reading of Adam Smith. He views the ascent of China most significantly as one piece of the general rise of the subordinated nations as a whole with respect to the dominant, inaugurating a fundamentally new form of accumulation not based on the hegemony of a single nation-state. An important consequence of Arrighi's argument, then, is that the decline of U.S. hegemony marks the end of hegemony based on a single nation-state—in imperialist, unilateralist, and all other forms—over the global economic and political system. The global order that emerges now must take a fundamentally novel form.[21]

The theorists and policymakers previously dedicated to U.S. hegemony who are intelligent enough to recognize this shift are now forced to find another paradigm of global order and confront the threat of global disorder. Their imaginations are so limited, though, that with the collapse of unilateralism to solve the problem of global order, they run quickly back to multilateralism, that is, an international order directed by a limited group of dominant nation-states in collaboration. Henry Kissinger declares it openly: "the world resembles Europe of the seventeenth century; it needs to become Europe of the nineteenth century."[22] In seventeenth-century Europe, before the Thirty Years' War, the world was chaotic. Only the Peace of Westphalia, which brought the war to an end, created a European order, the organizing principle of which was religion and absolute sovereignty. There was thus no international order outside of the agreements among sovereign powers and no structure that exercised power outside of the nation-states. By the nineteenth century, the Westphalian political world had reached its perfection, in Kissinger's view. The only difference desirable today, he adds, would be the disappearance of religion in favor of ideology, and thus the renovation of the plural concert of sovereign states. Even Kissinger recognizes that the sixteenth-century European principle *cuius regio, eius religio,* which links political rule to religious authority, cannot today serve as the foundation of planetary order. He focuses not on any clash of civilizations but on the multilateral concert among nation-states. Francis Fukuyama, having renounced neoconservative, unilateralist dreams, echoes Kissinger in his call for a multilateral order based on the collaboration of strong states. Fukuyama and Kissinger both, however, imagine a multilateral arrangement of states that does not rely on international institutions for support.[23] That is perhaps why Kissinger's imagination goes back to the nineteenth century to describe such an order.

The international system that could sustain a multilateral order has, in fact, completely fallen apart. All the international and supra-

national institutions constructed after 1945 to support the postwar
order are in crisis. With the creation of the United Nations, to take
just one of those, it was thought that an "ought," a juridical *sollen,*
could be constructed internationally and imposed by a concert of
nation-states. Today, however, multilateralist moral obligation has lost
its power. This is not to say that at the foundation of the United Nations the effort to constitutionalize fundamental aspects of the international order was in vain. Despite the injustices that it covered over
and its frequent manipulation by the dominant powers, the United
Nations did succeed at times in imposing a minimal standard of
peace. Consider simply some of the many disasters that the juridical
order of the United Nations dealt with during the cold war: in the
two great crises of 1956, for instance, at Suez and in Hungary, the
United Nations' realistic political orientation helped avoid much
more destructive world explosions. The U.N. order was not a "Holy
Alliance" or an imperial dictatorship but rather an international system of law, contradictory and always open to breakdowns but solid,
in the end, and realistically active. Its beginnings are rooted not really in the nineteenth century but rather in the twentieth-century
defeat of fascism, which unleashed so many democratic aspirations.
But its conditions of effectiveness have been exhausted. The letter
and the spirit of the United Nations Charter are now undone. In
short, a multilateral order, a new Westphalia capable of orchestrating
international agreement and collaboration, is impossible today in
large part because the institutional order on which it would rest—
from the United Nations to the Bretton Woods institutions—is no
longer effective.

The failure of unilateralism, then, cannot lead to the resurgence
of what seemed for a period its primary competitor: multilateralism.
In effect the international system could not survive the United
States' attempted coup d'état. In defeat, Samson pulled his enemies
down with him. But really the international institutions necessary to
support a multilateral order were already tottering before unilateralism dealt the decisive blow. In any case, with unilateralism defeated,
multilateralism and its international structures are not able to re-

spond—on the military, economic, ideological, or legal terrain—to the contemporary challenges. In this context it is thus not even possible to heed Kissinger's call for a return to Westphalia.

Imperial Governance

For those whose political imagination is populated only by previously existing forms of global order, once unilateralism has failed and multilateralism has been revealed as impossible, all that is left is disorder, a war of all against all with a kind of law of the jungle prevailing in global markets. It should be clear, however, that even in a situation of weakened unilateral and multilateral controls, globalization continues. We need to recognize the new forms of management, regulation, and control that are emerging to order the global system. Once we adopt a new perspective, in fact, we can begin to see that there already exists a complex network of global norms, structures, and authorities, which is partial, incomplete, and in some respects fragile but nonetheless real and effective.

Saskia Sassen's precise analyses of the emerging institutional forms of economic and political control give us a firm basis for investigating this new global order. She definitively puts to rest all of those useless debates that pit the continuing importance of nation-states against the processes of globalization as if the two were mutually exclusive. The emerging global order, she argues, is forming not only outside of nation-states but also, and more important, within them, initiating a process of the "denationalization" of certain components of the nation-state that makes them increasingly oriented toward global agendas and systems. The global is within the national, in other words, just as much as the national is within the global. Sassen thus proposes reading the emergent global political and institutional order in terms of assemblages in which "the nation-state and interstate system remain critical building blocks but they are not alone, and are profoundly altered from the inside out."[24] She demonstrates how the conditions of global order have changed such that, on the one hand, neither the United States nor any other pretender to the throne can exercise unilateral control and successfully conduct imperialist projects, and on the other, no multilateral interstate institutional structure can on its own manage and regulate the global system. The assemblages that she sees determining global order are constituted by a mixture of supranational, national, and nonnational institutions and authorities.

A wide variety of authors employ "governance," in contrast to "government," to explore the novelty of these authorities and assemblages forming within and outside the nation-state. The term "global governance" is generally used to refer to regulatory structures that function and produce norms, often in an ad hoc and variable fashion, in the absence of an overarching political authority, such as a hegemonic power or the international system.[25] The two most significant genealogies of the term coincide in some respects but inflect discussions very differently. First, "governance" derives from corporate discourse, where it highlights the structures of authority and the mechanisms of management and accountability typical of capitalist corporations in contrast to state structures. The allusion to corporate management serves, at the minimum, as a means to conceive of global order in a way not limited to state actors, as a hybrid system containing state, corporate, and other ruling bodies.[26] Second, the notion of governance also derives from a philosophical discourse, in particular the work of Michel Foucault and Niklas Luhmann, who, in very different ways, investigate the genealogy of a new concept of government, focusing attention on the creativity determined by the relationship between actors, regulation, and normativity in administrative processes. Luhmann and Foucault both attempt to transcribe traditional concepts of sovereignty and its power of dictation into more flexible structures of decision making and more open processes of negotiation. Governance marks, in this context, an inversion of the direction of political communication: a bottom-up process is substituted for a top-down one, and an inductive procedure replaces the deductive one, as the system's center of gravity shifts toward greater collaboration between state and non-state actors within the decision-making networks at multiple levels.[27]

These two primary genealogies of the concept of governance, the corporate and the philosophical, both help to open a new perspective from which to analyze the contemporary situation. Global governance is not a management model based on the unity of command and legitimation, deriving from a single center of power. It is rather a process of continual negotiation, an arrangement of instruments for consensual planning and coordination in which a multiplicity of state and non-state actors with vastly unequal powers work together. And only the collaboration among these actors can determine the processes of policymaking on the global terrain. The global order today is defined by a varied set of norms, customs, statutes, and laws that constitute a heterogeneous ensemble of demands and powers on the global horizon.

Different scholars develop the notion of governance to construct significantly different models of global order. One model, which derives primarily from economics and finance, focuses on "market values" as the measure of effectiveness in governance. The concrete institutional figures of this continuous activity are those that construct and manage the rules of international economic and social relations. This model conceives of governance as a polycentric and distributed mechanism of regulation enacted by state and non-state institutions but, since it derives primarily from the corporate notion, it generally understands the functions and structures of authority and rule only insofar as they facilitate and support commerce and profits.[28]

A second model, which derives from the neoinstitutional liberal tradition, conceives governance as a machine that can construct, within the relations of interests and jurisdictions, post-sovereign forms of global government. This model should be understood as a departure from, but still closely related to, the realist tradition in international relations, which focuses on states as the primary actors, thus highlighting the ways in which state and interstate institutions continue to function, sometimes transformed, in the new global context. This model proves useful, for example, in the innumerable fields of confrontation and negotiation that are opened domestically and internationally to resolve and regulate local conflicts. Neoinstitutional governance is not limited, though, to such activity but also has recourse to preventive police forces and ad hoc tribunals, and in this way creates a network of effective mechanisms for integrating and deploying governmental structures.[29]

A third model of governance draws on the neocorporative instruments of labor union institutions to manage directly collective interests, which cannot be treated effectively by procedures based at the individual level. Governance here is defined as a process of the self-regulation of exchanges among interests, driven by actors who consent to a plural and polyarchic jurisdiction, constraining states and governmental institutions to recede from the terrain of normative production to that of the production of shared rules, trying to construct, progressively, a single forum for a stable juridical order.[30] This model gives us a much more relevant view than the others for understanding the governance of Empire, which brings together an oligarchy of diverse political and economic bodies, including international institutions, the dominant nation-states, multinational corporations, continental and regional alliances, and so forth, which collaborate to create an open, constituent process. In effect, in light of this model, global capital seems to mix eclectically the Anglo-Saxon "gothic regime" and the Germanic "Puffendorf model" to construct a regulatory structure that articulates capitalist interests and the forces of organized labor with instruments of general mediation. "Trutina Statuum" is what the Duke of Rohan called it in the seventeenth century—a "balance" of states or, really, a mechanism that composes and decomposes the regulatory assemblages of state and non-state actors.[31] This is a far cry from the Hegelian state, which, in the philosophy of absolute spirit, dictates the unified march of history. The contemporary practices and structures of global governance provide instead an extraordinarily plural and flexible process.

All these models propose the idea of governance as a form of pluralistic regulation, which builds from below and is established in a network configured by a variable, multilevel, and/or polycentric geometry. Certainly states (some more than others) continue to be strategic sites where the connections among the diverse infrastructures of global policymaking are achieved, just as the major corporations and multinational firms at times offer (and impose) minimum governance standards of redistribution and social parity, which states have to enact. The various notions of governance thus share an idea of the deconstitutionalization and the governmentalization of *dispositifs* of the production of law that takes command away from sovereignty, makes it adequate to the market, and distributes it among a variety of actors.[32]

No one should confuse this governance, however, with democracy. Yes, it is composed of plural actors, it is relatively flexible and open, and it is formed "from below," at least with respect to the structures of state sovereignty. But its multiplicity is highly restricted to only a privileged set, an oligarchy of powers hierarchically related to one another, and its openness is severely limited by the effects of power and property. Its plurality and openness, in fact, might be best understood in relation to the structures and practices of market exchanges. Global governance is in this sense thoroughly permeated by "postdemocratic" practices of command.

These analyses of global governance should make clear, at the very least, that the ineffectiveness of unilateralist and multilateralist structures does not necessarily leave a power vacuum and chaos. In certain respects, after the failure of the U.S. coup d'état, collective capital has taken the reins of managing the economic, social, political, and military crisis. It is easy to understand at this point how the Empire emerging today might appear to some as a nonpolar world, to use the term we cited earlier. But once we put on a new set of glasses, we can see there is, in fact, a plurality of poles and a flurry of activity constructing assemblages of state and non-state actors, establishing new forms of authority, and determining new norms and practices of regulation and management. In this sense we might say that Davos, site of the annual World Economic Forum, is becoming more important than Washington. The global system is indeed in crisis in that its structures of authority and mechanisms of regulation are partial, often ineffective, and unevenly applied, but this crisis simply marks the interregnum in which the processes of global governance are constituting the infrastructure of the new Empire in formation.

The New Scramble for Africa

Recognizing that imperialism is over and a new imperial order is materializing does not in any way imply the end or even a lessening of division and hierarchy between and within societies. The claim by some proponents of capitalist globalization that the world is becoming "flat," that the global economy is becoming one smooth space and the conditions of economic opportunity and production are becoming more equal across the globe, is pure ideological mystification. The continuing and the new global divisions of labor and power may at times not be located along national boundaries—dividing China from Vietnam, for instance, France from Algeria, or Britain from Nigeria—but in fact the state-centered view of difference and hierarchy proved faulty too in many cases in the past. The important point is that divisions do not decline in the emerging imperial formation but in many cases become more severe. Numerous scholars, anthropologists and geographers foremost among them, demonstrate how the globalizing world is not flat but dramatically uneven, striated by old and new lines of difference and hierarchy.[33]

Most significant with regard to our analysis are the ways that divisions of labor and power serve as mechanisms of social control. Geographical unevenness and divisions still function, as they did in the imperialist era, to preserve hierarchies and displace (and thereby control) social antagonisms. The great imperialist Cecil Rhodes understood these functions well: "My cherished idea is a solution for the social problem, i.e., in order to save the 40,000,000 inhabitants of the United Kingdom from a bloody civil war, we colonial statesmen must acquire new lands to settle the surplus population, to provide new markets for the goods produced by them in the factories and the mines. The Empire, as I have always said, is a bread and butter question. If you want to avoid civil war, you must become imperialists."[34] There are no longer, of course, colonial administrations and colonial territories to maintain these geographical divisions, but the divisions are nonetheless still necessary for capital and its mechanisms of global governance as means to maintain hierarchy and displace social conflict. Sometimes today the unevenness is fit into much more compact areas, traversing the terrain of a single city. Geographical divisions, for example, particularly in Europe, between wealthy white urban centers and poor dark peripheries have developed into one model for creating and maintaining unevenness. The large cities of the Americas, from Los Angeles to Rio, present a different model, with a geographical pattern of divisions less concentrically defined. And the sprawling megalopolises of Lagos and Jakarta pose still other patterns of distribution and division. Divisions of labor and power also function at other scales, up to tracing transnational and intercontinental lines running north-south, east-west, and diagonally too. We do not intend to explore here the cartographies of these uneven developments, although that is an extremely important task. Our point is simply that these divisions remain in the formation of Empire, at times radically reorganized on different scales and often intensified, and that they are still necessary to maintain control, as Rhodes understood, by preserving hierarchy and displacing social conflict.

Recognizing how the present situation differs from Marx's analysis of the gradual historical shift from the formal subsumption of labor under capital to its real subsumption, corresponding to the processes of capitalist globalization, might clarify this point. For Marx subsumption remains *formal* when labor practices and relations created outside of capitalist production are imported intact under its rule. Consider, for instance, how methods of craft production are preserved and brought into manufacturing establishments or how noncapitalist agricultural practices are preserved in forms of capitalist agriculture. The formal subsumption, then, designates phenomena that are both inside and outside of capital. This subsumption becomes *real,* however, when capital creates new labor processes no longer tied to the noncapitalist forms and thus properly capitalist.

The forms of industrial labor produced in the factory are, for Marx, the prime example of real subsumption. Really subsumed labor is no longer at the border between outside and inside capital but wholly inside. Some of the great twentieth-century theorists of imperialism, such as Rosa Luxemburg, extend Marx's analysis beyond a single society to analyze imperialism as a process of the formal subsumption of noncapitalist economies under the dominant, capitalist economies. Formal subsumption, in this view, marks the borderline between capital and its outside, a division that imperialists use to maintain hierarchies and displace social conflicts. The process of globalization thus involves a general passage from formal to real subsumption, according to this view, pulling all societies within the circuits of capitalist production. Capital compels all nations, as Marx and Engels famously declare, to adopt on pain of extinction the capitalist mode of production, creating a world in its own image. Imagining the entire world in the stage of the real subsumption, a single capitalist whole, however, might lead easily to those visions of a flat or smooth world without geographical divisions of labor and power. We need, in fact, to recognize a reciprocal movement also under way in the process of globalization, from the real subsumption to the formal, creating not new "outsides" to capital but severe divisions and hierarchies within the capitalist globe. This does not, however, mark a return to the past: movements toward formal and real subsumption coexist in the globalizing capitalist world whose geography is striated by old and new boundaries and cleavages.[35]

The return movement from real to formal subsumption corresponds, in certain respects, to the recent reappearance of many antiquated, parasitical forms of capitalist appropriation. If there is any return to the nineteenth-century international arrangement, as Kissinger imagines, it is in that we are witnessing today a new "scramble for Africa," in which European nation-states in the final decades of that century vied for imperialist control over territory, carving the continent into colonies. Nineteenth-century Europeans were primarily dreaming of forms of wealth they could extract from Africa, such as ivory and gold. Today there is a renewed prominence of a similar kind of extraction from areas all over the world, which David Harvey calls accumulation by dispossession, a form of appropriation that involves not primarily the generation of wealth but rather taking possession of existing wealth, usually from the poor or the public sector, through legal or illegal means, and most often in situations where the limits of legality are unclear.[36] Old elements of the formal subsumption clearly reappear in this general competition among the powerful to accumulate by dispossessing others.

This scramble to appropriate is constantly supported and facilitated, of course, by extraeconomic violence. Naomi Klein names "disaster capitalism" the paradigm in which accumulation by dispossession and the imposition of neoliberal economic policies are initiated by some form of shock, which can range from a military coup or invasion to an ecological disaster. Capital, of course, has always found ways to profit from catastrophes, using them most often as a lever for the concentration of wealth and production. Klein maintains, though, that since the 1970s, and increasingly during the current period of interregnum and its disorders, economic transformation via disaster and appropriation by dispossession have come to constitute the dominant model.[37]

What we are calling here a new scramble for Africa is occurring, obviously, all over the world, but it does take particularly intense, brutal forms in Africa. From the diamond mines of Sierra Leone to the oil fields of Uganda, forms of mineral-extraction capitalism, often in the hands of foreign corporations and under the protection of informal militias, has come to dominate local economies. James Ferguson points out that, contrary to the standard narrative, stability, peace, and the rule of law do not correspond to economic growth in this context. Rather, he observes, "the countries that (in the terms of World Bank and IMF reformers) are the biggest 'failures' have been among the most successful at attracting foreign investment capital."[38] Whereas European states led the scramble a century ago, today it is primarily corporations dividing up the spoils under the cover of complex forms of global governance.

It should perhaps come as no surprise in this context that some old, seemingly outdated terms make a comeback to describe the unevenness and differences of the processes of capitalist globalization. One striking example is how some prominent Chinese historians return to Marx's notion of an "Asiatic Mode of Production" beginning in the 1980s. Marx uses the term, borrowing heavily from Hegel's theory of history, to designate an immobile and thus ahistorical apparatus of social production centered on a despotic state that appropriates surplus from self-sufficient village communities, which he contrasts to the dynamism of capitalist development in Europe. The notion of an Asiatic Mode of Production, as we noted in Part 2, has been thoroughly criticized by Marxists and non-Marxists alike for both historical inaccuracy and Eurocentrism. The Chinese historians who resurrected the term in the post–Mao era, however, Rebecca Karl explains, do so not to subordinate Asia in any new notion of general world history but rather to identify China's exceptional position in the global capitalist system. They conceive the "eternal standstill" of the Asian Mode of Production as a strength: the stability of Chinese rule over thousands of years affirms its model of state-centered capitalist development.[39] Leaving aside the utility of the concept of an Asiatic Mode of Production, which seems very questionable to us, the differences these historians point to are very real. We locate them, however, as marking not an *outside* but rather lines of division and hierarchy *within* the emerging global imperial formation.

The disorder and complexity of the current global situation—with the reappearance of a wide variety of outdated forms of violence, economic appropriation, political domination, and so forth—lead many to look to old models, such as unilateralist hegemony and multilateralist collaboration, to understand the terms of global order. Even though ghosts of the past continually spring up in this period of interregnum, however, we insist that the emerging world order has to be read in terms that are fundamentally new. "The hegemonic baton will likely be passed," maintains William Robinson, with an eye to this novelty, "from the United States, not to a new hegemonic nation-state or even to a regional bloc, but to a transnational configuration."[40] Once we focus on the assemblages and authorities being formed in the context of global governance, we can see that a new imperial formation is emerging that can function only through the collaboration of a variety of national, supranational, and nonnational powers. Our future politics will have to be cast in relation to this Empire.

4.3

GENEALOGY OF REBELLION

> Me, I hate the crowd, the herd. It always seems to me stupid or guilty
> of vile atrocities. . . . I have never liked the crowd except on days of
> riot, if even then! . . . On those days there is a great breath in the air—
> one feels intoxicated by a human poetry as *large* as that of nature, but
> more ardent.
>
> —Gustave Flaubert to Louise Colet, 31 March 1853

Revolt Breathes Life into History

In the course of this chapter we have outlined the major features of
the emerging Empire, its composition of state and non-state powers,
its assemblages of governance, its internal contradictions, its geographical hierarchies, and its divisions of power and labor. We should
begin to suspect, though, when we keep hearing about the instability and uncertainly of the present global order, that maybe these are
not just objective conditions but rather the result of conflicts and
antagonisms that are not readily visible, at least not from the standpoint of the powerful. In fact, if we are to make any further headway
in understanding the global order we will have to approach it from
the other side, from the standpoint of resistance and revolt. This
brings us back to the methodological principle we explored in Part
2, the axiom of freedom, which can be summarized in the following
way. Power can be exercised only over free subjects, and thus the
resistance of those subjects is not really posterior to power but an
expression of their freedom, which is prior. Revolt as an exercise of
freedom not only precedes but also prefigures the forms that power

will take in reaction. If we are to understand better the nature of the emerging Empire, then, we need to investigate the antagonisms, revolts, and rebellions that press against it. These struggles for freedom determine the entire development of the structures of power.[41]

From this principle it follows too that an empire also falls primarily from internal developments. The Roman Empire fell, for example, not really from the barbarian invasions but from the internal decline of its legitimacy and the rise of class struggle and forces counter to imperial command. Similarly the collapse of the Soviet Union resulted primarily not from cold war military and political pressures but from the internal revolt against unfreedom and, in particular, the contradiction between the socialist management of large-scale industry with extreme forms of discipline and the autonomy required by emerging forms of biopolitical production.[42]

Our task, then, is to investigate the organizational framework of antagonistic subjectivities that arise from below, based on the *indignation* expressed by subjects in the face of the unfreedoms and injustices of power, the severe forms of control and hierarchy, and the cruel forms of exploitation and expropriation in the disordered world of global governance. Indignation, as Spinoza notes, is the ground zero, the basic material from which movements of revolt and rebellion develop. Why, you might ask, should we go all the way back to the beginning? There are well-established oppositional parties and even some leftist governments that combat militarism, capitalist globalization, and various other injustices in countries throughout the world; there are trade unions that have negotiated in the name of workers for over a century; and there are nongovernmental organizations of every stripe that strive to serve and protect those in need of the basic necessities. Why should we try to reinvent the wheel? Why not, at this point in our analysis, simply investigate the established institutional forms of resistance? This certainly is an important task, and in our previous work we dedicated considerable energy to developing an extensive catalogue of the existing movements of the multitude against contemporary imperial command, highlighting how traditional models of contestation and rebellion have to be changed and are being changed in the current situation—how, for example, trade unions in the context of biopolitical production have to develop new strategies to include the poor and those with precarious employment; how social movements have to construct networks across national boundaries; and so forth.[43] In earlier chapters of this book, too, we examined movements of the multitude in altermodernity, for example, bringing together race and labor struggles. Here instead we want to approach the question from a more philosophical standpoint, starting from the most basic, abstract point and building logically to arrive back with a fresh perspective at the formation of the multitude. Consider this more philosophical approach a complement to empirical investigations.

Let us begin with indignation, then, as the raw material of revolt and rebellion. In indignation, as Spinoza reminds us, we discover our power to act against oppression and challenge the causes of our collective suffering. In the expression of indignation our very existence rebels.[44] Indignation thus includes a certain amount of violence. This relates closely to the fact, which we touched on earlier, that the resistance to power, the expression of freedom against the violence of power, always involves a dimension of force—when the worker confronts the boss, the colonized faces off against the colonizer, the citizen the state, and so forth.

The force and resistance that arise from indignation against the abuses and dictates of power, however, can appear immediate or spontaneous and thus naïve (though not for that reason any less powerful). Indignation is born always as a singular phenomenon, in response to a specific obstacle or violation. Is it possible, then, for there to be a *strategy* of indignation? Can indignation lead to a process of political self-determination?[45] In the history of modern political movements the great examples of self-organized rebellion based on indignation have often been called *jacqueries:* from the ferocious sixteenth- and seventeenth-century European peasant uprisings to the spontaneous worker revolts of the nineteenth and twentieth centuries, from anticolonial insurgencies to race riots, various forms of urban rebellion, food riots, and so forth. Normally such events are portrayed negatively in political histories. Yes, certainly, the standard version goes, these people are suffering and have just cause, but the spontaneity of their actions leads down the wrong path. The violence of the jacquerie, on the one hand, overflows reasonable measure and destroys the objects of its wrath seemingly indiscriminately: think of the tales of white colonists killed by revolting slaves in Haiti or the images of Detroit in flames during the riots of summer 1967. The spontaneity of the jacquerie, on the other hand, according to the standard narrative, leaves behind no organizational structure, no legitimate institution that can serve as an alternative to the power overthrown. The jacquerie burns out in a flash and is gone. The great poetry of François Villon is full of the brief adventures and tragic destinies of the jacqueries. And yet we have to recognize what some call the epidemic spread and constant presence of such uprisings punctuating modern history, from Europe and Russian to India and China, from Africa to the Americas and beyond.[46] Despite their brevity and discontinuity, the constant reappearance of these jacqueries profoundly determines not only the mechanisms of repression but also the structures of power itself.

Before addressing the political problem that jacqueries raise, we should observe that they are strongly characterized by the relations of production against which they strike. Riots are, from this perspective, much less generic and more intelligent than is often assumed: a jacquerie can be *zweckadequat,* in Max Weber's terms, that is, adequate to its goal and thus somewhat "organized" in its spontaneity. Peasant revolts throughout modernity rise up against the institutions of rent, recognizing and destroying the symbolic sites of aristocratic and colonial power. Industrial worker rebellions instead develop essentially through the sabotage of fixed capital and machinery. And most interestingly for us, struggles against the biopolitical regime of social production, such as the November 2005 events centered in the Paris suburbs, demonstrate a new intelligence by focusing on schools and public and private means of transportation, that is, the conditions of social mobility and division that are essential for the metropolitan exploitation of the social labor force.[47]

Revolt, the destruction of wealth, and social sabotage of the structures of power have in fact always been schools of organization. The terror of the jacqueries corresponds to the drive for liberation contained within them—against feudal lords, colonial powers, racist regimes, and so forth. Although in jacqueries organization arises as a set of singular demands, there is always a pressure to make common the action of the multitude, and this organizational initiative most often takes the form of the construction and reproduction of informal networks. In the past the organizations that arise from jacqueries were generally seen as insurrectional in the cities and nomadic in the countryside, in European history, for example, from the revolt of the *ciompi* in fourteenth-century Florence to the Masaniello revolt in seventeenth-century Naples, and from the sixteenth-century German peasant rebellions to all of those that arose against the ancien régime in France. The Russian Revolution might be considered in this respect a model of urban jacquerie (with coordinated activities also in the countryside) and the Chinese Revolution a model of nomadic, rural jacquerie all the way through the Long March. We will find as we go forward in our analysis, however, that today jacqueries, particularly with respect to metropolitan terrain, combine these two characteristics in a new organizational figure.

We should note at this point that reactionary theorists, particularly those in the great Spanish and German counterrevolutionary traditions, such as Carl Schmitt, also focus on jacqueries but attribute to them an opposite meaning, reading them as conservative events that legitimate and defend established powers against the transformations promoted by revolutionary movements.[48] One limit of these analyses, though, which in our view proves essential, is that they see only how jacqueries give "popular" legitimacy to a traditional ruling structure but are blind to the more profound legitimacy they give to a creative and nomadic power. Jacqueries, in their way, always express a double power: new power opposed to the ruling power, a form of life against a structure of exploitation, a project of liberation against a figure of command. The more the urban and rural models of jacqueries mix and overlap in the contemporary world, the more this double power emerges.

Often in our analyses, in this book and others, we focus on the rupture of the constituted order enacted by the refusal of relations of production by the producers and their organization of the material conditions of overturning them. Indeed the Marxist and communist revolutionary traditions, which constitute one of the primary points of departure for our work, understand the revolutionary process as taking place primarily within the field of economic production. Today, even for those who want to remain part of these traditions, the perspective of revolutionary action has to be conceived much more broadly, on the biopolitical horizon. As we insisted at length in Part 3, the sites of economic production have spread throughout the social terrain, and the production of economic value is increasingly indistinguishable from the production of social relations and forms of life. A worker revolution is no longer sufficient; a revolution in life, of life, is needed. Georges Sorel seems to intuit this shift but cannot conceive the material connection between the struggle against exploitation and the expressions of indignation against the corruption of the social order. Sorel formulates *le grand soir* as a myth—a necessary myth, he believes. What is really necessary instead, as Lenin rightly insists, is the link between ethico-political indignation and the unstoppable sequence of acts of violence, expropriation, and sabotage against the symbols and institutional realities of power that the jacqueries express.[49]

The central problem, though, adds Lenin, and we fundamentally agree, is how to translate every moment of insurgency into a moment of government, how to make insurrection lasting and stable, that is, how to make the jacquerie effective. For factory workers in many periods and in many parts of the world, the stabilization of the antagonistic relationship was achieved by translating it, through class struggle, into a wage issue (at both the individual and social levels, including welfare, social services, and the like). In the context of biopolitical production, however, it is increasingly impossible to translate the struggle over exploitation, welfare, and survival into monetary and wage issues. How can insurrectional action on the biopolitical horizon, then, be stabilized? The old socialist and communist responses have no place here. To explore new responses to this question we turn now to a political anthropology of resistance. We remain convinced that the expression of indignation and revolt in jacqueries is essential for a process of transformation but that without organization they cannot achieve it. Jacqueries are not sufficient, in other words, but they are necessary.

Anthropology of Resistance

At this point we need to develop a theory of "revolutionary biopolitics," or rather revolution in the biopolitical context, and to explore its bases we must begin by exploring the anthropological structures of politics today, that is, the conditions of obedience and resistance. In the Intermezzo we criticized the pessimistic tradition of political anthropology from Hobbes to Schmitt. Now to complete the scene we should add a critique of the liberal tradition from Locke to Kant, which constitutes an effective apology for the capitalist social order by planting its feet in an assumption of possessive individualism while its head seeks legitimacy in transcendental schema—but really the young Marx and C. B. Macpherson already critiqued this effectively.[50] It is perhaps more useful for us here to point out how the political anthropology implicit in contemporary neoliberal and neoconservative ideologies combine these two traditions. This amounts to an unlimited possessive individualism situated in a lifeworld of generalized insecurity and fear: an extraordinary mystification of a thoroughly capitalist society under the absolute rule of biopower.[51] Against these mystifications we have to recognize that exploitation remains the foundation of this society, that therefore living labor is required to sustain it, and that the multitude has to consent to capitalist authority. This is the sovereign against which indignation arises and revolt must be directed. If an entirely capitalist form of biopower constitutes the fundamental basis of all the anthropological conditions in contemporary society, then it is not hard to deduce that the forms of disobedience, revolt, and insurrection will similarly be biopolitical, that is, as singular expressions immersed in the reality of the common. "Indignation," according to

Spinoza's definition, "is hatred toward someone who has injured another."[52] This is how revolt is grounded in the common.

Indignation, disobedience, revolt, and rebellion constitute figures of rupture in the anthropological fabric of society but, paradoxically, also continuity. They constantly reappear as we saw in the contexts of jacqueries, and moreover they pose the conditions for lasting social organization. Michel Foucault insists on both the singular, local nature of revolt and the continuity of its lasting effects: "No one has the right to say, 'Revolt for me, it will contribute to the liberation of all humanity.' But I don't agree with those who say, 'It is useless to revolt, it will always be the same.' One shouldn't moralize with those who risk their lives against power. It is right or not to revolt? Let's leave the question open. People rise up, it's a fact. And that is how subjectivity (not that of great men but of whoever) is introduced into history and gives it its breath."[53] Not only is the rupture of revolt anthropologically continuous—"people rise up, it's a fact"—but moreover revolt is how the multitude makes history, how it breathes life into what would otherwise be dead.

In the revolutionary industrial workers' movement, "within and against" constituted the imaginary of worker action: within the factory and against capital. From the era of the professional industrial worker to that of the mass worker, this relation of "variable capital" within and against "constant capital" took various forms in relation to the technical composition of labor and the political composition of the organized proletariat. Today, in the context of biopolitical production, when the factory is no longer the primary site of the production of capital, this imaginary continues, but transformed: the proletariat is within society as a whole and produces there; and it is against this same social totality. This marks another anthropological condition of politics and revolt. The refusal of exploitation and alienation now more clearly is directed against the society of capital in its entirety and thus designates a process of exodus, a kind of anthropological (and ontological) separation from the domination of capital.

The political anthropology of resistance today is also characterized by a new temporality that reorganizes the relation of past, present, and future. We get a first approximation of this shift by looking at how the temporalities of labor and capitalist exploitation have changed. Marx and the Marxist tradition focus on two primary temporal divisions: the division between necessary labor-time (in which the value necessary to reproduce the worker is produced) and surplus labor-time (in which the value expropriated by the capitalist is produced); and the division between work time and life time. As we argued in Part 3, in biopolitical production both of these temporal divisions are breaking down. Necessary labor-time and surplus labor-time must today increasingly be conceived not in sequence but simultaneously; and similarly work time tends to spread throughout life time, investing it with its logics of exploitation and command. The capitalist temporality of valorization and expropriation, then, has to be understood no longer in terms of the succession of measured units of time but rather in a kind of simultaneity that constantly appears as an exception to linear temporality. Our earlier analyses of biopolitical production repeatedly returned to the figure of the poor to understand this progressive breakdown of the traditional capitalist divisions of time, this overlapping of production and exploitation, work and life. And from the standpoint of the poor we recognize a different character of this new temporality. The biopolitical productivity of the poor always exceeds all measure that is imposed on it, always overflows the mechanisms of capitalist exploitation. What we really confront here, then, are two temporalities, which both move beyond the old measures of time: the capitalist temporality of exception and the multitudinous temporality of exceeding. Previously capital and labor conflicted with asymmetric, nonsynchronic temporalities—with capitalist temporality well planted in the present, as Ernst Bloch says, and proletarian temporality oriented toward the future—but now they pose two alternatives on the same temporal horizon.[54] Today, in fact, revolution is no longer imaginable as an event separated from us in the future but has to live in the present, an "exceeding" present that in some sense already contains the future within it. Revolutionary movement resides on the same horizon of temporality with capitalist control, and its position of being within and against is manifest through a movement of exodus, which poses the exceeding productivity of the multitude against the exceptionality of capitalist command.

The struggles of 1968 probably revealed for the first time this coincidence of planes and temporalities on which capitalist development and social revolution conflict. In 1968, in fact, the socialist workers' movement entered the final stage of its history, since it is situated and moves according to a dialectical relation of exploitation and the contractual labor institutions. This dialectical duality was destroyed: a labor union "separated" from the labor process no longer makes sense, and neither does a boss "separated" from the common social intelligence that characterizes production. Hence the bourgeois hatred for the events of 1968. When the dialectical conditions of the labor movement were taken away, so too were removed the institutional mechanisms of mediation on which capital relies.

This is the situation to which capitalist governance has to bring order—a difficult and perhaps impossible task. And the structures of rule, as we argued earlier, can no longer stand above the social field to dictate the processes of exploitation but must reside, so to speak, within it. This is why the global order of governance is necessarily characterized by instability and insecurity.

This is also the situation in which we have to rethink the jacquerie. What can the jacquerie express when situated in this new anthropological condition, in light of its common ontological basis and its tendency toward exodus? How can the furor of indignation in revolt, its urgency and aggressiveness, be organized? What is the path from spontaneity to organization in this context? The anthropological conditions of resistance are in fact completely changed here. It is interesting that whereas in our other works we have often taken great pains to distinguish the multitude from the crowd, the mob, and the masses, here we see the possibility of recuperating these social formations when their indignation and revolt are directed and organized. This recomposition of all the subordinated classes, in fact, the enslaved, the oppressed, the exploited, has always been the work of class struggle. We might say, then, along with Flaubert in the epigraph to this section, that we hate the crowd except in its days of rebellion, when it achieves a kind of human poetry. This poetry of the future is what has to be composed to make the multitude.

Geographies of Rebellion

After having analyzed some of the temporal dimensions of the biopolitical transformations of labor, we need now to examine their spatial dimensions. We can begin from the claim we arrived at in Part 3 that the metropolis has become the primary locus of biopolitical production. By this we mean that the production of capital is no longer limited to the factory or any other separated site but rather spreads throughout the entire social territory. The qualities traditionally associated with the metropolis such as communication, unexpected encounters with social difference, access to the common, and the production of collective forms of life today increasingly characterize both urban and rural environments, and moreover these qualities are the central factors in biopolitical production. In this metropolitan territory, social life produces and is produced.

The flexibility and mobility imposed on biopolitical labor power along with migration pressures create an extraordinary dynamic of deterritorialization. When we talk about the breakdown of borders and nomadism, we should be clear that the breakdown of borders does not determine nomadism but instead nomadism itself breaks down borders and threatens the territorial stability of capitalist control.[55] The old development plan typical of industrial capital managed to link together urbanization, industrialization, and state formations, but biopolitical production breaks up this process. Collective capital is increasingly faced with a mobile and flexible multitude. From the perspective of command and exploitation, this can only appear chaotic and disordered. The task facing capital is thus constantly to rebuild borders, reterritorialize the laboring populations, and reconstruct the fixed dimensions of social space. Capital must pursue, in other words, ever new definitions of localized social hierarchies to rebuild the borders necessary for its order and command.

This creation of new lines of division and hierarchy is an example of the general process we described earlier that inverts the movement Marx indicated from formal to real subsumption. It should be clear, though, that the construction of borders and the movement to formal subsumption do not simply mark a return to old hierarchies, as if the division between peasant or craft labor and industrial labor or that between capitalist societies and colonial territories had reappeared. It is not a regression of an evolutionary process but rather a historical innovation.[56] This holds true also for figures of political authority and domination: even when it seems that outdated figures are reappearing, they are really new. But the difference here is that the figures of political rule are results, not causes, of the process of transformation. The political structures, which we used to call superstructural, maintain a relative independence with respect to the rhythms and the qualities of the social transformations. We will return to examine these new political structures in the remaining parts of the book.

The central characteristic of labor that results from the flexibility and mobility imposed on it in biopolitical production is its precarious nature, that is, its lack of guaranteed contracts, stable schedules, and secure employment, in which work time and life time blend together in the tasks and challenges of informal and changing jobs. The emblematic space of the precarious worker in the European context is the poor metropolitan periphery, the *banlieu*. The *banlieusards* traverse all the frontiers of the city just to make a living every day, and a large number of them participate during their lifetime in massive continental and intercontinental migrations—and yet their movement is subject constantly to a complex set of obstacles, stopped by police and the hierarchies of property on the subway, in the streets and the shopping centers, and throughout the city. The *banlieusards* are socially excluded at the same time that they are completely within the processes of economic and social production, and thus they serve as an adequate emblem for the modes of exploitation and control of precarious labor.[57]

In this world of precarious labor that continually breaks down the boundaries between inside and outside, there is clearly no longer any place for a political vanguard that would seek to lead or represent the masses. There is only the network of the laboring subjectivities that cooperate and communicate. This network often contains contradictory elements, of course, especially when the political centrality of the *banlieu* or the ghetto reappears not simply as a phenomenological element but as a political *dispositif*.[58] We said earlier that the structures of exploitation today require a reformulation of space and a continuous reconstruction of borders, maintaining the poverty and precariousness of social labor power. And yet in the passage through these diverse hierarchies there is a moment when indignation and its expression in jacqueries become essential. The political problem arises here when the poor, the precarious, and the exploited want to reappropriate the time and space of the metropolis. The central program must move from resistance to proposition and from jacquerie to organization—but that is an extremely difficult task, whose obstacles we must face head-on.

Both the temporality and the spatiality of biopolitical production and its networks are thus contradictory, but that contradictory nature at least indicates an opening, a potential. How is it possible that, through these networks, we pass from resistance to the defense of propositions allowing productive subjectivities to accumulate force? The question is not so much how to facilitate and extend the moments of revolt but rather how to identify the bases of the accumulation of power and the maturation of struggles. And yet the diverse temporalities explode in the event and the diverse spatial figures link up in the jacquerie. Like capitalist governance, the jacquerie reformulates social space, but it does so from the other side, destroying hierarchies, opening new paths of movement, and creating new territorial relations. How can this event of recomposition come about? How can such force become the soul of a social project, articulating the love that nourishes indignation? We should note that struggles over social reproduction, income, welfare, and the exercise of the rights of citizenship often take the form of reappropriating the life time and life space of the multitude. That is not sufficient to define an organizational program, but it is nonetheless a positive determination, an index of power. When economic-political demands are woven tightly together with the exercise of force by the multitude and successfully determine an event, that is when the force of rebellion engages with history and the rebirth of a revolutionary program begins to appear.

Against this development and even against its potential is deployed terror—terror against every form of resistance, which, paradoxically, is labeled "terrorist." Jacqueries, struggles of reappropriation, and metropolitan uprisings become the essential enemy of capitalist biopower. And yet these are only the social revolts born on the terrain of biopolitical production, which stand in relation to the metropolis just as the struggles of the industrial working class stood in relation to the factory. And as in the factory, here too there is a double relation: the *banlieusards,* standing within and against, want both to reappropriate and to destroy the metropolis, reappropriate its wealth, its networks of communication and cooperation, and destroy its hierarchies, division, and structures of command. This is a stubborn, fundamental contradiction.

The proposition of any solution and the definition of any program in this situation must be given within a global social space. The national sovereignties on their own, as we saw, are not able to organize global social space, and neither are the international institutions or the corporations or the NGOs. Even the hybrid assemblages of these different powers in regimes of global governance cannot succeed in determining global spatial arrangements. The only possible basis resides in the global movements of populations and their refusal of the global norms and rules of exploitation. Carrying rebellion onto the terrain of global social space on a cosmopolitical level means passing through the deepening of local resistances in the productive social networks, in the *banlieux,* the metropolises, and all the networks that connect the proletariat in its process of making the multitude. Constructing global public space requires that the multitude, in its exodus, create the institutions that can consolidate and fortify the anthropological conditions of the resistance of the poor.

In Parts 5 and 6 we will have to investigate political organization and revolution in terms much more concrete than we have used thus far. Before arriving at that point, however, we must work through the critique of political economy in the current situation and then develop a theory of political institutions. But we should remember here, before leaving this theme, that without the rebellion of the exploited and the jacqueries of the poor, there is no possibility of critical thought or a project for organization.

DE CORPORE 2: METROPOLIS

I will make inseparable cities with their arms about each other's necks.
  By the love of comrades,
    By the manly love of comrades.
                                                —Walt Whitman, "For You O Democracy"

The metropolis might be considered first the skeleton
and spinal cord of the multitude, that is, the built environment that
supports its activity, and the social environment that constitutes a
repository and skill set of affects, social relations, habits, desires,
knowledges, and cultural circuits. The metropolis not only inscribes
and reactivates the multitude's past—its subordinations, suffering,
and struggles—but also poses the conditions, positive and negative,
for its future. Such organic metaphors, however, can be misleading
since they are so often understood to imply functionalist and hierarchical relations: the head commands, the hand obeys, and so forth.
We understand the metropolis instead as the *inorganic body,* that is,
the body without organs of the multitude. "Nature," Marx writes,
in a passage that inspired Deleuze and Guattari, "is man's inorganic
body—that is to say, nature insofar as it is not the human body."[59]
Nature constitutes the wealth of the common that is the basis of
creative human activity, Marx explains, and in turn, past human activity is inscribed, registered in nature. In the era of biopolitical
production the metropolis increasingly fulfills this role as the inorganic body of the multitude.

When we focus on production, in fact, we arrive at a more

precise and suggestive analogy: *the metropolis is to the multitude what the factory was to the industrial working class.* The factory constituted in the previous era the primary site and posed the conditions for three central activities of the industrial working class: its production; its internal encounters and organization; and its expressions of antagonism and rebellion. The contemporary productive activities of the multitude, however, overflow the factory walls to permeate the entire metropolis, and in the process the qualities and potential of those activities are transformed fundamentally. We begin tracking down these changes by considering in turn the activities of the multitude in each of these domains: production, encounter, and antagonism.

The metropolis is the site of biopolitical production because it is the space of the common, of people living together, sharing resources, communicating, exchanging goods and ideas. Contemporary Italian, in fact, preserves the medieval Latin usage whereby the common—*il comune* in Italian—is the word for city. The common that serves as basis for biopolitical production, as we discovered in Part 3, is not so much the "natural common" embedded in the material elements of land, minerals, water, and gas, but the "artificial common" that resides in languages, images, knowledges, affects, codes, habits, and practices. This artificial common runs throughout metropolitan territory and constitutes the metropolis. The metropolis, then, is entirely inserted in and integral to the cycle of biopolitical production: access to the reserve of the common embedded in it is the basis of production, and the results of production are in turn newly inscribed in the metropolis, reconstituting and transforming it. The metropolis is a factory for the production of the common. In contrast to large-scale industry, however, this cycle of biopolitical production is increasingly autonomous from capital, since its schemas of cooperation are generated in the productive process itself and any imposition of command poses an obstacle to productivity. Whereas the industrial factory generates *profit,* then, since its productivity depends on the schema of cooperation and the command of the capitalist, the metropolis primarily generates *rent,* which is the only means by which capital can capture the wealth created autonomously. Urban real estate values are thus in large part expressions of the common or what economists call the "externalities" embedded in the surrounding metropolitan terrain. We explored these aspects of biopolitical production in Part 3, but now we can understand better how they are situated in the metropolis.

Biopolitical production is transforming the city, creating a new metropolitan form. One standard periodization of the city among architects and urban historians marks its changes in line with the shifts of its economic function. In societies dominated by agricultural production, and in precapitalist societies generally, cities provide a site for exchange. The *commercial city* is separate from production, since goods are primarily produced elsewhere, mined in the hills or grown in the fields. The formation of the great industrial cities from the eighteenth century on concentrates workers in the urban territory and brings into proximity a variety of industries—coke smelters with steel mills with auto plants. The *industrial city* is one of the primary levers that make possible the rise of capitalist production. There has always been some production within the city, of course, such as craft labor and manufacture, but the factory transfers there the economy's hegemonic instance of production. Although the space of the factory is within the city, it is still, however, separated. The industrial working class produces in the factory and then passes out through its wall into the city for its other life activities. Today, finally, the *biopolitical city* is emerging. With the passage to the hegemony of biopolitical production, the space of economic production and the space of the city tend to overlap. There is no longer a factory wall that divides the one from the other, and "externalities" are no longer external to the site of production that valorizes them. Workers produce throughout the metropolis, in its every crack and crevice. In fact, production of the common is becoming nothing but the life of the city itself.[60]

In addition to the immersion in the common produced by and productive of social life, another quality defines the metropolis:

the unpredictable, aleatory encounter or, rather, the encounter with alterity. The great European modernist literary representations of the metropolis, from Charles Baudelaire to Virginia Woolf and from James Joyce to Robert Musil and Fyodor Dostoyevsky, emphasize this relation between the common and the encounter. Village life is portrayed as a monotonous repetition of the same. You know everyone in your village, and the arrival of a stranger is a startling event. The metropolis, in contrast, is a place of unpredictable encounters among singularities, with not only those you do not know but also those who come from elsewhere, with different cultures, languages, knowledges, mentalities. Baudelaire, for example, conceives of entering the metropolis as "bathing in the multitude" *(prendre un bain de multitude),* which elicits the drunkenness of "universal communion" when one gives oneself completely to encounters, "to the unforeseen that arises, the unknown person who passes" *(à l'imprévu qui se montre, à l'inconnu qui passe).*[61] Although at first sight the common might seem to conflict or even contradict with multiplicity and encounters of singularities, actually, as we saw earlier in the context of biopolitical production, the common, in contrast to sameness, is entirely compatible. As Baudelaire demonstrates in the context of the metropolis, the common and unforeseen encounters are mutually necessary.

Once we define the metropolis by these qualities—embedded in the common and open to aleatory encounters—it becomes apparent that metropolitan life is becoming a general planetary condition. In quantitative terms this corresponds to the fact that world history has recently crossed a threshold: for the first time the majority of the planet's population lives in urban areas. But this quantitative view of urban space and world population does not grasp very well the transformation we want to highlight. Our qualitative standpoint gives a different view on how the traditional divisions between city and country, urban and rural have broken down and been reorganized. When Marx analyzes the political landscape of nineteenth-century France, for example, and distinguishes the political capacities of the urban proletariat from those of the peasantry,

his reasoning turns on communication and cooperation. The proletariat not only has access to news and information but also has the
ability to communicate internally, creating circuits of exchange and
debate among proletarians. The urban proletariat has ready-made
practices of cooperation in the factory, working side by side. The
nineteenth-century French peasantry, however, at least in Marx's estimation, was incommunicative in the sense that peasants were isolated in family or small community units scattered across the countryside, without a fabric of common relation and society. Or, to put
it differently, Marx sees peasants embedded in the "natural common" and proletarians in the "artificial common," which he deems
necessary for political action. Today, however, the circuits of communication and social cooperation are becoming generalized across
the planet. Rural life is no longer characterized by isolation and in-
communicability. There are, of course, different intensities of the
common, but the lines of division have increasingly less relation to
urban or rural environments.[62]

When we note the metropolitanization of the world, we in no
way mean to imply that all places are becoming the same but rather
that they should be distinguished by different qualities of the common and the encounters they present. As we saw earlier in the context of economic externalities, the common can be positive or negative: dynamic local cultural circuits in a metropolis are a positive
form of the common, whereas pollution, traffic, social conflicts, and
the like are negative forms. And similarly encounters can be beneficial or detrimental. When architects and architectural historians lament the rise of the "megalopolis" in the United States, the unregulated, formless sprawl that is replacing the classic, concentrated
metropolitan forms typical of 1930s Berlin, New York, and Shanghai, they are protesting the dilution of the common and the increasing obstruction of the encounters among singularities. What
the megalopolis most significantly lacks, they explain, is dense dif-
ferentiation of culture.[63] Similarly when Mike Davis uses the term
"slum" to define the increasingly general planetary condition, he
does so to emphasize not so much the poverty of those who reside

there but the negative forms of the common that surround them and the detrimental encounters to which they are subject.[64] All of these formations are metropolises, in our view, differentiated by degrees of intensity and qualities of the common and the encounters they present.

A series of recent studies investigate the specificity of African urban forms, the Afropolis, from Lagos and Kinshasa to Johannesburg. It is not sufficient, these scholars insist, simply to see them as slums or failed cities, although many are characterized by extreme deprivation and poverty. From an external standpoint it is clear that urban planning has been largely absent or ineffective in most African metropolises. But these scholars focus on the fact that, despite crumbling infrastructure and destitute populations, the metropolises actually work—most often through informal networks of communication, mobility, employment, exchange, and cooperation that are largely invisible to outsiders. The multitude of the poor, in other words, invents strategies for survival, finding shelter and producing forms of social life, constantly discovering and creating resources of the common through expansive circuits of encounter. That is not to say, of course: Don't worry about the poor, their life is lovely! All cities should be like these! The importance of these studies is to demonstrate, even in conditions of extreme adversity, what the poor can do, how they can produce the common and organize encounters.[65]

The concept of encounter we have used thus far as characteristic of the metropolis, however, is merely passive and spontaneous. In order for the metropolis to be for the multitude what the factory was for the industrial working class, it must be a site not only of encounter but also of organization and politics. This could be a definition of the Greek concept of *polis:* the place where encounters among singularities are organized politically. The great wealth of the metropolis is revealed when the felicitous encounter results in a new production of the common—when, for instance, people communicate their different knowledges, different capacities to form cooperatively something new. The felicitous encounter, in effect, produces a new social body that is more capable than either of the single bodies was alone. Not every encounter, of course, is a joyful one. The majority of spontaneous encounters with others in the metropolis are conflictive and destructive, producing noxious forms of the common, when your neighbors' noise keeps you up at night or you smell their garbage or, more generally, when the traffic congestion and air pollution of the metropolis degrade the life of all the residents. It is not easy to form with others a new relationship that promotes communication and cooperation, that creates a new, stronger social body and generates a more joyful common life. Infelicitous, conflictive encounters instead decompose the social body and corrupt the common life of the multitude. Often, in fact, since so many chance encounters are harmful, residents of the metropolis close themselves off to avoid encounters with others, walk silently past without seeing one another, erecting invisible walls in a common space, hardened to contact as if the skin had become callous, numb, mortified. And the privileged close themselves off in enclaves so that, even though they live near people radically different from them, they manage to interact only with those who are the same. This is when the defining characteristics of the metropolis degenerate, when it becomes no longer a space of the common and the encounter with the other, no longer the site of communication and cooperation.[66]

The politics of the metropolis is the organization of encounters. Its task is to promote joyful encounters, make them repeat, and minimize infelicitous encounters. This requires, first, an openness to alterity and the capacity to form relationships with others, to generate joyful encounters and thus create social bodies with ever greater capacities. Second, and perhaps more important, it requires learning how to withdraw from conflictive, destructive relationships and to decompose the pernicious social bodies that result from them. Finally, since so many of the spontaneous encounters are not immediately joyful, this politics of the metropolis requires discovering how to transform conflictive encounters, as much as possible, into joyful and productive ones.[67]

It should be clear at this point that the organization of encounters in the metropolis is not only a political matter but also
immediately an economic one. Joyful encounters are economically
significant acts and, in fact, are in many respects the pinnacle of the
biopolitical economy. In them the common is discovered and the
common is produced. This gives us a new view of the slogan we
proposed earlier: the metropolis is to the multitude what the factory was to the industrial working class. The organization of the
joyful encounters of the multitude corresponds to the productive
deployment of workers on the factory floor, in cooperative teams,
clustered around specific machines, or coordinated in the sequences
of the assembly line; but the biopolitical production of wealth—and
here is the central point—must be grasped from the other side, not
from the perspective of capital but rather from that of the multitude. Capital, in fact, is not able to organize joyful encounters in the
metropolis but can only capture or expropriate the common wealth
produced. The multitude must organize these encounters autonomously and put into play the kind of training required for a politics
of the metropolis. In the mid-1960s in the context of the Black
Power movement, when the major U.S. cities were becoming predominantly black, Grace and James Boggs proposed a similar politics of autonomous organization of the metropolis with the slogan
"The city is the black man's land."[68] Urban revolts under the banner of autonomy, in fact, were a prime motor leading to the crisis
of the industrial city along with, eventually, the crisis of U.S. hegemony. But today urban revolts, though still strongly defined by race,
are no longer led by those industrial figures. When metropolitan
production is embedded in capitalist valorization, urban uprisings
present original elements that herald new forms of organization,
just like the first industrial worker strikes, which set off epidemics
of sabotage against factories and their machines.

The multitude, however, is never allowed freely and peacefully
to manage the organization of the metropolis. In addition to the
common and encounters, the metropolis is defined also and perhaps most significantly by antagonism and violence. One last ety-

mology highlights this face: in ancient Greek, *metropolis* is the "mother city" that dominates and controls the colonies. This too is how the French term was used during the imperialist era: metropolitan France distinguished the European territory from the French colonies in Africa, Asia, the Pacific, and the Caribbean. Today "metropolis" still marks hierarchy, but its geography has shifted and become more complex. It is true, of course, that in general terms there remain significant inequalities among contemporary metropolises that echo colonial relations, between New York and Mexico City, for example, London and Mumbai, Paris and Dakar, Shanghai and Chengdu. In addition to these hierarchies, however, we need also to see those that exist within every metropolis, sometimes in extremely close proximity, among different neighborhoods and within each. This is a geography of intensities and thresholds, like those maps of the heat of the earth's surface as seen from space.

All contemporary metropolises are pathological in the sense that their hierarchies and divisions corrupt the common and block beneficial encounters through institutionalized racisms, segregations of rich and poor, and various other structures of exclusion and subordination. To say that São Paulo is a city of walls, for example, is to diagnose its illness.[69] And the pathology is that it not only prevents positive encounters but also bombards you with negative ones. In many dominant parts of the world, if you are poor and dark-skinned you cannot ride the subway or drive your car without being stopped by the police. In subordinated parts of the world your neighborhood is likely to be plagued by crime and diseases from lack of clean water and adequate sewage. The metropolis is a jungle, and the forms of the common and encounter it presents are ones you should run from!

The divisions of the metropolis are constantly produced and enforced economically by rent and real estate values. Gentrification is one weapon that creates and maintains social divisions, reproducing in every metropolis on a smaller scale the global hierarchies and inequalities. As we argued in Part 3, rent and real estate values derive directly from the common, what economists call the positive

and negative externalities of the surrounding metropolis. The relation of rent to the common, however, is not purely passive, parasitical. Certainly, in contrast to forms of industrial capital that generate
profit, rent does not have a direct relation to the organization of
production; but the capture and redistribution of wealth, preserving
and extending class divisions, nonetheless involves social production
and, specifically, the organization of the productivity of immaterial
labor-power. This helps explain why rent has become the paradigmatic economic instrument of neoliberalism and its regimes of financialization, which, as we will see in Part 5, are dedicated to the
production of services and immaterial goods, as well as redistribut-
ing wealth along class lines. Rent operates through a *desocialization
of the common,* privatizing in the hands of the rich the common
wealth produced and consolidated in the metropolis. The clear vi-
sual lines of Haussmann's Parisian avenues are not necessary for this
deployment of power. Rent and real estate are omnipresent apparatuses of segmentation and control that extend fluidly throughout
the urban landscape and configure the *dispositifs* of social exploitation. The very fabric of the contemporary metropolis wields a silent
economic control that is as vicious and brutal as any other form of
violence.[70]

This gives a third and final sense in which the metropolis is to
the multitude what the factory was to the industrial working class:
the metropolis, like the factory, is the site of hierarchy and exploitation, violence and suffering, fear and pain. For generations of workers the factory is where their bodies are broken, where they are
poisoned by industrial chemicals and killed by dangerous machinery. The metropolis is a dangerous and noxious place, especially for
the poor. But precisely because of this, the metropolis is also, like
the factory, the site of antagonism and rebellion. Since biopolitical
production requires autonomy, as we saw earlier, capital becomes
increasingly external to the productive process, and thus all of its
means to expropriate value pose obstacles and destroy or corrupt
the common. Capital becomes, perhaps paradoxically, a barrier to
the production of wealth. The indignation and antagonism of the

multitude is thus directed not only against the violence of hierarchy and control but also in defense of the productivity of the common and the freedom of encounters. But where exactly can this productive multitude rebel? For the industrial workers the factory provides the obvious site: the boss is in your face, the machines can be sabotaged, the plant occupied, production interrupted, and so forth.

It seems that the multitude in the metropolis has no comparable site for its rebellion and thus risks venting its rage in a void, but in recent years we have witnessed a series of metropolitan jacqueries that experiment with solutions to this problem. The *piqueteros* in Argentina beginning in 2001, for example, develop in literal terms our analogy between the factory and the metropolis: unemployed workers, who have no factory gates to block, decide instead to "picket" the city, blocking streets, obstructing traffic, bringing the metropolis to a halt. The *piqueteros* tested, in other words, a kind of wildcat strike against the metropolis. The Bolivian battles over water and gas in 2000 and 2003, which we analyzed in Part 2, developed similar tactics, frequently blocking the highway that links the major cities. At the peak of the struggle in 2003, the rebellious multitude descended from El Alto, the poor, predominantly indigenous suburb that encircles La Paz, and occupied the city center and its exclusive white neighborhoods, overflowing the barriers of racial segregation and wealth, creating panic among the elites. The 2005 rebellion born in the Paris suburbs similarly attacked racial and wealth hierarchies by blocking the mobility of the metropolis, burning cars and educational structures, both of which the *banlieusards* recognize as instruments of social mobility denied them. And like Bolivia, too, the French revolt combined race and labor antagonisms in a protest against the expropriation of the common and the impediments to encounters. These rebellions are not just *in* the metropolis but also *against* it, that is, against the form of the metropolis, its pathologies and corruptions.[71]

Jacquerie and spontaneous rebellions, however, as we argued earlier, are not necessarily beneficial and can often be self-destructive. The third task for the politics of the multitude in the metropolis, then, which must in most cases, in fact, come before promoting the production of the common and joyful encounter, is to organize antagonisms against the hierarchies and divisions of the metropolis, funnel the hatred and rage against its violence. There is joy also in destruction—attacking what you hate, the source of your suffering! The metropolitanization of the world does not necessarily just mean a generalization of structures of hierarchy and exploitation. It can also mean a generalization of rebellion and then, possibly, the growth of networks of cooperation and communication, the increased intensity of the common and encounters among singularities. This is where the multitude is finding its home.

PART 5

BEYOND CAPITAL?

The decadent international but individualistic capitalism, in the hands of which we found ourselves after the war, is not a success. It is not intelligent, it is not beautiful, it is not just, it is not virtuous—and it doesn't deliver the goods. In short, we dislike it, and we are beginning to despise it. But when we wonder what to put in its place, we are extremely perplexed.

—John Maynard Keynes, "National Self-Sufficiency"

5.1

TERMS OF THE ECONOMIC TRANSITION

> When the house is on fire one forgets even the dinner—Yes, but one
> recovers it from among the ashes.
> —Friedrich Nietzsche, *Beyond Good and Evil*

Neoliberal Zombies

The marriage between U.S. unilateralism and economic neoliberalism is a relatively recent union. The courtship may have begun with
the 1973 Chilean coup d'état led by Augusto Pinochet, which was
supported by the CIA and put into practice an economic plan authored by Milton Friedman and the "Chicago boys." Things got serious with Margaret Thatcher's election as U.K. prime minister in
1979. But the union was only consummated with Ronald Reagan
in the White House in the 1980s. At that point it began to seem
natural and inevitable that an economic policy of radical privatization of public goods and industries, unrelenting attack on labor organizations, and an ideology of free trade should go hand in hand
with U.S. dominance of global political and military affairs. Reagan
tore down the Berlin Wall, the myth goes, and vanquished not only
the Soviet Union but also socialism itself such that now there is no
alternative throughout the world to neoliberal economic policy
supported by U.S. power.[1]

There were alternatives, of course, despite all the rhetoric to
the contrary. In particular, as we saw in Part 4, various multilateralist
arrangements of global power, most often involving a concert among
the dominant European nation-states, competed with U.S. unilater-

alism throughout this period. The multilateralist options were not anticapitalist, of course, but they presented different mixtures of state control and privatization, welfare structures and free markets. In fact this competition was based, one might say, on which political arrangement can better guarantee the profits and continuity of the global capitalist system. The political decision for the union between neoliberalism and U.S. unilateralism—a decision, of course, that was not made in one boardroom or government office but across a wide spectrum of actors—elevated and centralized capitalist command in order to control the global economic transition, from Fordism to post-Fordism, as some economists say, or from a paradigm centered on industrial production to one centered on biopolitical production. This was an extreme decision, especially viewed in retrospect, but that extremity is an indication of the immensity of the task it was meant to fulfill and the difficulty of managing the transition.

With the collapse of U.S. unilateralism, the marriage fell apart. The political and military armory of unilateralism proved incapable of managing the capitalist transition and lately, through a decade or more of seemingly endless global war, economic disorder has only increased. The inadequacies came into plain view with the U.S. financial meltdown and the subsequent global economic crisis. It is obvious, in fact, when we look at the nature of the crisis and the transition of capital, that the weapons of unilateralism are completely unsuited to address the challenges facing neoliberalism.

The crisis is caused, to put it in the most synthetic terms, by the new ontology of biopolitical labor. The forms of intellectual, affective, and cognitive labor that are emerging in the central role in the contemporary economy cannot be controlled by the forms of discipline and command developed in the era of the factory society. We have argued elsewhere, in fact, that this transition toward the hegemony of biopolitical production was set in motion by the accumulation of struggles across the globe in the 1960s and 1970s against that imperialist and industrial disciplinary model of capitalist control. The transition was a response to the defeat of a form of capitalist production and command by workers' movements and social struggles.[2] Recourse to U.S unilateralism, with its imperialist imaginary, to manage this transition was really an attempt to treat a new disease with old remedies. In the final analysis, the primary responsibility for this decision to link capitalist economic strategy to unilateralism resides not so much in the U.S. government but in the world's jittery stock markets and the panicky souls of the wealthy. Beware bourgeois insecurity! It is not the first time, of course, that capital has looked to a strong central political authority to calm the markets and provide stability for profits. But it turns out that the nature of this transition and the conditions necessary for biopolitical production are inimical to those outdated forms of discipline and control.

When the failures of unilateralism become apparent, as we saw in political and military terms in Part 4, the major commentators and politicians unerringly run to multilateralism as the political support for neoliberalism. This has always been the official ideology, for example, of the World Economic Forum meetings, which bring together in Davos, Switzerland, government and corporate leaders from around the world. An ever more global world, the logic goes, needs increasingly to rely on a multilateral system of power—but such multilateral support is nowhere to be found. Unilateralism defeated multilateralism: the United States may have been too weak to rule on its own, but it was strong enough to block multilateral arrangements. That does not mean, though, that once unilateralism fails, multilateralism can take over. No, the foundations of multilateralism were already rotting before unilateralism gave it the coup de grâce. Neither unilateralism nor multilateralism is capable of supporting a neoliberal economic project. It may be useless, in fact, to search for a political form capable of supporting neoliberalism. Unlike those partisans of the "autonomy of the political," we do not believe that a political power can independently configure and maintain an economic system. The problem here is not only the lack of political support but also and more important the incapacities of neoliberalism itself.

To understand how neoliberalism has failed and, in fact, how it was never capable of being a program for capitalist production, we need to shift perspective and focus on the biopolitical terrain. All of the primary characteristics of neoliberal policy—strong private property rights and weak labor rights, privatization of common and public goods, free markets, and free trade—are focused on commerce and the redistribution of wealth. "The main substantive achievement of neoliberalization," David Harvey rightly claims, "has been to redistribute, rather than generate, wealth and income," primarily thanks to strategies of accumulation for the wealthy through dispossession of the public and the poor. In this sense, Harvey continues, neoliberalism is at base a project to restore class power.[3] Under neoliberal policies the wealthy have indeed grown much more wealthy and the poor correspondingly poorer within each nation and globally. Extraction processes—oil, gas, and minerals—are the paradigmatic industries of neoliberalism. But a large portion of the "generation" of wealth under neoliberalism has been achieved merely by feeding off the corpse of socialism, in the former second world as well as the first and third, transferring to private hands the wealth that had been consolidated in public property, industries, and institutions. Keep in mind that the essence of the capitalist mode of production is and must be to *produce* wealth; but this is exactly neoliberalism's weakness. The crisis of neoliberalism, then, is due not so much to the failure of unilateralism or multilateralism to provide an effective supporting political arrangement and guarantee its redistributions of property, but rather to the incapacity of neoliberalism to present a schema for stimulating and organizing production. No capitalist strategy can survive long without that.

The illusion that neoliberalism could be a sustainable economic program is testament to how difficult it is for many to recognize the nature of production in a postindustrial economy. It is easy, of course, to see and count the automobiles, steel beams, and refrigerators that roll out the factory gates or the tons of grain from the farm, but how can you put your finger on the immaterial products that become predominant in the biopolitical economy—the images, codes, knowledges, affects, and even social relations and forms of life?

To appreciate the novelty of this situation, consider, for example, a thumbnail sketch of the productive role of knowledge in capitalist economic history. Economic historians have insisted at length on the fact that knowledge, developed through practice and labor, was already a productive force in the mercantilist era.[4] In industrial capitalism knowledge remained a fundamental force of development, but increasingly, as the industrial paradigm took shape, its importance was not so much as an internal element, incarnated in the practice of workers and consolidated in their skills and know-how, but rather as an external one, independent of the workers and thus capable of controlling them. As industrial capitalism matured, knowledge became fundamental but completely absorbed within the system of command. In today's economy, in contrast, knowledge that is widespread across society—mass intellectuality—is becoming a central productive force, out of reach of the system of control, and this shift undermines the industrial paradigm. "The crisis of industrial capitalism," writes Carlo Vercellone,

> is in large measure the result of a social transformation that had already configured a model of alternative development structured on two principal axes: the reappropriation and socialization of knowledges that went well beyond the so-called scientific organization of labor, creating alternative forms of labor that reject productivism; and the expansion of the collective services of the welfare state (health, education, research, and so forth) as sectors and motors of a nonproductivist mode of development, based not on commodities but on intensive productions of knowledge aimed at the "production of man by man" and the reproduction of widespread intellectual capacities.[5]

Production, in other words, is becoming "anthropogenetic," generating forms of life. From this trajectory of knowledge within economic production, two important facts follow. First, knowledge is no longer merely a means to the creation of value (in the commodity form), but rather the production of knowledge is itself value creation.[6] Second, not only is this knowledge no longer a weapon of capitalist control, but also capital is in fact confronted with a paradoxical situation: the more it is forced to pursue valorization through knowledge production, the more that knowledge escapes its control.

Here we are touching on a dilemma that, in the era of biopolitical production, faces capital as such, not just its neoliberal forms. We will explore its consequences in more detail, but for the moment it is sufficient to recognize that neoliberalism has not gone into crisis only because it was tethered to unilateralism and is sinking along with it. Neoliberalism was already dead, in effect, because it fails to grasp and engage the biopolitical productive forces; it cannot provide a schema to foster production and increase the generation of wealth. Biopolitical production poses a problem for capital, in other words, and neoliberalism has no answer.

Socialist Illusions

Just as when the failure of unilateralism becomes evident the major commentators and politicians run back to multilateralism (without recognizing that it is already dead), so too when the failure of neoliberalism becomes clear the same figures turn to socialism or some form of government management and control of the economy (without understanding that its powers have already been completely exhausted). These two ideologies, neoliberalism and socialism, seem to be the only poles of the contemporary economic imaginary. And yet neither is able to control and stimulate production in the biopolitical economy.

Socialism did present a powerful model of economic production throughout the twentieth century on both sides of the cold war divide. It is important to understand that socialism and capitalism never were opposites, but rather, as many critical analysts of the Soviet Union claimed, socialism is a regime for the state management of capitalist production. Strong socialist elements—bureaucratic planning and regulation of the economy, state-run industries and public services, coordinated state regulation of capital and organized labor, and so forth—were also common throughout the capitalist countries. And the various forms of developmentalism that domi-nated the economic ideology of the subordinated countries in the latter half of the century, equally in countries aligned with the United States or the Soviet Union, were focused similarly on the increase of productive capacities through state intervention and bu-reaucratic planning. Programs of import substitution industrializa-tion, closely linked to dependency theories, were likewise centrally reliant on state control of markets and tariffs and intervention in the formation and regulation of national industries.[7] Socialism, in the final analysis, is a regime for the promotion and regulation of indus-trial capital, a regime of work discipline imposed through govern-ment and bureaucratic institutions. With the passage from the indus-trial to the biopolitical economy, however, socialist management and regulation lose all their effectiveness.

The incapacity of socialist ideology and rule to move beyond the industrial paradigm is one important element, for example, that led to the collapse of the Soviet Union. Standard narratives about the costs of the arms race, the military defeat in Afghanistan, and even the popular desire for commodities all have some explanatory power, but it is much more important, in our view, to look at the internal social dynamic and the obstacles to social production in the last decades of the Soviet Union. Alexei Yurchak demonstrates in a wonderful ethnographic study of "late socialism," the period from the 1960s to the 1980s, that Soviet society was far from the desert that cold war theorists of totalitarianism claimed, but rather an ex-traordinarily dynamic cultural and ideological environment. This dynamism, of course, was not promoted or fostered by the socialist regime; on the contrary, the regime presented unending obstacles to social and cultural creativity, resulting in a profound stagnation. Those who lived through the collapse, therefore, according to Yur-chak's suggestive formulation, found it both utterly unexpected and completely unsurprising: the power of the socialist regime seemed to them as if it would go on forever, but at the same time they knew it could no longer survive.[8] The socialist regime efficiently imposed discipline over an industrial society, but once the transition to biopolitical production began to emerge, socialist discipline became only a fetter to the social autonomy and cultural creativity that it required.

The incompatibility of socialism and biopolitical production goes for all forms of socialism, bureaucratic planning, state regulation, and so forth—not just the Soviet model. At the most fundamental and thus most abstract level, the two primary aspects of socialism, as we conceive it, public management of economic activity and a disciplinary work regime, directly conflict with biopolitical production. Earlier we argued that biopolitical labor is increasingly autonomous from capitalist control since its schema of cooperation is no longer provided externally, by capital, as it is in the factory, but generated within the productive process. Autonomy is equally required from state control and government forms of discipline. Perhaps you can "think on command" or "create affective relations to order," but the results will pale compared to what is accomplished through autonomous social activity. Furthermore, the results of biopolitical production, including social subjectivities and relations, forms of life, have an immediately ontological dimension. Value is generated in this process, but it is immeasurable, or rather it constantly exceeds the units of any accounting scheme; it overflows the corporation's double-entry ledgers and confounds the public balance sheets of the nation-state. How can you measure the value of an idea, an image, or a relationship? The autonomy of the biopolitical labor process and the immeasurable, overflowing nature of the value produced are two key elements of the current contradiction of capitalist command. To capture surplus value, capital must alienate the productive singularities, seize control of productive cooperation, neutralize the immaterial, exceeding character of the value, and expropriate the common that is produced—all of which pose obstacles to and undermine the production process itself. Government management and control produces the exact same contradiction. Whether the common is expropriated and its value corralled in private hands or by public means, under capitalist command or government control, the result is the same: the cycle of biopolitical production is stunted and corrupted.

In order to investigate what political regime can both foster and control production today, we have to explore further in economic terms what social production and social wealth means. Many economists use the concept "social capital" to delve into this question and get beyond crude economistic notions of production. We are not societies of atomized individuals, they explain, but rather are connected by a social fabric consisting of networks of understanding and trust, shared knowledges and norms of behavior, languages and habits, and so forth. Without trust and sympathy, market exchanges would not take place. Without social knowledges and norms, workers would not be able to cooperate and produce together. Social capital is thus a supplementary concept: the various forms of community constitute a stock of wealth that makes possible the functioning of industrial capital, finance capital, merchant capital, and all others.[9] This conception of social capital does successfully focus attention on the economic role of immaterial, social relations, but it conceives them as only peripheral to the productive process proper. Social capital, in other words, is not itself productive capital. And since it is conceived as subsidiary to the primary forms of capital, economists are constantly trying to make it conform to their schemes, devising formulas to measure social capital and close it within the lines of industrial accounting schedules. Such notions of social capital, however, since they are really aimed at complementing and completing the industrial paradigm of capitalist production, remaining within its conceptual order of quantities and equilibriums, do not solve any of the paradoxes of regulation and control raised by the transition to biopolitical production, its autonomous productivity, and its exceeding measure.

Traditional versions of social democracy continue today to be proposed as a just, humane, and sustainable politics to manage capitalist production and capitalist society; but these theories have no means to confront the challenges posed by biopolitical production and end up completely disoriented in this new situation. The social democratic doctrine of establishing agreement and trust between big business and the institutional labor unions, mediating any possible conflicts, and achieving modest gains for workers, not only has become completely blocked in the dead end of corporatism but also is increasingly estranged from growing categories of workers. Like the theories of social capital, social democracy can at best grasp the new figures of biopolitical production as supplements or appendages to Fordist industry and its mode of accumulation. Therefore the only figures of biopolitical labor that become politically relevant, from this perspective, are the ones that can be forced to fit into the traditional labor union structures. In effect, social democracy can see only the forms and relations of production that have continued from the past, and all the rest, from its perspective, simply do not exist.

The "third way" social democracy theorized by Anthony Giddens and practiced by Tony Blair does represent an analytical advance over doctrinaire socialisms to the extent that it recognizes that the corporatist trade union politics of the Fordist era has been (at least ideologically) surpassed. This revised social democracy essentially accepts some of the key elements of neoliberal policy—deregulation, privatization, and so forth—and combines them with a greater understanding of the economic value created through the social and cooperative development of biopolitical labor-power. What results is perhaps greater consciousness of biopolitical production and greater attempts to capture its results, making them available for capitalist profit and development, but still no means to solve the challenges it poses. No form of socialist regulation, even combined with elements of neoliberalism, can "rationalize" biopolitical production within its structures or promote its growth. Biopolitical production belongs to the common. Neither public nor private mechanisms can manage and contain it.

One also hears today urgent, desperate appeals for socialism or some form of government control of the economy as a result of the crises and the devastation that neoliberalism and unregulated capitalism have wrought. Capital is indeed destroying the common in both its physical and social forms at alarming rates. Climate change, resource depletion, and other ecological disasters are ever-increasing threats. Extreme social inequality, barriers and hierarchies of wealth, race, and nationality, crushing poverty, and a host of other menaces too are shattering social forms of the common. In the background of many accounts of the apocalyptic scenarios that face us, however, government management and regulation is the presumed solution. State regulation might at least avoid the worst scenarios of financial collapse! Surely some state control can save the planet, or at least slow down its ruin! At a minimum it can redistribute back to the poor some of the wealth that global elites have accumulated by dispossession! Socialism often functions as the default cure for the havoc wrought by unregulated capitalism. We agree wholeheartedly, of course, that governments have to stop the destruction of the planet and that it would be just and beneficial to redistribute wealth equitably across the globe. But the view of socialism that functions in these visions, much like that of neoliberalism that we critiqued earlier, sees it solely as a mechanism for the distribution of wealth, not its generation. Our primary point about the illusions of socialism, instead, is that, like neoliberalism, it cannot fulfill in the era of biopolitical production the task of promoting, managing, and regulating production.

Before closing this brief reflection on socialism, we should remember the difference between socialism and communism, a difference that has been thoroughly obscured through the last century. In standard journalistic usage today communism is likely to be used to mean centralized state control of the economy and society, a totalitarian form of government parallel to fascism. Sometimes when a concept has been so corrupted, it seems one ought to abandon it and find another way to name what we desire. But instead, in this case at least, we find it better to struggle over the concept and insist on its proper meaning. At a purely conceptual level we could begin to define communism this way: what the private is to capitalism and what the public is to socialism, the common is to communism.[10] But what does that mean? What would be an institution and a government of the common? That is one of the questions we will have to investigate in the remainder of this book.

The Global Aristocracy and Imperial Governance

All of the options on offer for political and economic global rule seem to have been disqualified. When unilateralism demonstrates its definitive failure, multilateralism has already collapsed on its rotting foundations; and when neoliberalism proves incapable of managing capitalist production, all versions of socialism and state management have already displayed their incapacity to engage and develop bio-political productive forces. And yet the global capitalist economy continues to function. How is production regulated and managed? How are profits maintained and guaranteed? There is no fully realized economic system in place to fill these needs. Just as the complex multilevel forms of imperial governance establish a form of rule during the current interregnum in terms of global power structures, so too an intricate patchwork of national and transnational legal and political structures together supports the functioning of the global economy during the current period of transition by regulating production, trade, finance, and property relations.

The characteristics of imperial governance that we discussed earlier apply equally on this economic terrain. Here too the tired debates that pit the role of the nation-state against globalization are of no help. When confronting the increasing globalization of capital, or more precisely the intensification and taking root of global capital, it is clear, on the one hand, that national structures alone are not adequate to the task of regulation and, on the other, that there is no global state to regulate global capital the way the nation-states regulated national capital. Instead *political interdependence* defines the mechanisms of economic management, regulation, and control. This is of course an extraordinarily mixed terrain, composed of, among other things, coordinated national mechanisms, bilateral and multi-lateral agreements, international and supranational institutions. The mixture is fragile not only because of the eclecticism of elements but also because the major international economic institutions on which it heavily relies, most of which were developed in the previous multilateralist global framework, are themselves weak and unstable. Increasingly today we see how these institutions, one after another, prove unable to address the crises for which they were designed: the International Monetary Fund cannot solve a currency crisis; the World Bank cannot solve a crisis of poverty; the Food and Agriculture Organization of the United Nations (FAO) cannot solve a food crisis; the World Trade Organization cannot solve a trade crisis; and so on. These institutions are not entirely useless, of course, but they do not constitute a sufficient basis for a lasting, stable global economic order. Capitalist globalization—the world market, the distribution networks, the linked productive structures, and so forth— has advanced far ahead of the structures of capitalist power.

This is not to say that no one is minding the store—that is, that global capital is functioning without political, legal, and institutional regulation and support. The global structures of capitalist power are functioning, but they are provisional and ad hoc, stitched together across the different levels of the system. Elsewhere we explored some of the specific mechanisms being developed on the terrain of global economic management and regulation, such as new legal conventions that reinterpret the old *lex mercatoria* in order to govern contracts not addressed adequately by national legal systems.[11] Here we want instead to consider the problem of a global capitalist power structure and its legal framework from a broader perspective and in relation to the structures of imperial governance.

What becomes immediately apparent from the perspective of imperial governance is the "aristocratic" nature of these global economic power structures. We describe the emerging Empire, drawing somewhat ironically on Polybius' eulogy to ancient Rome, as having a mixed constitution defined by a pyramidal structure, combining a single monarch, a limited aristocracy, and a broader (pseudo-) democratic base.[12] Joseph Nye presents the same pyramidal image of mixed Empire with a more modern analogy. "The agenda of world politics has become like a three-dimensional chess game," Nye explains, in which one can win only by playing vertically as well as horizontally. On the top board of classical interstate military issues, the United States is likely to remain the only superpower for years to come, and it makes sense to speak in traditional terms of unipolarity or hegemony. However, on the middle board of interstate economic issues, the distribution of power is already multipolar. The United States cannot obtain the outcomes it wants on trade, antitrust, or financial regulation issues without the agreement of the European Union (EU), Japan, and others. It makes little sense to call this distribution "American hegemony." And on the bottom board of transnational issues, power is widely distributed and chaotically organized among state and nonstate actors. It makes no sense at all to call this a "unipolar world" or an "American empire."[13]

The middle board of Nye's power game is where the aristocracy rules, primarily concerned, as he says, with global economic management and regulation—the realm of multilateral state relations, multi- and transnational corporations, and global economic institutions. Many scholars have recently documented the formation of a transnational or global capitalist class, closely associated with the corporations and the various state and institutional figures who regulate them, which functions as a new global aristocracy.[14] Our primary concern here, though, is not the sociological definition of this aristocracy but a structural view of the aristocratic functions of global economic management and regulation within the pyramidal arrangement of the imperial system.

One aspect to note first about this aristocratic level is that it is not composed of homogeneous, equal powers that collaborate peacefully. Aristocrats have always been a contentious bunch. When you look at the internal workings of the global aristocracy—at the World Economic Forum meetings, for example, or in World Trade Organization negotiations—the hierarchies among powers are obvious, as well as the devious maneuverings, with dominant states imposing their will and excluding others, subordinated states ganging up to counter them, and various other strategies and power plays regarding trade, antitrust actions, financial regulation, property law, and the like. And the dynamics between government regulatory structures and corporations, both nationally and internationally, is another field of contest within the aristocracy, which takes place inside and outside the courtroom. Reporting in the financial papers thus sometimes reads like the sports pages (when not the crime report).

The aristocracy is organized, of course, according to very different models in different countries. The "postsocialist" aristocracies are perhaps the newest models. In Russia an aristocracy has emerged composed of industrial and financial oligarchs together with mafia thugs and an array of government officials. In China instead the postsocialist model of aristocracy is anchored more closely to the state and party with tightly controlled participation of entrepreneurs and business elites. What remains of socialism in these postsocialist aristocracies is mainly the mechanisms of bureaucratic and party privilege along with the centralized circuits of power.

Equally significant or more so than the composition and internal dynamics of the aristocracy, however, are the complex relations of the global aristocracy considered as a whole with the other levels of the imperial structure. On one side we see constant conflict between the aristocracy and the monarch. Unilateralism, by which the monarch refused to listen to the pleading of the aristocrats, failed owing to not only the exhaustion of its military and political forces but also thousands of little aristocratic rebellions. The aristocratic complaints are loud and many: the other dominant nation-states as well as the subordinated ones want to participate in and reap the rewards of the global capitalist system; the corporations are aware that unilateralism with its endless wars is bad for business; and myriad others. As Nye says, it makes little sense to view the multipolar arrangement of this middle, aristocratic level of Empire as defined by "American hegemony." But these continual conflicts with the monarch should not fool us into thinking that the aristocracy is intent on putting an end to monarchy or siding with the multitude.

(Nineteenth-century French history is full of these ruses in which the aristocracy and the bourgeoisie trick the proletariat and the poor into fighting on the front lines, only to cut them off when the battle has been won and reestablish a new monarchical or imperial order.) The global aristocracy needs the monarch: it needs a central military power in Washington (or Beijing); a central cultural power in Los Angeles (or Mumbai); a central financial power in New York (or Frankfurt); and so forth. The aristocracy simply struggles constantly to negotiate a more advantageous relationship, forcing the monarch to collaborate and ensuring for itself a large share of the profits.

The global aristocracy must also negotiate and collaborate, on the other side, with those organisms and institutions that claim to represent "the people" on the third, lowest level of the imperial pyramid. In some instances the political elites of the subordinated nation-states masquerade as representatives of the global people, as do the various popes and imams of the major religions, but most often they are just poor cousins of the aristocracy trying to get their share of the loot; in others the various humanitarian NGOs and aid organizations are cast as representing the people (or at least their interests); and the dominant media, of course, are always happy to don the cloak of the voice of the people. This level of the imperial system is all smoke and mirrors, because in the end there is no adequate means of representation and no global people to represent. But the claims of representation nonetheless play an essential role. Specifically, with respect to the aristocracy, this third level affords mechanisms of mediation to contain the seething multitude. The one thing that unites all aristocrats and monarchs, after all, despite their constant bickering and competition, is fear of the plebs. Although the aristocracy is unable to engage and manage the multitude, its constant negotiations with the third level of the imperial system, even though they are conflictive, afford it some mechanisms of control and means to calm its fears.

There is no question, then, of any aristocratic secession from the imperial system. The global aristocracy will continually conflict with both the monarchical level above it and the "popular" level below, in addition to being plagued constantly by internal battles, but this will never amount to more than jockeying for position, claiming a greater portion of power, and negotiating the distribution of profits. The three levels of the imperial constitution need one another and cannot function on their own.

The real threat to the imperial system resides not in its internal conflicts and contradictions but in the resistances of the multitude. "So the reason why in practice [aristocratic] government is not absolute," Spinoza writes, "can only be this, that the multitude is an object of fear to the rulers, thereby maintaining some degree of freedom for itself, which it asserts and preserves, if not by express law, by tacit understanding."[15] The multitude of the poor, the forces of altermodernity, and the biopolitical productive forces, as we analyzed in the first half of this book, are all increasingly autonomous and exceed the forms of measure and control that have previously contained them. We need to descend once again to the terrain of the common to continue our analysis and explore what alternatives are emerging to challenge and eventually replace imperial rule.

5.2

WHAT REMAINS OF CAPITALISM

> But capitalist production begets, with the inexorability of a natural
> process, its own negation. This is the negation of the negation. It does
> not re-establish private property, but it does indeed establish individ-
> ual property on the basis of the achievements of the capitalist era:
> namely co-operation and the possession in common of the land and
> the means of production produced by labour itself.
>
> —Karl Marx, *Capital*

The Biopolitical Cycle of the Common

The key to understanding economic production today is the common, both as productive force and as the form in which wealth is
produced. But private property has made us stupid, as Marx says, so
stupid that we are blind to the common! It seems that economists
and politicians can only see the world as divided between private
and public, either owned by capitalists or controlled by the state, as if
the common did not exist. Economists do recognize the common,
in fact, but cast it generally outside of properly economic relations,
as "external economies" or simply "externalities." In order to understand biopolitical production, however, we need to invert this perspective and *internalize the productive externalities,* bringing the common to the center of economic life. The standpoint of the common
reveals how, increasingly in the course of the present transition, the
process of economic valorization becomes ever more internal to the
structures of social life.[16]

The concept of externality has a long history in economic
thought. In the early twentieth century Alfred Marshall uses the

term "external economy" to refer to economic activity and development that takes place outside the individual firm or industry, including knowledge and expertise that develop socially in industrial districts.[17] The term is used increasingly frequently in subsequent twentieth-century economics literature, but the meanings of the term are varied and often ambiguous. This should be no surprise, of course, since "external economy" is essentially a negative term, designating all that is outside the economy proper, outside the realm of exchanges of private property. For most economists, then, external economy simply names all that remains out there in the dark. In the 1950s J. E. Meade illuminates some of what the term designates by distinguishing between two types of external economy or "diseconomy": "unpaid factors," in which he includes the activity of bees to pollinate fruit trees; and "atmosphere," including the rainfall on the orchard.[18] It is easy to recognize, however, that each of these factors also has human, social components: unpaid human activities, such as domestic labor; and social atmospheres, including all those that affect the natural environment—the way, for instance, excessive logging affects rainfall. Even for the production of apples we can easily see how these "external" factors, which point toward the common, are centrally important. The question gets all the more interesting when economists, realizing they can no longer just ignore all that is external to the market, go on the offensive against it. External economies, according to some economists, are "missing markets" or even indications of "market failures." Nothing should be outside the market, and no productive goods should be "unowned," these economists maintain, because such externalities would escape the mechanisms of efficiency imposed by the market.[19]

The common has come into clearer view in recent years in large part thanks to the work not of economists but of lawyers and legal theorists. Debates about intellectual property make it impossible, in fact, not to focus on the common and its interaction with the public. "The most important resource we govern as an open commons," writes Yochai Benkler, "without which humanity could not be conceived, is all of pre–twentieth century knowledge and culture, most scientific knowledge of the first half of the twentieth century, and much of contemporary science and academic learning."[20] This common knowledge and culture we have inherited diverges and often conflicts with both the private and the public. The conflict of the common with private property is most often the focus of attention: patents and copyrights are the two mechanisms for making knowledge into private property that have played the most prominent roles in recent years. The relationship of the common to the public is equally significant but often obscured. It is important to keep conceptually separate the common—such as common knowledge and culture—and the public, institutional arrangements that attempt to regulate access to it. It is thus tempting to think of the relationships among the private, the public, and the common as triangular, but that too easily gives the impression that the three could constitute a closed system with the common between the other two. Instead the common exists on a different plane from the private and the public, and is fundamentally autonomous from both.

In the realm of the information economy and knowledge production it is quite clear that freedom of the common is essential for production. As Internet and software practitioners and scholars often point out, access to the common in the network environment—common knowledges, common codes, common communications circuits—is essential for creativity and growth. The privatization of knowledge and code through intellectual property rights, they argue, thwarts production and innovation by destroying the freedom of the common.[21] It is important to see that from the standpoint of the common, the standard narrative of economic freedom is completely inverted. According to that narrative, private property is the locus of freedom (as well as efficiency, discipline, and innovation) that stands against *public* control. Now instead the common is the locus of freedom and innovation—free access, free use, free expression, free interaction—that stands against *private* control, that is, the control exerted by private property, its legal structures, and its market forces. Freedom in this context can only be freedom of the common.

In the age of biopolitical production, the common, which previously was cast as external, is becoming completely "internalized." The common, in other words, in both its natural and artificial forms, is becoming the central and essential element in all sectors of economic production. Rather than seeing the common in the form of externalities as "missing markets" or "market failures," then, we should instead see private property in terms of the "missing common" and "common failures."

Once one adopts the standpoint of the common, many of the central concepts of political economy have to be rethought. In this context, for instance, valorization and accumulation necessarily take on a social rather than an individual character. The common exists in and is put to work by broad, open social networks. The creation of value and the accumulation of the common, then, both refer to an expansion of social productive powers. Economic growth, in this sense, has to be understood as the growth of society. "Social growth," however, may seem to be a concept too vague and abstract to be useful here. We can give this notion of accumulation more philosophical precision—recognizing, of course, that this will do little to satisfy the more economically minded—by conceiving it in terms of the social sensorium. Accumulation of the common means not so much that we have more ideas, more images, more affects, and so forth but, more important, that our powers and senses increase: our powers to think, to feel, to see, to relate to one another, to love. In terms closer to those of economics, then, this growth involves both an increasing stock of the common accessible in society and also an increased productive capacity based on the common.

One of the facts that make us rethink such concepts of political economy in social terms is that biopolitical production is not constrained by the logic of scarcity. It has the unique characteristic that it does not destroy or diminish the raw materials from which it produces wealth. *Biopolitical production puts bios to work without consuming it.* Furthermore its product is not exclusive. When I share an idea or image with you, my capacity to think with it is not lessened; on the contrary, our exchange of ideas and images increases my capacities. And the production of affects, circuits of communication, and modes of cooperation are immediately social and shared.

The characteristics of biopolitical production also force us to rethink the concept of economic cycle. Understanding business cycles is the essence of any course in macroeconomics. Capitalist economies under the hegemony of industrial production move periodically through a repeated sequence: expansion, peak, downturn, recession, expansion, and so forth. Economists generally focus on the "objective" causes of the cycle, such as inflation, unemployment rates, and disequilibria between supply and demand, and thus prescribe fiscal and monetary solutions to moderate the boom and bust periods, seeking to maintain rates of growth and employment while curbing inflation. When analyzing industrial business cycles in our previous work, we found it more illuminating to highlight the "subjective" causes, specifically the organized refusal and resistance of workers against capitalist command. Worker insurgency, of course, is often "behind" many of the objective economic indicators, such as inflation, imbalances of supply and demand, and disruptions of production and distribution. This perspective, for example, views the fiscal and economic crises of the 1970s in light of the proliferation and intensity of worker struggles in the 1960s.[22] Indeed, at least since the 1930s governments have sought to manage fluctuations of the business cycle with social policies that address the "subjective" causes through programs on wages, employment, and welfare. Whether viewed objectively or subjectively, however, the periodicity of the industrial business cycle through boom and bust remains, sometimes moderated but not negated by fiscal, monetary, and social policies.

The biopolitical cycle is very different. The economy is still subject to growth and recession, but these have to be understood now in relation to the *qualities* of the common. There are detrimental as well as beneficial forms of the common, as we have insisted repeatedly, and whereas some social institutions promote the common, others corrupt it. If biopolitical economic growth is conceived as a process of social composition, increasing our general social powers, then recession must be understood as social decomposition, in the sense that certain poisons decompose a body. Noxious forms of the common and institutions that corrupt it destroy social wealth and pose obstacles to social productivity. Since one of the central factors necessary for biopolitical productivity is the autonomy of the productive networks from capitalist command and from the corrupt social institutions, class struggle often takes the form of exodus, subtracting from control and establishing autonomy. The quantitative indicators of professional economists offer little insight on this biopolitical terrain, in particular since production of the common constantly exceeds not only relationships of control but also frameworks of measure. Useful economic indicators instead would have to be qualitative. What are the qualities of the common that constitute society? How accessible is the common to productive social forces? How autonomous are productive networks from forms of control? To what extent do social institutions promote or obstruct access to and productivity of beneficial forms of the common? If such indicators existed, they would trace a biopolitical cycle that is fundamentally arrhythmic, defined by thresholds of social composition and decomposition. But an adequate economic science of biopolitical production has yet to be invented.

The *Tableau économique* of the Common

In 1758 François Quesnay published the first version of his *Tableau économique,* which presents the equilibria of investment and consumption in the agricultural economy. His table traces the monetary exchanges throughout society in a zigzag fashion: artisans buy grain, agriculturalists buy craft goods, landlords exchange with foreign merchants, and so forth. The zigzag movements of money demonstrate the coherence of the economic system since each social class depends on the others for buying and selling. Quesnay's table is meant to demonstrate two claims that are central to Physiocratic doctrine: the wealth of a nation is defined not by the gold and silver in its coffers but by its net product; and agriculture is the only productive sector of the economy, since handicrafts and manufacture are seen as generating no more value than is invested in them. For

Quesnay, then, surplus value is primarily extracted by landlords in the form of rent.

Karl Marx was fascinated by the *Tableau économique,* and in many ways his analyses of the simple and expanded reproduction of capital strive to formulate for the industrial economy what Quesnay mapped for the agricultural, tracing the paths of value through the circuits of capitalist production, circulation, exchange, and consumption. Two of the important differences that define Marx's work with respect to Quesnay are that labor, not land, is the source of wealth in the capitalist economy, and the capitalist system is not a stable equilibrium but in constant need of expansion, continually searching for new markets, new materials, new productive forces, and so on. In this system surplus value is primarily extracted by capitalists in the form of profit.

We need to create today a new *Tableau économique* that traces the production, circulation, and expropriation of value in the biopolitical economy. This is not to say, of course, that industrial production is no longer an important sector of the economy, just as Marx's focus on industrial capital did not imply that agriculture had ceased to be significant. Our claim instead is that biopolitical production is becoming hegemonic in the contemporary economy, filling the role that industry played for well over one hundred years. In the same way that in the previous period agriculture had to industrialize, adopting industry's mechanical methods, wage relations, property regimes, and working day, industry now will have to become biopolitical and integrate ever more centrally communicative networks, intellectual and cultural circuits, the production of images and affects, and so forth. Industry and all other sectors of production, in other words, will gradually be constrained to obey the *Tableau économique* of the common.

Creating a new *Tableau économique,* however, runs into two immediate difficulties. First, the autonomy of biopolitical labor threatens the coherence of the table, taking away one side of Quesnay's zigzags. Capital still depends on biopolitical labor, but the dependence of biopolitical labor on capital becomes increasingly weak. In contrast to industrial labor, which is dependent on capitalist command or some other form of management to provide materials and enforce the cooperative relations necessary for production, biopolitical labor tends to have direct access to the common and the capacity to generate cooperation internally. Second, although economic tables are usually filled with quantities, social life, the common, and all the products of biopolitical production defy and exceed measure. How can one create an economic table filled with qualities? How can one balance the input and output of qualitative elements to determine the equilibrium of the system? Consider, for example, the fact that the production of subjectivity is increasingly central to the biopolitical generation of value. Subjectivity is a use-value, but one that has the capacity to produce autonomously; and subjectivity is an exchange-value, but one that is impossible to quantify. Evidently this will have to be a different kind of table.[23]

The terms that Marx develops for industrial production are still useful in the context of biopolitical production but have to be reformulated. He divides the working day, for example, between necessary labor-time, during which the value necessary to reproduce the society of workers is created, and surplus labor-time, when the surplus value appropriated by the capitalist is generated. In the biopolitical context *necessary labor has to be considered what produces the common,* because in the common is embedded the value necessary for social reproduction. In the context of industrial capital, wage relations were a primary field of class conflict over necessary labor, with workers struggling to raise what was considered socially necessary and capitalists trying to diminish it. In the biopolitical economy this conflict continues, but wage relations no longer contain it. This becomes increasingly a struggle over the common. Social reproduction based on the common might sound similar to positions promoted by theorists of "social capital," who, as we saw earlier, point toward the needs and mechanisms of social reproduction, insisting that they cannot be satisfied solely through wages. Generally the proponents of "social capital," however, fall back on social democratic proposals for government activity to guarantee social reproduction. Social reproduction based in the common, in contrast, has to be conceived outside of private or public management or command.

If necessary labor and the value it generates are conceived in terms of the networks of social reproduction in the common, then we have to understand surplus labor and surplus value as the forms of social cooperation and elements of the common that are appropriated by capital. What capital expropriates is not individual wealth but the result of a social power. The rate of surplus value, then, to rewrite Marx's definition, is the expression of the level of exploitation by capital on not only the labor-power of the worker but also the common powers of production that constitute social labor-power.[24] As a result, the contradiction that Marx often invokes between the *social* nature of capitalist production and the *private* character of capitalist accumulation becomes ever more extreme in the biopolitical era. And keep in mind that when capital accumulates the common and makes it private, its productivity is blocked or lessened. This is thus an extraordinarily violent and explosive situation in which the social productive forces, which are antagonistic and autonomous, inside and outside the market, are necessary for capitalist accumulation but threaten its command. Capital, so to speak, has the wolf by the ears: hold on and it will be bitten; let go and it will not survive.[25]

Capital is defined by crisis. Almost a century ago Rosa Luxemburg came to this conclusion when she recognized that the expanding cycles of capitalist reproduction led inevitably to interimperialist wars. Here we see the crisis also within the capital relation itself, with capital facing increasingly autonomous, antagonistic, and unmanageable forms of social labor-power. Two options seem available to maintain capitalist control: war or finance. The war option was attempted and in large measure exhausted with the unilateralist military adventures of recent years. Security measures, imprisonment, social monitoring, eroding the basic set of civil and human rights, and all the rest that comes with the war society might in the short run augment control, but it also undermines productivity, most dramatically in the biopolitical economy, where freedom, communication, and social interaction are essential. The global aristocracy helped put an end to unilateralism and its military regime, as we saw earlier, in part because it was bad for business. The finance option is much more effective. In many respects financialization has been the capitalist response to the crisis of the Fordist social relationship and the other social bases on which industrial capital relied. Only finance is able to follow the rapidly changing and increasingly global social production circuits of the biopolitical economy, extracting wealth and imposing command. Only finance is able to oversee and compel the flexibility, mobility, and precariousness of biopolitical labor-power while also reducing spending on social welfare! The key for finance is that it remains external to the productive process. It does not attempt to organize social labor-power or dictate how it is to cooperate. It grants biopolitical production its autonomy and manages nonetheless to extract wealth from it at a distance.[26]

A *Tableau économique* of the common cannot be created in the form used by Quesnay and Marx for the agricultural and industrial economies respectively. Those tables trace the lines of not only the exchanges but also the relations of interdependence among the various economic actors and, ultimately, the social classes. With the increasing autonomy of biopolitical labor embedded in the common, the reciprocity of those relations is broken. Capital, of course, still needs labor to produce the wealth it can appropriate, but it meets increasing antagonism and resistance from biopolitical labor. Instead of an economic table of exchanges, then, what we find here is a table of struggles, which we could organize, perhaps, in three columns. The first column is defined by the defense of the freedom of biopolitical labor. The composition of postindustrial labor-power is characterized by a forced mobility and flexibility, deprived of fixed contracts and guaranteed employment, having to migrate from one job to another in the course of a career and, at times, in the course of a working day, and in many cases having to migrate great distances across the city and across continents for work. Biopolitical labor does not reject mobility and flexibility per se (as if dreaming for a return to the fixity of the Fordist factory), but rejects only external control over them. The productivity of biopolitical labor requires autonomy to determine its own movements and transformation; it requires the freedom to construct productive encounters, form networks of cooperation, subtract itself from detrimental relationships, and so forth. The struggles in this first column, then, are struggles of the *common against work*—refusing the command of work, that is, in defense of free powers of creativity. The second column is defined by the defense of social life. In the Fordist system the wage, supplemented by state welfare services, was meant to guarantee the reproduction of the proletariat, although it often failed to fulfill that. The class of precarious workers today, the precariat, has an entirely different relation to the wage. It still depends on wages for its reproduction but is increasingly external to that relation with capital, relying ever more on income and means of reproduction that it can glean from other sources of social wealth. The struggles in this second column might thus be conceived in terms of *the common against the wage*—that is, in defense of an income to reproduce social life but against the increasingly violent and unreliable dependence dictated by wage relations. A third column of our table would have to be defined by the defense of democracy. These struggles are still in their infancy, but they will have to invent social institutions to achieve the democratic organization of social productive forces, providing a stable foundation for the autonomy of biopolitical production. The struggles in this third column will thus be struggles of *the common against capital*. Filling out the columns of this table is becoming the order of the day.

The One Divides in Two

In the mid-1960s, in the midst of the fervor of the Cultural Revolution, Chinese intellectuals following Mao Zedong proclaimed the slogan "The one divides into two" as a call to continuing class struggle and an affirmation of the proletarian perspective. Their opponents, they claimed, take the bourgeois perspective and are guided by the slogan "The two fuse into one."[27] This Maoist slogan captures the crisis of capital that we have been analyzing in this part of the book. As biopolitical labor becomes ever more autonomous from and antagonistic to capitalist management and command, capital has increasing difficulty integrating labor within its ruling structures.

In the context of industrial production the capacity of capital to integrate labor is taken for granted. Conceptually this is most clearly expressed when Marx, analyzing the production process, divides capital into constant capital—all the productive elements that merely transfer their value to the value of the product, such as raw materials and machines—and variable capital, that is, labor-power, the value of which varies in the sense that it contributes more value to the product than its own value, the wage. The concept of variable capital itself places labor-power, and hence the working class as a whole, within capital. This integration of labor within capital does not mean, of course, that labor is always peaceful and functional to capitalist development. On the contrary, the long history of radical industrial workers' movements reveals labor as within and against capital, blocking, sabotaging, and subverting its development. One of the great contributions of Mario Tronti's analyses in the 1960s was to demonstrate the priority of worker struggles with respect to capitalist development. "We have to invert the problem," he writes, "change direction, and start from the beginning—and the beginning is working-class struggle. At the level of socially developed capital, capitalist development is subordinated to worker struggles, comes after them, and has to make the political mechanism of its own reproduction correspond to them."[28] One could think of the working-class revolt that Tronti analyzes as an instance of the one dividing into two since in revolt the workers demonstrate their autonomy from and antagonism to the capitalist owners, but in subsequent moments, when the strike comes to an end, the two fuse back into one. Or better, Tronti's dialectic is a two-part movement: workers' struggles force capital to restructure; capitalist restructuring destroys the old conditions for worker organization and poses new ones; new worker revolts force capital to restructure again; and so forth. This two-part dialectic, however, as long as it does not pass over into revolutionary activity, never breaks apart the internal relation to capital.

The passage from the industrial to the biopolitical economy changes this situation, realizing and extending in certain respects the arrangement that Tronti foresaw in the factory. The industrial firm is no longer able, as it previously was, at least in the dominant countries, to centralize productive forces and integrate labor-power within capital. As we have seen, however, the exhaustion of the hegemonic and integrating powers of firm-based capital does not imply the end of capitalist development. In the place of firm-based capital has emerged a society-based capital in which society as a whole is the chief site of productive activity and, correspondingly, the prime site of labor conflict and revolt against capital.[29] On this social terrain of biopolitical production, in the context of society-based capital, the integrating mechanisms that functioned in firm-based capital no longer work. Here the one really divides into two: an increasingly autonomous labor-power and, consequently, a capital that becomes increasingly pure command. Labor-power is thus no longer variable capital, integrated within the body of capital, but a separate and increasingly oppositional force.[30]

This division in two results from a double movement. From one side, biopolitical labor increasingly asserts its autonomy. Not only is it progressively more capable of organizing productive cooperation and self-managing social production, but also all mechanisms of capitalist command imposed on it diminish its productivity and generate antagonism. From the other side, capital is ever more obliged to exclude labor from its relations, even while having to extract wealth from it. The characteristics of the technical composition of labor that we analyzed in Part 3 demonstrate this double movement. In biopolitical production, for example, there is a progressive dissolution of the working day. The Fordist industrial promise of eight hours' work, eight hours' leisure, and eight hours' sleep, which actually applied to relatively few workers globally, no longer serves as a regulative ideal. In the privileged and subordinated sectors of the economy alike, that division between work time and nonwork time is breaking down. And more important, the temporalities of factory life—its methods of managing time, its time precision, and time discipline, which had been generalized outside the factory to society as a whole—no longer apply. Workers are in many respects left to organize their own time, which is often an impossible task. German sociologists refer to an *Entgrenzung der Arbeit* (a delimitation or removal of boundaries of work) to name the spilling over of work into society (in spatial terms) and into life (in temporal terms).[31] A second and closely related example is the increasing precarity of labor in biopolitical production. Guaranteed, stable employment was in many ways the epitome of the internal nature of industrial labor within capital. At the extreme was the image of loyal workers and their families cared for by the firm throughout their working lives and beyond. By making labor increasingly precarious for an ever larger portion of the workforce, however, capital is casting labor out, expelling it, cutting ties of stability, welfare, and support. The dissolution of the working day and the increasing precarity of labor do not mean, of course, that workers are free from capitalist domination—far from it! Workers still have to arrange their lives in the world of commodities according to the commodified temporalities of capitalist social life. Precarious workers have to think of themselves still, even more so, as commodities. All workers remain in very important respects subject to capitalist domination.

When we declare that "the one divides in two," then, we are not proclaiming the demise of capital but rather identifying the growing incapacity of capital to integrate labor-power within itself and thus marking the rupture of the concept of capital into two antagonistic subjectivities. The resulting situation is characterized by a double production of subjectivity, or rather the production of two opposed, conflicting subjectivities that cohabit in the same social world. A capitalist power which is progressively losing its productive role, its ability to organize productive cooperation, and its capacity to control the social mechanisms of the reproduction of labor-power cohabits, often uneasily, with a multitude of productive subjectivities, which are increasingly acquiring the constituent capacities necessary to sustain themselves autonomously and create a new world.

Is it possible at this point to reintegrate the working class within capital? This is the illusion promoted by social democracy, which we analyzed earlier. It would mean, on the one hand, re-creating the mechanisms by which capital can engage, manage, and organize productive forces and, on the other, resurrecting the welfare structures and social mechanisms necessary for capital to guarantee the social reproduction of the working class. We do not believe, however, even if there were the political will among the elites, that this is possible. The cat is out of the bag, and, for better or worse, there is no way to get it back in. Or to put it in other terms, the old three-part dialectic, which would make a unity of the two conflicting subjectivities, will no longer work. Its claims of unity and integration at this point are just false promises.

The primary capitalist strategy for maintaining power in this divided situation, as we said earlier, is financial control. Marx anticipated this situation, in many respects, in his analyses of the dual nature of money. On its politically neutral face, money is the universal equivalent and medium of exchange that, in capitalist society, represents the value of commodities based on the quantity of labor consolidated within them. On its other face, though, money, as the exclusive terrain of the representation of value, wields the power to command labor. It is a representation of the wealth of social production, accumulated privately, that in turn has the power to rule over social production.[32] The world of finance, with its complex instruments of representation, extends and amplifies these two faces of money, which together are essential for expropriating the value of and exerting control over biopolitical production.

After identifying the two faces of money, Marx highlights the fact that they conflict with each other and thus register a social antagonism between the representation of the value of labor as the general equivalent of commodity exchange and the conditions of social production dominated by capital. One traditional anticapitalist strategy to confront the domination of money is to destroy both of its representational functions—eliminating not only capitalist command but also the role of money as general equivalent—by constructing a system of exchanges based on barter and/or ad hoc representations of value, while dreaming of the return to an antediluvian world of use-values. A second strategy is to defend the one face of money and attack the other: preserve money as the representation of value but destroy its power to represent the general social field of production, which is instrumental in command, with the ideal of fair trade and equal exchanges. Is a third strategy possible that would conserve both representational functions of money but wrest control of them away from capital? Might the power of money (and the finance world in general) to represent the social field of production be, in the hands of the multitude, an instrument of freedom, with the capacity to overthrow misery and poverty? Just as the concept of abstract labor was necessary for understanding the industrial working class as a coherent, active subject, including workers in a wide variety of different sectors, do the abstractions of money and finance similarly provide the instruments for making the multitude from the diverse forms of flexible, mobile, and precarious labor? We cannot answer these questions satisfactorily yet, but it seems to us that efforts to reappropriate money in this way point in the direction of revolutionary activity today. And this would mark a definitive break of the one divided in two.

5.3

PRE-SHOCKS ALONG THE FAULT LINES

> Capitalist performance is not even relevant for prognosis [of capital's future development]. Most civilizations have disappeared before they had time to fill to the full the measure of their promise. Hence I am not going to argue, on the strength of that performance, that the capitalist intermezzo is likely to be prolonged. In fact, I am now going to draw the exactly opposite inference.
>
> —Joseph Schumpeter, *Capitalism, Socialism, and Democracy*

Capital's Prognosis

All is not well with capital—and the traditional treatments are unable to cure its maladies. Neither private, neoliberal medicine (under unilateral or multilateral guidance) nor public, state-centered remedies (Keynesian or socialist) have any positive effect, and in fact only make things worse. We should do our best to search for a new cure, even though we are well aware that treating the disease seriously and aggressively could risk the demise of the patient. Euthanasia may in the end be the most humane course; but before being resigned to that fact, a conscientious doctor has to make every effort to discover the correct diagnosis and invent a successful treatment.

Capital is just fine, some might respond, despite its crises. Look at all those people getting rich! Look at how the stock markets rebound! Look at all those goods being produced! Well, as Joseph Schumpeter says in the epigraph to this section, these conventional measures of performance, as well as others such as the rate of profit, may not be the most relevant ones for judging health.[33] Capital is not immortal, of course, but came into being and will pass away just like all other modes of production. Our task is to discern the relevant symptoms, evaluate how they can be treated, and arrive at a prognosis for capital.

One symptom, which Schumpeter diagnosed over a half century ago, is the decline of capital's entrepreneurial capacities. Early in the twentieth century, working in Austria and surrounded by its nineteenth-century models of capitalist development, Schumpeter celebrated entrepreneurship as the vital force of capital. Many misunderstand the essence of the entrepreneurial function as risk-taking, he explains, but risk-taking is merely speculation. Schumpeter's entrepreneur is the one who introduces the new, the innovator driven by the joy of creation—a figure with strong overtones of a Nietzschean individual hero, giving capital its constant forward movement. By the mid-twentieth century, however, now in the United States and analyzing its increasingly bureaucratic corporate culture, Schumpeter foresees the obsolescence of capital's entrepreneurial function and its replacement by a mechanized, routine form of economic progress dictated by management rationality and the faceless gray suits that populate boardrooms. Once it loses its power of innovation and entrepreneurship, Schumpeter believes, capital cannot long survive.[34]

Many would claim, though, that today, in the computer age, the entrepreneurial function of capital has been reinvented and reinvigorated by figures like Microsoft chairman Bill Gates and Apple Computers' Steve Jobs. They do indeed play the part for the media, but they are not really entrepreneurs in Schumpeter's sense. They are just salesmen and speculators: they present the face of the corporation to sell the latest version of iPod or Windows, and they bet a portion of their fortune on its success, but they are not the locus of innovation. Corporations such as Apple and Microsoft survive by feeding off the innovative energies that emerge from the vast networks of computer and Internet-based producers that extend well beyond the boundaries of the corporation and its employees. Biopolitical production, in fact, is driven from below by a multitudinous entrepreneurship. Schumpeter was right, then, about the obsolescence of the capitalist entrepreneur as the fount of economic inno-vation, but he could not recognize that a hydra-headed multitude would emerge in its stead as biopolitical entrepreneur.

This points us to a second symptom of capital's illness: its fail-ure to engage and develop productive forces. When Marx and En-gels describe the centuries-long passage from feudal to capitalist re-lations of production in Europe, they focus on the expansion of productive forces: as feudal relations increasingly obstruct the devel-opment of productive forces, capitalist relations of property and ex-change emerge to foster them and spur them forward. "At a certain stage in the development of these means of production and of ex-change," Marx and Engels write in the *Manifesto,* "the conditions under which feudal society produced and exchanged, the feudal or-ganisation of agriculture and manufacturing industry, in one word, the feudal relations of property became no longer compatible with the already developed productive forces; they became so many fet-ters. They had to be burst asunder; they were burst asunder."[35] Every mode of production, capital included, at first powerfully expands productive forces but eventually holds them back, thereby generat-ing the foundation of the next mode of production. This is not an immiseration thesis. The question is not, Are people worse off than before? It is rather, Could their abilities and potential be developed more fully?

Capitalist relations of property are becoming increasingly such fetters today. One might object that capitalist development contin-ues at a high level: the speed and capacity of digital electronic de-vices, for instance, continue to double every two years. Such mea-sures of performance, however, are not reflective of the development of productive forces, which have to be gauged primarily in terms of human, social, and subjective powers, for which there is, in fact, no scientific measurement. We have to judge whether people's capaci-ties and creativity are fostered and developed to their fullest and, al-ternatively, how many lives are wasted. That is, at the most basic level, how the health of a mode of production has to be evaluated. We see increasing signs throughout the world today, in fact, that capitalist relations of production fetter the abilities of ever greater portions of the population. In the dominant regions one often hears of "growth without jobs," while in the subordinate regions an increasing number of people are becoming "disposable," useless from the perspective of capital. And in a more general sense, it is clear how little the majority of those who are employed by capital are allowed to develop their full productive capacities but are limited instead to routine tasks, far from their potential. In the context of biopolitical production this has nothing to do with full employment or giving everyone a job; rather it has to do with fostering the expansion of our powers to think and create, to generate images and social relationships, to communicate and cooperate. There is no need to pose this as a moral accusation, as if capital were duty bound to provide for the population. We mean to view the situation not as moralists but as doctors, evaluating the health of the patient. And it is a significant symptom of illness in an economic system that it cannot take advantage of existing productive forces and foster their growth, that it wastes the talents and abilities of the population.

These symptoms of capital's illness result in repeating crises of capitalist accumulation. The great financial and economic crises beginning in 2008 have refocused widespread attention on this fact. Traditionally capitalist crisis is conceived in objective terms, as we said, which from one perspective highlights blockages in the circuit from production to circulation to realization and back to production. When value, in either its money form or its commodity form, stands idle at any point in the circuit—because of labor shortages or strikes that halt production, for example, or transportation impasses that stop circulation, or insufficient demand to sell the goods and realize their value and profit—crisis results. Today crisis has to be viewed, instead, in subjective terms. Biopolitical goods—such as ideas, affects, codes, knowledges, information, and images—still have to circulate to realize their value, but that circulation is now internal to the production process. The biopolitical circuit is really all contained in the production of the common, which is also simultaneously the production of subjectivity and social life. The process can be understood as both, depending on one's perspective, the production of subjectivity through the common and the production of common through subjectivity. Crises of the biopolitical circuit should be understood, then, as a blockage in the production of subjectivity or an obstacle to the productivity of the common.

One day Monsieur le Capital, feeling ill, visits Doctor Subtilis and confesses that he is disturbed each night by a recurring dream. (We know. It is misleading shorthand to treat capital as if it were a subject with human attributes and desires, just as it is to ascribe to stock markets an emotional life: jittery, depressed, or buoyant. Instead of avoiding the trope, though, let's take it one step further!) In the dream, Monsieur le Capital explains, he is standing before a tree full of ripe fruit, glistening in the sun, but his arms are arthritic and he is unable to raise them high enough even to harvest the lower branches. He suffers hunger pangs but can only watch the delicious fruit in front of him. Finally, with great effort he somehow manages to grasp one of the fruits, but when he looks down at his hands, he sees, to his horror, that he is holding a withered human head! Doctor, please, what does it mean? Your problem, Doctor Subtilis responds, is not merely a disturbed consciousness but also a troubled body. In the era of biopolitical production, the traditional division between subjects and objects breaks down. No longer do subjects produce objects that subsequently reproduce subjects. There is a kind of short circuit whereby subjects simultaneously produce and reproduce subjects through the common. What you are trying to take in your hands, then, Monsieur le Capital, is subjectivity itself. But paradoxically, tragically, by laying your hands on the production of subjectivity, you destroy the common and corrupt the process, making productive forces wither. Monsieur le Capital, of course, is completely perplexed by this diagnosis but nonetheless presses the doctor for a cure. Well, Doctor Subtilis considers, the old medicines of private and public control, neoliberalism and social democratic strategies, will only make things worse. Finally, after much consideration, he responds enigmatically, All I can tell you, Monsieur le Capital, is this: don't touch the fruit!

By giving this gloomy prognosis for the future of capital we are not suggesting that it will collapse overnight. And we are not flirting with those old notions of capitalist apocalypse called *Zusammenbrückstheorien,* or collapse theories, which were meant to scare the bourgeoisie and incite revolutionary fervor among the proletariat.[36] Today, in fact, even in the face of dramatic crises, it seems that anyone who dares to speak of the eventual demise of capital is immediately dismissed as a catastrophe theorist. (It is remarkable how few contemporary economists confront the question, as Keynes and Schumpeter did in a previous era, of how and when the capitalist mode of production will come to an end.)[37] We are not preaching apocalypse but simply reading the symptoms of capital's illness with two basic assumptions: capital will not continue to rule forever, and it will create, in pursuing its own rule, the conditions of the mode of production and the society that will eventually succeed it. This is a long process, just as was the transition from the feudal to the capitalist mode of production, and there is no telling when it will cross the crucial threshold, but we can already recognize—in the autonomy of biopolitical production, the centrality of the common, and their growing separation from capitalist exploitation and command —the makings of a new society within the shell of the old.

Exodus from the Republic

The republican form that emerged historically as dominant, with its central aim of protecting and serving property, has long functioned as an adequate support for capital, fostering its development, regulating its excesses, and guaranteeing its interests. The republic of property, however, no longer serves capital well, and has instead become a fetter on production. Earlier we examined the difference between republic and multitude, along with the multitude's exodus from the republic, primarily from a political perspective. Now we have to approach this same question from the perspective of economic production, keeping in mind, of course, that in the biopolitical era economic and political processes are woven ever closer together, to the point at times of becoming indistinguishable. What

aspects of the republic block the development of productive forces
and the production of the common? What political and social arrangements can remove these obstacles, foster these developments,
and treat capital's ills? We will see in this section that for a new expansion of productive forces and an unfettered production of the
common—in order, in other words, to save capital—a politics of
freedom, equality, and democracy of the multitude is necessary.

We have already seen in the previous section one sense in
which freedom is required for the production of the common. The
multitude of producing subjectivities must today be autonomous
from either private/capitalist or public/state authority in order to
produce and develop the common. Previously production could
be—and even in many cases had to be—organized by the capitalist.
The capitalist provided the means of cooperation, bringing proletarians together in the factory, for instance, deploying them around the
machines, assigning them specific tasks, and imposing work discipline. The state also could organize production in the same way at
times, providing the means of cooperation and communication necessary for the productive process. The relation of the republic to
capital was characterized by this balance and alternative between
private and public, sustaining the authority of each over the multitude. Sometimes the republic focused more on the private and at
others more on the public, but these two poles, each of which served
as an authority to organize production, were the exclusive limits. In
biopolitical production, however, the cooperation and communication necessary for the organization of the multitude of productive
subjectivities is generated internally. It is no longer necessary for
the capitalist or the state to organize production from the outside.
On the contrary, any attempt at external organization only disrupts
and corrupts the processes of self-organization already functioning
within the multitude. The multitude produces efficiently, and moreover develops new productive forces, only when it is granted the
freedom to do so on its own terms, in its own way, with its own
mechanisms of cooperation and communication. This freedom re-

quires an exodus from the republic of property as an apparatus of control in both its private and public guises.

The freedom necessary here is clearly not an individualist freedom because the common can only be produced socially, through communication and cooperation, by a multitude of singularities. And neither is this freedom collectivist, as if all those producing subjectivities were unified in a homogeneous whole. This is the sense in which we said earlier that the metropolis is the space of freedom, the space of the organization of encounters among singular subjectivities. The requirement of freedom shows how the old formulas of the contract—both the contract between citizens and the state and that between workers and capital—are increasingly fetters on production. Whether security is exchanged for obedience or a wage for labor-time, the result of the contract is always the establishment and legitimation of authority, which always and inevitably dampens or even blocks the production of the common through subjectivity. The individualism of the parties who enter into the contract also blocks the production of the common—whether we view these individuals as preexisting or as results of historical-political processes. In the contract, individuals are drawn into a vertical relation with the figure of authority and not horizontal relations with others like them. An individual can never produce the common, no more than an individual can generate a new idea without relying on the foundation of common ideas and intellectual communication with others. Only a multitude can produce the common.

Just as political freedom is necessary for the interests of economic production, so too is political equality. Hierarchies segment the common and exclude populations from it, disrupting the necessary forms of cooperation and communication. The metaphor of a great conversation has become a conventional means to grasp the social circuits of biopolitical production. When the production of knowledge or affects is configured as a conversation, for example, it would be absurd and counterproductive to assume, on the one hand, that everyone already has the same knowledges, talents, and capacities and thus that everyone is saying the same thing. The conversation is productive precisely because of these differences. Equality, it is worth repeating, does not imply sameness, homogeneity, or unity; on the contrary. Production is also restricted when differences configure hierarchies and, for instance, only "experts" speak and others listen. In the biopolitical domain the production of the common is more efficient the more people participate freely, with their different talents and abilities, in the productive network. Participation, furthermore, is a kind of pedagogy that expands productive forces since all those included become through their participation more capable.

The metaphor of a great conversation, however, paints a picture of these productive relationships that is too harmonious and pacific, indifferent to the quality of encounters that constitute them. Many people are silenced even when included in a conversation. And simply adding more voices without adequate means of cooperation can quickly result in cacophony, making it impossible for anyone to understand anything. As we saw with regard to the metropolis in *De Corpore* 2, given the current state of society, most spontaneous encounters are infelicitous and result in a corruption of the common or the production of a negative, noxious form of it. Although the equality required to advance production and foster the expansion of productive forces is one that is characterized by participation in an open, expansive network of encounters that are as free as possible from hierarchies, then, our first course of action to achieve this will often require breaking off the conversation, subtracting ourselves from detrimental relationships and corrupt forms of the common. Such practices of rupture are, in many instances, the first step toward equality.

Freedom and equality also imply an affirmation of democracy in opposition to the political representation that forms the basis of hegemony. Two instances of representation are most relevant here, which, upon analysis, turn out to be very closely related. First is the representation required to construct a people out of a multitude. A people, of course, as Ernesto Laclau explains brilliantly, is not a natural or spontaneous formation but rather is formed by mechanisms of representation that translate the diversity and plurality of existing subjectivities into a unity through identification with a leader, a governing group, or in some cases a central idea. "There is no hegemony," Laclau makes clear, "without constructing a popular identity out of a plurality of democratic demands."[38] The second instance of representation, which is most clearly seen at the constitutional level, operates a disjunctive synthesis between the representatives and the represented. The U.S. Constitution, for instance, is designed simultaneously to link the represented to the government and at the same time separate them from it. This separation of the representatives from the represented is likewise a basis for hegemony.[39] The logic of representation and hegemony in both these instances dictates that a people exists only with respect to its leadership and vice versa, and thus this arrangement determines an aristocratic, not a democratic, form of government, even if the people elect that aristocracy.

The needs of biopolitical production, however, directly conflict with political representation and hegemony. The act of representation, insofar as it eclipses or homogenizes singularities in the construction of identity, restricts the production of the common by undermining the necessary freedom and plurality we spoke of earlier. A people might be able to conserve the existing common, but to produce new instances of the common requires a multitude, with its encounters, cooperation, and communication among singularities. The hegemony created by the division between the representatives and the represented, furthermore, is also an obstacle to the production of the common. Not only do all such hierarchies undermine biopolitical production, but also any instance of hegemony or control exerted from outside the multitude over the productive process corrupts and restricts it.

Democracy—not the aristocracy configured by representation and hegemony—is required to foster the production of the common and the expansion of productive forces, in other words, to avoid capital's biopolitical crises and treat its ills. This democracy of producers entails, in addition to freedom and equality, one more essential element: the power of decision, which would organize production, create forms of cooperation and communication, and push forward innovation. The mythology of the capitalist entrepreneur persists, although any attempt of an individual capitalist or even the class of capitalists to innovate by intervening in and organizing productive cooperation only corrupts the common and obstructs its production. What must arise instead (and is already emerging) is an entrepreneurship of the common, an entrepreneurship of the multitude, which functions within a democracy of producing subjectivities endowed together with the power of decision.

Finally, the exodus of the multitude from the republic of property, from the hierarchies of command over production, and from all other social hierarchies is perhaps the most significant example of a common decision. How is that decision to be made? Is there a vote? We are not yet in a position to describe the structures and function of such a democracy, but we can see clearly now, at least, that constructing it is necessary to treat the ills of capital and foster the expansion of biopolitical production.

Seismic Retrofit: A Reformist Program for Capital

Our analysis has led to the conclusion that capital is on a path of destruction, the destruction of not only others—the global environment and the poorest populations first of all—but also itself. Can capital be saved from its death drive? The last great economic thinker to propose a successful treatment for the ills of capital was John Maynard Keynes. On the basis of his work were developed regimes for the state regulation of production, welfare structures for producers, the stimulation of effective demand, and numerous other remedies. We have already seen, however, that today, in the biopolitical era, those old medicines no longer work and sometimes actually contribute to the disease. But that does not mean that reforms are no longer possible. It is not that difficult, on the basis of our argument, to come up with a list of beneficial reforms, but there is clearly something paradoxical about proposing such a program. It is unlikely, first of all, that the global aristocracy would be capable of enacting significant reforms today or deviating in any substantial way from its path of destruction. And second, if such reforms were actually instituted, they would, while treating capital's ills, also immediately point beyond capital toward a new mode of production. This situation reminds us of an old Yiddish joke. Question: What is the difference between a crow? Answer: Its two wings are the same length, except the left. Let us proceed in this same paradoxical spirit: working through the logic as far as we can, assuming it will eventually make sense, but knowing all the while it will eventually collapse in nonsense.

Capitalist crises today, as we have seen, have to be understood in not only their objective guise—credit crunch, inflation, recession, soaring energy prices, falling housing prices, currency crises, ecological devastation, and so forth—but also and more important their subjective guise. Innumerable obstacles are stacked against productive subjectivities: barriers preventing access to the common and corrupting it, lack of the necessities to create together and organize productive encounters, and so forth. The most urgent reforms needed are those to provide the necessities for developing the entrepreneurship of the common and the innovation of cooperative social networks. We do not expect the global aristocracy to come asking us for advice anytime soon, but here nonetheless are some possible reforms that could constitute a program for capital.

The first set of reforms is aimed at providing the infrastructure necessary for biopolitical production. Most obvious is the need for adequate physical infrastructure, which is lacking for the majority of the world. In the major metropolises of the subordinated parts of the world, vast populations are condemned to endure in misery on the brink of death in poisonous environments lacking clean drinking water, basic sanitary conditions, electricity, access to affordable food, and other physical necessities to support life. Rather than biopolitics, as Achille Mbembe suggests, this should be called a necropolitics, ruling over social death and physical death. Providing basic infrastructure needs is also immediately an environmental question since the devastation of the environment is a central obstacle to access to adequate food, clean air and water, and other needs for survival. Capital cannot just write off certain populations as disposable; it needs everyone to be productive in the biopolitical economy.[40]

Bare life, however, is not sufficient for biopolitical production. A social and intellectual infrastructure is also required to support productive subjectivities. In the age of biopolitical production the central tools are no longer the spinning loom or cotton gin or metal press, but rather linguistic tools, affective tools for constructing relationships, tools for thinking, and so forth. Humans already have brains, of course, linguistic abilities, and relationship capacities, but these have to be developed. That is why basic and advanced education is even more important in the biopolitical economy than it was previously. Everyone needs to learn how to work with language, codes, ideas, and affects—and moreover to work with others, none of which comes naturally. Something like a global education initiative would have to be instituted, which provides mandatory education for all, starting with literacy and working up to advanced education in the natural and social sciences as well as the humanities.[41]

As a corollary to education as a social and intellectual infrastructure, an open infrastructure of information and culture would have to be constructed to develop fully and put into practice the multitude's abilities to think and cooperate with others. Such an infrastructure must include an open physical layer (including access to wired and wireless communications networks), an open logical layer (for instance, open code and protocols), and an open content layer (such as cultural, intellectual, and scientific works). Such a common infrastructure would counter the mechanisms of privatization, including patents, copyrights, and other forms of immaterial property, which prevent people from engaging the reserves of existing ideas, images, and codes to use them to produce new ones. Such open access to the common also has the advantage of ensuring that all necessary goods, such as medicine and other fruits of scientific research, are available to all at affordable costs.[42]

Another necessary infrastructure reform is to provide sufficient funds to meet the technological requirements of advanced research.

One of the arguments for maintaining patents, for example, even though they restrict access to the common and thereby diminish productive capacities, is that corporations need profits to support research and development. It is indeed true that many types of research—such as in medicine, pharmaceuticals, computer science, and materials science—require large investments. If the enormous profits generated by patents and copyrights are taken away, some other source of funds must be provided, through either private or public institutions, to support such research.

In addition to reforms of the physical, social, and immaterial infrastructure, another set of reforms must provide the freedom required for biopolitical production. A first freedom necessary is the freedom of movement, by which we mean the freedom to migrate within and across national borders and also the freedom to stay in one place. As we saw at several points in our analysis earlier, biopolitical productivity depends on the ability to organize beneficial encounters and subtract from detrimental relationships and noxious forms of the common. Freedom of movement would thus configure a freedom of space, allowing the multitude to flow to where it can be the most creative, organize the most joyful encounters, and establish the most productive relationships. Establishing some form of open citizenship is the only means we see to support this freedom and thereby expand biopolitical production.

A second reform of freedom regards time, and the most significant portion of unfree time in our lives is spent at work. As we found earlier, all infringement on the autonomy of biopolitical labor, including the command of the boss, is an obstacle to productivity. (In fact in the biopolitical era, gauging how much time you are forced to waste—working in the call center, at the office desk, in the fields, or at the factory—is one good measure of exploitation.) A reform that would grant freedom of time is the establishment of a minimum guaranteed income on a national or global scale paid to everyone regardless of work. Separating income from work would allow everyone more control over time. Many authors, including ourselves, have argued for a guaranteed income on the basis of economic justice (wealth is produced across a widely dispersed social network, and therefore the wage that compensates it should be equally social) and social welfare (since nothing close to full employment can be achieved in the current economy, income must be provided also for those left without work). Here, however, we need to recognize how ensuring that the entire population has the basic minimum for life is in the interests of capital. Granting the multitude autonomy and control over time is essential to foster productivity in the biopolitical economy.[43]

The freedom required for biopolitical production also includes the power to construct social relationships and create autonomous social institutions. One possible reform to develop such capacities is the establishment of mechanisms of participatory democracy at all levels of government to allow the multitude to learn social cooperation and self-rule. As Thomas Jefferson argues, participating in government is a pedagogy in self-rule, developing people's capacities and whetting their appetites for more. Democracy is something you can learn only by doing.[44]

These are just a few of the reforms necessary to save capitalist production, and as we said earlier, we have no reason to believe that the global aristocracy that rules over economic relations is willing or able to institute them, even when facing enormous financial and economic crises. Reforms will come about only through struggle, only when capital is forced to accept them. Innumerable struggles demanding the physical and immaterial infrastructure for social life are already under way, as is too a struggle for the freedom and autonomy of the multitude. These will have to develop and intensify to achieve reforms.

Some readers might at this point begin to doubt our revolutionary intentions. Why are we suggesting reforms to *save* capital? Does that not just delay the revolution? We are working here with a different notion of transition. Ours is different, obviously, from the collapse theories that, promoting the slogan "The worse things are, the better things are," envision the end of capitalist rule resulting from catastrophic crises, followed by a new economic order that somehow rises whole out of its ashes. It is also different from the notion of socialist transition that foresees a transfer of wealth and control from the private to the public, increasing state regulation, control, and management of social production. The kind of transition we are working with instead requires the growing autonomy of the multitude from both private and public control; the metamorphosis of social subjects through education and training in cooperation, communication, and organizing social encounters; and thus a progressive accumulation of the common. This is how capital creates its own gravediggers: pursuing its own interests and trying to preserve its own survival, it must foster the increasing power and autonomy of the productive multitude. And when that accumulation of powers crosses a certain threshold, the multitude will emerge with the ability autonomously to rule common wealth.

DE HOMINE 2: CROSS THE THRESHOLD!

> If a man could write a book on Ethics which really was a book on
> Ethics, this book would, with an explosion, destroy all the other
> books in the world.
> —Ludwig Wittgenstein, "Lecture on Ethics"

What is the value of a company in the postindustrial era? Traditionally the value of an enterprise was established by calculating the cost of its initial outlay and adding it to labor costs, the amount paid for materials, plant maintenance, transportation of goods, and so forth. These might be complex calculations, but everything could fit in the columns of double-entry bookkeeping. Thomas Gradgrind, the soulless factory owner of Charles Dickens's *Hard Times,* can in this way confidently quantify all facets of life: "with a rule and a pair of scales, and the multiplication tables always in his picket . . . ready to weigh and measure any parcel of human nature, and tell you exactly what it comes to."[45] All value could be assessed with precision and, as the classics of political economy tell us, all value traced back to labor as its source. Value thus depended on the ability to discipline labor and measure its efforts, the very material efforts of thousands of workers and the harshness of organized command in manufacture.

Today the value of a company depends to an increasing degree on immaterial assets such as "goodwill" and other intangibles, which can at times be created and destroyed extraordinarily quickly. Economists define goodwill as the value derived from a company's reputation, position in the market, employee relations, managerial

talent, relations with government officials, and other immaterial assets. Quantifying goodwill and measuring other intangible assets is
thus an extremely difficult operation that torments accountants. In
fact the value of a company including its intangible assets is determined most often by the evaluations that stock exchanges, banks,
sellers and buyers, various entrepreneurs in the same sector, rating
agencies, and the industrialists and brokers of the immaterial agree
upon. The value of a company and its intangible assets appears to be
a monetary materialization of the functions of the market.[46] So is it
a question of value as goodwill versus value as labor? This alternative would be laughable had the financial markets not already made
it their own and contemporary capitalism adapted to it. It could almost make one question whether there still is any labor-power in
production today. Does wealth really flow from the brain of the
masters? No, of course it doesn't. Why, then, instead of mocking
notions of goodwill and demystifying intangible values, do we take
them so seriously?

In order to address the question of intangible value we need
to take a brief detour through traditional conceptions of the labor
theory of value. In the Marxist tradition, of which we see ourselves
part, the theory of value takes two forms. First, it is a theory of abstract labor, which is present in all commodities in so far as labor is
the common substance of all productive activity. Marxists analyze
how this qualitative conception is transformed into a quantitative
notion of the law of value centered on the problem of the measure
of the value of labor. The magnitude of value expresses the link between a certain commodity and the labor time necessary to produce it, which can be expressed in units of "simple labor." The fundamental problem posed by this quantitative theory of value,
according to Paul Sweezy, is to seek the laws that regulate the allo-
cation of the labor force to the various branches of production in a
society of commodity producers. "To use a modern expression,"
Sweezy explains, "the law of value is essentially a theory of general
equilibrium, developed in the first instance with reference to simple commodity production and later on adapted to capitalism."[47]

Behind every particular form assumed by labor in determinate instances lies a global social labor-power capable of being transferred from one use to another in accordance with social needs, the importance and development of which are dependent—in the last instance—on society's ability to produce wealth.

The law of value also takes a second form, which regards the value of labor as a figure of antagonism, as the subject of an open and ever present rupture in the system rather than an element of equilibrium. Throughout Marx's oeuvre, the concept of labor-power is regarded as an element of production that valorizes relatively independently of the functioning of the equilibrium sought by the first version of the law of value. This means that, instead of being idealized as measure, the "unity" is found in a relation to "necessary labor," which, rather than a fixed quantity, is a dynamic element of the system. Historically, necessary labor is determined by struggle and built on the ever-growing needs of the proletariat: it is the product of the struggle against work and the effort to transform productive activity. A second point of view thus emerges which considers the law of value as a motor of constitutional disequilibrium rather than equilibrium of the capitalist system. The law of value, from this perspective, is really part of the law of surplus value insofar as it helps generate a constitutional crisis of equilibrium. When the law of value is applied to capitalist development as a whole, it generates crisis—not only crises of circulation and disproportion (that is, phenomena that are reducible to the model of systemic equilibrium), but also crises caused by struggles and the subjective disequilibrium of the cycle, which result from the impossibility of containing the growth of demand, in other words, the needs and desires of productive subjects. In this framework the law of value/surplus value appears as both the law of the continual destructuring and restructuring of the cycle of capitalist development and the law of composition and recomposition of the multitude as power of transformation. The labor theory of value defined by classical political economy is thus being extinguished in the process of capitalist development as capital produces new forms of organization in the postindustrial era.[48]

This process of going beyond the law of value, however, brings back again and deepens all the contradictions it originally raised. The first of these is the opposition of "simple labor" to "skilled and complex labor." The latter cannot be reduced to a multiplier of the former, which is regarded as a unit of measure. Here lies the origin of the nonsensical claim that the greatest use-value of skilled labor (that is to say, its highest productivity level) can be deduced from the value of its product rather than explained by the "difference" inherent to the labor employed in production. The second contradiction is the opposition between "productive" and "unproductive" labor. Unlike unproductive labor, the classic definition tells us, productive labor directly produces capital. This definition, however, is terribly reductive of the notion of productivity and, more generally, productive force. Productive labor, if such a term is to be used, must be defined by its inscription in social cooperation rather than in relation to the quantity of units of simple labor that it assembles, and the more labor is subsumed under capital, the more this is the case. Cooperation and the common make labor productive, and cooperation grows as the productive forces develop and increasingly become common assets. Finally, the third contradiction is that biopolitical labor-power, including intellectual, scientific, communicative, and affective activity, is reducible neither to the sum of simple labor nor to cooperation (however complex it might be). Biopolitical labor is characterized by creativity—creativity as an expression of the common.

These contradictions have today become real, present, and significant, which is to say they no longer merely represent contradictory tendencies in the system. As capitalism developed, these contradictions have become concrete aporiae. The distinction between simple and complex labor may have been valid for the historical phase of capitalist development that Marx defined as simple cooperation, but already in the phase of manufacture it becomes an aporia. Similarly, the distinction between productive and unproductive labor which had some validity for manufacture becomes an aporia in the period of large-scale industry. And now, in the postindustrial era, the productive value of biopolitical labor has become hegemonic through the inclusion rather than exclusion of every other element of production. Because of this evolution it is clearly impossible to regard the law of value (in its classical formulation) as a *law of measure* of the global productivity of the economic system and as the rule of its equilibrium. Contemporary attempts to reinvent measure in terms of market values, goodwill, intangible assets, and the like demonstrate the inadequacy of the law of value for measuring productivity, but they do indicate a real change in the nature of productive power, which is still based on labor.[49] Even though measure remains indispensable for capital, all of the *dispositifs* intended to measure labor and value—such as productive and unproductive labor, labor-time and the organization of the working day, the hegemony of labor composition and/or industry over production as a whole, and working wages and social income—are now in crisis and cannot be applied in biopolitical society.

At this point we need a new theory of value. But will it really be a theory of value? In the sequence of discussions at the end of each part of this book, we have tracked figures in which labor-value exceeds the flows of the economy and power. In the first we insisted on how the biopolitical event exceeds the continuity of development, temporal routine, and the linear unfolding of history. In the second we emphasized that biopolitical reason and the production of knowledge exceed the instrumental norms of knowledge and power construed in modernity. In the third we discussed how love as a constituent social drive exceeds all constituted powers. In the Intermezzo, which functions in line with these discussions, we insisted on the fact that love, with its overflowing powers, also requires a training to guard against love gone bad and needs a force to combat evil. Finally, in the fourth we began to give concrete figure to the exceeding of the multitude in its production of the common in the metropolis. Now we are in a position to present the subjec-

tive relevance of this world of historical and ontological overflowing.

To determine what it means for biopolitics to exceed, we
need to establish the difference between this figure of *non-measure*
and the traditional models proposed to measure value. In the biopolitical context, value overflows any threshold of political and economic control. Its measure cannot be derived either from the quantity of time dedicated to the necessary reproduction of labor-power
as a whole or from the ensuing social order. Biopolitical value is
grounded on the common of cooperation. The needs interpreted
by valorization arise out of subjects and in turn continually transform them: the terrain of the common is animated by the production of subjectivity. "If two come together and unite their strength,"
Spinoza asserts, "they have more power, and consequently more
right over nature than either one alone: and the greater the number
so joined in alliance, the more right they will together possess."[50]
Value in the current situation must refer to life activity as a whole,
and therefore the immeasurability and overflowing of productive
labor is a process that traverses the entire biopolitical fabric of
society.[51]

Crossing the threshold gives us a first definition of the process
of biopolitical exceeding, which overflows the barriers that the tradition of modern political economy built to control labor-power
and the production of value. In epistemological terms, exceeding is
a linguistic act of rupture and innovation, which is not satisfied
with recomposing the continuity of language but instead reveals an
accumulated and still unexpressed power of meanings, on the one
hand, and an innovative expression of signs, on the other.[52] In physical terms, or rather what we would call the biophysics of bodies,
exceeding is the continual metamorphosis of modes of living and
the ever more accelerated invention of new forms of social life in
common. In the history of materialist philosophy, the physical innovation of bodies was always presented as a *clinamen,* the element
that intervenes in the fall of atoms to make them deviate from their
singular course and thus determine the event. Exceeding should be

understood as a *dispositif*, a dynamic of desire that not only recognizes its own formation but also experiments with it and intervenes in the process. Finally, in ethics, when viewed as an experience of training in love, this exceeding explodes in all its clarity—as Wittgenstein says in the epigraph to this chapter—no longer as the product of the biopolitical process but as its performative machine.[53]

In the history of philosophy there is a continuing legacy that, although continually repressed, defends the affirmation of value as an expression of life and interprets it as a power of creation. The principle of an exceeding of will over instrumental knowledge has, from ancient Greece onwards, faced strong opposition, confronted with the intellectual hierarchies imposed on life by dogmatic philosophy. But this alternative stream in the history of philosophy, of resistances and lines of flight, lives on. We can recognize it, for example, in Augustine's affirmation of a free will that elevates man to the threshold of transforming being itself. Against the intellectualism that identifies truth with instrumental rationality, Augustine affirms that free will permeates everything: "Voluntas est quippe in omnibus; imo omnes nihil aliud quam voluntates sunt."[54] We can also recognize it, as Ernst Bloch reminds us, in the "Aristotelian Left" of Ibn Sinā (Avicenna) and Ibn Rushd (Averroës), who insist on the creativity of matter and discover, with the *eductio formarum,* the human powers to interpret and develop the forces of life.[55] From Duns Scotus to Nicholas of Cusa, from Spinoza to Nietzsche and Deleuze, we could chart the development of these *dispositifs* of exceeding and ethical performativity. This alternative genealogy culminates, perhaps, with an understanding of love as will to power, that is, the ontological production of common subjectivities.

We still, however, need a new theory of value that is grounded in exceeding, crossing the threshold. We should note, first of all, that we are not expecting such a theory to reveal value as something other than the perception of a historical event. In the most powerful theoretical experience that runs from Marx to Nietzsche, value is already regarded as a historically determined innovation, that is, constituent activity. Wilhelm Dilthey aptly sums it up when he writes, "Everything man does in this socio-historical reality is produced by putting will into play; in will, the end becomes the agent under the guise of the motive."[56] Michel de Certeau similarly shows us how the *dispositifs* at work in Foucault's historical research provoke an explosion of life events, which build for the future, "like laughter."[57] But we need to go further. We are at the stage of the explosion, as Wittgenstein defines it: a singular, ethical, new, and irreducible determination.

All this means that a theory of value can and should be construed as a *dispositif* that, breaking away from determinism, redefines the temporality and spaces of life in creative terms. To exceed is a creative activity. A new theory of value has to be based on the powers of economic, political, and social innovation that today are expressions of the multitude's desire. Value is created when resistance becomes overflowing, creative, and boundless and thus when human activity exceeds and determines a rupture in the balance of power. Value is created, consequently, when the relations between the constituent elements of the biopolitical process and the structure of biopower are thrown out of balance. When control over development, which the state and the collective organisms of capital assume to define their own legitimacy, is no longer able to hold back the resistance of the multitude, labor-power, and the whole set of social singularities, only then will there be value.

This hypothesis leads to a series of political positions. First and foremost is *labor-power against exploitation*. The elements that determine the disequilibrium of capitalist command are insubordination, sabotage, industrial jacquerie, demands for basic income, the liberation and organization of the intellectual labor of the multitude, and so forth. Capitalist power can track and govern this disequilibrium in either a static or a dynamic manner. The choice between different techniques of containment and/or governance is dictated by the intensity of resistances. When the exceeding forces of the multitude win, the system enters a state of crisis, and repression can be imposed only at the most advanced and sophisticated levels of capitalist organization, or rather, starting from processes of reform in the structures of power.[58]

The second articulation of dispute, which poses the concept of exceeding activity from the perspective of resisting subjectivities, positions *singularity against identity.* We mentioned earlier and will return in Part 6 to analyze how identity represents a fundamental instrument of capitalist mystification and repression. In this context it acts to neutralize or crush the developments produced by singularities in the construction of the multitude and the common through a dialectics of identity. Singularities, however, can never be reduced to identity, just as the multitude can never be made a unity.

Third, the hypothesis poses *the common against the republic of property.* When labor and life exceed, they always point toward the construction of the common, which is the only sign of productivity today. The republic of property, however, tries to subjugate, exploit, and privatize the common in order to reallocate it in accordance with the laws of individual ownership and liberal political representation. This project asphyxiates singularities and neutralizes the power of the common. The bourgeois identity politics of capitalist exploitation and republican transcendence is really a necropolitics or thanatopolitics. Biopower reacts everywhere and always against the exceeding activity of biopolitical production.

What, then, is the definition of value in economic terms? This is a meaningless question unless we can make economics into bioeconomics with reference also to biopolitics and bio-society, as well as, obviously, bio-resistance, bio-revolution, and even bio-happiness! Whereas capitalists have destroyed economics by turning it into mathematics, it is up to us to bring it back to the terrain of life and the ancient meaning of *oikonomia.* Economic value is defined by the overflowing, exceeding process accomplished by cooperative activity (intellectual, manual, affective, or communicative) against and beyond the capitalist regulation of society exercised through the financial conventions of the market. If the *measure* of value is still to have any meaning, it must be determined through the democratic exercise of the production of the common. It would be useful to reclaim an old adage for ourselves as communists: freedom is not just a political value but above all an economic or, better, a biopolitical value. Starting from these political considerations, we can begin to account for the exceeding movement of social activity and common labor. The ontology of the present indicated by the biopolitics of production needs to be complemented, as we will see in Part 6, by a radically democratic structure.

We are proposing a steep path, but one that is already being traveled. When studying the development of worker resistance to industrial capitalism, Marx traces a similar process of training: "It took time and experience before workers learnt to distinguish between machinery and its employment by capital, and transfer their attacks from the material instruments of production to the form of society which utilises these instruments."[59] Contemporary proletarian subjects of biopolitical production also have to learn where to direct their attacks, and this is made easier only by the fact that the multitude is now established in the common, and capital is increasingly recognizable as merely an obstacle.

PART 6

REVOLUTION

We have frequently printed the word Democracy. Yet I cannot too often repeat this is a word the real gist of which still sleeps, still unawaken'd, notwithstanding the resonance and the many angry tempests out of which its syllables have come, from pen or tongue. It is a great word, whose history, I suppose, remains unwritten, because that history remains to be enacted.

—Walt Whitman, "Democratic Vistas"

6.1

REVOLUTIONARY PARALLELISM

> I have no race except that which is forced upon me. I have no country except that to which I'm obliged to belong. I have no traditions. I'm free. I have only the future.
>
> —Richard Wright, *Pagan Spain*

> As a *mestiza* I have no country, my homeland cast me out.... (As a lesbian I have no race, my own people disclaim me; but I am all races because there is the queer in me in all races.)
>
> —Gloria Anzaldúa, *Borderlands*

> I am of an inferior race for all eternity.
>
> —Arthur Rimbaud, "A Season in Hell"

Identity Politics in Purgatory

Identity politics has had a lot of bad press lately. On the one hand, the dominant reflex of the Right (as well as significant portions of the Left) is to maintain and police an ideological "identity-blind" standpoint by accusing anyone who speaks of the social hierarchies, segregations, and injuries of identity of having created them. The election of Barack Obama as U.S. president has only reinforced claims that we have entered a "postracial" era. Many on the radical Left, on the other hand, and more significantly for our purposes, critique identity politics for creating obstacles to revolution. The recognition and affirmation of identities—class, race, gender, sexuality, even at times religious identities—can reveal social wounds, the argument goes, demand redress of social ills, and create weapons for revolt and emancipation, but cannot operate the social metamorphosis, especially the self-transformation, necessary for revolution. And yet all revolutionary movements are grounded in identity. Here is the conundrum we face: revolutionary politics has to start from identity but cannot end there. The point is not to pose a division between identity politics and revolutionary politics but, on the contrary, to follow the parallel revolutionary streams of thought and practice within identity politics, which all, perhaps paradoxically, aim toward an abolition of identity. Revolutionary thought, in other words, should not shun identity politics but instead must work through it and learn from it.

It is inevitable that identity should become a primary vehicle for struggle within and against the republic of property since identity itself is based on property and sovereignty. On a first level, the rule of property is a means of creating identity and maintaining hierarchy. Property is so profoundly entangled with race, for example, not only because in many parts of the world the history of property rights is deeply embedded in the sagas of slave property but also because the rights to own and dispose of property are racialized, both with and without the aid of legalized schemes of segregation. Similarly, throughout the world male property privileges define female subordination, from notions of wife as property and the traffic in women to inheritance laws and more subtle forms of gendered property. On a second and more profound level, however, identity *is* property. Notions of the sovereign individual and possessive individualism, which constitute the seventeenth- and eighteenth-century origins of bourgeois ideology, pose identity as property in a philosophical sense: "Every man has a *property*," writes John Locke, "of his own *person*."[1] Identity also functions as property in material terms. Whiteness is property, for instance, Cheryl Harris explains, inasmuch as "the law has accorded 'holders' of whiteness the same privileges and benefits accorded holders of other types of property."[2] Though not alienable, like most forms of property identity is title and possession that wields the powers of exclusion and hierarchy. Identity is a weapon of the republic of property, but one that can be turned against it.

In our reading of the revolutionary projects in each of the identity domains we find three common tasks. The first is to reveal the violence of identity as property and thereby in some sense reappropriate that identity. The "primal scene" of African American identity in this respect, for example, might be considered Aunt Hester's scream: Frederick Douglass recounts in his autobiography how slave identity and blackness in general are rooted for him in the terror of hearing his aunt's cries as she is whipped by the master.[3] Recognizing the fact of blackness, as W. E. B. Du Bois and Frantz Fanon also testify in autobiographical accounts, is a discovery not just of difference but also and primarily of collective subordination and violence. And yet the violence of identity is largely invisible, especially to those not subject to it, making it all the more difficult to contest. This is one meaning of Du Bois's famous claim that a veil cordons off the subordinated from the view of dominant society. They are mysteriously hidden from sight, invisible, even when they are the ones who in broad daylight clean the houses, care for the children, produce the goods, and in general sustain the lives of the dominant. An initial task of insubordination, then, which is the most widespread form of identity politics today, requires attacking this invisibility, tearing down or rising above the veil, and revealing the structures of hierarchy that run throughout society.

The struggle to make visible the violences of identity may be even more urgent today, in an era when the dominant discourse, especially in North America and Europe, proclaims race, gender, and class hierarchies to have been overcome. Yes, there were regrettable social hierarchies, the story goes, there was slavery and Jim Crow laws, there was a generalized subordination of women under patriarchy, repression and genocide of native populations, the oppression of workers in factories and sweatshops—but since all that is now past, society must be "identity blind." A black man in the White House is posed as the ultimate confirmation of this discourse. The mandate of feminism, antiracist activism, worker struggles, and other identity politics are over, according to this view, and the social divisions of identity are only perpetuated by those who continue to speak of them. That is how those who promote consciousness of social inequalities along identity lines are cast as creating class, race, gender, and other identity divisions. And as a result we are increasingly facing paradoxical forms of "color-blind" racism, "gender-blind" sexism, "class-blind" class oppression, and so forth.[4]

Critical race scholars in the United States, for example, explain that by an ironic turn, a version of the civil rights legal paradigm has been victorious in the sense that, in the name of antiracism, today's prevailing dominant legal discourse mandates "race-blind" perspectives in legal thought and practice. This legal blindness to race, they argue, simply hides continuing racial hierarchies and makes them more difficult to confront with legal instruments.[5] Liberal oligarchies throughout Latin America have since independence mobilized a similarly "race-blind" ideology, attempting to Hispanicize the indigenous populations with the goal of eradicating the "Indian"—through education, intermarriage, and migration (when not through physical annihilation)—such that the vestiges of indigenous civilizations would be relegated to the museums and remain only as tourist curiosities. Such discourses of national integration have not, of course, eliminated or in most cases even lessened racial subordination but rather have only made the continuing colonization less visible and thus more difficult to combat.[6] Market ideology, to give one more example, is "class blind" in the sense that it views each individual as a free and equal commodity owner who comes to market with goods to sell: proletarians with their labor-power and capitalists bearing money and property. But this market ideology masks the hierarchy and command involved in the labor process itself, along with the "economic" violence of property and poverty and the "extraeconomic" violence of conquest, imperialism, exclusion, and the social control that creates and maintains class divisions. We are confident that readers are already quite familiar with these and parallel arguments in other identity domains, including hidden forms of sexual violence that women suffer, sometimes under the cover of marriage and the family, and the violence of homophobia and heteronormativity.

The violence and hierarchy of identity are not, of course, merely a matter of consciousness (or bigotry and prejudice); rather, like other forms of property, identity maintains hierarchy primarily through social structures and institutions. The initial positive task of identity politics in the various domains is thus to combat blindness and make visible the brutally real but too often hidden mechanisms and regimes of social subordination, segmentation, and exclusion that operate along identity lines. Making visible the subordinations of identity as property implies, in a certain sense, reappropriating identity. This first task of identity politics might thus be placed in the position that *the expropriation of the expropriators* fills in traditional communist discourse.

Too often, however, identity politics begins and ends with this first task, sometimes combining it with pallid declarations of pride and affirmation. Identity projects for revealing social violence and hierarchy run aground when they become wedded to injury, creating, Wendy Brown claims, a group investment in maintaining the injured status with an attitude of *ressentiment*. Identity is regarded as a possession, we might say, and is defended as property. What is most significantly missing from such identity politics, as Brown insists, is the drive for freedom that should be their basis.[7] Some of the most exciting recent scholarship in feminist theory and black studies, in fact, argues for a return to the discourse of freedom, which used to animate the center of feminism and black radicalism. Fred Moten, for instance, conceives blackness as not (or not only) the mark of subjection and subordination but a position of power and agency. The "performative essence of blackness" is the resistance to enslavement or, more generally, the quest for freedom.[8] Moten is to a certain extent echoing Du Bois's frequent reference to the powers of emancipation as one of the special gifts of black folk and Cedric Robinson's claims that freedom and power are central to the entire tradition of black radicalism.[9] Linda Zerilli, in parallel fashion, attempts to reclaim feminism as a practice of freedom, thus returning to some powerful currents of early second wave feminism. A freedom-centered feminism, in Zerilli's view, is concerned not so much with knowing (and revealing, for example, the ways in which women are socially subordinated) but rather with doing— "with transforming, world-building, beginning anew."[10] The tradition of revolutionary Marxism, to consider one more parallel example, presents proletarian identity as a weapon against capital and a motor of class struggle, not only by revealing the violence and suffering of the working class but also by constructing a figure of workers' power capable of striking back at capital and gaining freedom from it. The second task of identity politics, then, is to proceed from indignation to rebellion against the structures of domination using the subordinated identity as a weapon in the quest for freedom—thus filling the traditional role of *the conquest of state power.*

This second task of identity politics, the struggle for freedom, works against the risk of attachment to injury and focus on victimization but does not guarantee that the process will not become fixed on identity and grind to a halt. When freedom is configured as the emancipation of an existing subject, identity ceases to be a war machine and becomes a form of sovereignty. Identity as property, however rebellious, can always be accommodated within the ruling structures of the republic of property.

One version of identity politics that brings the process to a halt in this way, which was particularly widespread in the 1990s, poses it as a project of recognition, often guided by the logic of Hegelian dialectics. The struggle for recognition in the work of some of its most prominent proponents, such as Charles Taylor and Axel Honneth, aims at the expression of existing identities, the affirmation of their authenticity, and ultimately the construction of a multicultural framework of mutual respect and tolerance for all identity expressions. By substituting morality for politics in this way, recognition reduces the quest for freedom to a project of expression and tolerance. Here Marx's critique of Hegel's dialectic is once again useful: it merely affirms what exists rather than creating the new. Identity thus ceases to be a means and becomes an end.[11]

Another version of identity politics that brings the process to a halt in this way is characterized by nationalism, understood in a rather broad way as the effort to render identity sovereign. Black nationalism in the United States, for example, which takes inspiration from the anticolonial struggles and their goals of national liberation, is seldom configured in territorial terms but is aimed rather at the sovereignty of the racial identity, which implies separation and self-determination, controlling the economy of the community, policing the community, and so forth. It is easy to think of certain streams of feminist politics that are characterized similarly by gender nationalism, or gay and lesbian politics by gay and lesbian nationalisms, and there is a long and complex history of worker politics that takes the form of worker nationalism. The metaphor of nation, in each of the cases, refers to the relative separation of the community from the society as a whole and suggests the construction of a sovereign people. All these nationalisms, in contrast to the multiculturalist struggles for recognition, are combative formations that constantly rebel against structures of subordination. Such nationalisms do, however, end up reinforcing the fixity of identity. Every nationalism is a disciplinary formation that enforces obedience to the rules of identity, policing the behavior of members of the community and their separation from others. For reasons like these, some of the most revolutionary advocates of Black Nationalism, such as Malcolm X and Huey Newton, eventually move away from nationalist positions, as we will see shortly. The key to carrying through the first two tasks of identity toward a revolutionary politics is to make sure that rendering violence and subordination visible, rebelling against them, and struggling for freedom do not merely come back to identity and stop there. To become revolutionary, the politics of identity has to find a means to keep moving forward.

The terminological distinction between *emancipation* and *liberation* is crucial here: whereas emancipation strives for the freedom of identity, the freedom to be *who you really are,* liberation aims at the freedom of self-determination and self-transformation, the freedom to determine *what you can become.* Politics fixed on identity immobilizes the production of subjectivity; liberation instead requires engaging and taking control of the production of subjectivity, keeping it moving forward.

Revolution Is Monstrous

A third political task is necessary in order to support the first two tasks, keep the rebellious function of identity moving forward, and carry identity politics toward a revolutionary project: to strive for its own abolition. The self-abolition of identity is the key to understanding how revolutionary politics can begin with identity but not end up there. This paradoxical process might sound like a dialectical negation, but really, as we will see, it is a strictly positive movement of self-transformation and metamorphosis. This is the criterion, furthermore, that distinguishes the revolutionary streams of feminism, race politics, class politics, and other identity politics from all the nonrevolutionary versions.

The revolutionary communist tradition gives us perhaps the clearest example for understanding this paradoxical proposition. The proletariat is the first truly revolutionary class in human history, according to this tradition, insofar as it is bent on its own abolition as a class. The bourgeoisie seeks continually to preserve itself, as did the aristocracy and all previous ruling classes. "In order to struggle against capital," Mario Tronti writes, "the working class must struggle against itself inasmuch as it is capital.... Workers' struggle against work, struggle of the worker against himself"—identity politics, in other words, aimed at the abolition of one's own identity.[12] This communist proposition is not as paradoxical as it first appears, since revolutionary workers aim to destroy not themselves but the identity that defines them as workers. The primary object of class struggle, in other words, is not to kill capitalists but to demolish the social structures and institutions that maintain their privilege and authority, abolishing too, thereby, the conditions of proletarian subordination. The *refusal of work* is a central slogan of this project, which we have explored at length elsewhere. The refusal of work and ulti-

mately the abolition of the worker does not mean the end of production and innovation but rather the invention, beyond capital, of
as yet unimagined relations of production that allow and facilitate an
expansion of our creative powers.[13] This movement beyond workers'
identity summarizes and carries forward the first two tasks, making
visible the structural and institutional forms of violence and hierarchy that determine their subordination as workers and struggling for
freedom from them. There is no room here, of course, for recognition or affirmation of worker identity and the possession of identity
as property except as a weapon toward its abolition. The project for
the abolition of identity thus fills the traditional role of *the abolition
of property and the abolition of the state.* In order for revolutionary
communism to be a project of not emancipation but liberation—
not emancipation *of* work but liberation *from* work—it must launch
a process of self-transformation beyond worker identity.

This formulation helps clarify the distinction between revolutionary and nonrevolutionary forms of class politics. Revolutionary
politics are not aimed only at the amelioration of worker conditions
within capitalist social structures. By attaining better work conditions, higher wages, enhanced social services, greater representation
in government, and other reforms, workers can achieve recognition
and perhaps even emancipation but only by preserving their identity *as workers.* Revolutionary class politics must destroy the structures and institutions of worker subordination and thus abolish the
identity of worker itself, setting in motion the production of subjectivity and a process of social and institutional innovation. A revolutionary class politics also does not aim at workers taking power as
the new ruling class, and thereby continuing the long history of one
social class replacing another in the seat of power. Nor can it aim at
creating social equality by universalizing one of the existing class
identities, making either everyone bourgeois or everyone proletarian. Each of these nonrevolutionary projects leaves worker identity
intact, whereas a revolutionary process must abolish it. But what
would society be and how would it produce without capitalists and

workers? That is exactly what we explored in Part 5 and throughout the course of this book in terms of the autonomous production of common wealth.

Please suspend any fears you have that such a revolutionary abolition of identity would undermine the first two tasks of identity politics or lead to chaos and a social abyss of indifferentiation. We will return to consider these questions soon. First we want to extend this analysis to other identity domains and recognize how in each of them what is revolutionary is also defined, in parallel fashion, by the self-abolition of identity.

Revolutionary feminism is distinguished from other feminist perspectives by its aim at the abolition of gender. In addition to demonstrating that one is not born a woman but made one, revealing the violences of patriarchy, rebelling against its social institutions, demanding the equality and emancipation of women, revolutionary feminism seeks the abolition of woman as an identity. "Revolutionary feminism promised," Wendy Brown explains, "that we could become new women and men, that we could literally take in hand the conditions that produce gender and then produce it differently, that not simply laws and other institutions could be purged of gender bias but that humans themselves could be produced beyond gender as history has known it."[14] Gayle Rubin earlier articulated the goal as the "elimination of the social system which creates . . . gender."[15] Perhaps the contemporary streams of "freedom-centered" feminism, such as the work of Linda Zerilli we mentioned earlier, should be considered in line with this conception of revolutionary feminism, as long as the quest for freedom is conceived as a process of not emancipation but liberation, not preserving and affirming gender identity but abolishing identity and transforming gender relations. Donna Haraway calls this revolutionary proposition simply "the utopian dream of . . . a monstrous world without gender."[16] The revolutionary project goes beyond the reformist vision of emancipation—a world not without gender difference but without gender hierarchy—and seeks an abolition of identity itself. There will be differences, indeed a proliferation of singularities, but nothing that we currently recognize as gender. Revolutionary feminism is thus monstrous in the sense of Rabelais, overflowing with powers of creativity and invention.

Queer politics may be, from this perspective, the most clearly revolutionary form of identity politics since, in the work of its most significant proponents, such as Michael Warner, Judith Butler, and Eve Sedgwick, it links identity politics inextricably to a critique of identity. Queer politics, in other words, reveals the violences and subordinations of heteronormativity and homophobia along with other gender hierarchies, proposes projects to struggle against them, but at the same time seeks, often through processes of what José Muñoz calls "disidentification," to abolish (or at least destabilize and problematize) "the homosexual" as identity, as well as woman, man, and other gender identities. "Queer . . . is an identity category," Annamarie Jagose argues, "that has no interest in consolidating or even stabilizing itself. . . . [Q]ueer is less an identity than a *critique* of identity."[17] We should note, however, that in the work of many other authors and increasingly in public discourse today, "queer" is used not as a critique of identity but simply as another identity category, often as shorthand for LGBT (lesbian, gay, bisexual, and transgender/transsexual). Just as we have noted conceptual (and political) splits in other identity domains between nonrevolutionary and revolutionary streams, so too the fields of queer theory and queer politics are divided between advocacy projects that affirm queer as identity and propositions that wield queer as an anti-identity to undermine and abolish all gender identities and set in motion a series of becomings.[18]

Black radicalism, especially in North America, the Caribbean, Britain, and other diasporic locations, also has a strong tradition grounded in a revolutionary proposition parallel to those in other identity domains, which complements the rebellion against white supremacy with a process of the abolition of blackness. "I propose," Fanon writes early in his career, "nothing short of the liberation of the man of color from himself."[19] This liberation from himself is the self-abolition of identity—marking not only the destruction of racial hierarchy but also the abolition of race as we know it, and thus, in Fanon's terms, the creation of a new humanity. The quest for freedom we cited earlier in the work of Fred Moten and central to the tradition of black radicalism implies such a revolutionary proposition when freedom is conceived not as emancipation but as liberation and thus the transformation of humanity beyond racial identity. It is interesting to note, in this regard, that Malcolm X and Huey Newton eventually question and move away from Black Nationalist positions they earlier championed when they recognize a conflict between the nationalist affirmation of identity and revolutionary projects. Newton, in particular, progressively shifts the revolutionary framework from nationalism to internationalism and finally "intercommunalism" in an effort to designate a political framework for liberation that implies the abolition of racial identity and its structures of subordination.[20] We also read this revolutionary proposition, finally, as the basis of Paul Gilroy's efforts to shift the discourse of black politics toward an abolition of race. Whereas racial identity today, according to Gilroy, has become seemingly fixed and insurmountable, at best an object of recognition, he proposes instead to "demand liberation not from white supremacy alone, however urgently that is required, but from all racializing and raciological thought, from racialized seeing, racialized thinking, and racialized thinking about thinking."[21] Race has to be destroyed, of course, if we are to follow through Gilroy's proposition, not just as an object of thought but also and more important as social structures and institutions of hierarchy, segregation, and domination. The abolition of identity implies, once again, the abolition of property and sovereignty. Only a project of liberation that destroys not just blackness as an identity of subordination but blackness as such along with whiteness and all other racial identities makes possible the creation of a new humanity.[22]

These parallel revolutionary propositions that emerge from identity politics are met by two important critiques that emphasize essential aspects of the revolutionary project. The first claims that the proposition to abolish identity undermines the ability of identity politics to reveal and fight against social oppression—that our third task, in other words, contradicts the first two, depriving them of the necessary analytical and political tools. Striving to abolish identity, from this perspective, merely feeds into the dominant, reactionary strategy to make identity and its hierarchies invisible. Many feminist scholars, for example, criticize Judith Butler's work, particularly *Gender Trouble* and *Bodies That Matter,* for drawing into question and destabilizing the category of woman. Without gendered identity as foundation, it would be impossible to highlight and analyze gender hierarchies and struggle against them.[23] Paul Gilroy's arguments against race consciousness that suggest the goal of abolishing racial identity are met with parallel objections: without race thinking there is no way to make visible the violence of racism, and without black identity there is no figure of rebellion for the struggle against white supremacy.[24] Such critiques highlight the fact that the three tasks are inseparable. Without the first two, pursuing the third task—abolishing identity—is naïve and risks making existing hierarchies more difficult to challenge. But without the third task, the first two remain tethered to identity formations, unable to embark on a process of liberation. And furthermore, even though we have for clarity of explanation presented them in sequence—first, second, and third— these tasks must all be pursued simultaneously, without, for instance, deferring the revolutionary moment to some indefinite future.

A second critique of the revolutionary proposition in the various identity domains is made in the name of difference, with the warning that the abolition of identity will result in the destruction of difference as such, leaving us with an indifferent social field. Some fear, for instance, that queer and feminist utopias of a world beyond gender would be populated by androgynous beings, devoid of difference and desire. It is important to recognize that the abolition of identity—gender identity in this instance—does not imply the destruction of difference as such, thus making everyone the same. On the contrary, it initiates the release and proliferation of differences— differences that do not mark social hierarchies. Eve Sedgwick, for example, observes—or, really, complains—that all the myriad differences of our sexual desires are corralled into two categories, homosexual and heterosexual, defined solely by the gender of the object of our desires. If we could take off these blinkers, we would see that the universe of sexual desires is filled with innumerable differences that are often more significant than this one.[25] Once the heterosexual and the homosexual are abolished, along with the two gender identities, a multitude of sexual differences can surge forward—not two sexes or zero sexes, as Deleuze and Guattari like to say, but *n* sexes.[26] Paul Gilroy similarly uses the concept of diaspora to conceive of a nonracial society characterized by a proliferation of differences. The condition and perspective of diaspora, he explains, does not imply any nostalgia for an unchanging origin and its pure, fixed identity but on the contrary illuminates the richness and social creativity that mixture and movement make possible. Gilroy thus envisions a society defined by "conviviality," that is, the cohabitation and free interaction of social differences, a situation that he sees emerging in the multicultural social life of Britain's metropolises.[27] And a revolutionary project has to create, beyond the multicultural recognition of racial identities, a conviviality among proliferating differences we no longer recognize as racial.

At this point, having followed identity thus far, through its three primary political tasks, we need to reconsider the concept because, in fact, more adequate than identity for the process we are analyzing here is *singularity*, a concept with a long history in European thought, from Duns Scotus and Spinoza to Nietzsche and Deleuze. (See *De Homine* 2 at the end of Part 5 on this alternative line of European thought.) With respect to identity, the concept of singularity is defined by three primary characteristics, all of which link it intrinsically with multiplicity. First of all, every singularity points toward and is defined by a multiplicity outside of itself. No singularity can exist or be conceived on its own, but instead both its existence and definition necessarily derive from its relations with the other singularities that constitute society. Second, every singularity points toward a multiplicity within itself. The innumerable divisions that cut throughout each singularity do not undermine but actually constitute its definition. Third, singularity is always engaged in a process of becoming different—a temporal multiplicity. This characteristic really follows from the first two insofar as the relations with other singularities that constitute the social multiplicity and the internal composition of the multiplicity within each singularity are constantly in flux.[28]

Shifting our perspective from identity to singularity clarifies especially the revolutionary moment of the process. Whereas in terms of identity this process can be understood only in the negative, paradoxical terms of self-abolition, in terms of singularity it is rather a moment of metamorphosis. And in this context it is no mystery why the revolutionary process results in a proliferation of differences, since the nature of singularities is to become different. The concept of singularity, with its multiplicities and metamorphoses, thus also has the merit of dissolving all the dialectical illusions that too often plague discourses on identity. Singularity indicates the common as a field of multiplicities and thus destroys the logic of property. What identity is to property, singularity is to the common. The distinction between identity and singularity corresponds, therefore, to that between the two notions of achieving freedom we cited earlier: identities can be emancipated, but only singularities can liberate themselves.

This revolutionary process of the abolition of identity, we should keep in mind, is monstrous, violent, and traumatic. Don't try to save yourself—in fact, your *self* has to be sacrificed! This does not mean that liberation casts us into an indifferent sea with no objects of identification, but rather the existing identities will no longer serve as anchors. Many will pull back from the brink and try to stay who they are rather than dive into the unknown waters of a world without race, gender, or other identity formations. Abolition also requires the destruction of all the institutions of the corruption of the common we spoke of earlier, such as the family, the corporation, and the nation. This involves an often violent battle against the ruling powers and also, since these institutions in part define who we now are, an operation surely more painful than bloodshed. Revolution is not for the faint of heart. It is for monsters. You have to lose who you are to discover what you can become.

Revolutionary Assemblages

After having outlined the three primary tasks of identity politics —or, really, singularity politics—we need to analyze the relations among singularities. To what extent do race, class, gender, and sexuality struggles agree or conflict with one another? By highlighting the tasks common to the different identity domains, we have thus far emphasized the parallel nature of both the forms of subordination and the processes of rebellion and liberation. Now we need to focus on the conflicts and the means to address them.

Identity politics, by its very concept, assumes a certain parallelism—the structures of racial subordination share some common elements with those of gender subordination, class subordination, and so forth—which makes possible processes of translation among the analytical and political traditions. These translations, which have been extraordinarily productive for scholars and activists, do not imply sameness—the analytics and strategies through which race, class, gender, and sexuality hierarchies function and can be combated are qualitatively different—but translation does rely on the common.

This basis in the common does not deny that identities are divided and conflict. The concept of *intersectionality* usefully highlights division in two primary respects. First of all, multiple identities intersect, which is to say that structures of violence and hierarchy coincide in determinate subjects, such as black lesbians or Aymara peasants. This means that each identity is divided internally by others: racial hierarchies divide genders and classes, gender hierarchies divide races and classes, and so forth. (This internal multiplicity is one reason that makes singularity, as we said, a more adequate concept than identity.) Second, the political agendas of the various identities do not necessarily agree but rather are often divided, divergent, or even conflicting. Revealing and struggling against racial violence, for example, does not necessarily contribute to the struggle against gender subordination; historically, on the contrary, antiracist struggles along with worker struggles have most often ignored and even contributed to gender subordination. Intersectional analysis highlights the fact, in other words, that although the intersecting forms of violence and subordination that identities suffer are in some ways parallel, the political projects to address them can—and, according to some, necessarily do—conflict. In the context of our analysis, however, whereas struggles for the recognition, affirmation, and even emancipation of identities may in fact necessarily conflict, liberation movements of singularities have the potential to articulate with one another in parallel developments. Intersectional analysis demonstrates, nonetheless, that articulation and parallelism are not automatic but have to be achieved.[29]

When we think parallelism according to the model provided by Spinoza, in fact, it becomes a means for grasping and developing the lessons of intersectionality. Spinoza's so-called parallelism is defined by his proposition that "the order and connection of ideas is the same as the order and connection of things."[30] Spinoza insists that the two attributes, thought and extension, are relatively autonomous—the mind cannot cause the body to act or the body cause the mind to think—and yet the developments in the domains of thought and extension proceed in the same order and connection because they both participate in and express a common substance. Conceiving the identity domains in the position of attributes, then, emphasizes the relative autonomy of each. Just as the mind cannot cause the body to act, class struggle does not necessarily address gender oppression, race struggle does not necessarily attack homophobia and heteronormativity, and so forth. And yet the paths of rebellion and liberation, the metamorphoses of singularities in each domain can (and must, in our view) proceed in the same order and connection. In contrast to Spinoza's model, though, parallelism here is not given but must be achieved politically. A translation process is required to reveal and understand these potential correspondences, a process that both acknowledges the autonomy of the language of each domain and facilitates communication among them. And a political process of articulation is required to address their conflicts and link them together. What results is something like a swarm of political activity, with instances of rebellion and metamorphosis swirling around at once. We will have to investigate this swarm, its intelligence, and its internal organization in the next sections.

To claim this parallelism means, obviously, that no one domain or social antagonism is prior to the others. Slavoj Žižek, countering what he sees to be the reigning doctrine of multiculturalism promoted by identity politics, argues that class struggle is qualitatively different from (and superior to) race and gender struggles. "What the series race-gender-class obfuscates is the different logic of the political space in the case of class: while the antiracist and antisexist struggles are guided by a striving for the full recognition of the other, the class struggle aims at overcoming and subduing, even annihilating, the other—even if this [does] not mean direct physical annihilation, class struggle aims at the annihilation of the other's sociopolitical role and function."[31] We agree with Žižek's primary critique to the extent that it poses the danger we cited earlier that identity struggles become attached to identity as property and fail to engage a process of liberation. Žižek is wrong, however, to assume that class struggles are necessarily different from antiracist and antisexist struggles in this way. We have seen all too many forms of class politics that get stuck on identity, affirming worker identity and celebrating work. More important, though, Žižek fails to recognize the revolutionary forms of gender and race politics: just as revolutionary class struggle aims at the annihilation not of all bourgeois people but of their "sociopolitical role and function" (along with, we would add, the sociopolitical role and function of the worker), so too revolutionary feminist and antiracist politics attack not only sexists and racists, or even patriarchy and white supremacy, but the bases of gender and race identities as well. Žižek thus makes a false comparison by contrasting revolutionary class struggle with nonrevolutionary versions of race and gender struggles. In their nonrevolutionary versions—such as wage demands for workers, for example, legal protection from sexual violence, and social rights or affirmative action for subordinated groups—the various struggles, though often extremely important, are widely divergent and frequently conflicting. In their revolutionary versions, however, abolishing identity, property, and sovereignty, thus opening a field of multiplicities, they are parallel.

A Spinozian notion of parallelism has the added advantage of dispelling the frequent embarrassment that accompanies reproducing the catalogue race, class, gender, sexuality, and so forth. (The "and so forth" is especially embarrassing.) Spinoza maintains that there exist infinite attributes through which substance is expressed in parallel, but humans can recognize only two of them: thought and extension, mind and body. Perhaps in the same way we should say that, although in our society we can recognize only a limited number, there are infinite paths of struggle and liberation. The plurality and even the indefinite number is not the problem. Most important instead is how we articulate them along parallel lines in a common project.

One of the most significant challenges of revolution today, then, which this parallelism of singularities suggests, is that revolutionary action cannot be successfully conducted or even thought in one domain alone. Without its parallel developments any revolutionary struggle will run aground or even fall back on itself. A revolutionary race proposition that ignores or even exacerbates gender hierarchies will inevitably be blocked, as will a class proposition that fails to keep up with its parallels in the racial domain. Multiplicity and parallelism set the standard for evaluating revolutionary politics today: the multiple parallel paths of liberation either proceed through correspondences or do not proceed at all. The revolutionary process, in other words, is like walking on two legs in that after each pass forward, the one leg requires the other to take another step before being able to move again. It might hop alone for a few feet, but one is sure to fall on one's face soon. Except that there are many more than two legs in play here. Revolution can only move forward like a centipede or, really, as a multitude. Only on the field of biopolitical struggles, composed by parallelism and multiplicity, can a revolutionary struggle for the common be successfully pursued.

We hope to have demonstrated through our argument thus far

that the parallel coordination among the revolutionary struggles of singularities is possible, but it is by no means immediate or spontaneous. In the sections that follow, we must develop a logic of encounter and articulation among singularities, that is, a logic of democratic organization and decision making that governs the revolution. The parallel revolutionary struggles must discover how to intersect in insurrectional events and sustain their revolutionary processes in institutional forms, by which we mean not fixing them in bureaucratic procedures but making repeatable their constituent encounters and durable the process of transformation, creating lasting political bodies.

Before moving on we should note that, although it has become conventional today for scholars to identify revolution with modernity and, with expressions of mourning or celebration, proclaim it dead in the contemporary era, our argument suggests exactly the opposite. Since modernity, as we argued in Part 2, is always double, defined by hierarchy, coloniality, and property, modern revolution is finally impossible. Even the antimodern struggles that resist modern discipline and control are unable to arrive at a process of liberation that moves beyond resistance to create the world anew. All the revolutionary dreams and projects that emerged in the struggles between modernity and antimodernity—and there were so many!—pointed in the end beyond modernity. Only altermodernity, which we see emerging today, with its basis in the interplay between the common and the multitude of singularities, is the terrain proper to revolution. In the most schematic fashion, the triad identity–property–sovereignty that defines modernity is replaced in altermodernity by singularity–the common–revolution. Revolution is now, finally, becoming the order of the day.

INSURRECTIONAL INTERSECTIONS

> They were nothing more than people, by themselves. Even paired,
> any pairing, they would have been nothing more than people by
> themselves. But all together, they have become the heart and muscles
> and mind of something perilous and new, something strange and
> growing and great. Together, all together, they are the instruments of
> change.
>
> —Keri Hulme, *The Bone People*

Reactionary Intersections: Crises and Thermidors

Parallel struggles are not in themselves sufficient for revolutionary
movement. Insurrection against the existing order requires events in
which the parallel streams intersect, not only toppling the social
structures of hierarchy but also transforming the singularities in
struggle and multiplying their powers. Shortly we will analyze the
form such insurrectionary events have taken in the past and what
new potential they have today, in particular the potential for democratic decision making in the revolutionary process. Intersections,
however, are by no means necessarily revolutionary. We have already
seen how "intersectional analysis" explores the multiple axes of subordination that intersect in determinate social subjects—we are all
raced, gendered, defined by class position, and so forth—posing op-
portunities and limitations for identity politics. In this section we
investigate instead some of the ways that intersection is used as a
mechanism of control to maintain the existing political order, cor-
ralling and taming movements of rebellion and liberation.

The dominant modern political mode of control functions

through the *mediation* of identities, based most clearly in the North Atlantic world on elements of Kantian philosophy. (We have already emphasized, at different points in this book, that transcendental mediation is supported by an explicit metaphysics in which spiritual forms and ontological structures organize a priori the content of experience.) Just as in classical metaphysics the categories of substance and cause or modality and relation, which are posed as generic, are thought sufficient to define ontological processes, so too in transcendental philosophy the categories of mediation, which are posed as productive, configure transcendental schematism as something like a machine. In Kant's thought and Kantianism, transcendental schematism gains increasing autonomy in the construction of the structures of knowledge and power. Identities are thus at once mediated and confirmed in the formal unity of the transcendental.[32]

Modern political thought interprets these schemas of epistemological and ontological mediation in terms of *representation*. The traditional claim, in authors such as Rousseau and Hegel, is that representation is able to weave all social, cultural, and economic particularities into the generality of the state. On the contrary, Carl Schmitt recognizes rightly the antidemocratic nature of representation: "The representative character introduces precisely a nondemocratic element in this 'democracy.'"[33] We find it more accurate to understand the representative mechanisms typical of the modern republic as carrying out a double operation, a disjunctive synthesis, both linking the represented to political power and holding them separate from it. The mediation of identities in the transcendental sphere of representation achieves a similarly double result. On the one hand, concrete identities are transformed into abstract representations from which the structures of political mediation can produce (schematically) a formal unity. (The concept of the people is one such formal unity.) On the other hand, the logic of representation requires that identities remain static and separate: we are forced continually to perform our identities and punished for any deviation from them. Elizabeth Povinelli notes, for example, that the Austra-

lian state requires Aborigines, in order to obtain rights and public resources, to repeat faithfully the traditional indigenous identity,
conserving its memory and culture—in effect, to remain the same
or, really, to conform to a representation.[34] Such is the tyranny of
idealism. The link between rights and identity is a weapon that the
representational schema wields to trap all identities in logics of recognition and police the becomings of singularities. The seeming
paradox of political mediation is thus resolved on two separate
planes: abstract unity on the transcendental plane is maintained only
so long as on the social plane identities faithfully perform their separation and unchanging character.

Modern political representation, however, along with its mechanisms of mediation, have long been in crisis. A wide range of
twentieth-century political scientists, such as Max Weber, Robert
Michels, Gaetano Mosca, and Vilfredo Pareto, denounce how representation becomes bureaucratic through the actions of political parties, and thus the claims of representation to social universality become completely illusory, leaving political rule in the hands of
elites.[35] Numerous authors similarly analyze the crisis of representation—and hence the "democratic deficit"—in the global context,
where mechanisms of mediation and institutions of representation
are largely lacking, and those that do exist have proved ineffective.[36]
Such analyses of the crisis of representation generally fit within the
project of "the liberal critique of liberalism," that is, critiques aimed
at repairing and restoring liberalism.

The primary response of systems of power to the crisis of representation, however, has been the construction of new mechanisms
of social mediation in the form of governance. Governance, as we
saw in Part 4, does not rely on any transcendental schematism and
does not in general function through fixed structures. It is instead an
aleatory form of government that rules over contingency through
legal processes which Gunther Teubner describes as "constitutional-
ization without the state."[37] Governance does not restore the schema
for the representation of identities central to republican regimes of
tolerance (in both their multicultural and universalist forms) but in-

stead attempts to create social order without representation; it does not resolve the crisis but seeks to manage it. What is lacking, as we suggested in *De Homine* 2 at the end of Part 5, are the mechanisms of *measure* that identity and representation require. Just as capital is no longer able to command productive processes through disciplinary regimes based on the measure of value but rather must rely on abstract and flexible financial apparatuses of capture, so too representative mediation cannot order society without the measure of identities and must instead rely on the abstract and flexible control of governance. The abstraction and flexibility of these mechanisms highlight the contingent nature of the structures of order and the thin line separating them from chaos. Governance in this sense is a system for the management of the exception. Without the representational mechanisms of mediation, the governance of identities and the management of social hierarchies alternate between two poles: enforced "identity-blind" perspectives, as if the hierarchies did not exist, and "identity panic" when those hierarchies become undeniable factors of social life.

Governance, of course, serves to maintain the ruling powers and support the interests of capital, but it never succeeds in solving the crisis and bringing it to an end. In fact processes of negotiation and struggle are constantly reopened on the terrain of governance. In some respects, then, governance is analogous to the old terrain of trade union struggles, and indeed, some authors propose confronting the current forms of governance with the models of negotiation and agreement of labor law.[38] When the old labor leaders used to say, "There is no end to negotiations," they never questioned the ultimate hegemony of capital but still appreciated the importance of the struggle. We should not underestimate the fact that governance is an open space of conflict and struggle between (sovereign) powers and (social) counterpowers.

In contrast, given the abstract and flexible mechanisms of governance, which run constantly on the border of instability, it is easy to see why neoconservatism and other contemporary right-wing ideologies attempt to resolve the crisis of representation not by restoring any transcendental schematism but by grounding the theory of measure solidly on the immutable terrain of natural law. Certainly conservatism, from Burke and Hegel to Leo Strauss and Michael Oakeshott, always has an element of relativism, since it constantly refers to custom and tradition, but this is really only the background for an ontological foundation of constant measure. Neoconservative strategies thus run counter to governance, opposing its contingency and fluidity with the concrete fixity of values and identities, and even conflict at times with the emerging forms of capitalist control, insofar as they tolerate or even encourage the flux of economic and social values. Neoconservatives aim instead for a new Thermidor, which attempts to fix absolutely the criteria of value regarding property and social hierarchies in order to restore the ancien régime or, really, make social reality conform to the representation of an imagined past. Neoconservatives are thus actually theocrats even when they express secular beliefs: their gods are the Central Bank and the Supreme Court as the ultimate guarantors of the stability of value.

Democratic Decision Making?

Democratic decision making transforms the parallel struggles of identities into an insurrectional intersection, a revolutionary event that composes the singularities into a multitude. That definition is correct but embarrassingly naïve. Such conceptual abstractions never really account for the complexity and richness of the passions behind the construction of democratic decision making. Some of these passions line up perfectly in the direction of revolution—the rationality and joy of the multitude stand against fear and sadness, and indignation against tyranny and the resistance against oppression arm disobedience and revolt—but liberation movements are also always plagued by internal conflicts and misunderstandings among the oppressed. The translation process that communicates among the parallel paths, which we mentioned earlier, pushing each of them forward, making them stronger, often breaks down in a cacophony of misinterpretations. Disagreement is the daily, normal condition of revolutionary movements. The task of democratic decision making is thus not only to chart the path of liberation but also to provide a structure for resolving the (often mundane and tedious) conflicts within the multitude. We need to investigate how decision making can be structured so as continually to move forward the making of the multitude and the process of revolution.

When we speak of intersections that contribute to the making of the multitude, we have in mind something different from what is traditionally conceived of as *alliance* or *coalition*. The multitude is composed through the encounters of singularities within the common. Alliance and coalition movements are, of course, organized against a common enemy, often with recognition of the parallel subordinations and struggles of the different social groups: industrial workers and peasants, for example, or women and African Americans, or trade unions and churches.[39] But alliances and coalitions can never get beyond the fixed identities striving for emancipation that form them. The process of articulation accomplished in insurrectional intersections does not simply couple identities like links in a chain but transforms singularities in a process of liberation that establishes the common among them. This articulation is an ontological process that transforms social being in the making of the multitude. "Politics is the sphere of activity of a common," writes Jacques Rancière, "that can only ever be contentious."[40] The making of the multitude must arrive at the point of a *partage,* dividing and sharing the common. Making the multitude, and thus the event of insurrection, we should repeat, is not a process of fusion or unification, as Jean-Paul Sartre suggests, but rather sets in motion a proliferation of singularities that are composed by the lasting encounters in the common.[41] Democratic decision making must determine and sustain this process of articulation and composition.

It should be clear at this point that the conception of revolution we put forward here departs significantly from that proposed and practiced by the twentieth-century communist movements. The major streams of that tradition pose insurrection and revolution in terms of the creation of a new identity: a vanguard subject separate from and capable of leading the rest of society. Lenin, for example, conceives of the articulation of the social groups in struggle under the hegemony of the party, which forms a counterpower, mirroring in certain respects the identity of the central power it opposes. Trotsky, recounting the course of the Russian Revolution, similarly warns against naïve notions of the spontaneity of the masses. Mass insurrection, he maintains, requires a "conspiracy" of revolutionary leadership, which takes responsibility for planning and decision making. Lenin's and Trotsky's conceptions may have been a realistic and pragmatic means to address the realities of late-nineteenth- and early-twentieth-century Russia and indeed were more effective at arriving at a decision for revolutionary action than were the various positions that socialist movements of that era produced, but as theories of subjectivity and revolutionary decision making they are completely inappropriate to our contemporary world. Indeed today we are a long way from the construction of a political figure adequate to the revolutionary process, but however it emerges it will have to take a path radically different from that tradition. What is required is an organizational process that establishes revolutionary decision making and the overthrow of the ruling power from within, not above, the movements of the multitude.[42]

The communist tradition does, however, provide a useful method for investigating the new potential for democratic decision making today through the analysis of the transformations of labor and production. Earlier, in Part 3, we examined the changing technical composition of capital (which is really the technical composition of labor-power) in relation to the organic composition of capital (that is, the relation between variable and constant capital). Now we need to explore the technical composition of the proletariat in relation to its political composition. The terminology might make this sound obscure, but the basic premise is simple: what people do at work and the skills they exercise there (technical composition) contribute to their capacities in the field of political action (political composition). If, as we have argued throughout this book, the technical composition of the proletariat has changed such that biopolitical production has become hegemonic, as its qualities are imposed over the sectors of production, then a new political composition is possible, corresponding to the capacities specific to biopolitical labor. The transformation of the technical composition does not spontaneously create a new political figure of struggle and revolution—that requires organization and political action—but it does indicate a new possibility that can be grasped. Today, we argue, the nature and qualities of biopolitical production make possible a process of political composition defined by democratic decision making.

Posing this relation between technical and political composition, we should note, historicizes the question of vanguard organizations, casting it in a very different light. This can be clarified by sketching a rough periodization. In the early twentieth century, when industrial production is characterized by hierarchical ranks of professional workers, the Bolshevik Party, the German *Räte,* and the various council movements propose political figures to interpret that technical composition: the vanguard party corresponds to the vanguard of professional workers in the factory. In the mid-twentieth century, when industrial production is characterized by great masses of relatively deskilled workers, mass parties—the Italian Communist Party at times plays this role—attempt to create a political figure adequate to this new situation, treating the trade union simply as a "transmission belt" for the party and employing strategies that alternate between blocking industrial production and demanding a continuous rise in salaries and social welfare. Insisting on the relation between technical and political composition in this way does validate (or at least explain) such political organizations insofar as it recognizes how they are rooted in the reality of their situations, attempting to interpret politically the organization and capacities of workers in production. In doing so, however, it relegates them irrevocably to the past. Today, when the technical composition of labor has changed so profoundly, to repropose any such vanguard political formation is anachronistic at best.[43]

The emerging hegemony of biopolitical production today brings with it new democratic capacities. Three overlapping developments, which we emphasized in Parts 3 and 5, are crucial here.

First, whereas in the era of the hegemony of industrial production capitalists generally provided workers with the means and schemas of cooperation that organized production, in biopolitical production labor is increasingly responsible for generating cooperation. Second, and consequently, biopolitical labor becomes ever more autonomous from capitalist command, which tends to block production and reduce productivity whenever it intervenes. Third, in contrast to the vertical, hierarchical forms of cooperation dictated by capitalist command, biopolitical labor tends to create horizontal network forms. These three characteristics of biopolitical labor—cooperation, autonomy, and network organization—provide solid building blocks for democratic political organization. Remember Lenin's claim that since people are trained to need bosses at work, they also need bosses in politics: "Human nature as it is now . . . cannot do without subordination, control, and 'managers.'"[44] Today's biopolitical production shows how much human nature has changed. People don't need bosses at work. They need an expanding web of others with whom to communicate and collaborate; the boss is increasingly merely an obstacle to getting work done. The focus on the technical composition of labor thus gives us one view of the democratic capacities that people exercise in everyday life. These democratic capacities of labor do not immediately translate into the creation of democratic political organizations, but they do pose solid ground on which to imagine and create them.

We should note the important strategic advances that contemporary democratic organizational forms present with respect to vanguard organizations. Historically the vanguard carried the responsibility for *destabilizing* the capitalist system to set in motion the revolutionary process. In the 1970s communist and autonomist movements in western Europe, which were both anti-Stalinist and opposed to the national communist parliamentary parties, reformulated and extended this proposition: the tactics of destabilizing capitalism must be complemented by the strategy of a deep and profound *destructuring* of capitalist society, dismantling its configurations of hierarchy and command.[45] The democratic organizational forms

suggested by biopolitical labor add another element to the definition of revolutionary activity: to the fire of destabilizing tactics and
destructuring strategy they add the project of constructing a new
power, a new type of power, by which the multitude is capable of
managing the common. Revolution is thus aimed at the generation
of new forms of social life. This implies a new form of political decision making. On the biopolitical terrain, the knowledge and will
required for decision are embedded, so to speak, in historical being
such that decision making is always performative and results in the
real, anthropological transformation of the subject involved or, as
Jean-Luc Nancy puts it, an ontological transformation of the conditions of decision making itself.[46]

Some readers might be made uneasy by how our method here
brings together the economic and the political, even perhaps sus-
pecting us to be guilty of economism, as if we believed that economic forces determine all other realms of social life. No; when we
insist that investigating the aptitudes, competencies, and skills expressed at work are a means to understand the generalized capacities
of the multitude in everyday life, it is only one among many—but it
is an important one! Hannah Arendt, as we have said before, dis-
counts the relevance of the economic for political life because she
believes the capacities of labor (the rote repetition of tasks, following
commands, and so forth) have no bearing on political life, which
requires autonomy, communication, cooperation, and creativity.
Biopolitical labor, however, is increasingly defined by these properly
political capacities, and thus these emerging capacities in the economic sphere make possible in the political sphere the development
of democratic organizations, demonstrating in fact the increasingly
broad overlap between the two spheres. In this regard our argument
can be situated in a long line of revolutionary appeals that combine
economic and political demands. The seventeenth-century English
partisans of the multitude we spoke of in Part 1 posed freedom
against property. The rallying cry of the Soviet Revolution was
"peace, land, and bread." Our slogan to combine the economic and
the political might be "poverty and love" or (for those who consider

such terms too sentimental) "power and the common": the liberation of the poor and the institutional development of the powers,
of social cooperation. In any case, recognizing the intersection of
the political and the economic is not only essential for the description of contemporary social life but also fundamental for the construction of the mechanisms and practices of democratic decision
making.

Insurrection and Institution

Insurrection, in order to open a path for revolution, must be sustained and consolidated in an institutional process. Such an institutional conception of insurrection should not be confused, of course,
with the coup d'état, which merely replaces the existing state institutions with comparable, homologous ones. The multitude, as we
have said, has no interest in taking control of the state apparatuses,
not even in order to direct them to other ends—or, better, it wants
to lay its hands on state apparatuses only to dismantle them. It regards the state as not the realm of freedom but the seat of domination, which not only guarantees capitalist exploitation and defends
the rule of property but also maintains and polices all identity hierarchies. Political engagement with state institutions is no doubt useful and necessary for struggles against subordination, but liberation
can only be aimed at their destruction. This might seem to imply
that insurrection is inimical to institutions, but in fact insurrection,
as we said, needs institutions—just institutions of a different sort.

A long-standing division in the history of social theory poses a
major line that conceives the *social contract* as the basis of institutions
against a minor line that considers *social conflict* their basis. Whereas
the major line seeks to maintain social unity by casting conflict out
of society—your consent to the contract forfeits your right to rebel
and conflict—the minor line accepts conflict as internal to and the
constant foundation of society. Thomas Jefferson contributes to this
minor line of thought, for example, when he asserts that periodically
(at least once a generation, which he considers to be every twenty
years) the multitude should rebel against the government and form

a new constitution.[47] Machiavelli and Spinoza, two other prominent proponents of the minor line, conceive of the conflict that grounds institutions along not only the clearly defined paths of resistance and rebellions against authority and oppression but also, and more important, the fractured and changing paths of conflict within the multitude.[48] The development of social institutions can be democratic, authors of the minor line insist, only if it remains open to and constituted by conflict.

As long as we can conceive institutions only along the major line, insurrection seems to be blocked at an impasse. On the one hand, revolts and rebellions that fail to develop institutional continuity are quickly covered over and absorbed within the dominant order, like stones that fall into a pool only to see the tranquil surface immediately restored. On the other hand, entering into the dominant form of institution, which is based in identity, functions through representation, and demands unity and concord, serves to neutralize the social rupture opened by revolt. How many times have we heard leaders of rebellions who enter into government declare: "You must go home now and lay down your weapons. We will represent you"? An institutional process based in conflict, however, according to the minor line, can consolidate insurrection without negating its force of rupture and power. As we saw in our discussion of jacqueries earlier, revolt becomes powerful and long-lasting only when it invents and institutionalizes a new set of collective habits and practices, that is, a new form of life. Jean Genet, for example, in his journeys among the Palestinian refugees and fedayeen in Jordan and the Black Panthers in the United States, was captivated by the "style" of these groups, by which he meant their invention of new forms of life, their common practices and behaviors as well as their original set of gestures and affects.[49] It would certainly be useful, if we had the talents and tools of historians, to investigate how a range of contemporary revolts has been consolidated in alternative institutional forms— how, for example, the disruptive force of the 1969 Stonewall rebellion in New York City was continued through the formation of a variety of gay and lesbian organizations; how during the South

African struggle against apartheid revolts like the 1976 Soweto uprising became part of the fabric of an institutional process; how Italian worker revolts in the 1970s in the factories of Porto Marghera,
Pirelli, and FIAT among others were prolonged and developed
through the construction of new forms of worker committees and
other political institutions; or how the 1994 Zapatista uprising in
Mexico developed through the creation of autonomous assemblies,
caracoles or base community structures, and *juntas* of good government. The key is to discover in each case how (and the extent to
which) the institutional process does not negate the social rupture
created by revolt but extends and develops it.

We now have several elements at hand for a new definition of
institution. Institutions are based on conflict, in the sense that they
both extend the social rupture operated by revolt against the ruling
powers and are open to internal discord. Institutions also consolidate
collective habits, practices, and capacities that designate a form of
life. Institutions, finally, are open-ended in that they are continually
transformed by the singularities that compose them. This notion of
institution corresponds closely to what we called earlier "training in
love" in that it does not reduce the multiplicity of singularities but
creates a context for them to manage their encounters: to avoid the
negative encounters, which diminish their strength, and prolong and
repeat the joyful ones, which increase it. Institutions thus conceived
are a necessary component in the process of insurrection and revolution.

One can arrive at a similar definition of institution based on
the common experiences of productive activity in cybernetic networks. We should keep in mind, of course, a series of myths that
characterized the enthusiasm of some of the early writings about
the political implications of networks: that networks cannot be controlled, for example, that the transparency of networks is always
good, and that the cybernetic swarm is always intelligent.[50] Experience with network technologies has nonetheless led to the development of novel decision-making processes characterized by multiplicity and interaction. Whereas the old socialist elites used to dream

of a "decision-making machine," the experiences of networkers and net users have configured an *institutional decision making* composed of a myriad of micropolitical paths. "Become the media" is a line of institutional construction of communication in which the collective control of expression in networks becomes a political weapon. Here too we find a definition of institution defined by conflict and multiplicity, composed of collective habits and practices, and open to transformation by singularities.[51]

Two basic objections to our definition of institution immediately come to mind, which really serve to mark its distance from the standard assumptions of sociologists and political scientists. We imagine a sociological objection that our conception does not adequately account for the individuality and identity of those who interact with institutions. According to the conventional sociological notion, in effect, individuals enter institutions and come out as identities. In other words, institutions silently compel individuals to follow established patterns of behavior, providing them with formulas for living such that, for example, the desire for love is channeled into marriage and the desire for freedom channeled into shopping. These created behavior patterns, however, are by no means uniform throughout society but instead define identity formations by compelling people to conform to race, gender, and class attributes as if they were natural and necessary. Our conception of institution, in contrast, does not begin with individuals, end with identities, or function through conformity. Singularities, which are in revolt against the ruling power and often in conflict with one another, enter into the institutional process. By definition, as we said, singularities are always already multiple and are constantly engaged in a process of self-transformation. This institutional process allows singularities to achieve some consistency in their interactions and behaviors, creating in this way a form of life, but never are such patterns fixed in identity. The central difference, perhaps, has to do with the locus of agency: whereas according to the conventional sociological notion institutions form individuals and identities, in our conception singularities form institutions, which are thus perpetually in flux.

We imagine an objection from political scientists and legal theorists that our notion of institution cannot form the basis of sovereignty. This perspective assumes that the life of individuals in the economic and social worlds, as in the state of nature, is characterized by risk, danger, and scarcity. Only when individuals enter into institutions, and thereby transfer at least a portion of their rights and powers to a sovereign authority, can their protection be guaranteed. Legal theorists make a similar point when they emphasize that the relationship between legal claim and obligation in institutions must be invariable to establish and maintain social order. Institutions must serve as the foundation for the constituted power, that is, the constitutional order of sovereignty. According to our conception, in contrast, institutions form a constituent rather than a constituted power. Institutional norms and obligations are established in regular interactions but are continually open to a process of evolution. The singularities that compose the multitude do not transfer their rights or powers, and thus they prohibit the formation of a sovereign power, but in their mutual encounters each becomes more powerful. The institutional process therefore provides a mechanism of protection (but with no guarantees) against the two primary dangers facing the multitude: externally, the repression of the ruling power, and internally, the destructive conflicts among singularities within the multitude.

The extension of insurrection in an institutional process that transforms the fabric of social being is a good first approximation of revolution. Immanuel Kant comes close to this definition when he declares that the French Revolution should be understood as not revolution but "the evolution of a constitution founded on natural law [Naturrecht]." He emphasizes, in particular, the public and universal nature of the process. "This event consists neither in momentous deeds nor crimes committed by men ... nor in ancient splendid political structures which vanish as if by magic while others come forth in their place as if from the depths of the earth. No, nothing of the sort. It is simply the mode of thinking of the spectators which reveals itself *publicly* in this game of great revolutions, and manifests such a universal yet disinterested sympathy for the players on one side against those on the other."[52] Revolution is insurrection once it has become an institutional process, a form of government, which Kant defines as public and we would call common.

Kant goes on to explain that revolution's transformation of social being constitutes an innovation in history and points toward the future. "Owing to its universality, this mode of thinking demonstrates a character of the human race at large and all at once; owing to its disinterestedness, a moral character of humanity, at least in its predisposition, a character which not only permits people to hope for progress toward the better, but is already itself progress in so far as its capacity is sufficient for the present."[53] Revolution, as a new form of government, is in fact, despite Kant's confidence in progress, squeezed in the vise between past and future, leaving it very little room for maneuver. It constantly has to battle the pressures of the established constituted power and the accumulated social weight of the past. Think, for example, of the gothic façades of French and Catalan cathedrals desecrated by revolutionaries who have broken off the heads of saints and kings. Yes, we too are indignant at their destruction of precious cultural heritage, but we understand their attempt to destroy physically the symbols of a power that continues to haunt them. Often, even when revolutionaries think their actions are sufficient to launch us into the future, the past bursts through to reimpose itself. Tocqueville, for example, describes how the past sometimes surreptitiously insinuates itself and reappears in revolutionary futures, but that is not a law of history and the inevitable destiny of revolutions, as reactionaries often claim, but simply one possible outcome. We can share Kant's faith in progress, then, when it is, first, posed not as a natural law but grounded in revolutionary struggle and, second, consolidated and reinforced in institutional form. Revolution's creation of a new form of government holds off the past and opens toward the future.

GOVERNING THE REVOLUTION

> A revolutionary law is a law whose object is to maintain the revolu-
> tion and to accelerate or regulate its course.
> —Condorcet, *On the Meaning of the Word Revolutionary*

The Problem of Transition

Too much of revolutionary thought does not even pose the problem
of transition, paying attention only to the overture and neglecting
all the acts of the drama that must follow. Defeating the ruling powers, destroying the ancien régime, smashing the state machine—
even overthrowing capital, patriarchy, and white supremacy—is not
enough. That might be sufficient, perhaps, if one were to believe
that the formation of the multitude was already achieved, that we
were all already somehow not only purified of the hierarchies and
corruptions of contemporary society but also capable of managing
the multiplicity of the common and cooperating with one another
freely and equally—in short, that democratic society was already
complete. If that were the case, then, yes, maybe the insurrectional
event destroying the structures of power would be sufficient and the
perfect human society already existing beneath the yoke of oppression would spontaneously flourish. But human nature as it is now is
far from perfect. We are all entangled and complicit in the identities,
hierarchies, and corruptions of the current forms of power. Revolution requires not merely emancipation, as we said earlier, but liberation; not just an event of destruction but also a long and sustained
process of transformation, creating a new humanity. This is the prob-

lem of transition: how to extend the event of insurrection in a process of liberation and transformation.

Condorcet proclaims, and Hannah Arendt echoes him almost two hundred years later, that "the word 'revolutionary' applies only to revolutions that have freedom as their object."[54] We would extend this to say that revolutions must have democracy as their object and thus that the direction and content of revolutionary transition must be defined by the increase of the capacities for democracy of the multitude. People are not spontaneously, by nature, capable of cooperating with one another freely and together governing the common. W. E. B. Du Bois, for example, studying the promises, betrayals, and failures of Reconstruction after the U.S. Civil War, is keenly aware that emancipation alone is not sufficient. In addition to all the traps and subterfuges of the U.S. government and dispossessed Southern slaveholders, in addition to the color and class hierarchies created by Northern carpetbagger capitalists, Du Bois also focuses on the problem that even after the abolition of slavery the vast majority of the population, white and black alike, remains poor and ignorant, lacking the capacities for democracy. Emancipation is only the beginning.[55]

In the annals of modern revolutionary thought Lenin provides the locus classicus for understanding the revolutionary transition. Lenin recognizes, as we noted earlier, that human nature as it is now is not capable of democracy. In their habits, routines, mentalities, and in the million capillary practices of everyday life, people are wedded to hierarchy, identity, segregation, and in general corrupt forms of the common. They are not yet able to rule themselves democratically without masters, leaders, and representatives. Lenin thus proposes a dialectical transition composed of two negations. First, a period of dictatorship must negate democracy in order to lead society and transform the population. Once a new humanity has been created, capable of ruling itself, then dictatorship will be negated and a new democracy achieved.[56] Lenin has the great merit of posing the problem clearly, but his dialectical solution is today widely and rightly discredited, not only because "transitional" dictatorships so stubbornly hold on to power, resisting the dialectical inversion in democracy, but more important because the social structures of dictatorship do not foster the training in democracy necessary to make the multitude. On the contrary! Dictatorship teaches subservience. Democracy can be learned only by doing.

The problem of transition must be given a positive, nondialectical solution, leading toward democracy through democratic means. Our analysis in the previous section has already developed some elements for such a democratic transition. The insurrectional event, we explained, must be consolidated in an institutional process of transformation that develops the multitude's capacities for democratic decision making. Making the multitude is thus a project of democratic organizing aimed at democracy. Rather than counting on the boomerang effect of the dialectic to thrust the process at the final moment to the opposite end of the spectrum, this notion of transition delineates an asymptotic approach such that even if the movement never reaches a conclusion, the distance between transition and goal, between means and end becomes so infinitesimal that it ceases to matter. This process should not be confused with old reformist illusions that insist on gradual change and constantly defer revolution into the indefinite future. No; rupture with contemporary society and its ruling powers must be radical: as much as insurrection is swept up in the process of transition, transition must constantly renew the force of insurrection. Often in evaluating the state of the present society, in other words, the point is not to haggle over whether the glass is half empty or half full but to break the glass!

The process of transition, however, as we said, is not spontaneous. How can the transition be governed? What or who draws the *political diagonal* that guides the transition? The political line, after all, is not always straight and immediately obvious but moves diagonally through mysterious curves. These questions, though, throw us back into the dilemmas of vanguards, leadership, and representation. Revolutionary movements have repeatedly in history allowed the helm to be taken and the process steered by charismatic figures or leadership groups—the party, the junta, the council, the directorate, and so forth—who represent (to different degrees) the masses. And how many times have we heard the need for leadership as an argument to privilege one social group (with superior knowledge, consciousness, or position in the production process) over others in the revolutionary struggle, breaking the potential parallelism we spoke of earlier? Industrial workers have claimed to lead peasants, white workers to lead black workers, male workers to lead female workers, and so forth. Often the establishment of leadership has been accompanied by claims of the "autonomy of the political" with respect to the social, the economic, the private, or the merely cultural.[57]

Our argument seems to have led us into an impasse. On the one hand, the process of transition is not spontaneous but must be guided according to a political diagonal. On the other hand, however, allowing any social identity or vanguard group or leader to take control of the process undermines the democratic function the transition must serve. There seems to be no path for the revolutionary process to walk between the danger of ineffectiveness and disorder on the one side and that of hierarchy and authority on the other.

The way out of the impasse is to bring the *political diagonal* back to the *biopolitical diagram,* that is, to ground it in an investigation of the capacities people already exercise in their daily lives and, specifically, in the processes of biopolitical production. In the terms we proposed earlier, this means to explore the technical composition of the productive multitude to discover its potential political composition. Here we get the political payoff of all our economic analyses in Parts 3 and 5. In the biopolitical context, as we saw, the production of ideas, images, codes, languages, knowledges, affects, and the like, through horizontal networks of communication and cooperation, tends toward the autonomous production of the common, which is to say, the production and reproduction of forms of life. And the production and reproduction of forms of life is a very precise definition of political action. This does not mean that the revolution has already begun and the problem of transition has been solved because, first, the autonomy of biopolitical production is only partial, since it is still directed and constrained under the command of capital; and second, these economic capacities are not immediately expressed as political capacities. It does mean, though, that in the common fabric of the biopolitical diagram rest latent, potential, chrysalis-like the capacities for the multitude to determine autonomously the political diagonal of the transition. Realizing this potential, by means of political action and organization, would mean carrying forward the parallel revolutionary struggles through the insurrectional event of intersection to an institutional process of managing the common.

Antonio Gramsci's notion of "passive revolution" and its limitations helps us understand how the relation between political diagonal and biopolitical diagram addresses the conundrum of the transition. As he does with many of his key concepts, Gramsci employs "passive revolution" in a variety of contexts with slightly different meanings, using multiple standpoints to give the concept greater amplitude. His first and primary usage is to contrast the passive transformation of bourgeois society in nineteenth-century Italy with the active revolutionary process of the bourgeoisie in France. Passive revolution, Gramsci explains, is a revolution without a revolution, that is, a transformation of the political and institutional structures without there emerging centrally a strong process for the production of subjectivity. The "facts" rather than social actors are the real protagonists. Second, Gramsci also applies the term "passive revolution" to the mutations of the structures of capitalist economic production that he recognizes primarily in the development of the U.S. factory system of the 1920s and 1930s. "Americanism" and "Fordism" name what Marx calls the passage from the "formal" to the "real subsumption" of labor within capital, that is, the construction of a properly capitalist society. This structural transformation of capital is passive in the sense that it evolves over an extended period and is not driven by a strong subject. After using "passive revolution" as a descriptive tool of historical analysis, regarding both the superstructural and structural changes of capitalist society, Gramsci seems to employ it, third, to suggest a path for struggle. How can we make revolution in a society subsumed within capital? The only answer Gramsci can see is a relatively "passive" one, that is, a long march through the institutions of civil society.[58]

Gramsci's various political proposals coalesce as a Leninist critique of Leninism. He is critical of Leninism in that he emphasizes not the "war of movement" but the "war of position," proposing, in other words, not the insurrectional blow against the ruling powers but an extended series of battles in the cultural and political spheres in the effort to wrest hegemony away from the bourgeoisie.[59] Gramsci's critique, however, remains Leninist. Passive revolution, for the nineteenth-century Italian bourgeoisie or the twentieth-century proletariat, is not superior to active revolution but merely an alternative when the primary avenue is not possible, when there is no active subject to lead the revolutionary process. All the core ideas of Gramsci's politics—including war of position, hegemony, and passive revolution—are aimed at inventing revolutionary activity for nonrevolutionary times, but this is oriented nonetheless toward the horizon of active revolution, when sometime in the future this becomes possible.

Gramsci is thus in many ways a prophet of the biopolitical diagram. He understands that the vanguard of industrial workers can no longer serve as the subject of an active proletarian revolution and, at least with respect to their "leadership" of the peasantry, questions the desirability of the worker vanguard. Gramsci also recognizes in Fordism that the subsumption of society under capital leads to a transformation of the technical composition of the proletariat, and he seems to intuit that eventually, within the biopolitical diagram, capitalist production will spill over the factory walls to invest the entire social sphere, breaking down the divisions between structure and superstructure, bringing culture and social relations directly into the realm of economic value and production. He even grasps that the new technical composition implies a new production of subjectivity:"In America rationalization has determined the need to elaborate a new type of man suited to the new type of work and productive process."[60] But Gramsci fails to foresee—and how could

he foresee it?—that with the development of the biopolitical diagram opens up the possibility of a new political diagonal. The making of the multitude and the composition and consolidation of its
capacities for democratic decision making in revolutionary institutions is exactly the kind of production of subjectivity that Gramsci
sees as necessary for an active rather than passive revolution. Such a
return to the Leninist Gramsci on the biopolitical terrain allows us
to bring together the seemingly divergent strands of his thought. We
are not faced with an alternative—either insurrection or institutional struggle, either passive or active revolution. Instead revolution
must simultaneously be both insurrection and institution, structural and superstructural transformation. This is the path of the
"becoming-Prince" of the multitude.

Revolutionary Violence

This is the point in the discussion where inevitably someone asks,
"Does revolution have to be violent?" Yes, it does, but not always
in the ways you think. Revolution does not necessarily require
bloodshed, but it does call for the use of force. The better question,
then, is not if violence is necessary but what kind of violence. And,
according to our analysis of the link between insurrection and institution, this question has to be considered separately in two different
arenas: the struggle against the ruling powers and the making of the
multitude.[61]

Force is required to gain freedom, in the first arena, because
the ruling powers impose it. The Jewish slaves of Egypt would have
happily left in peace with Moses, but Pharaoh wouldn't let them go
without a fight; in general, rulers react violently when their power is
threatened. Liberation requires a defensive struggle against the ruling powers and thus civil war, a prolonged battle between camps
that divide society, but even war does not always call for lethal weapons and bloodshed. Gramsci distinguishes the different types of force
and weapons appropriate to specific situations with the distinction
we cited earlier between "war of movement" (typically armed insurrection, such as storming the Winter Palace in St. Petersburg or the

Moncada Barracks in Santiago de Cuba) and "war of position" (which generally involves protracted, unarmed struggle in the cultural and political spheres). Gramsci has nothing in principle against armed struggle—and neither do we. The point is simply that arms are not always the best weapons. What is the best weapon against the ruling powers—guns, peaceful street demonstrations, exodus, media campaigns, labor strikes, transgressing gender norms, silence, irony, or many others—depends on the situation.

We know that the response "It depends on the situation" is not very satisfying. All we can do, though, is offer criteria for determining the best weapon in each situation. The first and most obvious criterion is, What weapons and strategy are most likely to be effective and win the struggle? Keep in mind that the one with the most firepower does not always win. In fact our estimation is that increasingly today a "disarmed multitude" is much more effective than an armed band and that exodus is more powerful than frontal assault. Exodus in this context often takes the form of sabotage, withdrawal from collaboration, countercultural practices, and generalized disobedience. Such practices are effective because biopower is always "subject" to the subjectivities it rules over. When they evacuate the terrain, they create vacuums that biopower cannot tolerate. The alterglobalization movements that flourished in the years around the turn of the millennium functioned largely in this way: creating breaks in the continuity of control and filling those vacuums with new cultural expressions and forms of life. Those movements have left behind, in fact, an arsenal of strategies of disobedience, new languages of democracy, and ethical practices (for peace, care for the environment, and so forth) that can eventually be picked up and redeployed by new initiatives of rebellion.

The second criterion is even more important: What weapons and what form of violence have the most beneficial effect on the multitude itself? Making war always involves a production of subjectivity, and often the most effective weapons against the enemy are the ones that have the most poisonous effects on those who wage the struggle. Thomas Jefferson seems to forget this second criterion when he overzealously defends the violence of the French Revolution in 1793. "The liberty of the whole earth was depending on the issue of the contest," he writes to William Short, "and was ever such a prize won with so little innocent blood? My own affections have been deeply wounded by some of the martyrs to this cause, but rather than it should have failed, I would have seen half the earth desolated. Were there but an Adam & an Eve left in every country, & left free, it would be better than as it now is."[62] We certainly do not share the acceptance of mass bloodshed Jefferson expresses here— and Jefferson himself is clearly overstating the position for effect in this passage—but he also seems to neglect the need for revolutionary action to bolster the production of the common and aid the process of making the multitude. (We are not fond of the slogan "liberty or death," but we have no sympathy for the notion of "liberty and death.") Aside from the issue of mass bloodshed, then, the question is, What does Jefferson mean by Adam and Eve? If he is satisfied with a notion of bare life, returning humanity to some imagined original, natural, or base condition, then we oppose him. But perhaps, from a perspective closer to ours, Jefferson imagines Adam and Eve to mark the creation of a new humanity that results from a revolutionary process. In any case, in evaluating the weapons and forms of violence in revolutionary struggle, the question of effectiveness against the enemy should always be secondary to that of its effects on the multitude and the process of building its institutions.

This leads us directly to the second arena in which revolution requires the use of force: the field for making the multitude, engaging and resolving conflicts within it, leading the singularities that compose it to ever more beneficial relationships, but also overcoming the obstacles to the kinds of transformation required for liberation. The force of institutions fills this role in part. Louis de Saint-Just, writing like Jefferson in 1793, insists on the revolutionary function of institutions: "Terror can rid us of monarchy and aristocracy but what will deliver us from corruption? ... Institutions."[63] We have already cast in doubt the first part of Saint-Just's remark, questioning the effectiveness and the desirability of armed struggle—let alone terror—for the battle against the current ruling powers and their social hierarchies; but what interests us more is his affirmation, in the second part, of the force of institutions against corruption. Saint-Just admittedly may understand corruption as deviation from the line established by revolutionary leaders and the institution as a means of generating conformity, but we are tempted to proclaim the same slogan—institutions against corruption—with a very different meaning.

At various points in this book we have analyzed the corruption of the common in terms of both its destruction by means of the imposition of social hierarchies (through privatization, for example) and the perpetuation of negative forms of the common in institutions which decrease the powers of the multitude, block its production of subjectivity, and exacerbate its internal conflicts. Part of revolutionary activity, then, is the destruction of what we called earlier the institutions of the corrupt forms of the common, such as the family, the corporation, and the nation. The struggles against them will take place on multiple fronts, many of which we probably have not yet even imagined, and we can be certain that the battles, even without bloodshed, will be violent, ugly, and painful, testing us in unknown ways. Think of how violently those are punished who even in small ways threaten the corrupt institution of the family, in terms of reproductive rights, for example, or sexuality, kinship structures, the sexual division of labor, or patriarchal authority. This and other institutions that corrupt the common will not fall without intense, extended combat. Saint-Just makes clear, though, that the struggle involves not only destroying the corrupt institutions but also constructing new ones. New institutions are needed to combat corruption, as we have said, not by unifying society and creating conformity to social norms, but by facilitating the production of the beneficial forms of the common, keeping access to it open and equal, and aiding the joyful encounters of singularities that compose the multitude—and at the same time combating all obstacles that stand in its way. This is perhaps just a restatement in more concrete, practical terms of our earlier proposition that the training in love has to be armed with the means to combat evil.

The most terrifying violence confronting revolutionaries may be the monstrous self-transformation we find in the revolutionary streams of identity politics. The abolition of identity, leaving behind who you are, and constructing a new world without race, gender, class, sexuality, and the other identity coordinates is an extraordinarily violent process, not only because the ruling powers will fight every step of the way but also because it requires us to abandon some of our core identifications and become monsters. Even Saint-Just and his bloody colleagues could not imagine such terror!

Constituent Governance

Revolution must be governed not only to guide and regulate its movements but also to establish the forces of constituent power as a new form of life, a new social being. We have discussed the role of novel institutional processes to compose and consolidate insurrection in the revolutionary procedure, both combating the ruling powers and their corruptions and establishing new collective habits and practices. We have also explored how in the biopolitical context forms of democratic decision making can generate the political diagonal that marks the path of transition. But that is not yet enough. All of this must be supported in a governmental, constitutional, and juridical framework. Here, though, our argument runs into another impasse because at numerous points in our analysis we have already explained that existing governmental forms and structures are obstacles to revolution. We have criticized in the name of democracy numerous propositions of revolutionary government: the notion of taking power in the sense of laying hold on the existing, ready-made state machinery of the bourgeoisie (to use Marx's phrase); the projects to create a "counterpower" that is homologous to the existing state structures; the mechanisms that close down the development of constituent power in the structures of a constituted power; and the dialectical notions of revolutionary transition that govern through some form of dictatorship. And yet we are fully aware that the revolutionary process is not spontaneous and must be governed. How can we invent a democratic form of rule adequate to the revolutionary process? This would have to be democratic not in the false sense that we are fed every day by politicians and the media, with their pretenses of representation, but in the active and autonomous self-rule of the multitude as a whole.

We find some help for overcoming this impasse in what may at first seem an unlikely source: the structures of governance that are emerging as the primary forms of rule within Empire. We argued in Part 4 that the contemporary global order does not take the form of a "world state" or even reproduce the governmental structures created in the context of the nation-state, but instead is increasingly characterized by emerging forms of governance that rule without relying on an overarching political authority to manage and regulate in an ad hoc and variable fashion. We traced the genealogy of the concept of governance, in part, to the structures of regulation, management, and accountability of capitalist corporations, and indeed the characteristics of corporate governance remain strongly present in the various deployments of governance in the imperial constitution. Global governance is "postdemocratic" in the sense that it shuns the representative structures that have in the past served to legitimate state power in favor of pluralistic forms of regulation controlled, often indirectly, by oligarchic forces, such as those of property. As a result, governance structures have the flexibility and fluidity constantly to adapt to changing circumstances. They do not need stability and regularity to rule, but instead are designed to manage crises and rule over exceptional conditions.

Those prone to oppositional habits of thought are likely to respond to this analysis of "governance without government" in Empire with proposals in the contrary direction: we need to oppose Empire, they might say, with the fixed juridical structures and regularized normative processes of government. We tend in general, however, toward subversive rather than oppositional responses. The governance mechanisms of Empire do have the merit, in fact, of interpreting the biopolitical context and registering the increasing autonomy of the networks of singularities, the overflowing and unmeasurable forms of value produced by the multitude, and the ever greater power of the common. Our inclination is to appropriate this concept of governance, subvert its imperial vocation, and reformulate it as a concept of democracy and revolution.

We find some potential in the notion of federalism by which some theorists understand functions of global governance. In contrast to traditional models, such as those of the United States and Switzerland, for example, this federalism is not oriented toward state sovereignty but rather serves to articulate a wide variety of powers and mediate diverse political institutions with different and separate objectives. In the space between the nation-state and Empire, federalism constructs an array of diverse territorial mediations. The seeming multiplicity of federalism, however, quickly closes down, as its mechanisms of mediation merely seek to create a kind of nomadic state-form, reproducing forms of sovereignty and control.[64]

Much more useful are the analyses of governance by legal theorists, especially a group of German legal theorists who build on Niklas Luhmann's systems theories, which emphasize two primary characteristics of global governance: one *exceeding* the limits of fixed legal systems and their normative structures, and another *fragmenting* legal systems because of conflicts in global society and colliding norms. The passage from government to governance is thus conceived in legal terms as the movement from a unitary and deductive normative structure to a pluralistic and plastic one. Governance gives up any vain attempt to bring unity to global legal systems (based on international law or consensus among nation-states) and tries instead to establish a network logic that can manage conflicts and achieve a normative compatibility among the fragments of global society. Governance conceived in this way does "rule over the exception," but in a way completely different than Carl Schmitt imagines when he famously uses that phrase to define sovereignty. The exception here is not a punctual event that demands a decision but is spread over time and throughout society. Since the society they regulate and manage is full of exceptions, the structures of governance always remain contingent and aleatory—floating structures, we could say, on the clashing waves of global society.[65]

Some of the elements of governance, as conceived by these legal theorists, fit so closely with our analyses of biopolitical society that they could be seen as a summary of a string of passages in this book. Where they read fragmentation, we see a multiplicity of singularities; the overflowing they read in the relation between society and normative structures we recognize in the relation between labor and value; the network logic they read in the governance of exceptional normative situations we analyze in the cooperation of biopolitical production; and the social conflict they read as the basis for contingent legal frameworks we propose as the basis for the revolutionary notion of institution. Does this mean that these legal theorists are masked revolutionaries? No; in fact from our perspective they maintain a detached, skeptical, even cynical standpoint on the potential for social transformation. The proximity of their analyses of global governance to our analyses of the multitude, however, does identify the point on which the imperial notion of governance can be turned inside out, subverted, and transformed into a revolutionary concept. This is not an ideal operation of dialectical inversion but a practical, subversive path.

It should come as no surprise, in fact, that the structures of imperial governance so strongly correspond to the movements of the multitude. Governance is forced to register and represent, according to new diagrams, the juridical claims and political forces that the multitude expresses, like impressions of footprints in the sand. The struggles of the multitude are primary with respect to power, as we have insisted at various points in our analysis, in the sense that they are the locus of social innovation, whereas power can only react by attempting to capture or control their force.

A constituent governance that inverts the imperial form would have to present not simply a normative figure of rule, and not only a functional structure of social consensus and cooperation, but also an open and socially generalized schema for social experimentation and democratic innovation. This would be a constitutional system in which the "sources of law" and their means for legitimation are based solely on constituent power and democratic decision making. Just as insurrection has to become institutional, so too must revolution, in this way, become constitutional, building, through struggle after struggle, on successive levels that indefatigably overflow every systemic equilibrium, toward a democracy of the common.

Whereas revolt and insurrection may be episodic and short-lived, there is running throughout the revolutionary process something like a will to institution and constitution. We have in mind here as analogy the great Viennese art historian Alois Riegl's notion of *Kunstwollen,* which although difficult to translate can be rendered as "will to art." Riegl analyzes how, in another period of transition, late Roman art revolts against the ancient forms and establishes not only new techniques and a new "industry" but also new ways of seeing and experiencing the world. He conceives the late Roman *Kunstwollen* as the force governing this transformation of the plastic arts, the desire that articulates all the singular artistic expressions as a coherent institutional development, demonstrating not only the continuity but also the innovation of the process. The *Kunstwollen* accomplishes both the overcoming of the historical threshold and the organization of the exceeding, overflowing social forces in a coherent and lasting project.[66] A revolutionary process today will have to be governed by a *Rechtswollen,* that is, an institutional and constitutional will, which, in a parallel way, articulates the singularities of the multitude, along with its diverse instances of revolt and rebellion, in a powerful and lasting common process.

DE SINGULARITATE 2:

INSTITUTING HAPPINESS

> Through its buildings, pictures, and stories, humanity is preparing, if it must, to survive civilization. And, above all, it does so laughing.
> —Walter Benjamin, "Experience and Poverty"

> We have it in our power to begin the world over again. A situation, similar to the present, hath not happened since the days of Noah until now.
> —Thomas Paine, *Common Sense*

Welcome to Year 0! Prehistory ends not with a bang but a sigh of relief, after centuries of darkness and blood. The beginning of history does not mean the end of social strife, but rather that we all have the potential to address conflicts and transform them into peaceful, productive relationships. Nor does the beginning of history mean that our powers have been fully realized; if that were the case, history would be over before it had even begun. It is rather the beginning of a process of education and training in which we are engaged collectively in constituting social life, putting into action democratic government.

Enlightenment revolutionaries, from Diderot and Fontanelle to Jefferson, following the ancient Greeks and Romans, pose the ultimate political goal as public happiness. Happiness should become once again today a political concept, in some ways that the eighteenth-century thinkers understood and in others that they could not yet imagine. By happiness they mean, first of all, a long-lasting condition rather than a passing feeling, such as pleasure. Happiness is a pleasure that lasts and repeats. They insist too on the collective nature of happiness, emphasizing that it is public, not private. Already with these first two characteristics it is clear why happiness should be the primary object of government. It is a collective good, perhaps the ultimate collective good, which must take on an institutional character to guarantee its longevity. Happiness, however, is not something that leaders or representatives simply provide for the population. It is an active not a passive affect. The multitude must govern itself in order to create a durable state of happiness (and thus rather than "public" we would call it "common happiness"). Happiness is not a state of satisfaction that quells activity but rather a spur to desire, a mechanism for increasing and amplifying what we want and what we can do. Humans, of course, are not born with the fully developed capacities to govern ourselves, to resolve conflicts, to form lasting, felicitous relationships, but we do all have the potential for all that. Finally, then, happiness is the process of developing our capacities of democratic decision making and training ourselves in self-rule.[67]

The demand for happiness is thus an affirmation and celebration of the goals of the Enlightenment. The core of the Enlightenment that interests us is not any claim that some or all of us have already achieved or will ever reach an enlightened state of absolute mastery, self-control, knowledge, or the like. It is instead the recognition that humans are trainable, that we can improve ourselves individually, collectively, and over the course of history. And in the realm of government this must involve learning by doing. "The qualifications for self-government in society," Thomas Jefferson explains, "are not innate. They are the result of habit and long training."[68] Democracy must be not only the goal of a multitude with the already developed powers necessary for self-government but also a learning mechanism, a *dispositif,* that expands those powers, increasing not only the capacity but also the desire to participate in government. This is where Diderot and Machiavelli come together, because the call for happiness is an entirely realistic political project, based on humanity as it is now, as Machiavelli often insists, but with an equally lucid recognition of how humans can become different, how they can learn, improve themselves, and realize goals that were previously unimaginable. The point is to bring about our new and ever greater capacities, to set out on a political project for which democracy is both the end and the means.

Enlightenment thinkers have long been ridiculed for their faith in progress since the past is full of examples of human-wrought catastrophes and folly and since so many claims to progress have led to disaster and ruin. Some point to the way Nazi adminis-trative rationality led to genocide and gas chambers, others to the way scientific "advances" led to environmental devastation and nu-clear destruction. There is indeed no automatic movement of prog-ress, no guarantee that tomorrow will be better than today; but the recognition of such contingency should not lead anyone to a cyni-cal conclusion, to ignore the fact that we do have the power to im-prove our world, our society, ourselves. This is a materialist teleol-ogy that has no illusions about invisible hands or final causes pulling history forward. It is a teleology pushed forward only by our desires and our struggles, with no final end point. Progress will be measured by our growing powers to realize common happiness and form a democratic world in which we are all together permit-ted, able, and willing to rule.

Instituting happiness, therefore, is not only a political but also an ontological project. With each increase of our power we become different, adding to what we are, expanding social being. Being is not fixed once and for all in some otherworldly realm but con-stantly subject to a process of becoming. Human nature similarly is not immutable but rather open to a process of training and educa-tion. This does not mean that there are no limits to what we can do or that we can break absolutely from the past to create a clean slate: there are no leaps in nature, as the evolutionary biologists like to say. What it does mean, though, is that change is possible at the most basic level of our world and our selves and that we can inter-vene in this process to orient it along the lines of our desires, to-ward happiness.

Intellectual historians recount one version of how the political concept of happiness was lost: eighteenth-century happiness is turned inward in the nineteenth century and made sentimental. Bernard de Fontenelle's *Traité du bonheur* gives way to Adam Smith's *Theory of Moral Sentiments;* Saint-Just's proclamations of public happiness yield to the domestic sentiments of nineteenth-century novels; Jefferson's claim of happiness as a political right cedes to narratives of individual contentedness. Happiness is separated from reason, to which it was so strongly tied in the eighteenth century, and becomes and remains today merely a passion, something we feel, not something we do—an individual sentiment stripped of political meaning. Sympathy and pity present mechanisms of association and social constitution, but ones that are powerless and even block our power.

It is useful, therefore, to look to earlier authors to understand the political and ontological project of happiness. The aim of Spinoza's philosophy and politics, for instance, is joy *(gaudium),* an active affect that marks the increase of our power to act and to think. Joy is thus not a static state, as contentment might be, but rather a dynamic process that continues only so long as our powers continue to increase. We still don't know, Spinoza says, what a body can do and a mind can think. And we will never know the limits of their powers. The path of joy is constantly to open new possibilities, to expand our field of imagination, our abilities to feel and be affected, our capacities for action and passion. In Spinoza's thought, in fact, there is a correspondence between our power to affect (our mind's power to think and our body's power to act) and our power to be affected. The greater our mind's ability to think, the greater its capacity to be affected by the ideas of others; the greater our body's ability to act, the greater its capacity to be affected by other bodies. And we have greater power to think and to act, Spinoza explains, the more we interact and create common relations with others. Joy, in other words, is really the result of joyful encounters with others, encounters that increase our powers, and the institution of these encounters such that they last and repeat.

Before Spinoza, Dante Alighieri proposed joy and love as pro-

ductive of not only being but also being-in-common, that is, social
life. For Dante love is an accident that transforms the world and
creates a "vita nuova," a new life—going beyond the conceptions of
his predecessors, both the sentimental notions of love (in Guido
Guinizelli, for instance, for whom love produces emotions) and the
rationalist views (in Guido Cavalcanti love produces knowledge).
Dante tells us that love is a practice of the common. Love is able,
traversing the city, to generate new forms of conviviality, of living-
together, that affirm the autonomy and interaction of singularities
in the common.[69]

How can we restore or reinvent such political conceptions of
happiness, joy, and love for our world? A conventional answer to
such a question might offer a political program against misery,
meaning by misery not only the lack of wealth and resources but
also and more generally the lack of power to create and innovate, to
rule oneself. Misery is the condition of being separated from what
one can do, from what one can become. And indeed we have already mentioned the basic outlines of a program that can and
should be demanded of existing governments and the various institutions of global governance.

A first platform must demand the support of life against misery, that is, simply, that governments must provide everyone with
the basic means of life. In many national contexts important proposals have been debated about providing a guaranteed income to
all citizens, a basic income sufficient for the necessities of a productive, dignified existence. Many governments too, particularly in the
wealthiest countries, already guarantee basic health care to all their
citizens. But the majority of those living in misery, those most in
danger of famine and disease, reside elsewhere. What is necessary is
a global initiative to provide the basic means of life for all, throughout the world, a global guaranteed income and truly universal
health care, whether furnished through global institutions such as
UN agencies, citizen organizations, or other bodies.

Since the guarantee of a bare life for all is not enough to escape misery, a second platform must demand equality against hier-

archy, allowing everyone to become capable of participating in the constitution of society, collective self-rule, and constructive interaction with others. Everyone needs access to a basic education, of course, and a series of basic social and technical knowledges and skills. These are some of the prerequisites necessary for any political participation. Armed with these basic elements everyone will not be the same, of course, but will be able to participate equally in the collective management of society. But even when people have the skills, knowledges, and capacities required for government today, they are separated from power. We want a government that is not only open to the participation of all but also trains everyone to participate in democratic decision making, allowing people to move across borders and reside where they like. In the national contexts, the kind of political equality demanded by this platform has often been called citizenship. What we intend here is something like a global citizenship, then, which provides to all both the means and the opportunity to participate equally in the government of global society.

A third platform must demand open access to the common against the barriers of private property. It is possible today for everyone to have free and equal use of resources and wealth, and be able in turn to produce with them. In the context of scarcity in the past, of course, the demand for such equal access to resources often created an insolvable puzzle. If you grow crops on that field, it is not available for someone else to farm it; if you use that machine to produce, no one else can use it at the same time. Increasingly today, though, production and wealth cease to obey the logic of scarcity. If you use that idea productively, I can use it too, at the very same time. In fact the more of us that work with an idea and communicate about it, the more productive it becomes. To favor the increase of productive common wealth and to allow everyone free access to it is in the common interest. Government must support, in particular, the accumulation of knowledges: scientific knowledges and codes, of course, which are increasingly central in production, but also social knowledges and skills, the means of avoiding social conflicts and facilitating felicitous encounters, the means of promoting productive communication and exchange.

These three platforms are just and reasonable demands to make on today's ruling powers. They are nothing but the conditions that most favor the constituent encounters that we said earlier constitute the wealth of the multitude in the metropolis: ensuring that everyone has the basic means to life and good health; creating the conditions that we meet in a relation of equality, with the knowledge and skills to interact socially; and providing all open access to accumulated common wealth that serves as the basis for and is also enriched by our encounters. Remember, too, that we have already seen in our analysis that large portions of the global population already possess many of these capacities, in the networks of biopolitical production, in the life of the metropolis, and in the fabric of everyday social life. We can demand of the ruling powers that they be guaranteed and made universal.

But today's ruling powers unfortunately have no intention of granting even these basic demands. In the face of this arrogance of power, the most adequate response, rather than lamenting our poor lot and wallowing in melancholy, is laughter. Laughter, mind you, is a very serious matter. It is not consolation for our weakness but an expression of joy, a sign of our power. "Don't think that one has to be sad to be a militant," Michel Foucault reminds us, "even if the combat is abominable. It is the connection of desire to reality (and not its retreat into the forms of representation) that possesses revolutionary force."[70] The process of instituting happiness will constantly be accompanied by laughter.

Ours is, first of all, a knowing laugh, which accompanies our realistic critique of the dominant powers. The rulers, destroyers, and corrupters are not as strong as they think, and we are more powerful than they will ever know. Increasingly today in the biopolitical context the one divides in two, that is, productive forces are becoming ever more autonomous in their production of common goods, such as ideas, codes, affects, images, and the like. Capital still manages to expropriate the common that is produced, and ruling powers continue to exert their control, but we laugh with the recognition of what their weakness portends for our future.

Ours is also a laugh of creation and joy, anchored solidly in the present. Our free and equal access to the common, through which we together produce new and greater forms of the common, our liberation from the subordination of identities through monstrous processes of self-transformation, our autonomous control of the circuits of the production of social subjectivity, and in general our construction of common practices through which singularities compose the multitude are all limitless cycles of our increasing power and joy. While we are instituting happiness, our laughter is as pure as water.

Ours is finally a laugh of destruction, the laugh of armed angels which accompanies the combat against evil. Happiness has a dark side. Spinoza describes the joy of destroying what does harm to a friend.[71] This destruction has nothing to do with hatred, from which, indeed, nothing good can come. And this joy has nothing to do with *Schadenfreude,* enjoyment derived from the misfortune of others. The destruction of what causes harm is secondary to the increase of power and joy released by its removal. The extirpation in ourselves of our attachments to identity and, in general, the conditions of our enslavement will be extraordinarily painful, but still we laugh. In the long battles against the institutions that corrupt the common, such as the family, the corporation, and the nation, we will spill no end of tears, but still we laugh. And in the struggles against capitalist exploitation, the rule of property, and the destroyers of the common through public and private control, we will suffer terribly, but still we laugh with joy. They will be buried by laughter.

NOTES / ACKNOWLEDGMENTS / INDEX

NOTES

PREFACE

1. For some recent arguments for the common in various fields, see Nick Dyer-Witherford, *Cyber-Marx* (Urbana: University of Illinois Press, 1999); Augusto Illuminati, *Del comune* (Rome: Manifestolibri, 2003); Massimo De Angelis, *The Beginning of History* (London: Pluto, 2007); Peter Linebaugh, *The Magna Carta Manifesto* (Berkeley: University of California Press, 2008); Naomi Klein, "Reclaiming the Commons," *New Left Review,* no. 9 (May–June 2001), 81–89; Donald Nonini, ed., *The Global Idea of "the Commons"* (New York: Berghahn Books, 2007); and Michael Blecher, "Reclaiming the Common or the Beginning of the End of the (Legal) System," in *Entgrenzungen und Vernetzungen im Recht: Liber Amicorum Gunther Teubner,* ed. G.-P. Callies, Andreas Fischer-Lescano, Dan Wielsch, and Peer Zumbansen (New York: DeGruyter, forthcoming).

2. Gilles Deleuze, "What Is a *Dispositif?*" in *Michel Foucault, Philosopher,* ed. Timothy Armstrong (New York: Routledge, 1992), pp. 159–168.

3. Walter Benjamin, "Experience and Poverty," in *Selected Writings,* vol. 2 (Cambridge, Mass.: Harvard University Press, 2005), p. 732. See Patrick Greaney's excellent analysis of the concept of poverty in Benjamin and other modern European poets and philosophers, *Untimely Beggars* (Minneapolis: University of Minnesota Press, 2008).

4. See Luce Irigaray, *Éthique de la différence sexuelle* (Paris: Minuit, 1984), pp. 27–39; Diotima, *Il pensiero della differenza sessuale* (Milan: La Tartaruga, 1987); and Adriana Cavarero, *Nonostante Platone* (Rome: Editori Riuniti, 1990).

5. Reading Marx and Spinoza, Franck Fischbach identifies a very similar notion of joy and happiness based in productivity and differences grounded in the common. See *La production des hommes* (Paris: PUF, 2005), p. 145.

6. See Jacques Derrida, *D'un ton apocalyptique adopté naguère en philosophie* (Paris: Galilée, 1983).

7. Jean-Luc Nancy, *The Birth to Presence,* trans. Brian Holmes and others (Stanford: Stanford University Press, 1994), p. 407, n. 56.

1. REPUBLIC (AND THE MULTITUDE OF THE POOR)

1. For an example of leftist accusations of fascism centered on the U.S. government, see Naomi Wolf, "Fascist America, in 10 Easy Steps," *The Guardian,* 24 April 2007. For an example of the right-wing usage of "islamofascism," see Norman Podhoretz, *World War IV: The Long Struggle against Islamofascism* (New York: Doubleday, 2007).

2. Among recent scholarship that focuses on sovereignty, the work of Giorgio Agamben is undoubtedly the most sophisticated and significant. See in particular *Homo Sacer: Sovereign Power and Bare Life,* trans. Daniel Heller-Roazen (Stanford: Stanford University Press, 1998); and *State of Exception,* trans. Kevin Attell (Chicago: University of Chicago Press, 2005). See also Jean-Claude Monod, *Penser l'ennemi, affronter l'exception: Réflexions critiques sur l'actualité de Carl Schmitt* (Paris: La découverte, 2007).

3. Léon Robin, *La pensée grecque et les origines de l'esprit scientifique* (Paris: Renaissance du livre, 1923), pp. 209–212.

4. Immanuel Kant, introduction to *Critique of Pure Reason,* ed. Paul Guyer and Allen Wood (Cambridge: Cambridge University Press, 1997), A11, B25, p. 149.

5. For our previous analyses of the Kantian forms of juridical thought, see Michael Hardt and Antonio Negri, *Labor of Dionysus: A Critique of the State-form* (Minneapolis: University of Minnesota Press, 1994), pp. 217–261; and Antonio Negri, *Alle origini del formalismo giuridico* (Padua: Cedam, 1962), chap.1.

6. Alfred Sohn-Rethel, *Intellectual and Manual Labour* (Atlantic Highlands, N.J.: Humanities Press, 1978), p. 35.

7. Thomas Jefferson Samuel Kercheval, 12 July 1816, in *Writings,* ed. Merrill Peterson (Washington, D.C.: Library of America, 1984), p. 1396.

8. Emmanuel-Joseph Sieyès, *Écrits politiques,* ed. Roberto Zapperi (Paris: Éditions des archives contemporaines, 1985), p. 81.

9. For an excellent historical presentation of republican thought in England, which integrates the results of Quentin Skinner's and J. G. A. Pocock's analyses, see Jonathan Scott, *Commonwealth Principles* (Cambridge: Cambridge University Press, 2004).

10. On the notion of material constitution, see Costantino Mortati, *La costituzione in senso materiale* (Milan: Giuffrè, 1940); and Ernst Forsthoff, *Rechtsstaat im Wandel* (Stuttgart: Kohlhammer, 1964).

11. Charles Beard, *An Economic Interpretation of the Constitution of the United States* (New York: Macmillan, 1913), p. 324.

12. John Adams, "Defense of the Constitutions of Government of the United

States," in *The Works of John Adams*, 10 vols., ed. Charles Francis Adams (Boston: Little, Brown & Co., 1850), 6:9.

13. On the right to bear arms, see J. G. A. Pocock, "Historical Introduction," in *The Political Works of James Harrington* (Cambridge: Cambridge University Press, 1977), pp. 138–143; Antonio Negri, *Insurgencies*, trans. Maurizia Boscagli (Minneapolis: University of Minnesota Press, 1999), pp. 163–164; and Joyce Lee Malcolm, *To Keep and Bear Arms: The Origins of an Anglo-American Right* (Cambridge, Mass.: Harvard University Press, 1994).

14. *The Federalist*, no. 51, ed. Benjamin Fletcher Wright (Cambridge, Mass.: Harvard University Press, 1961).

15. See Negri, *Insurgencies*, pp. 205–212 and 235–236.

16. Henry Cachard, ed., *The French Civil Code* (London: Stevens and Sons, 1895), p. 134.

17. On the Haitian Revolution as an unthinkable event, see Michel-Rolph Trouillot, *Silencing the Past: Power and the Production of History* (Boston: Beacon Press, 1995), pp. 70–107. On the place of Haiti in the pantheon of modern revolutions, see Nick Nesbitt, *Universal Emancipation: The Haitian Revolution and the Radical Enlightenment* (Charlottesville: University of Virginia Press, 2008); Laurent Dubois, *Avengers of the New World: The Story of the Haitian Revolution* (Cambridge, Mass.: Harvard University Press, 2004); and Sibylle Fischer, *Modernity Disavowed: Haiti and the Cultures of Slavery in the Age of Revolution* (Durham: Duke University Press, 2004).

18. See Ranajit Guha, *A Rule of Property for Bengal: An Essay on the Idea of Permanent Settlement*, 2nd ed. (Durham: Duke University Press, 1983).

19. Evgeny Pashukanis, *General Theory of Law and Marxism*, in *Selected Writings on Marxism and Law*, ed. Piers Bierne and Robert Sharlet (London: Academic Press, 1980), p. 69. On Pashukanis, see Hans Kelsen, *The Communist Theory of Law* (New York: Praeger, 1955); and Antonio Negri, "Rileggendo Pashukanis," in *La forma stato* (Milan: Feltrinelli, 1979), pp. 161–195. More generally, on the relation between private and public law, see Karl Renner, *The Institutions of Private Law and Their Social Functions*, trans. Agnes Schwarzschild (London: Routledge and Kegan Paul, 1949); John R. Commons, *Legal Foundations of Capitalism* (New York: Macmillan, 1924); and, from a historical point of view, Franz Wieacker, *The History of Private Law in Europe*, trans. Tony Weir (Oxford: Clarendon Press, 1995).

20. Immanuel Kant, "An Answer to the Question: 'What is Enlightenment?'" in *Political Writings*, 2nd ed., ed. H. S. Reiss (Cambridge: Cambridge University Press, 1991), pp. 54–60.

21. For a reading of the minor Kant relatively close to our own, see Michel

Foucault, "What Is Enlightenment?" in *Ethics: Subjectivity and Truth,* ed. Paul Rabinow (New York: New Press, 1997), pp. 303–320; and Foucault, introduction to Immanuel Kant, *Anthropologie d'un point de vue pragmatique* (Paris:Vrin, 2008), pp. 11–79. Many brilliant and original books have been published in recent years that provide alternative images of Kant that differ to varying degrees from the minor Kant who interests us here. See in particular Peter Fenves, *Late Kant* (New York: Routledge, 2003); and Kojin Karatani, *Transcritique: On Kant and Marx,* trans. Sabu Kohso (Cambridge, Mass.: MIT Press, 2003).

22. For an example of Habermas's early work on intersubjectivity, see Jürgen Habermas, "Labor and Interaction: Remarks on Hegel's Jena *Philosophy of Mind,*" in *Theory and Practice,* trans. John Viertel (Boston: Beacon Press, 1973), pp. 142–169. For his later work on the communicative public sphere, see primarily *The Theory of Communicative Action,* 2 vols., trans. Thomas McCarthy (Boston: Beacon Press, 1984). For Rawls, both elements we identify in his work can be found in John Rawls, *A Theory of Justice* (Cambridge, Mass.: Harvard University Press, 1971). One can follow the movement in his thought away from schemas of redistribution in *Collected Papers,* ed. Samuel Freeman (Cambridge, Mass.: Harvard University Press, 1999).

23. For some representative works, see Anthony Giddens, *The Consequences of Modernity* (Stanford: Stanford University Press, 1990); Giddens, *The Third Way: The Renewal of Social Democracy* (Cambridge: Polity, 1998); Ulrich Beck, Anthony Giddens, and Scott Lash, *Reflexive Modernization* (Cambridge: Polity, 1994); and Ulrich Beck, *Risk Society: Towards a New Modernity,* trans. Mark Ritter (London: Sage, 1992).

24. For a critique of "global social democracy" in terms somewhat different from ours, see Walden Bello, "The Post-Washington Dissensus" (Washington, D.C.: Foreign Policy in Focus, September 24, 2007).

25. Karl Marx, *Economic and Philosophical Manuscripts,* in *Early Writings,* trans. Rodney Livingstone and Gregor Benton (London: Penguin, 1975), p. 336.

26. On Althusser's conception of the break in Marx's thought, see Louis Althusser, *For Marx,* trans. Ben Brewster (New York: Pantheon, 1969). For the Frankfurt School, see, for example, Max Horkheimer and Theodor Adorno, *The Dialectic of Enlightenment,* trans. Edmund Jephcott (Stanford: Stanford University Press, 2002).

27. Mario Tronti, *Operai e capitale* (Turin: Einaudi, 1964), p. 89. See also the anthology *Socialisme ou barbarie* (Paris: Acratie, 2006); and Ranajit Guha and Gayatri Spivak, eds., *Selected Subaltern Studies* (New York: Oxford University Press, 1988).

28. See Raniero Panzieri, *Lotte operaie nello sviluppo capitalistico* (Turin: Einaudi, 1976), pp. 88–96; Cornelius Castoriadis, "Recommencer la revolution," *Socialisme ou barbarie,* no. 35 (January 1964), p. 136; and Hans-Jürgen Krahl, *Kostitution und Klassenkampf* (Frankfurt: Neue Kritik, 1971), chap. 31.

29. See, for example, Georg Lukács, *The Destruction of Reason,* trans. Peter Palmer (Atlantic Highlands, N.J.: Humanities Press, 1980).

30. *Briefwechsel zwischen Wilhelm Dilthey und dem Grafen Paul Yorck von Wartenburg, 1877–97,* ed. Sigrid von der Schulenburg (Halle: Niemeyer, 1923).

31. Reiner Schürmann, *Des hégémonies brisées* (Toulouse: T. E. R., 1996), p. 650.

32. On the relationship between Foucault and Merleau-Ponty, see Daniel Liotta, *Qu'est-ce que une reprise? Deux études sur Foucault* (Marseille: Transbordeurs, 2007).

33. See, for example, Frantz Fanon, *Black Skin, White Masks,* trans. Charles Markmann (New York: Grove, 1967), p. 116.

34. On the way new medical technologies have shifted the boundaries of racial discourse, see Paul Gilroy, *Against Race: Imagining Political Culture beyond the Color Line* (Cambridge, Mass.: Harvard University Press, 2000), pp. 44–48.

35. Marx explains the metaphysical character of commodities in the famous passage on fetishism in *Capital,* vol. 1, trans. Ben Fowkes (New York: Vintage, 1976), pp. 163–177.

36. Michel Foucault, "L'esprit d'un monde sans esprit" (interview with Pierre Blanchet and Claire Brière), in *Dits et écrits,* vol. 3 (Paris: Gallimard, 1994), p. 749. See also Foucault, "Téhéran: la foi contre le chah," ibid., pp. 683–688. English translations of Foucault's essays and interviews on the Iranian Revolution are included as the appendix of Janet Afary and Kevin Anderson, *Foucault and the Iranian Revolution* (Chicago: University of Chicago Press, 2005), pp. 179–277.

37. For a sustained argument for the continuing importance of nationalism and national thought, particularly in the subordinated countries, see Pheng Cheah, *Spectral Nationality* (New York: Columbia University Press, 2003), and *Inhuman Conditions: On Cosmopolitanism and Human Rights* (Cambridge, Mass.: Harvard University Press, 2006).

38. Frantz Fanon, *Wretched of the Earth,* trans. Richard Philcox (New York: Grove, 2004).

39. On blackness and freedom, see Cedric Robinson, *Black Marxism* (London: Zed Press, 1983); and Fred Moten, *In the Break: The Aesthetics of the Black Radical Tradition* (Minneapolis: University of Minnesota Press, 2003).

40. Marx, *Economic and Philosophical Manuscripts,* p. 351.

41. David Wootten, ed., *Divine Right and Democracy* (New York: Penguin, 1986), p. 273. We are grateful to Russ Leo for his guidance in studying the role of the multitude in seventeenth-century English thought.

42. Nahum Tate, *Richard the Second,* 2.1.25, cited in Wolfram Schmidgen, "The Last Royal Bastard and the Multitude," *Journal of British Studies* 47 (January 2008), 64.

43. *The Putney Debates,* ed. Geoffrey Robertson (London: Verso, 2007), p. 69.

44. Robert Filmer, "Observations upon Aristotle's Politiques," in *Patriarchia and Other Writings,* ed. Johann Sommerville (Cambridge: Cambridge University Press, 1991), p. 236. On Filmer's refusal of the power of the multitude, see also ibid., pp. 1–68.

45. Thomas Hobbes, *The Elements of Law Natural and Politic,* ed. J. C. A. Gaskin, pt. 2 (Oxford: Oxford University Press, 1994), chap. 21, p. 125. For the mandate to reduce the multitude to a unity, see also Hobbes, *Leviathan,* ed. C. B. Macpherson (London: Penguin, 1968), chaps. 16 and 17, in particular pp. 220–221 and 227–228. For the distinction between the multitude and the people, see Hobbes, *De Cive* (New York: Appleton Century-Crofts, 1949), chap. 12, sec. 8, p. 135.

46. Cited in Wolfram Schmidgen, "Empiricist Multitudes in Boyle and Locke," paper delivered at the Conference of the Society for Literature, Science, and the Arts, Chicago, Fall 2005. We follow Schmidgen's analysis throughout this paragraph.

47. On the Hobbes-Boyle controversies and the relation between scientific debates and political questions of social order, see Steven Shapin and Simon Schaffer, *Leviathan and the Air-Pump: Hobbes, Boyle, and the Experimental Life* (Princeton: Princeton University Press, 1985).

48. The differences between Spinoza and Boyle are explored in detail in Spinoza's correspondence with Henry Oldenburg. For recent analyses of this polemic, see Luisa Simonutti, "'Dalle sensate esperienze' all'ermeneutica biblica," in *Spinoza: Ricerche e prospettive,* ed. Daniela Bostrenghi and Cristina Santinelli (Naples: Bibliopolis, 2007), pp. 313–326; and Elhanan Yakira, "Boyle et Spinoza," *Archives de philosophie* 51, no. 1 (1988), 107–124.

49. See Antonio Negri, *The Savage Anomaly* (Minneapolis: University of Minnesota Press, 1991).

50. On the legal theory of Franciscanism in relation to poverty, see Giovanni Tarello, "Profili giuridici della questione della povertà nel francescanesimo prima di Ockham," in *Scritti in memoria di Antonio Falchi* (Milan: Giuffrè, 1964), pp. 338–448. On the Franciscan affirmation of poverty as a contemporary political perspective, in the context of liberation theology, see

Leonardo Boff, *Saint Francis: A Model for Human Liberation* (New York: Crossroad, 1982). On Marsilius's affirmation of "supreme poverty," see *Defender of Peace,* trans. Alan Gewirth (New York: Columbia University Press, 1956), in particular Discourse Two, chaps. 12–14, pp. 187–233.

51. See Franz Mehring, *Absolutism and Revolution in Germany, 1525–1848* (London: New Park Publications, 1975).

52. See Peter Linebaugh and Marcus Rediker, *The Many-Headed Hydra* (Boston: Beacon Press, 2000).

53. Jacques Rancière, *Disagreement,* trans. Julie Rose (Minneapolis: University of Minnesota Press, 1999), p. 11.

54. Adolphe Thiers cited in Jeffrey Schnapp and Matthew Tiews, eds., *Crowds* (Stanford: Stanford University Press, 2006), p. 71.

55. Pope Benedict XVI, *God Is Love* (San Francisco: Ignatius Press, 2006).

56. Martin Heidegger, "Die Armut," in *Heidegger Studies,* vol. 10 (Berlin: Duncker & Humblot, 1994), pp. 5–11. Translations are our own. For the account of the scene of Heidegger's lecture, we follow Philippe Lacoue-Labarthe's excellent introduction to the French edition of the text, Martin Heidegger, *La pauvreté* (Strasbourg: Presses Universitaires de Strasbourg, 2004), pp. 7–65. F.-W. von Herrmann explains in his editorial note (p. 11) to the original publication of the text in *Heidegger Studies* that Heidegger added in the margin the sentence about world history.

57. Ibid., p. 8.

58. Ibid., pp. 8, 9.

59. Slavoj Žižek similarly shows how Heidegger translates his anticommunism into an ontological argument in his 1942 lectures on Hölderlin's hymn "The Ister," focusing on Heidegger's explanation of "the essence of victory" with reference to the battle of Stalingrad. More generally, Žižek claims that central elements of Heidegger's ontology function as an apology for Nazi militarism. See Slavoj Žižek, *The Parallax View* (Cambridge, Mass.: MIT Press, 2006), pp. 275–285.

60. See Theodor Adorno, Else Frenkel Brunswik, Daniel Levinson, and R. Nevitt Sanford, *The Authoritarian Personality* (New York: Harper & Brothers, 1950).

61. Henry Louis Gates Jr. and Cornell West, *The Future of Race* (New York: Knopf, 1996), p. xiii.

62. On the hypothesis of a strong theoretical relationship between Heidegger and Schmitt, see Jean-Claude Monod, *Penser l'ennemi* (Paris: La découverte, 2007); and Carlo Galli, *Genealogia della politica: Carl Schmitt e la crisi del pensiero politico moderno* (Bologna: Il Molino, 1996).

63. Thomas Hobbes, *Behemoth,* ed. Ferdinand Tönnies (New York: Barnes & Noble, 1969), Dialogue 3, p. 126.

64. Niccolò Machiavelli, *Florentine Histories,* trans. Laura Banfield and Harvey Mansfield Jr. (Princeton: Princeton University Press, 1988), bk. 3, chap. 13, pp. 122–123.

65. Niccolò Machiavelli, *The Golden Ass,* in *Machiavelli: The Chief Works,* 3 vols., ed. Allan Gilbert (Durham: Duke University Press, 1965), chap. 8, vv. 118–123, 2:772 (translation modified).

66. Baruch Spinoza, *Ethics,* in *Complete Works,* trans. Samuel Shirley (Indianapolis: Hackett, 2002), bk. 3, Proposition 2, Scholium, p. 280.

67. Karl Marx, "Economic Manuscript of 1861–63," trans. Ben Fowkes, in Karl Marx and Frederick Engels, *Collected Works,* vol. 30 (New York: International Publishers, 1982), p. 40. See also *Grundrisse,* trans. Martin Nicolaus (New York: Vintage, 1973), pp. 295–296. We fundamentally concur with Dussel's readings of the successive drafts of *Capital* on this topic. It is not surprising, given his interest in and association with liberation theology, that Dussel would be especially sensitive to Marx's focus on poverty. See Enrique Dussel, *Towards an Unknown Marx: A Commentary on the Manuscripts of 1861–63,* trans. Yolanda Angulo, ed. Fred Moseley (London: Routledge, 2001), esp. pp. 6–11 and 240–245.

68. Beverly Silver makes a similar point when she highlights that boundaries are drawn around what counts as the working class in a way that often neglects how gender and race are constitutive of class identities. To analyze how working classes are made and unmade, she brings together a Polanyi model (emphasizing exploitation as expropriation and violence) and a Marx model (focusing on economic phenomena). See Beverly Silver, *Forces of Labor: Workers' Movements and Globalization since 1870* (Cambridge: Cambridge University Press, 2003), esp. pp. 16–25. For an excellent discussion of these issues in relation to Marx's notion of primitive accumulation, see Sandro Mezzadra, "Attualità della preistoria: Per una rilettura del cap. 24 del Capitale, I," in *La condizione postcoloniale* (Verona: Ombre corte, 2008), pp. 127–154.

69. See François Ewald, *L'État-providence* (Paris: Grasset, 1986); and Roberto Esposito, *Bios: Biopolitics and Philosophy,* trans. Timothy Campbell (Minneapolis: University of Minnesota Press, 2008).

70. See Agamben, *Homo Sacer;* and Jean-Luc Nancy, *The Inoperative Community,* trans. Peter Connor, Lisa Garbus, Michael Holland, and Simona Sawhney (Minneapolis: University of Minnesota Press, 1991). Jacques Derrida's early works, such as *Writing and Difference* and *Margins of Philoso-*

phy, although they take an entirely different approach, arrive at similar results. In some respects Derrida's later work attempts to define a political approach in "biopolitical" terms. See in particular *Specters of Marx,* trans. Peggy Kamuf (New York: Routledge, 1994); and *Politics of Friendship,* trans. George Collins (London: Verso, 1997).

71. See, for example, Noam Chomsky and Michel Foucault, *The Chomsky-Foucault Debate* (New York: New Press, 2006).

72. Michel Foucault, "The Subject and Power," in Hubert Dreyfus and Paul Rabinow, *Michel Foucault: Beyond Structuralism and Hermeneutics* (Chicago: University of Chicago Press, 1982), pp. 221–222.

73. On linguistic innovation in Foucault, see Judith Revel, *Foucault* (Paris: Bordas, 2006); and Arnold Davidson, *The Emergence of Sexuality: Historical Epistemology and the Formation of Concepts* (Cambridge, Mass.: Harvard University Press, 2001).

74. The theory of the event runs throughout Badiou's work. For a representative treatment, see Alain Badiou, *Being and Event,* trans. Oliver Feltham (New York: Continuum, 2005), pts. 4 and 5, pp. 173–261. For Badiou's claim that contemporary political movements cannot break from the "dominant political subjectivities" with the current mechanisms of domination, see "Prefazione all'edizione italiana," in Badiou, *Metapolitica* (Naples: Cronopio, 2001), pp. 9–15, esp. pp. 13–14.

75. Luciano Bolis, *Il mio granello di sabbia* (Turin: Einaudi, 1946), p. 4.

76. Gilles Deleuze, *Negotiations,* trans. Martin Joughin (New York: Columbia University Press, 1995), p. 176.

77. Reiner Schürmann, ed. and commentary, *Meister Eckhart: Mystic and Philosopher* (Bloomington: Indiana University Press, 1978), p. 4.

78. Charles Peirce, *Elements of Logic,* in *Collected Papers of Charles Sanders Peirce,* ed. Charles Hartshorne and Paul Weiss (Cambridge, Mass.: Harvard University Press, 1960), p. 474.

2. MODERNITY (AND THE LANDSCAPES OF ALTERMODERNITY)

1. On the double nature of modernity and the hierarchical relationship that defines it, see Michael Hardt and Antonio Negri, *Empire* (Cambridge, Mass.: Harvard University Press, 2000), pp. 69–92.

2. Walter Mignolo, *The Idea of Latin America* (Cambridge: Blackwell, 2005), p. xiii. On the definition of modernity as the management of the center-periphery relation in the world-system, see also Enrique Dussel, *Etica de la liberación* (Madrid: Trotta, 1998), pp. 19–86.

3. Dussel invents the term "transmodernity" to name a notion of modernity

that is not a European but a planetary phenomenon. See Enrique Dussel, *The Invention of the Americas,* trans. Michael Barber (New York: Continuum, 1995).

4. Ranajit Guha, *Dominance without Hegemony: History and Power in Colonial India* (Cambridge, Mass.: Harvard University Press, 1997), pp. 97–98.

5. James Lockhart, *The Nahuas after the Conquest* (Palo Alto: Stanford University Press, 1992), p. 14. See also Michael Ennis, "Historicizing Nahua Utopias" (Ph.D. diss., Duke University, 2005).

6. See, for example, Serge Gruzinski, *The Conquest of Mexico: The Incorporation of Indian Societies into the Western World, 16th–18th Centuries,* trans. Eileen Corrigan (Cambridge: Polity Press, 1993).

7. On Iroquois federalism, see Iris Marion Young, "Hybrid Democracy: Iroquois Federalism and the Postcolonial Project," in *Political Theory and the Rights of Indigenous Peoples,* ed. Duncan Ivison, Paul Patton, and Will Sanders (Cambridge: Cambridge University Press, 2000), pp. 237–258; and Donald Grinde and Bruce Johansen, *Exemplar of Liberty: Native America and the Evolution of Democracy* (Berkeley: University of California Press, 1991).

8. Guha, *Dominance without Hegemony,* p. 89.

9. We are drawing in very general terms on Jacques Lacan's notion of foreclosure *(forclusion).* See Dylan Evans, *An Introductory Dictionary of Lacanian Psychoanalysis* (New York: Routledge, 1996), pp. 64–66.

10. See, for example, Matthew Sparke, *In the Space of Theory: Postfoundational Geographies of the Nation-State* (Minneapolis: University of Minnesota Press, 2005); and James Ferguson and Akhil Gupta, "Spatializing States: Toward an Ethnography of Neoliberal Governmentality," *American Ethnologist* 29, no. 4 (November 2002), 981–1002.

11. World-systems theory presents the best-articulated and most influential center-periphery model. See Immanuel Wallerstein, *World-Systems Analysis: An Introduction* (Durham: Duke University Press, 2004).

12. See Neil Lazarus, "The Fetish of 'the West' in Postcolonial Theory," in *Marxism, Modernity, and Postcolonial Studies,* ed. Crystal Bartolovich and Neil Lazarus (Cambridge: Cambridge University Press, 2002), pp. 43–64.

13. See Jürgen Habermas, "Modernity: An Unfinished Project," in *Habermas and the Unfinished Project of Modernity,* ed. Maurizio Passerin d'Entrèves and Seyla Benhabib (Cambridge, Mass.: MIT Press, 1997), pp. 38–58; and *The Philosophical Discourse of Modernity,* trans. Frederick Lawrence (Cambridge, Mass.: MIT Press, 1987).

14. See Susan Buck-Morss, "Hegel and Haiti," *Critical Inquiry* 26, no. 4 (Summer 2000), 821–865.

15. On the contradictions of slaves and property in the development of capitalism, with an accent on the origins of financial speculation, see Ian Baucom, *Specters of the Atlantic: Finance Capital, Slavery, and the Philosophy of History* (Durham: Duke University Press, 2005).

16. Marx to Pavel Vasilyevich Annenkov, 28 December 1846, in Karl Marx and Frederick Engels, *Collected Works,* vol. 38 (New York: International Publishers, 1982), pp. 101–102.

17. On the historical relationship between slavery and capitalist production, see Sidney Mintz, *Sweetness and Power: The Place of Sugar in Modern History* (New York: Penguin, 1985); Immanuel Wallerstein, *The Modern World-System: Mercantilism and the Consolidation of the European World-Economy, 1600–1750* (New York: Academic Press, 1980); and Robin Blackburn, *The Making of New World Slavery* (London: Verso, 1998).

18. On the centrality of race to modernity, see Paul Gilroy, *The Black Atlantic* (Cambridge, Mass.: Harvard University Press, 1993).

19. On the significance of the Haitian Revolution for understanding the nature of modernity and specifically on the notion of disavowal, see Sibylle Fischer, *Modernity Disavowed: Haiti and the Cultures of Slavery in the Age of Revolution* (Durham: Duke University Press, 2004). See also the 1805 Haitian Constitution, which Fischer includes as an appendix, pp. 275–281. Note that even in the Haitian Constitution private property is declared sacred and inviolable (Article 6).

20. This Foucaultian perspective resembles in some ways that of George Rawick, *From Sundown to Sunup: The Making of the Black Community* (Westport, Conn.: Greenwood Press, 1972).

21. Baruch Spinoza, *Theological-Political Treatise,* trans. Samuel Shirley (Indianapolis: Hackett, 2001), chap. 17, p. 185.

22. See Robin Blackburn, *The Overthrow of Colonial Slavery* (London: Verso, 1988); and Yann Moulier Boutang, *De l'esclavage au salariat: Économie historique du salariat bridé* (Paris: PUF, 1998).

23. W. E. B. Du Bois, *Black Reconstruction* (New York: Russell & Russell, 1935), p. 67.

24. W. E. B. Du Bois, *The Gift of Black Folk* (New York: AMS Press, 1971), p. 139.

25. See Furio Ferraresi and Sandro Mezzadra, introduction to Max Weber, *Dalla terra alla fabbrica: Scritti sui lavoratori agricoli e lo Stato nazionale (1892–1897)* (Bari: Laterza, 2005), pp. vii–xliv; and Moulier Boutang, *De l'esclavage au salariat,* pp. 109–130.

26. See Orlando Patterson, *Slavery and Social Death* (Cambridge, Mass.: Har-

vard University Press, 1985). On "bare life," see Giorgio Agamben, *Homo Sacer: Sovereign Power and Bare Life,* trans. Daniel Heller-Roazen (Stanford, Stanford University Press, 1998).

27. Edward Said, *Orientalism* (New York: Pantheon, 1978).

28. Gayatri Spivak, *A Critique of Postcolonial Reason* (Cambridge, Mass.: Harvard University Press, 1999).

29. Pope Benedict XVI, "Inaugural Address of the Fifth General Conference of the Bishops of Latin America and the Caribbean," 13 May 2007, www. vatican.va.

30. Stokely Carmichael and Charles Hamilton, *Black Power* (New York: Vintage, 1967).

31. Barnor Hesse, "Im/Plausible Deniability: Racism's Conceptual Double Bind," *Social Identities* 10, no. 1 (2004), 24. See also Hesse, "Discourse on Institutional Racism," in *Institutional Racism in Higher Education,* ed. Ian Law, Deborah Phillips, and Laura Turney (London: Trentham Books, 2004), pp. 131–148. More generally, on the centrality of racial hierarchy to the development of the modern state, see David Theo Goldberg, *The Racial State* (Oxford: Blackwell, 2002).

32. Throughout this paragraph we follow the illuminating analysis of Irene Silverblatt, *Modern Inquisitions: Peru and the Colonial Origins of the Civilized World* (Durham: Duke University Press, 2004).

33. Nathan Wachtel, *The Vision of the Vanquished: The Spanish Conquest of Peru through Indian Eyes, 1530–1570,* trans. Ben Reynolds and Siân Reynolds (New York: Barnes & Noble, 1977).

34. See Roman Rosdolsky's critique of Engels, *Engels and the "Nonhistoric" Peoples: The National Question in the Revolution of 1848,* trans. and ed. John-Paul Himka (Glasgow: Critique Books, 1986); and more generally Eric Wolf, *Europe and the People without History* (Los Angeles: University of California Press, 1982).

35. See, for example, Karl Marx, "The British Rule in India" and "The Future Results of British Rule in India," in *Surveys from Exile,* vol. 2 of *Political Writings,* ed. David Fernbach (London: Penguin, 1973), pp. 301–307 and 319–325.

36. Weber's famous lectures on science and politics as a calling or vocation lament our inability to liberate the historical condition from economism. See Max Weber, *The Vocation Lectures,* trans. Rodney Livingstone (Indianapolis: Hachett, 2004).

37. For critiques of these aspects of the Marxist tradition, see Cedric Robinson, *Black Marxism* (London: Zed Books, 1983), pp. 9–63; and Ward

Churchill, ed., *Marxism and Native Americans* (Boston: South End Press, 1983).

38. We are grouping together here the work of authors such as Immanuel Wallerstein and Giovanni Arrighi even though there are significant differences among them. Arrighi is the only one, in our view, to articulate successfully in the era of globalization the problem of discontinuity in cyclical economic development. In particular, he foresees a new cycle characterized by a relatively peaceful Chinese hegemony over the processes of globalization that will determine a new phase of social and political relations. See *Adam Smith in Beijing* (London: Verso, 2007). On the importance of Arrighi's work and world-systems theory more generally in contemporary political and theoretical debates, see Perry Anderson, "Jottings on the Conjuncture," *New Left Review,* no. 48 (November–December 2007), 5–37.

39. Rosa Luxemburg, *The Accumulation of Capital,* trans. Agnes Schwarzschild (New York: Monthly Review, 1951), pp. 466–467.

40. V. I. Lenin, *Imperialism: The Highest Stage of Capitalism* (New York: International Publishers, 1939), p. 10 (1920 preface to the French and German editions).

41. See Mao Tsetung, *A Critique of Soviet Economics,* trans. Moss Roberts (New York: Monthly Review, 1977).

42. Wang Hui, *China's New Order* (Cambridge, Mass.: Harvard University Press, 2003), p. 150. See also Jean-Louis Rocca, *La société chinoise vue par ses sociologues* (Paris: Presses de Sciences Po, 2008).

43. Marx to Nicolai Mikhailovsky [also known as the "Letter to Otechestvenniye Zapiski"], November 1877, in Karl Marx and Frederick Engels, *Collected Works,* vol. 24 (New York: International Publishers, 1989), p. 200.

44. Karl Marx, "First Draft of Letter to Vera Zasulich," March 1881, ibid., p. 360.

45. On Marx's letters about the Russian commune, see Étienne Balibar, *The Philosophy of Marx* (London: Verso, 1995), pp. 106–112; and Enrique Dussel, *El último Marx (1863–1882) y la liberación latinoamericana* (Ixtapalapa, Mexico: Siglo XXI, 1990), pp. 238–293.

46. José Carlos Mariátegui, *Seven Interpretive Essays on Peruvian Reality* (Austin: University of Texas Press, 1971), p. 57. On the relationship between "Inca communism" and European communisms in Mariátegui, see esp. pp. 35–44, 74–76; and "Prologue to *Tempest in the Andes,*" in *The Heroic and Creative Meaning of Socialism: Selected Essays of José Carlos Mariátegui,* ed. Michael Pearlman (Atlantic Highlands, N.J.: Humanities Press, 1996), pp. 79–84.

47. For a useful history of developmentalist discourses, see Gilbert Rist, *The History of Development* (London: Zed Books, 2002). For critiques of developmentalist ideologies and political economy, see Arturo Escobar, *Encountering Development* (Princeton: Princeton University Press, 1994); and Giuseppe Cocco and Antonio Negri, *GlobAL* (Rome: Manifestolibri, 2006).

48. This is the critique Althusser directed against Lenin in the midst of his polemic against the destructive effects of Soviet ideology. See Louis Althusser, *Lenin and Philosophy,* trans. Ben Brewster (New York: Monthly Review Press, 1971).

49. Wallerstein argues that in the great ideological confrontation between Wilsonianism and Leninism, which continued in the latter half of the century between capitalist modernization theory and socialist dependency theory, both sides shared a common ideology of national development. See Immanuel Wallerstein, "The Concept of National Development, 1917–1989: Elegy and Requiem," *American Behavioral Scientist* 35, no. 4–5 (March–June 1992), 517–529.

50. On the concept of "extremism of the center," see Étienne Balibar, introduction to Carl Schmitt, *Le léviathan dans la doctrine de l'état de Thomas Hobbes* (Paris: Seuil, 2002), p. 11.

51. Ernesto Guevara, "Socialism and Man in Cuba," in *Che Guevara Reader,* ed. David Deutschmann (Melbourne: Ocean Press, 2003), p. 217 (translation modified). On Che's critique of the orthodoxy of Soviet economic policy, see Ernesto Che Guevara, *Apuntes críticos a la economía política* (Havana: Centro de estudios Che Guevara, 2006).

52. See Silvia Federici, *Caliban and the Witch* (New York: Autonomedia, 2004); and Luisa Muraro, *La Signora del Gioco* (Milan: Feltrinelli, 1976).

53. Karl Marx, *Capital,* vol. 1, trans. Ben Fowkes (New York: Vintage, 1976), p. 91.

54. Max Horkheimer and Theodor Adorno, *The Dialectic of Enlightenment,* trans. Edmund Jephcott (Palo Alto: Stanford University Press, 2002), p. xvi

55. William Shakespeare, *The Tempest,* 1.2.311–313.

56. Roberto Fernández Retamar, *Caliban and Other Essays,* trans. Edward Baker (Minneapolis: University of Minnesota Press, 1989), p. 14.

57. See Aimé Césaire, *A Tempest,* trans. Richard Miller (New York: TGC Translations, 2002), esp. act 3, scene 5. See also Paget Henry, *Caliban's Reason: Introducing Afro-Caribbean Philosophy* (New York: Routledge, 2000).

58. Spinoza to Pieter Balling, 20 July 1664, in Baruch Spinoza, *Complete Works,* trans. Samuel Shirley (Indianapolis: Hackett, 2002), p. 803.

59. For an astute analysis of and ample bibliography on Spinoza's letter, see Augusto Illuminati, *Spinoza atlantico* (Milan: Mimesis, forthcoming). See

also Michael A. Rosenthal, "'The black, scabby Brazilian': Some Thoughts on Race and Early Modern Philosophy," *Philosophy and Social Criticism* 31, no. 2 (2005), 211–221; and Warren Montag, *Bodies, Masses, Power: Spinoza and His Contemporaries* (London: Verso, 1999), pp. 87–89 and 123. On Kant's racism, see Emmanuel Chukwadi Eze, "The Color of Reason: The Idea of 'Race' in Kant's Anthropology," in *Postcolonial African Philosophy* (Oxford: Blackwell, 1997), pp. 103–140.

60. On the powers of the imagination in Spinoza, see Antonio Negri, *The Savage Anomaly* (Minneapolis: University of Minnesota Press, 1991), esp. pp. 86–98. See also Daniela Bostrenghi, *Forme e virtù della immaginazaione in Spinoza* (Naples: Bibliopolis, 1996).

61. Frantz Fanon, *The Wretched of the Earth,* trans. Richard Philcox (New York: Grove, 2004), p. 155.

62. Ibid., p. 160. On Fanon's notion of a new humanity, see Lewis Gordon, *Fanon and the Crisis of European Man* (New York: Routledge, 1995).

63. See, for example, Elizabeth Povinelli, *The Cunning of Recognition: Indigenous Alterities and the Making of Australian Multiculturalism* (Durham: Duke University Press, 2002); and Manuhuia Barcham, "(De)Constructing the Politics of Indigeneity," in *Political Theory and the Rights of Indigenous Peoples,* ed. Duncan Ivison, Paul Patton, and Will Sanders (Cambridge: Cambridge University Press, 2000), pp. 137–151.

64. Guillermo Bonfil Batalla, "Utopía y revolución," in *Utopía y revolución: El pensamiento político contemporáneo de los indios en América Latina,* ed. Bonfil Batalla (Mexico City: Nueva Imagen, 1981), p. 24. See also Bonfil Batalla, *México profundo: Una civilización negada* (Mexico City: Grijalbo, 1987).

65. See Leslie Marmon Silko, *Ceremony* (New York: Penguin, 1977); *Almanac of the Dead* (New York: Penguin, 1991); and *Gardens in the Dunes* (New York: Simon and Schuster, 1999).

66. The argument in this paragraph is drawn from Shannon Speed and Alvaro Reyes, "Rights, Resistance, and Radical Alternatives: The Red de Defensores Comunitarios and Zapatismo in Chiapas," *Humboldt Journal of Social Relations* 29, no. 1 (2005), 47–82.

67. See René Zavaleta, *Las masas en noviembre* (La Paz: Juventud, 1983); and *Lo nacional popular en Bolivia* (Mexico City: Siglo XXI, 1986). On Zavaleta's notion of Bolivia as a *sociedad abigarrada,* see Walter Mignolo, "Subalterns and Other Agencies," *Postcolonial Studies* 8, no. 4 (November 2005), 381–407; Luis Atezana, *La diversidad social en Zavaleta Mercado* (La Paz: Centro Boliviano de Estudios Multidisciplinares, 1991), pp. 109–160; and Luis Tapia, *La producción del conocimiento local* (La Paz: Muela del Diablo Editores, 2002), pp. 305–325.

68. See Alvaro García Linera, *Re-proletarización nueva clase obrera y desarrollo del capital industrial en Bolivia (1952–1998)* (La Paz: Muela del Diablo Editores, 1999); and "La muerte de la condición obrera del siglo XX," in Alvaro García Linera, Raquel Gutiérrez, Raúl Prada, and Luis Tapia, *El retorno de la Bolivia plebaya* (La Paz: Muela del Diablo Editores, 2000), pp. 13–50.

69. Alvaro García Linera, introduction to *Sociología de los movimientos sociales en Bolivia,* ed. García Linera (La Paz: Diakonía/Oxfam, 2004), p. 17.

70. For Zavaleta's use of the term "multitude," see René Zavaleta, "Forma classe y forma multitud en el proletariado minero en Bolivia," in *Boliva, hoy,* ed. Zavaleta (Mexico City: Siglo XXI, 1983), pp. 219–240. For the use of the concept by contemporary scholars, see the work of the "Comuna" group, including Raquel Gutiérrez, Alvaro García Linera, Raúl Prada, Oscar Vega, and Luis Tapia. Representative texts include Raquel Gutiérrez, Alvaro García Linera, and Luis Tapia, "La forma multitud de la política de las necesidades vitales," in *El retorno de la Bolivia plebeya,* pp. 133–184; García Linera, "Sindicato, multitud y comunidad: Movimientos sociales y formas de autonomía política," in *Tiempos de rebelión* (La Paz: Muela del Diablo Editores, 2001), pp. 9–79; and Raúl Prada, "Politica de las multitudes," in *Memorias de Octubre* (La Paz: Muela del Diablo Editores, 2004), pp. 89–135. On the difference between Zavaleta's use of the term "multitude" and that of the group Comuna, see García Linera, "Sindicato, multitud y comunidad," p. 39, n. 30.

71. Two excellent sources on the basis of the 2003 rebellion in the existing structures of self-government in El Alto highlight different aspects: for an emphasis on the neighborhood councils, see Raúl Zibechi, *Dispersar el poder: Los movimiento como poderes antiestatales* (Buenos Aires: Tinta Limón, 2006), pp. 33–60; and for an emphasis on the Aymara community structures, see Pablo Mamani, *El rugir de las multitudes* (La Paz: Ediciones Yachaywasi, 2004), pp. 139–159. On rebellious forms of youth and student subjectivity in El Alto, including the role of hip-hop and other cultural forms, see Jiovanny Samanamud, Cleverth Cárdenas, and Patrisia Prieto, *Jóvenes y política en El Alto* (La Paz: PIEB, 2007). Finally, for a philosophical reflection on the role of the multitude in the 2003 uprising in El Alto, see Raúl Prada, *Largo octubre* (La Paz: Plural, 2004). We are grateful to Lia Haro for sharing with us her research in Bolivia.

72. See, for example, Ulrich Beck and Christoph Lau, "Second Modernity as a Research Agenda: Theoretical and Empirical Explorations in the 'Meta-Change' of Modern Society," *British Journal of Sociology* 56, no. 4 (December 2005), 525–557. On the question of hypermodernity and postmodernity, see also Antonio Negri, *Fabrique de porcelaine* (Paris: Stock, 2006).

73. Jean-Marie Vincent analyzes the overcoming of modernity in terms of the confluence of the capitalist "totalization" of civilization and a process of cultural "discouragement." See Jean-Marie Vincent, *Max Weber ou la démocratie inachevée* (Paris: Éditions du Félin, 1998), pp. 184–189. See also Massimo Cacciari, *Krisis: Saggio sulla crisi del pensiero negativo da Nietzsche a Wittgenstein* (Milan: Feltrinelli, 1976).

74. The weak versions of postmodernism, from Jean-François Lyotard and Richard Rorty to Jean Baudrillard and Gianni Vattimo, offer this kind of aestheticized reaction to the crisis, at times veering into theology.

75. See Jonathan Israel, *Radical Enlightenment* (Oxford: Oxford University Press, 2001).

76. Michel Foucault, "Le pouvoir psychiatrique," in *Dits et écrits,* 4 vols. (Paris: Gallimard, 1994), 2:686. See also Jacques Derrida's critique of Foucault, "Cogito and the History of Madness," in *Writing and Difference,* trans. Alan Bass (Chicago: University of Chicago Press, 1978), pp. 31–63; and Foucault, "Réponse à Derrida," in *Dits et écrits,* 2:281–295.

77. See Johannes Fabian, *Out of Our Minds: Reason and Madness in the Exploration of Central Africa* (Berkeley: University of California Press, 2000).

78. In addition to Henry, *Caliban's Reason,* which we cited earlier, see Walter Mignolo, "The Geopolitics of Knowledge and the Colonial Difference," *South Atlantic Quarterly* 101, no. 1 (Winter 2002), 57–96. For a good overview of the varieties of feminist epistemologies, see Linda Alcoff and Elizabeth Potter, eds., *Feminist Epistemologies* (New York: Routledge, 1993); and Sandra Harding, ed., *The Feminist Standpoint Theory Reader* (New York: Routledge, 2004).

79. See Donna Haraway, "A Cyborg Manifesto" and "Situated Knowledges: The Science Question in Feminism and the Privilege of Partial Perspective," in *Simians, Cyborgs, and Women: The Reinvention of Nature* (New York: Routledge, 1991), pp. 149–181 and 183–201.

80. See, for instance, Antonio Gramsci's illuminating discussion of "common sense" in "Critical Notes on an Attempt at Popular Sociology," in *Selection from the Prison Notebooks,* trans. Quintin Hoare and Geoffrey Nowell Smith (New York: International Publishers, 1971), pp. 419–472. On "common notions" in Spinoza, see Martial Guéroult, *Spinoza,* vol. 2, *L'âme* (Paris: Aubier-Montaigne, 1974), pp. 324–333.

81. Michel Foucault, *Society Must Be Defended,* trans. David Macey (New York: Picador, 2003), p. 9.

82. Ludwig Wittgenstein, *Philosophical Investigations,* trans. G. E. M. Anscombe (Oxford: Blackwell, 1953), no. 241, p. 75.

83. Ibid., no. 19, p. 7.

84. For a Wittgensteinian argument for the move from knowing to doing and

from epistemology to political action, see Linda Zerilli, *Feminism and the Abyss of Freedom* (Chicago: University of Chicago Press, 2005).

85. Philippe Descola, *Par-delà nature et culture* (Paris: Gallimard, 2005), pp. 129–131.

86. Claude Lévi-Strauss, ed., *L'identité: Seminaire interdisciplinaire* (Paris: PUF, 1983), p. 331.

87. Eduardo Viveiros de Castro, "Exchanging Perspectives: The Transformation of Subjects into Objects in Amerindian Ontologies," *Common Knowledge* 10, no. 3 (2004), 474–475.

88. Eduardo Viveiros de Castro, *From the Enemy's Point of View: Humanity and Divinity in an Amazonian Society,* trans. Catherine Howard (Chicago: University of Chicago Press, 1992) [originally *Araweté: Os deuses canibais* (1986)].

89. See Bruno Latour, *Politics of Nature,* trans. Catherine Porter (Cambridge, Mass.: Harvard University Press, 2004).

90. Baruch Spinoza, Letter 50 to Jarig Jelles, in *Complete Works,* pp. 891–892.

91. See Gianfranco Pala, ed., "L'inchiesta operaia di Marx" (1880), *Quaderni rossi,* no. 5 (April 1965), 24–30.

92. On the logic of teach-ins in the 1960s, see, for instance, Marshall Sahlins, "The Future of the National Teach-In: A History" (1965), in *Culture in Practice* (New York: Zone Books, 2000), pp. 209–218.

93. Michel Foucault, "Le jeu de Michel Foucault," in *Dits et écrits,* 3:299–300.

94. See Romano Alquati, *Sulla Fiat ed altri scritti* (Milan: Feltrinelli, 1975); and *Per fare conricerca* (Turin: Velleità alternative, 1993).

95. See, for example, Charles Hale, "Activist Research v. Cultural Critique," *Cultural Anthropology* 21, no. 1 (2006), 96–120.

96. See, for example, MTD Solano and Colectivo Situaciones, *La hipótesis 891* (Buenos Aires: De mano en mano, 2002); Collettivo edu-factory, ed., *L'università globale* (Rome: Manifestolibri, 2008); and Marta Malo, ed., *Nociones comunes: Experiencias y ensayos entre investigación y militancia* (Madrid: Traficantes de Sueños, 2004).

97. Robin Kelley, *Freedom Dreams* (Boston: Beacon Press, 2002), p. 8.

98. We substitute "confirmation" for "analogy" when we paraphrase Melandri here, without, we hope, departing too far from his meaning. See Enzo Melandri, *La linea e il circolo* (Macerata: Quidlibet, 2004), p. 810.

3. CAPITAL (AND THE STRUGGLES OVER COMMON WEALTH)

1. On the emerging hegemony of immaterial production, see Michael Hardt and Antonio Negri, *Multitude* (New York: Penguin, 2004), pp. 103–115.

2. André Gorz, *L'immatériel* (Paris: Galilée, 2003), p. 35.

3. Robert Boyer, *La croissance, début de siècle* (Paris: Albin Michel, 2002), p. 192.

4. Christian Marazzi, "Capitalismo digitale e modello antropogenetico di produzione," in *Reinventare il lavoro,* ed. Jean-Louis Laville (Rome: Sapere 2000, 2005), pp. 107–126.

5. On the feminization of work, see Guy Standing, "Global Feminization through Flexible Labor: A Theme Revisited," *World Development* 27, no. 3 (March 1999), 583–602; V. Spike Peterson, *A Critical Rewriting of Global Political Economy* (London: Routledge, 2003), pp. 62–65; Valentine Moghadam, *Globalizing Women* (Baltimore: Johns Hopkins University Press, 2005), pp. 51–58; and Nazneed Kanji and Kalyani Menon-Sen, "What Does the Feminisation of Labour Mean for Sustainable Livelihoods," International Institute for Environment and Development, August 2001.

6. Chandra Mohanty, "Women Workers and Capitalist Scripts," in *Feminist Genealogies, Colonial Legacies, Democratic Futures,* ed. M. Jacqui Alexander and Chandra Mohanty (New York: Routledge, 1997), p. 20. See also Peterson, *A Critical Rewriting of Global Political Economy,* pp. 65–68.

7. Michael Foucault, "Entretien" (with Duccio Tromadori), in *Dits et écrits,* 4 vols. (Paris: Gallimard, 1994), 4:74 [in English, *Remarks on Marx* (New York: Semiotext(e), 1991), pp. 121–122]. At this point in the interview Foucault is discussing his differences from the Frankfurt School.

8. See, for example, David Harvey's analyses of neoliberalism in *The New Imperialism* (Oxford: Oxford University Press, 2003); and *A Brief History of Neoliberalism* (Oxford: Oxford University Press, 2005). See also Aihwa Ong, *Neoliberalism as Exception* (Durham: Duke University Press, 2006).

9. Naomi Klein, *The Shock Doctrine* (New York: Metropolitan Books, 2007).

10. On the economies of extraction in southern and central Africa, see James Ferguson, *Global Shadows: Africa in the Neoliberal World Order* (Durham: Duke University Press, 2006), pp. 194–210.

11. On primitive accumulation, see Jason Read, *The Micro-Politics of Capital* (Albany: SUNY Press, 2003); and Sandro Mezzadra, "Attualità della preistoria," in *La condizione postcoloniale* (Verona: Ombre corte, 2008), pp. 127–154.

12. John Locke, *Second Treatise of Government* (Indianapolis: Hackett, 1980), p. 18.

13. Thomas Jefferson to Isaac McPherson, 13 August 1813, in *The Writings of Thomas Jefferson,* ed. Andrew A. Lipscomb and Albert Ellery Bergh, 20 vols. (Washington, D.C.: Thomas Jefferson Memorial Association, 1905), 13:333.

14. On the concept of alienation with regard to affective labor, see Kathi Weeks, "Life within and against Work: Affective Labor, Feminist Critique, and Post-Fordist Politics," *Ephemera* 7, no. 1 (2007), 233–249. See also

Christophe Dejours, ed., *Plaisir et souffrance dans le travail,* 2 vols. (Paris: Ao-cip, 1987–88); and Yves Clot, *La fonction psychologique du travail* (Paris: PUF, 1999).

15. On cooperation, see Karl Marx, *Capital,* vol. 1, trans. Ben Fowkes (New York: Vintage, 1976), pp. 439–454.

16. On externalities in economics, see Yann Moulier Boutang, *Le capitalisme cognitif* (Paris: Amsterdam, 2007); and Carlo Vercellone, ed., *Capitalismo cognitivo* (Rome: Manifestolibri, 2006).

17. See Carlo Vercellone, "Finance, rente, et travail dans le capitalisme cognitif," *Multitudes,* no. 32 (March 2008), 32–38.

18. John Maynard Keynes, *The General Theory of Employment, Interest and Money* (London: Macmillan, 1936), p. 376.

19. See again Klein, *The Shock Doctrine.*

20. On the forms of crisis conceived by traditional political economy, see Adelino Zanini, *Economic Philosophy* (Oxford: Peter Lang, 2008).

21. See Michel Crozier, Samuel Huntington, and Joji Watanuki, *The Crisis of Democracy* (New York: NYU Press, 1975), p. 61.

22. On precarity in Europe, see Anne Gray, *Unsocial Europe: Social Protection or Flexploitation?* (London: Pluto Press, 2004); Andrea Fumagalli, *Bioeconomia e capitalismo cognitivo* (Rome: Carocci, 2007); Evelyne Perrin, *Chômeurs et précaires, au cœur de la question sociale* (Paris: La dispute, 2004); Pascal Nicolas-Le-Strat, *L'expérience de l'intermittence* (Paris: L'Harmattan, 2005); and An-toniella Corsani and Maurizio Lazzarato, *Intermittents et précaires* (Paris: Amsterdam, 2008).

23. Danny Hoffman, "The City as Barracks: Freetown, Monrovia, and the Organization of Violence in Postcolonial African Cities," *Cultural Anthropology* 22, no. 3 (2007), 400–428.

24. Bernard Mandeville, *The Fable of the Bees,* cited in Marx, *Capital,* 1:764.

25. Richard Florida claims that the "creative class" thrives in a society characterized by tolerance, openness, and diversity; see *The Rise of the Creative Class* (New York: Basic Books, 2002).

26. Fredric Jameson provides an excellent analysis of the problem of ground rent in the context of architecture and finance capital in "The Brick and the Balloon: Architecture, Idealism, and Land Speculation," in *The Cultural Turn: Selected Writings on the Postmodern, 1983–1998* (London: Verso, 1998), pp. 162–190.

27. See, as just one example of a vast literature, Edward Glaeser, "Market and Policy Failure in Urban Economics," in *Chile: Political Economy of Urban Development,* ed. Glaeser and John R. Meyer (Cambridge, Mass.: Harvard School of Government, 2002), pp. 13–26.

28. See Antonio Negri and Carlo Vercellone, "Le rapport capital / travail dans le capitalisme cognitif," *Multitudes,* no. 32 (March 2008), 39–50.

29. On the common in urban spaces, see Henri Lefebvre, *Critique of Everyday Life,* 3 vols., trans. John Moore (London: Verso, 1991).

30. See Georg Simmel, "The Metropolis and Mental Life," in *The Sociology of Georg Simmel,* ed. Kurt Wolff (Glencoe, Ill.: Free Press, 1950), pp. 409–424.

31. For excellent analyses of money as equivalent, money as means of circulation, and money as capital, see Michel Aglietta, *Macroéconomie financière* (Paris: La découverte, 2002); and Aglietta and André Orléan, *La monnaie: Entre violence et confiance* (Paris: Odile Jacob, 2002).

32. See Christian Marazzi, *E il denaro va: Esodo e rivoluzione dei mercati finanziari* (Turin: Bollati Boringhieri, 1998); and *Capital and Language: From the New Economy to the War Economy,* trans. Gregory Conti (New York: Semiotext(e), 2008).

33. See Giovanni Arrighi, *The Long Twentieth Century* (London: Verso, 1994).

34. Georg Simmel, *The Philosophy of Money,* 3rd ed., ed. David Frisby, trans. Tom Bottomore and David Frisby (New York: Routledge, 2004), p. 129.

35. Judith Butler creatively reads Antigone's claim against Creon as a way to think the freedom to construct alternative kinship structures outside the rule of heteronormative family in *Antigone's Claim: Kinship between Life and Death* (New York: Columbia University Press, 2000). See also Valerie Lehr, *Queer Family Values* (Philadelphia: Temple University Press, 1999).

36. See Lee Edelman, *No Future: Queer Theory and the Death Drive* (Durham: Duke University Press, 2004).

37. On the struggles of working couples in the United States to balance work and family, see Arlie Russell Hochschild, *The Time Bind: When Work Becomes Home and Home Becomes Work,* 2nd ed. (New York: Holt, 2001); and Kathi Weeks, "Hours for What We Will: Work, Family, and the Movement for Shorter Hours," *Feminist Studies* 35, no. 1 (Spring 2009).

38. Pheng Cheah offers one of the most sustained arguments in favor of the nation as a center of thought and politics and as the locus of freedom, especially in the subordinated parts of the world. See *Spectral Nationality: Passages of Freedom from Kant to Postcolonial Literatures of Liberation* (New York: Columbia University Press, 2003); and *Inhuman Conditions: On Cosmopolitanism and Human Rights* (Cambridge, Mass.: Harvard University Press, 2007).

39. See Hardt and Negri, *Multitude.*

40. Pierre Macherey, "Présentation," Citéphilo, Palais des Beaux-Arts, Lille, 19 November 2004.

41. Ernesto Laclau, *On Populist Reason* (London: Verso, 2005), p. 153.

42. See Paolo Virno, "Il cosidetto 'male' e la critica dello Stato," *Forme di vita,* no. 4 (2005), 9–36.

43. See Étienne Balibar, "Spinoza, the Anti-Orwell: The Fear of the Masses," in *Masses, Classes, Ideas,* trans. James Swenson (New York: Routledge, 1993), pp. 3–38; and "Potentia multitudinis, quae una veluti mente dicitur," in *Ethik, Recht und Politik,* ed. Marcel Senn and Manfred Walther (Zurich: Schulthess, 2001), pp. 105–137.

44. See Slavoj Žižek, *The Parallax View* (Cambridge, Mass.: MIT Press, 2006), pp. 261–267.

45. Alain Badiou, "Beyond Formalization: An Interview," trans. Bruno Bosteels and Alberto Toscano, *Angelaki* 8, no. 2 (August 2003), 125.

46. See Judith Butler, *Gender Trouble: Feminism and the Subversion of Identity* (New York: Routledge, 1990); and *Bodies That Matter: On the Discursive Limits of "Sex"* (New York: Routledge, 1993).

47. Anne Fausto-Sterling, *Sexing the Body: Gender Politics and the Construction of Sexuality* (New York: Basic Books, 2000), p. 4. On the question of bone development and sex, see Fausto-Sterling, "The Bare Bones of Sex: Part 1—Sex and Gender," *Signs* 30, no. 2 (2005), 1491–1527. More generally on gender and corporeality in science studies, see Elizabeth Wilson, *Psychosomatic: Feminism and the Neurological Body* (Durham: Duke University Press, 2004).

48. On the ontologically constituent character of the modes in Spinoza, see Gilles Deleuze, *Expressionism in Philosophy: Spinoza,* trans. Martin Joughin (New York: Zone Books, 1990); Antonio Negri, *The Savage Anomaly: The Power of Spinoza's Metaphysics and Politics* (Minneapolis: University of Minnesota Press, 1991); and, more recently, Laurent Bove, *La stratégie du conatus* (Paris: Vrin, 2001).

49. Many feminist theorists come to analogous conclusions negotiating poststructuralism and identity demands. See, for example, Rey Chow, "The Interruption of Referentiality: or, Poststructuralism's Outside," in *The Age of the World Target* (Durham: Duke University Press, 2006), pp. 45–70.

50. Hannah Arendt, *The Human Condition* (Chicago: University of Chicago Press, 1958), p. 233.

51. V. I. Lenin, *State and Revolution* (New York: International Publishers, 1971), p. 43.

52. Macherey, "Présentation."

53. Karl Marx, *Grundrisse,* trans. Martin Nicolaus (London: Penguin, 1973), p. 712.

54. Daniel Bensaïd seems particularly uncomfortable with our use of the con-

cept of love. See *Un monde à changer* (Paris: Textuel, 2003), pp. 69–89; and "Antonio Negri et le pouvoir constituent," in *Résistances* (Paris: Fayard, 2001), pp. 193–212.

55. See Franz Rosenzweig, *The Star of Redemption,* trans. Barbara Galli (Madison: University of Wisconsin Press, 2005), p. 234.

56. Friedrich Nietzsche, *Thus Spoke Zarathustra,* trans. Adrian Del Caro (Cambridge: Cambridge University Press, 2006), pp. 44–45.

57. Arendt, *The Human Condition,* in particular pp. 50–57.

58. Adam Smith, *The Wealth of Nations,* ed. Edwin Cannan (New York: Modern Library, 1994), p. 15.

59. On pollination as an example of a positive externality, see Boutang, *Le capitalisme cognitif.*

60. Félix Guattari, *The Anti-Oedipus Papers,* ed. Stéphane Nadaud, trans. Kélina Gotman (New York: Semiotext(e), 2006), p. 179.

61. Gilles Deleuze and Félix Guattari, *A Thousand Plateaus,* trans. Brian Massumi (Minneapolis: University of Minnesota Press, 1987), pp. 10.

INTERMEZZO

1. See Helmuth Plessner, *Macht und menschliche Natur* (Frankfurt: Suhrkamp, 1981). On Plessner's notion of intraspecies aggressiveness, see Paolo Virno, "Il cosidetto 'male' e la critica dello Stato," *Forme di vita,* no. 4 (2005), 9–36.

2. Baruch Spinoza, *Theologico-Political Treatise,* in *Complete Works,* trans. Samuel Shirley (Indianapolis: Hackett, 2002), pp. 389–390.

3. See Immanuel Kant, *Religion within the Boundaries of Mere Reason and Other Writings,* ed. and trans. Allen Wood and George Di Giovanni (Cambridge: Cambridge University Press, 1998). On the ambiguities and contradictions of Kant's theory of evil, see Victor Delbos, *La philosophie pratique de Kant* (Paris: Félix Alcan, 1905), p. 621. More generally, see Richard Bernstein, *Radical Evil* (Cambridge: Polity, 2002). On the figures of juridical formalism, which give law a regulative function based on formal, a priori elements, see Antonio Negri, *Alle origini del formalismo giuridico* (Padua: Cedam, 1962).

4. See Baruch Spinoza, *Ethics,* pt. 3, Proposition 9, Scholium, in *Collected Works,* p. 284; and Michel Foucault and Noam Chomsky, "Human Nature: Justice vs. Power," in *The Chomsky-Foucault Debate* (New York: New Press, 2006), p. 51.

5. Baruch Spinoza, *Political Treatise,* chap. 6, in *Complete Works,* pp. 700–701.

6. Karl Marx and Frederick Engels, *The Holy Family,* in *Collected Works,* vol. 4 (New York: International Publishers, 1975), p. 128.

7. For his discussions of pain, see Ludwig Wittgenstein, *Philosophical Investigations,* trans. G. E. M. Anscombe (Oxford: Blackwell, 1984).

8. See Antonio Negri, *Lenta ginestra* (Milan: Sugarco, 1987).

9. Carl Schmitt, *The Nomos of the Earth,* trans. G. L. Ulmen (New York: Telos, 2003), pp. 59–60. Giorgio Agamben displays the erudition and brilliance typical of his work in his reading of this Pauline passage in *The Time That Remains,* trans. Patricia Dailey (Stanford: Stanford University Press, 2005), pp. 108–112. Paolo Virno proposes the *katechon* as key to the institution of the multitude in *Multitude: Between Innovation and Negation* (New York: Semiotext(e), 2008), pp. 56–67.

4. EMPIRE RETURNS

1. See, for example, Philip Gordon, "The End of the Bush Revolution," *Foreign Affairs* 85, no. 4 (July–August 2006), 75–86.

2. Richard Haass, "The Age of Nonpolarity: What Will Follow U.S. Dominance," *Foreign Affairs* 87. no. 3 (May–June 2008), 44–56. See also Haass's analysis of the end of U.S. dominance in the Middle East, "The New Middle East," *Foreign Affairs* 85, no. 6 (November–December 2006), 2–11. For a similar view, see Fareed Zakaria, *The Post-American World* (New York: Norton, 2008).

3. See Michael Hardt and Antonio Negri, *Empire* (Cambridge, Mass.: Harvard University Press, 2000).

4. Giovanni Arrighi situates the failure of the coup and its imperialist project in an even longer historical frame: "The new imperialism of the Project for a New American Century probably marks the inglorious end of the sixty-year long struggle of the United States to become the organizing center of a world state. The struggle changed the world but even in its most triumphant moments, the U.S. never succeeded in its endeavor." Giovanni Arrighi, *Adam Smith in Beijing* (London: Verso, 2007), p. 261.

5. For arguments for the use of "soft power," see primarily Joseph Nye, *Soft Power* (New York: Public Affairs, 2004); and *The Paradox of American Power* (Oxford: Oxford University Press, 2002).

6. David Frum and Richard Perle, *An End to Evil: How to Win the War on Terror* (New York: Random House, 2003), p. 7.

7. Niall Ferguson is the most prominent pro-imperialist critic of the United States, chastising it for not doing what it takes to be a proper imperialist power. See *Colossus* (New York: Penguin, 2004).

8. For an example of a neoconservative who attempts to break with the ideology, see Francis Fukuyama, *After the Neocons* (London: Profile, 2006). For

examples of those who maintain the faith, see the essays by Richard Perle, Norman Podhoretz, Max Boot, and others organized in the symposium "Defending and Advancing Freedom," *Commentary* 120, no. 4 (November 2005).

9. For two of the more intelligent examples of this line of scholarship, see Ellen Wood, *Empire of Capital* (London: Verso, 2003); and Tariq Ali, *Bush in Babylon: The Recolonisation of Iraq* (London: Verso, 2003).

10. For our analysis of the "revolution in military affairs" and its application in Iraq, see Michael Hardt and Antonio Negri, *Multitude* (New York: Penguin, 2004), pp. 41–62.

11. See Jennifer Taw and Bruce Hoffmann, *The Urbanization of Insurgency* (Santa Monica, Calif.: Rand Corporation, 1994); and Stephen Graham, "Robo-War Dreams: Global South Urbanization and the United States Military's 'Revolution in Military Affairs,'" LSE Crisis States Working Papers, 2007.

12. Stephen Graham, "Imagining Urban Warfare," in *War, Citizenship, Territory,* ed. Deborah Cohen and Emily Gilbert (New York: Routledge, 2007), pp. 33–56.

13. See Eyal Weizman, *Hollow Land: Israel's Architecture of Occupation* (London: Verso, 2007).

14. Noam Chomsky is a tireless chronicler of U.S. interventions that have undermined democratic governments throughout the world. See, among his other books, *Hegemony or Survival: America's Quest for Global Dominance* (New York: Owl Books, 2004). Specifically with regard to Latin America, see Greg Grandin, *Empire's Workshop: Latin America, the United States, and the Rise of the New Imperialism* (New York: Metropolitan Books, 2006).

15. Emmanuel Todd is a good example of a European who previously believed in the benefits of U.S. global hegemony and became disillusioned. See *After the Empire: The Breakdown of the American Order,* trans. C. Jon Delogu (New York: Columbia University Press, 2003).

16. Thomas Friedman, "Restoring Our Honor," *New York Times,* 6 May 2004.

17. For a nuanced analysis of how "blood for oil" is an insufficient frame for understanding the 2003 invasion of Iraq, see Retort, *Afflicted Powers: Capital and Spectacle in a New Age of War* (London: Verso, 2005), pp. 38–77.

18. On the clean slate model of neoliberal transformation, see Naomi Klein, *The Shock Doctrine: The Rise of Disaster Capitalism* (New York: Metropolitan Books, 2007). On the economic project of the U.S. occupation of Iraq, see Klein, "Baghdad Year Zero," *Harpers* (September 2004), 43–53, and *The Shock Doctrine,* pp. 389–460.

19. Arrighi, *Adam Smith in Beijing,* p. 384. See also pp. 198–202.

20. We share some aspects of the analysis of Paul Krugman, *Conscience of a Liberal* (New York: Norton, 2007).

21. Arrighi, *Adam Smith in Beijing,* p. 8. See also Giovanni Arrighi, *The Long Twentieth Century* (London: Verso, 1994).

22. Henry Kissinger, Speech at the International Bertelsmann Forum, 23 September 2006, cited in Daniel Vernet, "Le monde selon Kissinger," *Le monde,* 25 October 2006.

23. Francis Fukuyama, *State-Building* (Ithaca: Cornell University Press, 2004).

24. Saskia Sassen, *Territory, Authority, Rights* (Princeton: Princeton University Press, 2006).

25. For useful introductions to the term "global governance," see Gianfranco Borrelli, ed., *Governance* (Naples: Dante & Descartes, 2004); and David Held and Anthony McGrew, eds., *Governing Globalization* (Oxford: Polity, 2002).

26. See, for example, Robert Cobbaut and Jacques Lenoble, eds., *Corporate Governance: An Institutionalist Approach* (The Hague: Kluwer Law International, 2003).

27. On Foucault's notion of governmentality, see Graham Burchell, Colin Gordon, and Peter Miller, eds., *The Foucault Effect: Studies in Governmentality* (Chicago: University of Chicago Press, 1991). For Luhmann and the autopoiesis school, see Niklas Luhmann, *Legitimation durch Verfahren* (Frankfurt: Suhrkamp, 1969); Gunther Teubner, *Law as an Autopoietic System* (Oxford: Blackwell, 1993); and Alessandro Febbraio and Gunther Teubner, eds., *State, Law, and Economy as Autopoietic Systems* (Milan: Giuffrè, 1992).

28. Sabino Cassese, *Lo spazio giuridico globale* (Bari: Laterza, 2003); and *Oltre lo Stato* (Bari: Laterza, 2006).

29. See, for example, Robert Keohane and Joseph Nye, "Between Centralization and Fragmentation: The Club Model of Multilateral Cooperation and Problems of Democratic Legitimacy," Kennedy School of Government Working Paper no. 01–004, February 2001; and Robert Keohane, *Power and Governance in a Partially Globalized World* (New York: Routledge, 2002).

30. See, for example, Bob Jessop, "The Regulation Approach and Governance Theory," *Economy and Society* 24, no. 3 (1995), 307–333; and Mary Kaldor, *Global Civil Society* (Oxford: Polity, 2003).

31. Hans Maier, *Die ältere deutsche Staats—und Verwaltungslehre,* 2nd ed. (Munich: C. H. Becksche, 1980), p. 223. Maier refers to Friedrich Meinecke, *Weltbürgertum und Nationalstaat* (Munich: R. Oldenbourg, 1911).

32. See Sandro Chignola, ed., *Governare la vita* (Verona: Ombre corte, 2006).

See also Ulrich Beck, *Politik der Globalisierung* (Frankfurt: Suhrkamp, 2003); and Ulrich Beck and Edgard Grande, "Empire Europa," *Zeitschrift für Politik* 52, no. 4 (2004), 397–420.

33. See, for instance, with respect to East Asia, Aihwa Ong, *Neoliberalism as Exception* (Durham: Duke University Press, 2006); and, with respect to Africa, James Ferguson, *Global Shadows: Africa in the Neoliberal World Order* (Durham: Duke University Press, 2006). James Mittelman develops the notion of global divisions of labor and power in *The Globalization Syndrome* (Princeton: Princeton University Press, 2000).

34. Cecil Rhodes, quoted in V. I. Lenin, *Imperialism* (New York: International Publishers, 1939), p. 79.

35. On real and formal subsumption, see Karl Marx, *Capital,* vol. 1, trans. Ben Fowkes (New York: Vintage, 1976), pp. 1019–38. On Rosa Luxemburg's analysis of imperialism as capital's internalization of its outside, see *The Accumulation of Capital,* trans. Agnes Schwarzchild (New York: Monthly Review Press, 1968). For our previous analyses of formal and real subsumption in the context of globalization, see *Empire,* esp. pp. 254–256.

36. See David Harvey, *The New Imperialism* (Oxford: Oxford University Press, 2003); and *A Brief History of Neoliberalism* (Oxford: Oxford University Press, 2005).

37. Klein, *The Shock Doctrine.*

38. Ferguson, *Global Shadows,* p. 196. See also Patrick Bond, *Looting Africa* (London: Zed Books, 2006).

39. Rebecca Karl, "The Asiatic Mode of Production: National and Imperial Formations," *Historein* 5 (2005), 58–75.

40. William Robinson, *A Theory of Global Capitalism* (Baltimore: Johns Hopkins University Press, 2004), p. 129.

41. The axiom of freedom that we express here in Foucaultian terms is a continuation of the methodological principles of the "workers' standpoint" studies conducted in the 1960s and 1970s by authors such as E. P. Thompson, Mario Tronti, and Karl-Heinz Roth.

42. We make this argument about the collapse of the Soviet Union in *Empire,* pp. 276–279.

43. This theme runs throughout our *Multitude.*

44. On Spinoza's notion of indignation, see Laurent Bove, *La stratégie du conatus* (Paris: Vrin, 1997); and Filippo Del Lucchese, *Tumulti e indignation: Conflitto, diritto e moltitudine in Machiavelli e Spinoza* (Milan: Ghibli, 2004).

45. For a theory of social struggles that respond to the experience of injustice, see Emmanuel Renault, *L'expérience de l'injustice* (Paris: La découverte, 2004). Renault's investigation relies on Axel Honneth's hypothesis that

brings the analyses of communicative "transcendentals" back to social contradictions and the exploitation of labor. See Honneth, *Kritik der Macht* (Frankfurt: Suhrkamp, 1988); and *The Struggle for Recognition* (Cambridge: Polity, 1995).

46. For an analysis of the continuously emerging conflicts within the capitalist system, see Guido Rossi, *Il conflitto epidemico* (Milan: Adelphi, 2003).

47. See Alain Bertho, *Nous autres, nous mêmes* (Paris : Du Croquant, 2008).

48. Carl Schmitt, *Theorie des Partisanen* (Berlin: Duncker & Humblot, 1963).

49. For Georges Sorel, see primarily his interpretation of Walter Benjamin in *Reflections on Violence,* ed. Jerome Jennings (Cambridge: Cambridge University Press, 1999). For Lenin, see primarily *What Is to Be Done?* and *State and Revolution,* as well as Antonio Negri, *Thirty-three Lessons on Lenin* (New York: Columbia University Press, forthcoming).

50. See C. B. Macpherson, *The Political Theory of Possessive Individualism* (Oxford: Clarendon Press, 1962); and Karl Marx, *A Contribution to the Critique of Hegel's Philosophy of Right* and *Economic and Philosophical Manuscripts,* in *Early Writings,* trans. Rodney Livingstone and Gregor Benton (London: Penguin, 1975).

51. The philosophical antecedents of neoconservative thought are found not generally in the European reactionary tradition but rather in natural right theories, particularly those of Leo Strauss and Michael Oakeshott, which bring together individualism and a transcendental, Hobbesian definition of power.

52. Baruch Spinoza, *Ethics,* in *Complete Works,* trans. Samuel Shirley (Indianapolis: Hackett, 2002), pt. 3, Definitions of the Affects, no. 20, p. 314.

53. Michel Foucault, "Inutile de se soulever?" *Le monde,* 11–12 May 1979, reprinted in *Dits et écrits,* vol. 3 (Paris: Gallimard, 1994), p. 793.

54. Ernst Bloch, *The Principle of Hope,* 3 vols., trans. Neville Plaice, Stephen Plaice, and Paul Knight (Cambridge, Mass.: MIT Press, 1986).

55. See Sandro Mezzadra, *Diritto di fuga* (Verona: Ombre corte, 2006); and Enrica Riga, *Europa di confine* (Rome: Meltelmi, 2007).

56. For an argument against evolutionary assumptions with respect to the transformations of labor power, see André Gorz, *L'immatériel* (Paris: Galileé, 2003).

57. See Robert Castel, *L'insécurité sociale* (Paris: Seuil, 2003). On precarious labor in France, see Antonella Corsani and Maurizio Lazzarato, *Intermittents et précaires* (Paris: Amsterdam, 2008). On the social conditions of French *banlieux,* see Stéphane Beaud and Michel Pialoux, *Violence urbaines, violence sociale* (Paris Fayard, 2003); and Loïc Wacquant, *Parias urbains* (Paris: La découverte, 2006).

58. See Judith Revel, *Qui a peur de la banlieue?* (Paris: Bayard, 2008).

59. Karl Marx, *Economic and Philosophical Manuscripts,* in *Early Writings,* p. 328. For Deleuze and Guattari's interpretation of this passage, see *Anti-Oedipus,* trans. Robert Hurley, Mark Seem, and Helen Lane (Minneapolis: University of Minnesota Press, 1983), pp. 4–5.

60. Saskia Sassen traces a similar genealogy of urban forms and paradigms of production to define the contemporary "global city," which is centered on the activities of finance. As is often the case, our thinking here is very close to that of Sassen, but our focus on biopolitical production rather than finance gives a significantly different view of the life and potential of the contemporary metropolis.

61. Charles Baudelaire, "La foule," in *Œuvres complètes,* ed. Marcel Ruff (Paris: Seuil, 1968), p. 155.

62. For our argument about the twilight of the peasant world as defined by a lack of the political capacities of communication and cooperation, see *Multitude,* pp. 115–127. For Marx's views on the political capacities of peasants in nineteenth-century France, see *The Eighteenth Brumaire of Louis Bonaparte* (New York: International Publishers, 1998), pp. 123–129.

63. On megalopolis, see Kenneth Frampton, "Towards a Critical Regionalism," in *The Anti-Aesthetic,* ed. Hal Foster (Port Townsend, Wash.: Bay Press, 1983), pp. 26–30.

64. See Mike Davis, *Planet of Slums* (London: Verso, 2006).

65. See, for example, Achille Mbembe and Sarah Nuttall, eds., *Johannesburg: The Elusive Metropolis* (Durham: Duke University Press, 2008); Filip de Boeck and Marie-Françoise Plissart, *Kinshasa: Invisible City* (Ghent: Ludion, 2004); AbdouMaliq Simone, *For the City Yet to Come* (Durham: Duke University Press, 2004); and Rem Koolhaas, ed., *Lagos: How It Works* (Baden: Lars Müller, forthcoming).

66. For a philosophical elaboration of the encounter, see Gilles Deleuze's interpretation of Spinoza's theory of the affects in relation to joyful and sad passions in *Expressionism in Philosophy: Spinoza,* trans. Martin Joughin (New York: Zone Books, 1990). For a political elaboration of different forms of encounter, see El Kilombo and Michael Hardt, "Organizing Encounters and Generating Events," *Whirlwinds: Journal of Aesthetics and Protest* (2008), www.joaap.org.

67. In his investigation of Mumbai, Arjun Appadurai presents a similar notion of the politics of the metropolis as the organization of encounters from below, which he identifies as "deep democracy." See "Deep Democracy: Urban Governmentality and the Horizon of Politics," *Public Culture* 14, no. 1 (2002), 21–47.

68. Grace and James Boggs, "The City Is the Black Man's Land," *Monthly Review* 17, no. 11 (April 1966), 35–46.

69. Teresa Caldeira, *City of Walls: Crime, Segregation, and Citizenship in São Paulo* (Berkeley: University of California Press, 2000).

70. On urban rent and finance, see Carlo Vercellone, "Finance, rente et travail dans le capitalisme cognitive," *Multitudes,* no. 32 (March 2008), 27–38, as well as the other essays in this issue. See also Agostino Petrillo, "La rendita fondiaria urbana e la metropolis," Presentation at Uninomade, Bologna, 8 December 2007. On gentrification, see Neil Smith, *The New Urban Frontier: Gentrification and the Revanchist City* (New York: Routledge, 1996); and for an international perspective, Rowland Atkinson and Gary Bridge, eds., *Gentrification in a Global Context: The New Urban Colonialism* (New York: Routledge, 2005).

71. On the French revolt in October and November 2005, see Revel, *Qui ha peur de la banlieue?;* Bertho, *Nous autres, nous meme;* and Guido Caldiron, *Banlieue* (Rome: Manifestolibri, 2005).

5. BEYOND CAPITAL?

1. Two excellent narratives that recount this link between neoliberalism and U.S. unilateralism, from Pinochet to Reagan and beyond, are David Harvey, *A Brief History of Neoliberalism* (Oxford: Oxford University Press, 2005); and Naomi Klein, *The Shock Doctrine* (New York: Metropolitan Books, 2007).

2. See Michael Hardt and Antonio Negri, *Empire* (Cambridge, Mass.: Harvard University Press, 2000), pp. 260–303.

3. Harvey, *A Brief History of Neoliberalism,* p. 159.

4. See David Landes, *The Wealth and Poverty of Nations* (New York: Norton, 1999); and Michael Polanyi, *The Tacit Dimension* (London: Routledge, 1967).

5. Carlo Vercellone, "Sens et enjeux de la transition vers le capitalisme cognitif," paper presented at the conference "Transformations du travail et crise de l'économie politique" at the University of Paris 1, Panthéon-Sorbonne, 12 October 2004. See also Robert Boyer, *The Future of Economic Growth* (Cheltenham: E. Elgar, 2004).

6. See, for example, Kenneth Arrow, "The Economic Implications of Learning by Doing," *Review of Economic Studies* 29, no. 3 (June 1962), 155–173.

7. For an analysis of dependency theories from the perspective of globalization, see Giuseppe Cocco and Antonio Negri, *GlobAL* (Buenos Aires: Paidos, 2006).

8. Alexei Yurchak, *Everything Was Forever, Until It Was No More: The Last Soviet*

Generation (Durham: Duke University Press, 2006). For our earlier account of the collapse of the Soviet Union, which develops this point further, see Hardt and Negri, *Empire,* pp. 276–279.

9. For a good overview of the various uses of the concept, see David Halpern, *Social Capital* (Cambridge: Polity, 2005).

10. Nick Dyer-Witherford coins the term "commonism" to name the society based on the common and common wealth. See "Commonism," *Turbulence* 1 (June 2007), 81–87; and *Cyber-Marx* (Urbana: University of Illinois Press, 1999).

11. Michael Hardt and Antonio Negri, *Multitude* (New York: Penguin, 2004), pp. 169–171. The *Indiana Journal of Global Legal Studies* is an excellent resource on these issues.

12. Hardt and Negri, *Empire,* pp. 304–324.

13. Joseph Nye, "U.S. Power and Strategy after Iraq," *Foreign Affairs* 82, no. 4 (July–August 2003), pp. 60–73.

14. See, for example, William Robinson, *A Theory of Global Capitalism* (Baltimore: Johns Hopkins University Press, 2004), pp. 33–84.

15. Baruch Spinoza, *Political Treatise,* in *Complete Works,* trans. Samuel Shirley (Indianapolis: Hackett, 2002), chap. 8, para. 4, p. 725 (translation modified).

16. On the internalization of economic externalities in the context of "cognitive" production, see Carlo Vercellone, ed., *Sommes-nous sortis du capitalisme industriel?* (Paris: La Dispute, 2003); and, with some reservations regarding this view, Yann Moulier Boutang, *Le capitalisme cognitif* (Paris: Éditions Amsterdam, 2007).

17. On Marshall's notion of external economies, see Renee Prendergast, "Marshallian External Economies," *Economic Journal* 103, no. 417 (March 1993), 454–458; and Marco Bellandi, "Some Remarks on Marshallian External Economies and Industrial Tendencies," in *The Economics of Alfred Marshall,* ed. Richard Arena and Michel Quéré (New York: Palgrave Macmillan, 2003), pp. 240–253.

18. J. E. Meade, "External Economies and Diseconomies in a Competitive Situation," *Economic Journal* 62, no. 245 (March 1952), 54–67.

19. See Andreas Papandreou, *Externality and Institutions* (Oxford: Clarendon Press, 1994), pp. 53–57. We follow Papandreou's excellent history of the concept of externality throughout this paragraph.

20. Yochai Benkler, "The Political Economy of the Commons," *Upgrade* 4, no. 3 (June 2003), 7.

21. See, for example, Lawrence Lessig, *Free Culture* (New York: Penguin, 2004); and Kembrew McLeod, *Freedom of Expression: Resistance and Repression in*

the Age of Intellectual Property (Minneapolis: University of Minnesota Press, 2007).

22. For an example of interpreting workers' struggles as the motor of economic cycles and crises, see Antonio Negri, "Marx on Cycle and Crisis," in *Revolution Retrieved,* trans. Ed Emery and John Merrington (London: Red Notes, 1988), pp. 43–90.

23. For analyses that highlight in very different ways the autonomy and creativity of biopolitical labor, see McKenzie Wark, *A Hacker Manifesto* (Cambridge, Mass.: Harvard University Press, 2004); and Richard Florida, *The Rise of the Creative Class* (New York: Basic Books, 2002).

24. For Marx's definition of the rate of surplus value, which we rewrite here, see Karl Marx, *Capital,* vol. 1, trans. Ben Fowkes (New York:Vintage, 1976), p. 326.

25. Thomas Jefferson uses this phrase—"we have the wolf by the ears"—to capture why in his view the United States could neither continue the system of black slavery nor abolish it. See Jefferson to John Holmes, 22 April 1820, in *Writings,* ed. Merrill Peterson (New York: Library of America, 1984), pp. 1433–35.

26. See Christian Marazzi, *Capital and Language,* trans. Gregory Conti (Cambridge, Mass.: MIT Press, 2008).

27. This ideological episode of the Cultural Revolution has inspired, among others, Debord and Badiou. See Guy Debord, *The Society of the Spectacle,* trans. Donald Nicholson-Smith (New York: Zone Books, 1994), p. 35; and Alain Badiou, *The Century,* trans. Alberto Toscano (Cambridge: Polity, 2007), pp. 58–67.

28. Mario Tronti, *Operai e capitale,* 2nd ed. (Turin: Einaudi, 1971), p. 89.

29. We call this situation, following Marx, the real subsumption of society within capital. On Marx's notion of the real subsumption, see *Capital,* 1:1019–38.

30. For an analysis that anticipates this situation in the 1970s, see Antonio Negri, "Marx on Cycle and Crisis," in *Revolution Retrieved,* trans. Ed Emery and John Merrington (London: Red Notes, 1988), pp. 43–90.

31. On industrial time discipline and its progressive generalization throughout society, see E. P. Thompson, "Time, Work-Discipline, and Industrial Capitalism," *Past & Present,* no. 38 (1967), 56–97. On the debates among German sociologists about the *Entgrenzung der Arbeit,* see Karin Gottschall and Harald Wolf, "Introduction: Work Unbound," *Critical Sociology* 33 (2007), 11–18. We are grateful to Stephan Manning for drawing our attention to this literature.

32. For an interpretation of the "Chapter on Money" in Marx's *Grundrisse,* see Antonio Negri, *Marx beyond Marx,* trans. Harry Cleaver, Michael Ryan, and Maurizio Viano (New York: Autonomedia, 1991), pp. 21–40.

33. On the failing rate of profit and economic crisis, see Robert Brenner, *The Boom and the Bubble: The U.S. in the World Economy* (London: Verso, 2002).

34. On the characteristics of the entrepreneur, see Joseph Schumpeter, *The Theory of Economic Development* (1911), trans. Redvers Opie (Cambridge, Mass.: Harvard University Press, 1934), pp. 128–156. On the obsolescence of the entrepreneur, see Schumpeter, *Capitalism, Socialism, and Democracy* (New York: Harper & Brothers, 1942), pp. 131–134.

35. Karl Marx and Friedrich Engels, *The Communist Manifesto* (Oxford: Oxford University Press, 1992), p. 8.

36. See, for example, Henryk Grossmann, *The Law of Accumulation and Breakdown of Capitalist Systems: Being Also a Theory of Crises* (1929), trans. Jairus Banaji (London: Pluto Press, 1992).

37. Some contemporary heterodox economists sketch the outlines of a postcapitalist future. See, for example, J. K. Gibson-Graham, *A Postcapitalist Politics* (Minneapolis: University of Minnesota Press, 2006); and Michael Albert, *Parecon: Life after Capitalism* (London: Verso, 2003).

38. Ernesto Laclau, *On Populist Reason* (London: Verso, 2005), p. 95.

39. For our most extended discussion of the conflict between political representation and democracy, see Hardt and Negri, *Multitude,* pp. 241–247.

40. See Achille Mbembe, "Necropolitics," *Public Culture* 15, no. 1 (2003), 11–40. On the disastrous physical conditions of metropolises in subordinated parts of the world, see Mike Davis, *Planet of Slums* (London: Verso, 2006).

41. Christopher Newfield emphasizes the need in the biopolitical economy for a public with higher education in the humanities and social sciences. See *Unmaking the Public University* (Cambridge, Mass.: Harvard University Press, 2008).

42. On the need for a common intellectual, cultural, and communication infrastructure, see Yochai Benkler, *The Wealth of Networks* (New Haven: Yale University Press, 2006).

43. Many economists have detailed how such a guaranteed income is feasible in the dominant countries—serious proposals have been advanced in Europe and the United States—but obviously in the subordinated parts of the world, where the percentage of the population whose capacities are thwarted by poverty is much higher, such a system would be even more important. The Brazilian government's experiment with the "family stipend" *(bolsa família),* which distributes money to poor families in a way

that approximates a guaranteed income, is an important example because it demonstrates the feasibility of such a program even outside the wealthiest countries.

44. On Jefferson's proposal of a "ward system" as a training in self-rule for the multitude, see Michael Hardt, *Thomas Jefferson: The Declaration of Independence* (London: Verso, 2007). On contemporary experiments in participatory democracy, see America Vera-Zavala, *Deltagande demokrati* (Stockholm: Agora, 2003).

45. Charles Dickens, *Hard Times* (Ware, Hertfordshire: Wordsworth Classics, 1995), p. 4.

46. On goodwill and intangible assets, see Michel Aglietta, "Le capitalisme de demain" (Paris: Fondation Saint-Simon, 1998); and Baruch Lev, *Intangibles: Management, Measurement, and Reporting* (Washington, D.C.: Brookings Institute, 2001).

47. Paul Sweezy, *The Theory of Capitalist Development* (New York: Oxford University Press, 1942), p. 53.

48. On the theory of value, see Isaak Rubin, *Essays on Marx's Theory of Value,* trans. Miloš Samardžija and Fredy Perlman (Detroit: Black and Red, 1972); Ronald Meek, *Studies in the Labour Theory of Value* (London: Lawrence and Wishart, 1956); and Claudio Napoleoni, *Smith, Ricardo, Marx,* trans. J. M. A. Gee (Oxford: Blackwell, 1975). On the reduction of the law of value to the law of surplus value, see Mario Tronti, *Operai e capitale* (Turin: Einaudi, 1966); and Negri, *Marx beyond Marx.* On the theory of crisis, see Negri, "Marx on Cycle and Crisis."

49. See André Orléan, *Le pouvoir de la finance* (Paris: Odile Jacob, 1999).

50. Spinoza, *Political Treatise,* chap. 2, para. 13, p. 686 (translation modified).

51. See Maurice Nussenbaum, "Juste valeur et actifs incorporels," *Revue d'économie financière,* no. 71 (August 2003), 71–85.

52. On this double method, see Giorgio Agamben, *Signatura rerum* (Milan: Bollati Boringhieri, 2008).

53. Here we refer to Deleuze's interpretation of Spinoza's *Ethics.* See Michael Hardt, *Gilles Deleuze* (Minneapolis: University of Minnesota Press, 1993); and Antonio Negri, "Kairos, Alma Venus, Multitudo," in *Time for Revolution,* trans. Matteo Mandarini (London: Continuum, 2003).

54. Augustine, *De civitate dei,* bk. 14, chap. 7, cited in Heinz Heimsoeth, *Les six grands thèmes de la métaphysique* (Paris: Vrin, 2003), p. 223.

55. Ernst Bloch, *Avicenna und die Aristotelische Linke* (Berlin: Rütten & Loening, 1952).

56. Wilhelm Dilthey, *Einleitung in die Geisteswissenschaften,* vol. 1 of *Gesammelte Schriften* (Leipzig: Teubner, 1914), p. 47.

57. Michel de Certeau, "Le rire de Michel Foucault," *Revue de la Bibliothèque Nationale,* no. 14 (Winter 1984), 10–16.

58. For an interpretation of economic innovation as historical rupture, in Schumpeter's work in particular, see Adelino Zanini, *Economic Philosophy: Economic Foundations and Political Categories,* trans. Cosma Orsi (Oxford: Peter Lang, 2008).

59. Marx, *Capital,* 1:554–555.

6. REVOLUTION

1. John Locke, *Second Treatise on Government* (Indianapolis: Hackett, 1980), p. 19. See also C. B. MacPherson, *The Political Theory of Possessive Individualism* (London: Oxford University Press, 1964).

2. Cheryl Harris, "Whiteness as Property," *Harvard Law Review* 106, no. 8 (June 1993), 1731. See also George Lipsitz, *The Possessive Investment in Whiteness,* 2nd ed. (Philadelphia: Temple University Press, 2006).

3. See Saidiya Hartman's invocation of Douglass and his Aunt Hester in *Scenes of Subjection: Terror, Slavery, and Self-Making in Nineteenth-Century America* (Oxford: Oxford University Press, 1997).

4. See, for example, Eduardo Bonilla-Silva, *Racism without Racists: Color-Blind Racism and the Persistence of Racial Inequality in the United States* (Lanham, Md.: Rowman & Littlefield, 2003).

5. See, for example, Gary Peller, "Race Consciousness," in *Critical Race Theory,* ed. Kimberlé Williams Crenshaw et al. (New York: New Press, 1996), pp. 127–158.

6. See, for example, Silvia Rivera Cusicanqui, *"Oppressed but not defeated": Peasant Struggles among the Aymara and Qhechwa in Bolivia, 1900–1980* (Geneva: United Nations Research Institute for Social Development, 1987).

7. Wendy Brown, *States of Injury* (Princeton: Princeton University Press, 1995).

8. Fred Moten, *In the Break: The Aesthetics of the Black Radical Tradition* (Minneapolis: University of Minnesota Press, 2003). See also Robin Kelley, *Freedom Dreams: The Black Radical Imagination* (Boston: Beacon Press, 2002).

9. On the tradition of black radicalism, see Cedric Robinson, *Black Marxism* (London: Zed, 1983).

10. Linda Zerilli, *Feminism and the Abyss of Freedom* (Chicago: University of Chicago Press, 2005), p. 65.

11. See Charles Taylor, *Multiculturalism: Examining the Politics of Recognition* (Princeton: Princeton University Press, 1994); Axel Honneth, *The Struggle for Recognition* (Cambridge, Mass.: MIT Press, 1996); and Nancy Fraser's

useful critique of the politics of recognition in *Justice Interruptus* (New York: Routledge, 1996).

12. Mario Tronti, *Operai e capitale* (Turin: Einaudi, 1966), p. 260.

13. For a brief definition of the refusal of work, see Paolo Virno and Michael Hardt, eds., *Radical Thought in Italy* (Minneapolis: University of Minnesota Press, 1994), p. 263. See also Antonio Negri, *Books for Burning: Between Civil War and Democracy in 1970s Italy,* trans. Timothy Murphy and Arianna Bove (London: Verso, 2005); and Mario Tronti, "The Strategy of Refusal," in *Autonomia: Post-Political Politics, Semiotext(e),* 2nd ed., ed. Sylvère Lotringer and Christian Marazzi (Cambridge, Mass.: MIT Press, 2008), pp. 28–34.

14. Wendy Brown, *Edgework* (Princeton: Princeton University Press, 2005), p. 108.

15. Gayle Rubin, "The Traffic in Women," in *The Second Wave of Feminism,* ed. Linda Nicholson (New York: Routledge, 1997), p. 54.

16. Donna Haraway, "A Cyborg Manifesto," in *Simians, Cyborgs, and Women* (New York: Routledge, 1991), p. 181.

17. Annamarie Jagose, *Queer Theory: An Introduction* (New York: NYU Press, 1996), p. 131.

18. For excellent summaries of this division within queer theory and, more generally, the variations of what is meant by "queer," see Nikki Sullivan, *A Critical Introduction to Queer Theory* (New York: NYU Press, 2003), pp. 37–56; and Jagose, *Queer Theory,* pp. 101–132.

19. Frantz Fanon, *Black Skin, White Masks* (New York: Grove, 1967), p. 8. Lewis Gordon emphasizes Fanon's call for a new humanism in *Fanon and the Crisis of European Man* (New York: Routledge, 1995).

20. For Malcolm X, see "The Young Socialist Interview," in *By Any Means Necessary* (New York: Pathfinder, 1992), pp. 179–188, esp. p. 181; and Angela Davis, "Meditations on the Legacy of Malcolm X," in *The Angela Y. Davis Reader,* ed. Joy Jones (Oxford: Blackwell, 1998), pp. 279–288. For Huey Newton, see Erik Erikson and Huey Newton, *In Search of Common Ground* (New York: Norton, 1973), pp. 27–32; Judson Jeffries, *Huey P. Newton: The Radical Theorist* (Jackson: University of Mississippi Press, 2002), pp. 62–82; and Alvaro Reyes, "Huey Newton e la nascita di autonomia," in *Gli autonomi,* vol. 2, ed. Sergio Bianchi and Lanfranco Caminiti (Rome: Derive/approdi, 2008), pp. 454–476.

21. Paul Gilroy, *Against Race* (Cambridge, Mass.: Harvard University Press, 2000), p. 40.

22. Parallel to black revolutionary traditions there has emerged in the United States a "new abolitionism" aimed at destroying whiteness. We must abol-

ish the white race by any means necessary, these authors write in appealingly inflammatory rhetoric, by which they mean abolish the privileges of whiteness. See David Roediger, *Towards the Abolition of Whiteness* (New York: Verso, 1994); and Noel Ignatiev and John Garvey, eds., *Race Traitor* (New York: Routledge, 1996).

23. Toril Moi, for example, drawing primarily on Simone de Beauvoir, argues that the category of woman is not as problematic as Butler suggests. See *What Is a Woman? and Other Essays* (Oxford: Oxford University Press, 1999), pp. 3–120.

24. Hortense Spillers, for example, does not contest the goal of "racelessness" but questions Gilroy's route to reach that destination. See "Über against Race," *Black Renaissance/Renaissance Noire* 3, no. 2 (Spring 2001), 59–68.

25. Eve Kosofsky Sedgwick, *Epistemology of the Closet* (Berkeley: University of California Press, 1990), pp. 1–66.

26. See Gilles Deleuze and Félix Guattari, *Anti-Oedipus,* trans. Robert Hurley, Mark Seem, and Helen Lane (Minneapolis: University of Minnesota Press, 1983), p. 296.

27. On Gilroy's notion of diaspora and hybridity, see Paul Gilroy, *Against Race* (Cambridge, Mass.: Harvard University Press, 2000), pp. 97–133. On conviviality, see his *After Empire* (Oxfordshire: Routledge, 2004), p. xi and passim.

28. Singularity functions as a technical term in the vocabularies of Gilles Deleuze, Alain Badiou, and several other contemporary French philosophers. Our definition of the concept shares with theirs a focus on the relation between singularity and multiplicity.

29. For a classic proposition of intersectional analysis, see Kimberlé Williams Crenshaw, "Mapping the Margins: Intersectionality, Identity Politics, and Violence against Women of Color," *Stanford Law Review* 43, no. 6 (July 1991), 1241–99.

30. Baruch Spinoza, *Ethics,* in *Complete Works,* ed. Samuel Shirley (Indianapolis: Hackett, 2002), pt. 2, Proposition 7, p. 247.

31. Slavoj Žižek, *The Parallax View* (Cambridge, Mass.: MIT Press, 2006), p. 362.

32. See H. J. De Vleeschauwer, *The Development of Kantian Thought* (New York: T. Nelson, 1962); and Ernst Cassirer, *The Problem of Knowledge* (New Haven: Yale University Press, 1959), which develops the work of the Marburg School, particularly the teachings of Hermann Cohen.

33. Carl Schmitt, *Verfassungslehre,* 6th ed. (Berlin: Duncker & Humblot, 1983), p. 218. See also Olivier Beaud, "'Repräsentation' et 'Stellvertretung': Sur une distinction de Carl Schmitt," *Droits,* no. 6 (1987), 11–20.

34. Elizabeth Povinelli, *The Cunning of Recognition: Indigenous Alterities and the Making of Australian Multiculturalism* (Durham: Duke University Press, 2002).

35. See Antonio Negri, "Lo stato dei partiti," in *La forma stato* (Milan: Feltrinelli, 1977), pp. 111–149.

36. See our presentation of contemporary positions regarding the crisis of democracy in the global context in Michael Hardt and Antonio Negri, *Multitude* (New York: Penguin, 2004), pp. 231–37.

37. Gunther Teubner, "Societal Constitutionalism: Alternatives to State-Centered Constitutional Theory?" in *Transnational Governance and Constitutionalism,* ed. Christian Joerges, Inger-Johanne Sand, and Gunther Teubner (Oxford: Hart, 2004), pp. 3–28.

38. See Alain Supiot, *Au-delà de l'emploi* (Paris: Flammarion, 1999).

39. Robin Kelley analyzes from a historical perspective a series of revolutionary alliances that border on insurrectional intersections in *Freedom Dreams.*

40. Jacques Rancière, *Disagreement,* trans. Julie Rose (Minneapolis: University of Minnesota Press, 1999), p. 14.

41. Jean-Paul Sartre, *Critique of Dialectical Reason,* vol. 1, trans. Alan Sheridan-Smith (London: Verso, 2004).

42. For Lenin, see primarily *What Is to Be Done?* (New York: International Publishers, 1969). On Lenin, see also Antonio Negri, *La fabbrica della strategia: 33 lezioni su Lenin,* 2nd ed. (Rome: Manifestolibri, 2004); and Slavoj Žižek, ed., *Revolution at the Gates: Žižek on Lenin, the 1917 Writings* (London: Verso, 2004). For Trotsky, see *The History of the Russian Revolution,* trans. Max Eastman (New York: Simon & Schuster, 1932), esp. chap. 43, "The Art of Insurrection."

43. This periodization of vanguard political figures clarifies our difference from the propositions of Slavoj Žižek and Ernesto Laclau. Žižek's return to Lenin is not so much a reversion to Lenin's method (designing political composition on the basis of the current technical composition of the proletariat) but, on the contrary, a repetition of the vanguard political formation without reference to the composition of labor. Laclau instead remains faithful to the conception of hegemony typical of the next phase, specifically the one promoted by the Italian Communist Party in its populist rather than its workerist face.

44. V. I. Lenin, *State and Revolution* (New York: International Publishers, 1971), p. 43.

45. On the development of communist movements in the 1970s, see Negri, *Books for Burning.*

46. Jean-Luc Nancy, "The Decision of Existence," in *The Birth to Presence,*

trans. Brian Holmes et al. (Stanford: Stanford University Press, 1993), pp. 82–109.

47. See Michael Hardt, "Thomas Jefferson, or, The Transition of Democracy," in Thomas Jefferson, *The Declaration of Independence* (London: Verso, 2007), pp. vii–xxv.

48. See Filippo Del Lucchese, *Tumulti e indignatio: Conflitto, diritto e moltitudine in Machiavelli e Spinoza* (Milan: Ghibli, 2004).

49. Jean Genet, *Prisoner of Love,* trans. Barbara Bray (Hanover, N.H.: University Press of New England, 1992).

50. On these myths of network politics, see Carlo Formenti, *Cybersoviet* (Milan: Raffaele Cortina, 2008), pp. 201–264.

51. On the political possibilities of network structures, see Tiziana Terranova, *Network Culture* (London: Pluto, 2004); Geert Lovink, *Uncanny Networks* (Cambridge, Mass.: MIT Press, 2003); Olivier Blondeau, *Devenir média* (Paris: Amsterdam, 2007); and Alexander Galloway and Eugene Thacker, *The Exploit* (Minneapolis: University of Minnesota Press, 2007).

52. Immanuel Kant, *The Conflict of Faculties,* trans. Mary Gregor (Lincoln: University of Nebraska Press, 1992), p. 153 (emphasis added).

53. Ibid., p. 153.

54. Condorcet, "Sur le sens du mot révolutionnaire," in *Œuvres de Condorcet,* ed. A. Condorcet and F. Arago, 12 vols. (Paris: Firmin Didot, 1847), 12:615. See also Hannah Arendt, *On Revolution* (London: Penguin, 1963).

55. W. E. B. Du Bois, *Black Reconstruction* (New York: Russell & Russell, 1935), p. 206.

56. See primarily Lenin, *State and Revolution*.

57. For one version of the argument for the "autonomy of the political," see Mario Tronti, *Sull'autonomia del politico* (Milan: Feltrinelli, 1977).

58. See Antonio Gramsci, *Selections from the Prison Notebooks,* trans. Quintin Hoare and Geoffrey Nowell Smith (New York: International Books, 1971), pp. 105–120 (on passive revolution) and pp. 279–318 (on Americanism and Fordism).

59. On the distinction between war of movement and war of position, see ibid., pp. 229–235.

60. Ibid., p. 286.

61. We have addressed the question of revolutionary violence at various moments in our past work, but our analysis in this book allows us to offer some new insights. See Negri, *Books for Burning;* and Hardt and Negri, *Multitude,* pp. 341–347.

62. Jefferson to William Short, 3 January 1793, in Thomas Jefferson, *Writings,* ed. Merrill Peterson (New York: Library of America, 1984), p. 1004.

63. Saint-Just, "Fragments sur les institutions républicaines," in *Œuvres choisies,* ed. Dionys Mascolo (Paris: Gallimard, 1968), p. 310.

64. See Olivier Beaud, *Théorie de la fédération* (Paris: PUF, 2007).

65. See, for example, Gunther Teubner and Andreas Fischer-Lescano, "Regime Collisions: The Vain Search for Legal Unity in the Fragmentation of Global Law," *Michigan Journal of International Law* 25, no. 4 (2004), 999–1046.

66. See Alois Riegl, *Late Roman Art Industry* (Rome: Giorgio Brentschneider, 1985). Regarding the controversies surrounding the concept of *Kunstwollen,* see Jas' Elsner, "From Empirical Evident to the Big Picture: Some Reflections on Riegl's Concept of *Kunstwollen,*" *Critical Inquiry,* no. 32 (Summer 2006), 741–766. For an illuminating analysis of Walter Benjamin's transformation of Riegl's concept along lines similar to what we suggest here, see Katherine Arens, "*Stadtwollen:* Benjamin's *Arcades Project* and the Problem of Method," *PMLA* 122, no. 1 (January 2007), 43–60.

67. See Vivasvan Soni, "Affecting Happiness: The Emergence of the Modern Political Subject in the Eighteenth Century" (Ph.D. diss., Duke University, 2000).

68. Jefferson to Edward Everett, 27 March 1824, in Thomas Jefferson, *Writings,* vol. 16, ed. Andrew Lipscomb (Washington, D.C.: Thomas Jefferson Memorial Association, 1904), p. 22.

69. On Dante and love, see Giorgio Agamben, *Stanzas,* trans. Ronald Martinez (Minneapolis: University of Minnesota Press, 1993); and Giorgio Passerone, *Dante: Cartographie de la vie* (Paris: Kimé, 2001).

70. Michel Foucault, preface to Deleuze and Guattari, *Anti-Oedipus,* pp. xi–xiv.

71. See Spinoza's definition of "indignation" in *Ethics,* pt. 3, Definition 20, p. 314.

ACKNOWLEDGMENTS

It would be impossible to thank all those who contributed to the writing of this book. We would like simply to acknowledge here those with whom we discussed elements of the manuscript and those who helped us with translations: Alain Bertho, Arianna Bove, Beppe Caccia, Cesare Casarino, Giuseppe Cocco, Antonio Conti, Patrick Dieuaide, Andrea Fumagalli, Stefano Harney, Fredric Jameson, Naomi Klein, Wahneema Lubiano, Matteo Mandarini, Christian Marazzi, Sandro Mezzadra, Timothy Murphy, Pascal Nicolas-Le Strat, Charles Piot, Judith Revel, Alvaro Reyes, America Vera-Zavala, Carlo Vercellone, Lindsay Waters, Kathi Weeks, Robyn Wiegman, and Tomiko Yoda. We are grateful to these friends for all they have taught us.

INDEX